Depression:

BEHAVIORAL, BIOCHEMICAL, DIAGNOSTIC AND TREATMENT CONCEPTS

Depression:

BEHAVIORAL, BIOCHEMICAL, DIAGNOSTIC AND TREATMENT CONCEPTS

Edited by
Donald M. Gallant, M.D., Tulane University School of Medicine
New Orleans, Louisiana

and

George M. Simpson, M.D., Rockland Psychiatric Center
Orangeburg, New York

S P Books Division of
SPECTRUM PUBLICATIONS, INC.
New York

Distributed by Halsted Press
A Division of John Wiley & Sons

New York   Toronto   London   Sydney

SPECTRUM PUBLICATIONS, INC..
86-19 Sancho Street, Holliswood, N.Y. 11423

Distributed solely by the Halsted Press division of John Wiley & Sons, Inc., New York

Library of Congress Cataloging in Publication Data

Main entry under title:

Depression—behavioral, biochemical, diagnostic, and
    treatment concepts.

    Includes index.
    1. Depression, Mental. I. Gallant, Donald M.
II. Simpson, George M. [DNLM: 1. Depression—Con-
gresses. WM170 D424 1974]
RC537.D4276   616.8'9   75-37679
ISBN 0-470-01375-3

Contributors

JAMES L. CLAGHORN, M.D.
Assistant Director
Texas Research Institute of Mental Sciences
Houston, Texas

C. KEITH CONNERS, Ph.D.
Associate Professor of Psychiatry
Western Psychiatric Institute and Clinics
University of Pittsburg School of Medicine
Pittsburg, Pennsylvania

DONALD M. GALLANT, M.D.
Professor of Psychiatry
Director of the Psychopharmacology Research
    Unit
Tulane University School of Medicine
New Orleans, Louisiana

MAX HAMILTON, M.D.
Nuffield Professor of Psychiatry
Department of Psychiatry
University of Leeds
Leeds, England

ROBERT G. HEATH, M.D.
Professor and Chairman
Department of Psychiatry and Neurology
Tulane University School of Medicine
New Orleans, Louisiana

EDGAR HEIM, M.D.
Director of the Psychiatric Clinic "Schloessli",
    Zurich
PD, Department of Psychiatry
University of Zurich, Switzerland

DONALD F. KLEIN, M.D.
Director of Research and Evaluation
Department of Psychiatry
Long Island Jewish-Hillside Medical Center
Glen Oaks, New York
Professor of Psychiatry
School of Medicine
State University of New York
Stony Brook, New York

MORRIS A. LIPTON, M.D.
Director of the Biological Sciences Research
    Center
University of North Carolina School of Medicine
Chapel Hill, North Carolina

WILLIAM T. MCKINNEY, JR., M.D.
Professor of Psychiatry
University of Wisconsin Medical School
Madison, Wisconsin

CONTRIBUTORS

JOE MENDELS, M.D.
Professor of Psychiatry
Chief, Depression Research Unit
Department of Psychiatry
University of Pennsylvania Medical School and
    Veterans Administration Hospital
Philadelphia, Pennsylvania

DAVID H. MIELKE, M.D.
Assistant Professor of Psychiatry
Co-Director of the Psychopharmacology
    Research Unit
Tulane University School of Medicine
New Orleans, Louisiana

CARLO PERRIS, M.D.
Professor and Chairman
Department of Psychiatry
University of Umea
Umea, Sweden

FELIX POST, M.D.
Consultant Psychiatrist to Bethlem Royal
    Hospital and Maudsley Hospital
London, England

ALLEN RASKIN, Ph.D.
Research Psychologist
Psychopharmacology Research Branch
National Institute of Mental Health
Rockville, Maryland

MOGENS SCHOU, M.D.
Professor of Biological Psychiatry
Aarhus University
Risskov, Denmark

GEORGE M. SIMPSON, M.B.
Principal Research Psychiatrist
Rockland Psychiatric Center
Orangeburg, New York

ERVIN VARGA, M.D.
Senior Research Psychiatrist
Rockland Psychiatric Center
Orangeburg, New York

MYRNA M. WEISSMAN, Ph.D.
Assistant Professor of Psychiatry (Epidemiology)
Director, Depression Research Unit of the
    Connecticut Mental Health Center
Yale University School of Medicine
New Haven, Connecticut

JOHN S. WERRY, M.B.
Professor and Head
Department of Psychiatry
University of Auckland School of Medicine
Auckland, New Zealand

MAX WILHELM, Ph.D.
Group Director of Exploratory Research
CIBA Pharmaceutical Company
Summit, New Jersey

We would also like to express our appreciation to Dr. Rachel Gittelman-Klein, Director, Child Development Clinic, Department of Psychiatry, Long Island Jewish-Hillside Medical Center, Glen Oaks, New York, and to Dr. A. Delini-Stula, Head, Psychopharmacology Unit, Pharmacology Section, Research Department, CIBA-Geigy, Ltd., Basel, Switzerland, for the valuable information they presented during the second day of the symposium.

Preface

Depression is the most common emotional disorder, afflicting approximately 50 percent of North Americans and western Europeans at one time or another; the depressive syndrome is the presenting problem in approximately one-half of all admissions to psychiatric institutions. The National Institutes of Mental Health recently warned that 15 percent of adults or about 20,000,000 people between the ages of eighteen and seventy-four in the United States may be suffering from serious depressive disorders in any given year. Depression is a serious illness which carries a high mortality rate. The suicide rate has increased in the past ten years, and approximately 20,000 deaths per year are a result of this illness. These facts emphasize the immediate need for a higher national priority for research and treatment of this illness, which affects a majority of United States citizens at some time in their lives regardless of income or race.

The introduction of ECT, lithium, tricyclic, MAOI and, more recently, tetracyclic antidepressant drug therapy has proved to be of immense help for 60 to 90 percent of these depressed patients. However, this figure also represents the reality that a significant number of depressed patients with ostensibly the same illness respond poorly to the available therapeutic agents, suggesting that the diagnostic entities of depression are still not well defined. It is essential that the rational, scientific approach be used routinely in the search for the biochemical and environmental causes of depression as well as in the evaluation of the specific treatment approaches. This book reviews the present state of the basic biochemical and clinical concepts of depression, presents specific guidelines for future research in both animals and humans in order to improve treatment methods for the patient with depression, and offers specific guidance as to the best-known available modes of therapy for the various clinical subgroups of depression. That one volume could cover such a wide subject in its entirety is not possible; a certain amount of selectivity was therefore essential.

In the choice of participants in this conference, for both the presentations and discussions, the editors selected authorities from a variety of disciplines in basic and clinical research. As a result of the different viewpoints, experience and disciplines represented, there were many valuable disagreements in the discussions (Commentaries), which were often, in the view of the editors, as essential and enlightening as the original manuscripts. It is hoped that these freely expressed disagreements will provide the reader with thought-provoking material and additional insight in his own thinking and in reaching his own conclusions.

D. M. G.
G. M. S.

Foreword

Clarification of the pathogenesis of depression within the next few years is a reasonable expectation in light of the recent rapid progress of physiologic and biochemical research on this problem. Understanding of the specific biologic mechanisms involved will lead to the development of more effective—perhaps specific—pharmacologic treatments. Such a prospect makes this conference, attended by many of those responsible for these promising developments, an exciting and timely gathering.

The absence of a structural abnormality is probably the principal reason for failure to elucidate the pathogenesis of depression earlier—during the heyday of cellular pathology after development of the microscope. Many of us here today may witness in our lifetimes all the evolutionary stages in the understanding of this syndrome—from the initial description-classification through the dynamic explanation to the understanding of the cellular-molecular mechanisms responsible for the clinical symptoms.

The recent encouraging developments are the result of new technology. It is now possible to localize pathologic function by methods other than visualization of structural change and to identify a probable biochemical lesion that is not associated with cellular destruction. The first demonstration of a physiologic mechanism of the brain that functioned to produce pleasure and alerting took place here at Tulane. Inasmuch as diminution-to-absence of pleasure is characteristic of depression, our findings suggested that impairment of the rostral septal area was basic to the syndrome. Physiologic data, principally electroencephalographic changes, support these findings. The cellular anomaly in depression which impairs the functioning of this system remains to be clarified. Pharmacologic agents that produce symptomatic relief of depression shed some light on this process, and this subject is the main focus of many of the papers to be presented in this symposium.

As Chairman of the Department of Psychiatry at Tulane, I have been privileged to follow the progress in this field through the activities of Dr. Gallant and his associates in their Early Clinical Drug Evaluation Unit.

Final elucidation of the specific molecular aberration involved in depression requires not only more basic animal research, but also many more trials with new agents in patients who suffer from depression. No animal model can ever be completely satisfactory. The clinical effect of new agents requires an assessment of changes in feelings, a largely subjective variable, and these data are available only through reporting of the depressed subject; animals cannot talk. Thus future progress in the area of depression, as well as the entire field of psychiatry, depends on a free intellectual research climate which would foster ethical human investigation.

R. G. Heath

Acknowledgments

We wish to express our deep appreciation to all whose efforts and cooperation have made this book possible: to Tulane University, which served as host for the symposium; to the sponsoring organization, CIBA Pharmaceutical Company, which provided complete and unrestricted editorial freedom, and its representatives who attended the symposium, Dr. Richard H. Roberts and Mr. John N. Zaccheo. Special thanks to Luciana Dameron-Smith, for her time and efforts toward making the meeting a success, and to Dianne Gallant, the art editor; our gratitude to Linda Terranova and Jane Sosnow for their time, patience and cooperation in the preparation of the manuscript. Most of all, we are grateful to Joyce Cooper Gallant for her continued interest, advice and many freely given hours of editorial assistance which have helped to bring about the prompt publication of this book.

Contents

Preface — D.M. Gallant and G.M. Simpson
Foreword — R.G. Heath
Contributors
Acknowledgments

I	Animal Models of Depression *W.T. McKinney, Jr.*	1
II	Biological Concepts of Depression *J. Mendels, S. Stern and A. Frazer*	19
III	Frequency and Hereditary Aspects of Depression *C. Perris*	75
IV	Recent Advances in Blood Levels of Antidepressant Agents: Assay Procedures, Reliability, and Relationship to Therapeutic Outcome and Side Effects *G.M. Simpson, T.B. Cooper, and J.H. Lee*	109
V	Differential Diagnosis and Treatment of the Dysphorias *D.F. Klein*	127
VI	Clinical Evaluation of Depression: Clinical Criteria and Rating Scales, Including a Guttman Scale *M. Hamilton*	15
VII	Classification and Treatment of Childhood Depression and Depressive Equivalents *C.K. Conners*	181
VIII	Diagnosis of Depression in Geriatric Patients and Treatment Modalities Appropriate for the Population *F. Post*	205

IX   Some Problems in Clinical Trails of New Antidepressant Agents   235

     A. Issues in the Evaluation of New Drugs: A Double-Blind
        Trail of Maprotiline (Ludiomil) and Amitriptyline
        (Elavil) in Outpatient Depressives
          M.M. Weissman   235

     B. Double-Blind Evaluations in Psychopharmacology: A
        Double-Blind Study of Maprotiline (Ludiomil), Imipramine
        (Tofranil) and Placebo in Depressed Outpatients
          J.L. Claghorn   250

X   Adverse Reactions of Thymoleptics
      D.H. Mielke   273

XI   Prophylactic and Maintenance Therapy in Recurrent Affective
Disorders
      M. Schou   309

XII   Concluding Remarks
      G.M. Simpson   332

      Index

CHAPTER I

Animal Models of Depression

W. T. McKinney, Jr.

Animal models, though widely used and accepted in many medical specialties, have only become available for psychiatric disorders in recent years. Certain problems present themselves when one attempts to create models for behavioral disorders, but there is no intrinsic reason to preclude the creation of models for psychopathological disorders in general; indeed, several of them have already been produced. Animal models of depression must be viewed in the larger context of the problems of creating animal models for psychopathological states as a whole. It is impossible to give a detailed exposition of any one area, whether it be social isolation, separation, or behavioral changes occurring as a consequence of experimental biogenic amine depletion. Therefore, I have chosen to provide a general outline of the approaches currently being used in our laboratory to create experimental animal models for human psychopathological states.

Prior to outlining the major approaches being used in the creation of animal models, I will deal with some of the philosophical issues concerning work in this field.

PHILOSOPHICAL ISSUES

During the last ten years experimental psychopathology in nonhuman primates has undergone considerable development. It is now possible by utilizing certain social and biological induction methods to produce syndromes of abnormal

1

behavior which can be objectively documented and studied. If behavioral and biochemical studies whose findings may subsequently be applied to human beings are to be performed, ideally one should use a species as close to man as possible. From this viewpoint, the great apes might be the logical choice. However, due to the scarcity, difficulties and expense in working with large primates in a laboratory, much of the work to be reviewed in this paper has utilized only rhesus monkeys as subjects. Also, the life span of monkeys is considerably telescoped in comparison to that of man or the apes, thus facilitating longitudinal studies.

The skepticism with which animal behavior work has been received by clinicians is due partly to the history of the field and partly to the attitudes of some psychiatrists who have been unwilling to accept animal work as relevant to human disorders. With regard to the former, much of the early work in experimental psychopathology utilized very specialized conditioning techniques whose terms and relevance to clinical phenomena were poorly understood. Clinical terms were thrown about far too loosely to describe certain behavioral states in animals, with little attention being paid to the theoretical problems implicit in using nonhumans to study human psychopathology. Consequently, the interest of most clinicians in the experimental simulation of abnormal behavior states in nonhumans has ranged from excessive anthropomorphism to indifference to hostility or confusion.

One of the leading spokesmen for those psychiatrists who refuse to accept animal work as relevant to human disorders has been Kubie (1939). He states, "Thus, the imitation in animals of the emotional states which attend neuroses in man is not the experimental production of the essence of neuroses itself." Kubie's contention is that behavior is only the "sign language" of an underlying symbolic disorder which is the real core of psychopathology. He feels that animals do not have symbolic capacities and, therefore, it is not possible to produce a true neurotic or psychotic state in nonhumans. This position of Kubie's is predicated on an assumption about human psychopathology that many psychiatrists would disagree with: namely, that behavior is important only as an indicator of something more important which is the "real" disorder. Others would insist that observations of behavior are critical ingredients in reliably defining disorders. Also, the assumption that higher-order primates do not have symbolic capacities is now open to serious question (Premack, 1970; Gardner and Gardner, 1971). However, Kubie and his criticisms did focus on an important issue. Various terms have been applied far too loosely to the abnormal behavior states created in different species. Labels such as "experimental neuroses," "phobia," "anxiety," "behavioral disorder," "chronic emotional disorder," "experimental neurasthenia" and "depression" have been utilized often without adequate behavioral descriptions. This laxity in labeling has often alienated the clinicians, who fail to see the similarities between conditions used to produce abnormal behavior in many animal studies and those that are thought to predispose to human psychopathology.

Many criticisms of this field are justified, as will be apparent from a later section of this paper. It has been pointed out by Seligman (Seligman and Groves,

1969; Seligman and Maier, 1967; Seligman et al., 1968) and by McKinney and Bunney (1970) that the difficulty in moving from a dramatic analogue to true animal models has been due in large part to the lack of ground rules or criteria which might validate the model. Historically, much work in this area has suffered from the lack of prior criteria by which the syndromes produced could be evaluated, and the establishment of such criteria for animal model research in recent years has been a major advancement and one with considerable heuristic value.

The following criteria have been proposed as being useful in evaluating nonhuman experimental psychopathology research; in considering animal models of depression, these criteria should be kept in mind.

1. The behavioral manifestations of the syndrome being modeled should be similar to those seen in the human condition.
2. These behavioral changes should be capable of being objectively detected by independent observers and different laboratories.
3. The behavioral state induced should be persistent and generalizable.
4. Conditions which produce abnormal behavior in animals should be similar to those etiologic conditions responsible for human psychopathology.
5. Treatment modalities effective in reversing the human disorder should be effective in primates.
6. There must be sufficient reference control data available on the species under study.

While these criteria suggest research strategies for the creation of models, it should also be remembered that the condition being modeled is often itself poorly defined from a behavioral standpoint. While this point can be used as a rebuttal to critics who demand more preciseness from model research than is currently available, it also delineates one of the potential values of animal model research, i.e., to aid in more clearly defining human syndromes from a behavioral standpoint.

In essence, what is being attempted in the creation of experimental models in animals is the production of syndromes which meet the criteria outlined above. The value of the model system in animals is that it lends itself to more direct manipulation of social and biological variables than is possible in human beings from ethical and/or practical standpoints. This is not to contend that monkeys are humans or vice versa. Obviously, there are differences; the similarities, however, far outweigh most differences, especially with regard to social development and affectional systems. As a matter of fact, investigators should start paying more attention to the differences among species, as these in themselves may have considerable relevance for human social organizations.

In most other medical specialties, of course, animals are frequently used as models for some conditions. Psychiatry has not had this tradition. Yet there is little question that there is a great need for animal models with regard to depression and other forms of psychiatric disorder. Ethical and practical issues confront one who seeks to answer many of the critical questions in psychiatry by studies in human beings. Also, some of the critical questions with regard to human depression and psychopathology involve prospective and longitudinal studies that many investigators have been reluctant to undertake because of the length of time involved. The advantage of the greatly telescoped life span of the rhesus monkey and other primates as compared to the human being has already been mentioned. This enables one, for example, to evaluate the role of early experiences in the production of abnormal behavior later in the development, a question which is of particular concern with regard to clinical psychiatric practice even though it has been difficult to study in humans in a prospective and controlled manner.

APPROACHES TO INDUCING ABNORMAL
BEHAVIOR IN ANIMALS

Following is a discussion of the major approaches being used in our laboratory, as well as one line of work in another laboratory. The major approaches can be broadly divided into social induction methods, biological induction methods and rehabilitation studies.

Social Induction Methods

The major social induction methods currently available for producing psychopathological syndromes in primates include social isolation rearing, mother-infant separation, peer separation, vertical chamber confinement and learned helplessness.

The technique of social isolation involves rearing animals from birth in either total social isolation, where they have no social contact with other animals, or in barbed wire cages, where their only contact is visual and auditory. In social isolation, as contrasted to separation, one never allows attachment bonds to develop. The effects of isolating rhesus monkeys for the first six to twelve months of life have been amply described in the literature (Harlow, 1964; Harlow et al., 1964, 1966; Harlow and Harlow, 1971; McKinney, 1974; Mason, 1963a, 1963b, 1968; Mason and Sponholz, 1963). There are both short- and long-term effects. Animals so reared and then removed and tested socially with other animals spend most of their time huddled alone in a corner, rocking, self-clasping and refusing to enter into play or other normal social encounters with their peers. They may show stereotyped behaviors and also engage in self-aggression or in inappropriate and unpredictable aggression against, for example, a large dominant male. Appropriate sexual behaviors are virtually absent among isolation reared monkeys when they reach puberty and adulthood. Females, when they do become pregnant, are very inadequate mothers with their first infants. Isolation reared monkeys have also been reported to show polyphagia and polydipsia when they become adults (Miller et al., 1969). There is very little data available concerning possible mechanisms underlying the dramatic effects of total social isolation. It is particularly striking that there are minimal data concerning possible neurophysiological and/or neuroendocrinological substrates of the isolation syndrome. Heath (1971) has reported electroencephalographic studies in isolation reared monkeys and has found abnormalities from limbic system structures and from sensory relay nuclei for vestibular and proprioceptive function in the cerebellum and in the somato-sensory thalamus. The significance of the above findings remains to be evaluated.

It is clear that investigation of the isolation syndrome in nonhuman primates potentially provides one avenue for clarifying the interactions among rearing conditions, their possible neurobiological consequences and social behavior. In this sense its utility as an animal model should be quite helpful, regardless of what clinical label one attaches to the isolate animals.

As demonstrated by recent social and biological rehabilitation studies, the social isolation syndrome is not irreversible as once thought. Previous attempts to socialize isolate monkeys by providing experience with equal age peers and/or with older animals have been strikingly unsuccessful. On the other hand, when isolate animals were paired with monkeys who were chronologically three months younger, the younger subjects spent much more time gently clinging to the isolate animals when they engaged in their abnormal behaviors. This kind of experience plus the opportunity to observe the younger animals engaging in normal behavior among themselves resulted in striking improvement in the isolate animal's behavior (Suomi et al., 1972; Harlow, 1971b). In a broader sense, equal-aged animals may be providing too many stimuli for the withdrawn isolate animals to respond to except with more huddling, self-clasping, etc., whereas the younger animals did not present this stimulus overload. Chlorpromazine treatment has also been shown to be beneficial for monkeys that were disturbed as a result of early partial social isolation (McKinney et al., 1973). Chlorpromazine resulted in dramatic decreases in most forms of self-directed disturbance behaviors. One value of such rehabilitation studies, both social and biological, lies in the possibilities they present for a better understanding of the mechanisms underlying the isolation syndrome. Also, isolated monkeys or monkeys that have other forms of socially induced psychopathology may be used in some future preclinical drug trials and thereby improve the quality of such drug trials before human subjects can be used.

Another social induction method involves the experimental use of separation experiences. This technique involves allowing attachment bonds to develop between animals and then experimentally disrupting such bonds. Separation experiences are thought, of course, to precede the development of severe depression as well as other forms of psychopathology in some human beings. However, the theories that postulate the importance of separation are largely based on retrospective studies that start with the population of clinically depressed people who have undergone separation but do not include a control group who have undergone separation but are not depressed. There is certainly little understanding of the mechanisms involving the apparent connection between separation and depression, though the terms have become well-accepted phrases among clinicians. Unfortunately, separation is becoming a greatly overused term in the sense that its usage has far outstripped our basic understanding of its meaning. We need to redefine it in terms of many parameters, and if this is not done there exists the risk that the term will continue to be used so broadly and loosely as to become meaningless. Many variables may determine a response to separation, and these need identification and study before the connection between what is called separation and depression can be understood. Also, depression may not be the only response to separation or, if it is, may manifest itself differently depending on many factors which almost certainly include genetic and neurochemical ones, prior experiences with separation, the conditions surrounding separation, and age, to mention only a few.

It is in the area of clarifying some of these mechanisms underlying separation that primate models may be especially useful. Rhesus monkeys develop strong affectional systems and form close social bonds, factors that have facilitated the study of separation and depression. Space will not permit a detailed discussion of the rather vast literature on mother-infant (Seay et al., 1962, 1965; Hinde et al., 1966; Hinde and Spencer-Booth, 1971; Jensen and Tvemen, 1962) and peer (Suomi et al., 1970; McKinney et al., 1971a; McKinney et al., 1972a) separation. In general, if one allows rhesus infants and their mothers to live together for the first three to six months of life and then experimentally separates them, the infant exhibits a biphasic response to this separation. During the first twenty-four to thirty-six hours following separation, he is hyperactive and his behavior is characterized by increased vocalizations, increased activity, and frantic attempts to get back to the mother. This phase has been labeled the "protest" stage. It eventually subsides and the "despair" stage ensues. This stage is characterized by the infant being very withdrawn, retreating to a corner, becoming inactive, and engaging in some combination of huddling and self-clasping behaviors. He ceases his attempts to regain access to the mother. This stage has been described as lasting several weeks with some periods of improvement and, in some animals, gradual spontaneous recovery over a four- to six-week period. However, some infants have died during this stage, perhaps, but not always, in association with lowered intake. This type of mother-infant separation study has been carried out in many laboratories and with quite a few variations in terms of separation technique. There are some important species differences as illustrated by the work of Kaufman and Rosenblum (1967a, 1967b; Rosenblum and Kaufman, 1968), who found that bonnet infants do not show this kind of response following separation from their mother, whereas pigtail infants do. This difference is probably due to the fact that pigtail infants and mothers form dyadic bonds with each other, whereas the bonnet infants and mothers when they are living in a group do not do this; rather, mothering is shared among several members of the group, and when the infant's biological mother is removed other adults help with the care of the infant. Consequently, he does not show the protest and despair reactions.

The above reaction to maternal separation has been the more or less classic one described in the literature with variations, depending on how the separation is accomplished and the conditions that exist during the separation period. Recent work in our laboratory would suggest that life is not quite this simple but that this type of separation experiment nevertheless has potential in terms of a technique of preclinical drug evaluation. It, along with peer separation, is probably the best social model of human depression currently available. One can, by controlling the conditions of separation, produce a prolonged protest stage or a situation where the infants go very quickly into the despair stage. Thus it becomes possible to do drug rehabilitation studies to answer a variety of questions. For example, once an animal is in the despair stage, what are the effects of antidepressants on shortening or alleviating the intensity of this stage? What would be the effects of antidepressants and/or antianxiety agents given to the animal before or during the protest stage? Might it be possible to prevent the occurrence of this separation reaction by appropriate prior drug treatment? These types of studies and others done in a more socially analogous paradigm than that in which preclinical drug trial studies are now conducted might offer great potential for the study of antidepressant and/or antianxiety drugs.

Biological studies of rhesus infants undergoing this maternal separation reaction are also currently under way. Infants exhibiting behaviors typical of the protest stage have been found to show elevated levels of each of the catecholamine synthesizing enzymes in the adrenal gland and increases in serotonin levels in the hypothalamus (Breese et al., 1973). There were no changes in norepinephrine, dopamine or serotonin levels in any of the other brain regions examined. However, this particular study, which was the initial study in the series, focused on absolute levels, and we are not able to say anything yet about possible differences in turnover rates. Monkey infants exhibiting behaviors typical of the despair stage are currently being studied with regard to possible neurochemical changes in the brain and adrenal gland.

A series of recent peer separation studies also provides another approach for the creation of animal models for depression and perhaps a more practical one than maternal separation. It has been found that monkeys reared only with peers under a year of age exhibit when separated a biphasic reaction very similar to that shown by infant separation from their mothers. In contrast, two studies of adolescent rhesus monkeys who underwent peer separation found only a uniphasic type of reaction with behaviors characteristic of the protest stage appearing throughout the separation. There was no evidence of the despair stage. Thus age and developmental stages are quite important factors in determining an animal's response to separation. Also, it has been shown that rhesus monkeys two years of age respond to peer separation quite differently, depending on the nature of their background (Young et al., 1973). Animals with a history of vertical chamber confinement responded to peer separation with a significant increase in most self-directed disturbance behaviors, whereas nonseparated peer reared rhesus monkeys respond to separation with increases in locomotion and hyperactive type behaviors. Upon reunion, the normal monkeys also showed much ventral clinging and reunion behaviors whereas the early chambered animals did not. Therefore, early experience appears to be another important variable influencing the rhesus monkey's response to separation.

One other approach to creating animal models for depression involves the vertical chamber apparatus. This apparatus, created by Professor Harlow, is created on an intuitive basis to simulate the feelings of helplessness and hopelessness that are felt by some to be among the key features in depression. Pilot studies with this apparatus showed that rhesus monkeys that were confined at six weeks of age for six weeks exhibited many abnormal behaviors when removed and tested socially (Harlow and Suomi, 1970; Harlow and Harlow, 1971). These behaviors included huddling, rocking, self-clasping and social withdrawal. The mechanisms by which the vertical chamber apparatus exerts its effects are undetermined at this point. However, it does appear that short periods of confinement in this chamber at certain ages are effective in producing a snydrome of abnormal behavior. Rhesus monkeys three years of age when subjected to lengthy periods of vertical chamber confinement become quite passive, locomotion scores drop, and they tend to spend most of their time clinging to each other (McKinney, et al., 1972b). Thus, though they were also affected by a period of confinement in the vertical chamber, the nature of the effect differs significantly from that of the younger animals. It is not yet clear what syndrome is being modeled with the vertical chamber apparatus, and its analogy to the human situation is somewhat questionable at this point. Whether or not it is indeed simulating feelings of helplessness and hopelessness, it may prove to be useful as another way of studying effects of early environmental deprivation.

Another social induction method, studied by Professor Seligman at the University of Pennsylvania, is that which has been termed "learned helplessness" (Seligman and Groves, 1970; Seligman and Maier, 1967; Seligman et al., 1968). This term has been used by Professor Seligman to describe the interference with adaptive responding produced by inescapable shock. Most of this work has been done with dogs, but a similar phenomenon occurs in rats, cats, fish, mice and men. In general, it involves giving subjects a series of inescapable random electrical shocks. Twenty-four hours later the subjects are given trials of electrical shocks which may be avoidable if they jump a barrier. Failure to jump leads to a shock which continues until the subject jumps the barrier. Learned helplessness is an operational concept applied to subjects who have learned that shock is uncontrollable and subsequently fail to initiate responses to escape shock or are very much slower to make responses than naïve animals. In other words, after an initial experience in which responding cannot control reinforcers, that is, uncontrolled shock, the animals ceased to respond, even when responding could now control the reinforcers. Such a model for learned helplessness has been suggested as another type of animal model for certain aspects of human depression. This type of model also lends itself to both social and biological rehabilitation studies.

Biological Induction Methods

This approach in animal models involves experimental alteration of brain and/or peripheral amine levels and the study of the effects of these changes on the animal's social behavior. Prior to the social studies described above, the most prevalent animal model for depression was the reserpine model in rats. This model has severe limitations in terms of its behavioral analogies to depression and of its nonsocial nature. Because of its prevalence, however, we initially studied the effects of reserpine on rhesus monkeys (McKinney et al., 1971a). Not surprisingly, it is capable of producing social withdrawal, decreased locomotion, decreased activity and increased huddling scores. However, the effects are temporary and clearly related to the administration of the drug. Once the drug is stopped, the behavior of the animal returns to normal. Alpha-methyl-paratyrosine (AMPT) is a drug that inhibits tyrosine hydroxylase and thereby blocks norepinephrine synthesis. When given to both stumptail (Redmond et al., 1971a, 1971b) and rhesus monkeys it produces a syndrome very similar to that described for the reserpine treated animals but again, it is dose and time dependent. By contrast, when parachlorophenylalanine (PCPA), an inhibitor of serotonin synthesis, is given to both stumptail (Redmond et al., 1971a, 1971b) and rhesus monkeys, it produces no major behavioral changes. The above studies would point to an important role of norepinephrine and/or dopamine in the regulation of primate social behaviors.

However, with none of the above drugs is it possible to discriminate the behavioral effects due to the effects on the brain amine systems from those due to the effects on the peripheral amine systems. A possible tool to evaluate this has become available in recent years, and work with this drug is being pursued in primate models. Intraventricular administration of 6-hydroxydopamine (6 OHDA) is thought to produce a specific destruction of noradrenergic nerve terminals in the brain but not in the periphery. With this tool, it was thought that it should be possible to evaluate the relative contribution of brain and peripheral amines in the regulation of social behavior and their influence on the pattern of urinary metabolite excretion. An extensive series of studies with this drug has been done in rhesus monkeys, the details of which are impossible to present here. It is a very complicated situation and the results are not easily summarized. Perhaps it is more important to focus on the concept involved in using this drug which illustrates one of the potential values of an animal model. That is, by giving a drug which presumably produces one of the experimental lesions postulated to be important in depression and by giving this drug in a species which has a wide repertoire of social behaviors, one can evaluate in a controlled manner its effects on a series of behavioral and biological parameters. Such studies are not feasible in humans. The data from these studies, which will be reported in a series of forthcoming papers, force one to reevaluate the nature of the relationship between the brain noradrenergic system and social behavior. Certainly they provide additional data to force one away from any kind of simplistic or deterministic explanation of this relationship.

Rehabilitation Studies

Before ending, let me say one brief word about rehabilitation studies. Rehabilitation studies, both social and biological, are important in terms of validating animal models. This, of course, has been one of the criteria originally proposed, and it has had considerable heuristic value. Rehabilitation methods can theoretically be tried with both socially and biologically induced abnormal behavior syndromes. Experiments with both social and biological rehabilitation methods for each of these induction techniques could be done. The more usual thing, of course, is to pair socially induced syndromes with both social and biological rehabilitation but to confine biologically induced syndromes to biological treatment only. However, the possibility that biologically induced syndromes of abnormal behavior can be reversed by strictly social means merits investigation in primate models. Also, the interactive and possible facilitative effects of combined therapeutic approaches can be pursued. I am intrigued by rehabilitation studies in terms of their potential for understanding mechanisms of a syndrome under study as well as developing systems for doing improved preclinical drug evaluations in animal models. I have personally been concerned that many of our drug evaluation methods are inadequate in this regard and that there is too big a jump from trials in a laboratory in a relatively asocial model in animals to human clinical trials. It would seem worthwhile to try to develop something more meaningful in between and something in a more social context. This holds for antidepressants as well as other classes of therapeutic agents.

OVERVIEW

Experimental psychopathology in animals is both a new and an old field. Historically, it has suffered from many faults. The rest of medicine, however, has long used animal models to advance knowledge, and there is no intrinsic reason why psychiatrists should not do the same. The major drawback has been the lack of stable behavioral syndromes in nonhumans that can be studied from both social and biological perspectives and in which rehabilitative approaches could be tried. This presentation has described several attempts to create such syndromes and how they might be useful in this study of human psychopathology. I am encouraged by the recent widespread interest in animal models within psychiatry, even on the part of some groups that one might think would not be so concerned, and by the increasing sophistication in terms of being able to evaluate animal models with regard to their possible benefits as well as their limitations.

COMMENTARIES

DR. LIPTON: I agree with Dr. McKinney that animal model work is important. For too long psychiatrists have assumed that the emotional ills of man are unique to him and that animal models are useless. In marked contrast to the remainder of medicine, which has always sought, found and profited from research with animal models, the mainstream of psychiatry has shunned such models as being too primitive and hence irrelevant. Although we couch it in different language, we are almost saying that emotional ills are diseases of the soul, that only man has a soul, and so the study of any other species is worthless. Yet we have known, at least since Darwin, that animals are capable of expressing emotions and that they have affectional bonds and social systems. What has been needed are investigators who would systematically experiment with animal psychopathology as Dr. McKinney has done.

Clearly, he has produced severe animal psychopathology, but both he and we have trouble naming it. I am especially intrigued by the work he has done on rehabilitating these animals. The animals produced by mother-infant separation or by peer separation have features which anthropomorphically we would identify as resembling severe anaclitic depression, autism or schizophrenia. The fact that they can be rehabilitated by interaction with baby monkeys, whose own needs for contact make them persistently approach and contact the withdrawn monkey, makes it clear that the condition is reversible. The fact that it can also be done with chlorpromazine along with gradual introduction of the disturbed animals into a social milieu gives us a clear demonstration that in such psychopathology, pharmacotherapy and psychotherapy are perhaps interchangeable and raises the possibility of similar applications in some conditions in man. The very provocative question of whether or not pharmacotherapy and psychotherapy are also interactive or even additive remains a subject for future work. I cannot stress sufficiently that the question of how drugs and psychotherapy relate to each other in man is among the most important psychiatric issues of the day. It is very difficult to study in man, however, and only a few studies, like those of Weissman and Paykel (1974) in depression, have offered evidence of additive effects. The animal experiments may offer us a powerful strategy for future research. Yet even this must be approached with caution. I was pleased when Dr. McKinney described his work with chlorpromazine, because this drug works well with psychoses and poorly with neuroses. Hence, on pharmacological grounds, one might call the monkeys psychotic. Dr. McKinney has been understandably reluctant to label his animals in human terms, and this is one illustration of the hazards attendant upon such labeling.

There are other implications of Dr. McKinney's work that deserve comment. The first has to do with genetics. In man there is increasing evidence that the diathesis to depression, as contrasted to realistic grief, has genetic components. If Dr. McKinney has really produced depression, we have the question of whether or not his monkeys have a gene which predisposes them to this condition. If this is the case, then breeding experiments, impossible in man, could be conducted to generate strains susceptible to and resistant to depression. Genetic experiments in monkeys, while difficult, are still more feasible than in man.

Transcultural experiments could also be carried out. Dr. Kaufman in Denver is doing such experiments with bonnets and pigtails. Bonnet monkeys raise their infants in a type of group mothering program so that if the biological mother is removed the infant turns to a surrogate. Pigtails have a one-to-one relationship with their biological mothers. Bonnet infants do not appear depressed when separated from their mothers; pigtails do. Probably these infant rearing patterns are genetically determined, but they need not be totally so. What will happen if bonnet babies are reared by pigtail mothers and vice versa? The data are not yet in, but it will be fascinating to see whether rearing in a different cultural pattern can protect or predispose to depression. This can yield important insights into the psychological factors involved in converting a genotype into a phenotype.

A second area of investigation that comes to mind deals with the modalities of sensory input that are required to maintain affectional bonds. Given the five senses of touch, sight, smell, taste and sound, perhaps all are required or alternatively perhaps some are more important than others. I'm still not clear, Dr. McKinney, whether or not the pitted animal can hear his mother?

DR. MCKINNEY: They cannot; in a separated situation they may or may not, depending on how you set up the paradigm.

DR. LIPTON: Then, you could in future investigations, establish experimental conditions in which you eliminated sensory inputs one at a time or in combinations and then measured the consequences for establishment of psychopathology or for protection against it.

Another comment I want to make has to do with the use of this kind of model for therapeutics, particularly pharmacotherapeutics. There is tremendous potential here, but given the expense of raising and breeding animals, I suspect that results will come rather slowly and may be difficult to interpret. We tend to label drugs in terms of their first known clinical use. Yet Dr. Klein has shown that imipramine is useful not only as an antidepressant but also in the treatment of phobias. One can hardly conclude that if an antidepressant works on an animal model, it is working on a depressive state rather than what might be an extremely phobic state in the animal. It is very difficult to determine which nosological state it really is from the clinical utility of the drug; so I don't feel that animal models, this kind of animal model at least, will offer us a quick and easy answer to the preclinical drug trials that we would like to have. Parenthetically, I would like to mention that I feel the rat is the least useful of the animal models since there seem to be no affectional bonds or strong social structure.

Finally, I would agree with Dr. McKinney that the animal model is uniquely useful for the study of biological pathogenesis. What is going on in the brain in severely disturbed behavioral states? In man this problem can only be approached indirectly, but in animals one can decapitate and analyze the brain chemically and even morphologically. That has a lot of potential. Dr. Breese of our laboratory has collaborated with Dr. McKinney in such preliminary experiments. Those which have been completed thus far have shown that infant monkeys stressed by separation show changes in their adrenals, but no changes have been found thus far in their brains.

DR. GALLANT: I agree with Dr. McKinney's statement that investigators should start paying more attention to the differences within species as having considerable relevance for the understanding of human social organizations. One example of this variation is the difference in cooperative behavior within a species. As emphasized by Scott and his associates (1973), there are genetic and environmental differences that affect the general motivational system for attachment and separation behavior. Dr. McKinney mentioned one example, the bonnet infant monkeys who are handled by several mothers and do not develop a depressive reaction after removal from the original mother. The huddling together of the bonnet monkeys in groups infers that a genetic factor is *strongly* influencing the social organization. This possible genetic variation within a species has to be taken into account when comparing frequency of depressive problems in various cultures as well as differences in pharmacologic treatment results. In the human species, attempts to separate environmental influences from genetic differences are somewhat more complex. While genetic factors may be of relatively great importance in explaining some of the differences between the cultures of southeast Asia and the West in family groups and rearing of offspring, the relatively rapid trend from the large extended families to small nuclear families in the United States during the past century is obviously more dependent upon socioeconomic and environmental modifications. The relative importance of genetic factors, as compared to environmental factors, in determining the depressive reaction may have some correlation with response to antidepressant drug therapy and will be described in several of the other presentations.

Dr. McKinney's description of the treatment of isolate monkeys by pairing them with younger subjects and his opinion that animals of the same age may provide too many stimuli for the withdrawing isolate animals reminds me of the problem we have concerning environmental stimulation of the depressed patient. As has been recognized for many years, the environmental stimulation surrounding all patients is one of the major variables affecting the treatment response of the subject. Environmental stimuli should be decreased for manics and increased for patients recovering from depressions. However, the timing of the stimulation may have an important effect on the treatment outcome. Excessive stimulations (which could be the problem when pairing equal aged animals with the social isolates) or premature stimulation of the depressed patient can only increase his feelings of inadequacy and hopelessness at a time when he is unable to respond to the stimulation. These variables of quantity of timing as well as quality of environmental stimuli must be kept in mind when one is dealing with both animal and human research.

The importance of using animal models as predictors of psychopharmacologic activity was emphasized by Dr. McKinney when he stated that chlorpromazine treatment has been shown to be beneficial for monkeys who were displaying disturbed behavior as a result of early partial social isolation. The importance of the animal model for the psychopharmacologic treatment of depression has been shown by Scott and his associates (1973). After they produced distress at the absence of the familiar and fear of the strange in beagles who were exposed to prolonged separation, administration of imipramine apparently decreased this symptomatology. The symptoms of distress at the absence of the familiar and fear of the strange may be related to separation anxiety in children or what is known as "school phobia." Whether or not this symptomatology is related to some of the depressive symptomatology observed in man remains to be determined.

Another important point raised in Dr. McKinney's paper was the possibility that biologically induced syndromes of abnormal behavior could be reversed by strictly social means. The obvious inference that environmental changes can result in a normalization of biologically induced syndromes of abnormal behavior and mood is most encouraging. The increased efficacy resulting from the combination of drug maintenance therapy with psychotherapy in depressed patients, as shown by Dr. Weissman and her associates (1974), would then have even greater implications for future directions in evaluating combinations of environmental (e.g., psychotherapeutic or behavioral) and pharmacologic drug therapy in the treatment of various mental disorders. The quantum leap from drug trials in research institutions to complex outpatient trials in patients residing at home is just as big a jump as from investigations in laboratory animals under sterile social conditions to early human clinical trials.

It should be quite evident by this time that these animal models are essential for the understanding of depression and other mental and mood disorders in human subjects. In fact, with the trend toward increased restrictions of human research in the United States, it may well be that all of the clinical pharmacologists in this country will become almost solely dependent upon these animal models for the development of new drugs and for the elaboration of the understanding of these new agents in relation to their metabolism and therapeutic effects.

Concerning the specific problem of depression, it is important to remember that the depressive reaction is one type of final common pathway toward which a number of causes converge, as the etiology may be multiple. The appropriate combination of environmental and biochemical treatment methods may facilitate therapeutic results, and this *interaction* must be thoroughly explored in both controlled animal and human studies.

I have one question for Dr. McKinney which was alluded to by Dr. Lipton. In your opinion, would it be feasible to inbreed, using artificial insemination if necessary, those monkeys that are *least* susceptible to the protest-despair separation type of reactions and compare them with those inbred monkeys who are *most* susceptible to this syndrome in order to obtain more homogeneous samples for biochemical, neurophysiologic and psychopharmacologic research? I am referring to the use of the reactors at both ends of the normal curve in order to obtain control comparison groups of animals.

DR. MCKINNEY: It should be feasible but it has not been done. It would take a relatively long time to build up that population, but it may be worth the effort.

DR. LIPTON: My recollection of imipramine in the beagle study is that it did work in a specific manner by diminishing the vocalization during the separation phase without sedating the animals.

DR. HEATH: We did have a number of Dr. Harlow's monkeys who were implanted with depth electrodes in specific subcortical sites, and extensively recorded in chronic implantation studies. I also had a group of twenty-three isolation reared monkeys from Bill Mason. His study was an attempt to address himself to the question of what sensory modalities are involved, a point that was raised by Dr. Lipton. The Harlow monkeys were raised in severe isolation and show recording changes at the same specific brain sites where we had almost identical recording changes in psychotic patients. So there was a correlation between recordings at specific deep brain sites and behavioral phenomena in these animals, just as there had been in our human population. I want to point out that the altered brain activity in the human was associated with psychotic behavior, not with schizophrenia particularly. These results should not be misinterpreted because there are many causes of psychosis. Schizophrenia is one type of psychosis, and the recording changes we get are essentially the same and at the same site for all psychoses. Thus it appears that the isolation raised monkeys are a model for a type of psychotic behavior. The recordings resemble essentially what we have in psychotic people.

Abnormal behavior in humans cannot give any indication of the specific etiology of schizophrenia. The recording changes are in the pleasure system and are focused around the septal region and interconnected sites, areas which have been correlated with emotionality. The changes were also in the sensory relay nuclei, and we have worked out connections between these sites that are important in emotional expression and the sensory relay nuclei. In the schizophrenics, there does seem to be some alteration in uptake of transmitter amines which might be basic to the recording changes; however, I want to reiterate that this particular biochemical alteration from transmitter amines or in enzymes as well as the physiological recordings are not specific to a given pathology; they are not necessarily specific for schizophrenia. We can produce these same recording changes in monkeys and similar behavioral changes by passively transferring to them immunoglobulins that we obtain from schizophrenics, which also affect the uptake of transmitter amines rather profoundly; I would say this gets closer to explaining what the pathology might be in the etiology of schizophrenia. I consider the animal models to be extremely useful, but I think they have some limitations in what they precisely demonstrate compared to what is seen clinically in patients.

DR. MCKINNEY: When Dr. Lipton asked me how one would label these isolated animals, I studiously avoided the word schizophrenia and used the term undifferentiated psychosis. I still don't know what it means. I think Dr. Heath's points are very good ones in terms of semantics of the psychosis.

In terms of combined pharmacotherapy and psychotherapy, it looks as if the models are useful for evaluating how these two areas can fit together. For example, one can use chlorpromazine to reduce quickly the level of disturbance in behaviors, while at the same time gradually introducing different levels of milieu therapy to animals. We first start with the very young and then gradually introduce animals closer in age to the isolate, meanwhile maintaining the isolated animals on chlorpromazine. That combination works quite well. One can get the isolated animals to a point where they can interact normally with equal-age peers. Frankly, the evaluation of the combination of these two treatment approaches is the one use of the animal models that I am quite excited about at the present time.

REFERENCES

Breese, G. R., Smith, R. D., et al. (1973). Induction of adrenal catecholamine synthesizing enzymes following mother-infant separation. *Nature/New Biol.* 246: 94–96.
Gardner, B. T., and Gardner, T. A. (1971). Two-way communication with an infant chimpanzee. In A.M. Schrier and F. Stolenitz, eds., *Behavior of Non-Human Primates*, Vol. 4. New York: Academic Press.
Harlow, H. F. (1964). Early social deprivation and later behavior in the monkey. In A. Abrams, H. H. Garner and J. E. P. Tomal, eds., *Unfinished Tasks in the Behavioral Sciences*. Baltimore: Williams & Wilkins, pp. 154–73.
———— and Harlow, M. K. (1971). Psychopathology in monkeys. In H. D. Kimmel; ed., *Experimental Psychopathology: Recent Research and Theory*. New York: Academic Press.
———— and Suomi, S. J. (1970). Induced psychopathology in monkeys. *Engineer Sci.* 33:8–14.
————and Suomi, S. J. (1971a). Productionof depressive behaviors in young monkeys. *J. Autism Child Schiz.* 1:246–55.
———— and Suomi, S. J. (1971b). Social recovery by isolation-reared monkeys. *Proc. Nat. Acad. Sci.* 68:1534–38.

————, Harlow, M. K., et al. (1966). Maternal behavior of rhesus monkeys deprived of mothering and peer associations in infants. *Proc. Am. Philos. Soc.* 110:58–66.

————, Rowland, G. L., et al. (1964). The effect of total social deprivation on the development of monkey behavior. In P. Solomon and B. C. Glueck, eds., *Recent Research on Schizophrenia.* American Psychiatric Assn., pp. 116–35.

Heath, R. G. (1971). Electroencephalographic studies in isolation-raised monkeys with behavioral impairment. *Dis. Nerv. Syst.* 33:157-63.

Hinde, R. A. and Spencer-Booth, Y. (1971). Effects of brief separation from mother on rhesus monkeys. *Science* 173:111–18.

————, Spencer-Booth, Y., et al. (1966). Effects of 6-day maternal deprivation on rhesus monkey infants. *Nature* 210:1021–23.

Jensen, G. D., and Tvemen, C.W. (1962). Mother-infant relationship in the monkey, macaca nemestrina: the effect of brief separation and mother-infant specificity. *J. Comp. Physiol. Psychol.* 55:131–36.

Kaufman, I. C., and Rosenblum, L. A. (1967a). Depression in infant monkeys separated from their mothers. *Science* 155:1030–31.

————and Rosenblum, L. A. (1967b). The reaction to separation in infant monkeys: anaclitic depression and conservation-withdrawal. *Psychosom. Med.* 29:648–75.

Kubie, L. S. (1939). The experimental induction of neurotic reaction in man. *Yale J. Biol. Med.* 11:541–45.

McKinney, W. T. (1974). Primate social isolation: psychiatric implications. *Arch. Gen. Psychiat.* 31:422–26.

————, and Bunney, W. F. (1969). Animal model of depression: review of evidence. *Arch. Gen. Psychiat.* 21:240.

————, Eising, R. G., et al. (1971a). Effects of reserpine on the social behavior of rhesus monkeys. *Dis. Nerv. Syst.* 32:735–41.

————, Suomi, S. J., et al. (1971b). Depression in primates. *Am. J. Psychiat.* 127:1313–20.

————, Suomi, S. J., et al. (1972a). Repetitive peer separations of juvenile age rhesus monkeys. *Arch. Gen. Psychiat.* 27:200–03.

————, Suomi, S. J., et al. (1972b). Vertical chamber confinement of juvenile age rhesus monkeys. *Arch. Gen. Psychiat.* 26:223–28.

————, Young, L. D., et al. (1973). Chlorpromazine treatment of disturbed monkeys. *Arch. Gen. Psychiat.* 29:490–95.

Mason, W. A. (1963a). Social development of rhesus monkeys with restricted social experience. *Percept. Motor Skills* 16:263-70.

———— (1963b). The effects of environmental restriction on the social development of rhesus monkeys. In C. H. Southwick, ed., *Primate Social Behavior.* Princeton, N.J.: Van Nostrand, pp. 161–73.

———— (1968). Early social deprivation in the non-human primates: implications for human behavior. In D. C. Glass, ed., *Environmental Influences.* New York: Rockefeller University & Russell Sage Foundation, pp. 70–100.

————and Sponholz, R. R. (1953. Behavior of rhesus monkeys raised in isolation. *J. Psychiat. Res.* 1:298-306.

Miller, R. E., Mirsky, I. A., et al. (1969). Hyperphagia and polydipsia in socially isolated rhesus monkeys. *Science* 165:1027–28.

Premack, D. A. (1970). A functional analysis of language. *J. Exp. Anal. Behav.* 14:107-25.

Redmond, D. E., Maas, J. W., et al. (1971a). Changes in primate social behavior after treatment with alpha-methyl-paratyrosine. *Psychosom. Med.* 33:97-113.

————, Maas, J. W., et al. (1971b). Social behavior of monkeys selectively depleted of monoamines. *Science* 174:428–31.

Rosenblum, L. A., and Kaufman, I. C. (1968). Variations in infant development and response to maternal loss in monkeys. *Am. J. Orthopsychiat.* 83:418–26.

Scott, J. P., Stewart, J. M., and DeGhett, V. J. (1973). Separations in infant dogs: emotional responses and motivational consequences. In J. P. Scott and E. C. Senay, eds., *Separation and Depression*. Washington, D. C.: AAAS Publ. No. 94.

Seay, W., Hansen, E., et al. (1962). Mother-infant separation in monkeys. *J. Child Psychol. Psychiat.* 3:123–32.

Seay, W., and Harlow, H. F. (1965). Maternal separation in the rhesus monkey. *J. Nerv. Ment. Dis.* 140:434–41.

Seligman, M. E. P., and Groves, D. (1970). Non-transient learned helplessness. *Psychol. Sci.* 19:191–92.

———and Maier, S. F. (1967). Failure to escape traumatic shock. *J. Exp. Psychol.* 74:1-9.

———, Maier, S. F., et al. (1968). The alleviation of learned helplessness in the dog. *J. Abn. Soc. Psychol.* 73:256-62.

Suomi, S. J., Domak, C. J., et al. (1970). Effectos of repetitive infant-infant separation of young monkeys. *J. Abn. Psychol.* 76:161–72.

———, Harlow, H. F., et al. (1972). Monkey psychiatrists. *Am. J. Psychiat.* 128:927–32.

Weissman, M. M., and Paykel, E. J. (1974). *The Depressed Woman*. Chicago, Ill.: Univ. of Chicago Press.

Young, L. D., Suomi, S. J., et al. (1973). Early stress and later response to separation in rhesus monkeys. *Am. J. Psychiat.* 130:400-05.

CHAPTER II

Biological Concepts of Depression

J. Mendels, S. Stern and A. Frazer

The past decade has seen an unprecedented expansion of investigation into, and theorization about, the biological changes associated with clinical depression and mania.* The demonstration that drugs can alleviate the symptoms of depression and mania while others induce symptoms suggestive of depression, together with increasing evidence that genetic factors play an important role in the development of some forms of affective illness, has constituted the major spur to this line of inquiry (Schildkraut, 1970; Mendels, 1974; Mendels, 1975).

This upsurge of interest does not exclude or even diminish the possibility that psychological, social or developmental factors play an important role in the genesis of affective illness. Rather than engage in fruitless debates as to whether biological or psychological factors are more important, we should recognize that we do not have the necessary information to resolve the issue and that we are probably dealing with an interaction between a variety of factors. Certainly this is true with such conditions as diabetes, hypertension and cardiovascular disease, among

---

*At key points in this manuscript, major review articles are cited which contain many of the references for the material discussed in that section. The large amount of material summarized in this review prohibits individual citation of each item discussed. Thus we have adopted the general policy of citing several recent reviews and/or books which will contain specific references to the material discussed here, and the interested reader can refer to these. In addition, certain key references or more recent papers which may not be included in the general reviews are also cited. This policy has been adopted to avoid what would otherwise be an unwieldy format. It is hoped that individual investigators whose work is discussed in this review will find this acceptable.

others. Why should it not apply to the major psychiatric disorders?

Several points must be borne in mind in evaluating our current knowledge and in planning future investigations in this area. These include:

Heterogeneity of Depression

Depression is almost certainly a heterogeneous condition with a variety of manifestations, pathologies and etiologies (Mendels, 1970; Klerman, 1971; Robins and Guze, 1972; Becker, 1974; Klein, 1974). Unfortunately, while most investigators recognize this, it is only recently that they have begun to design studies and analyze data accordingly. For many years most investigators simply studied hospitalized depressed patients as a group, perhaps dividing them on the basis of severity of the illness or some other clinical variable. As a consequence, it is possible that a significant abnormality in a relatively small subgroup of patients may have been obscured by the findings from a larger group of patients in whom no abnormality was present.

We know from general medicine that this approach can be misleading. For example, pernicious anemia is different from other forms of anemia, in terms of etiology, pathology and treatment. This had led to the need to *identify* this particular type of anemia, and *then* institute specific treatment with vitamin B_{12}. If one simply treated one hundred consecutive anemic patients with vitamin B_{12}, then the improvement rate for the group would have been insignificant, and the investigators would have concluded that vitamin B_{12} was of no value in the treatment of anemia. As a generalization, this, of course, is true. It required the recognition of the specific condition — pernicious anemia — and its association with vitamin B_{12} to form the basis for an adequate evaluation.

There have been many attempts to divide depressed patients into meaningful groups. In the main, these have been conducted by clinicians, statisticians or psychometricians who have conducted studies aimed at separating depressed patients into nosological categories using such descriptive terms as endogenous, reactive, neurotic, psychotic, involutional, agitated, retarded, presenile, and so forth. More recently the terms bipolar and unipolar* have come into prominence following on the initial observations by Leonhard and the subsequent descriptions by Perris and others, and the suggestion that these constitute two independent types of depression. This approach has yielded interesting findings which will be summarized later. However, it is probable that these two groups may each contain more than one type of illness.

The important point is that investigators must be on the alert for clusters of patients with a particular pathology. Our studies investigating the possible anti-

---

*Bipolar depression describes patients who have both depressive and manic episodes, while unipolar depression refers to patients with recurrent depressive episodes without evidence of mania or hypomania. It is probably advisable to exclude from the unipolar group patients with a family history of bipolar illness but who themselves have never been manic or hypomanic.

depressant effects of lithium carbonate constitute an example of the potential importance of this approach. Several investigators have advanced the general argument that lithium is not an effective antidepressant drug. Certainly if lithium were given to an unselected group of depressed patients it would not be of value for the group as a whole. However, if we are able to identify and isolate a subgroup of depressed patients who are lithium-responsive, then this would provide a rational approach for further investigation. Using this strategy we now have evidence suggesting that there is a specific group of depressed patients who are lithium-responsive and who accumulate proportionately more of the cation in their erythrocytes than do nonresponders (Mendels, et al., 1972b; Mendels and Frazer, 1973). While this group probably constitutes only a small percentage of the total population of depressed patients, it does serve as an example of the strategy which must be adopted if we are to advance our understanding of this complex disorder.

Primary and Secondary Biochemical Changes

The biological changes associated with depression may be primary (associated with the etiology and/or development of the condition) or secondary either to the primary biochemical change or to the illness itself. It is possible that the secondary changes may obscure the primary manifestations. Certainly some of the changes noted in depressives are not specific for that condition, and may be associated with concomitant anxiety or psychosis. Even if it were demonstrated that certain biological changes anteceded the clinical appearance of the depression, we could not assume that these changes are of etiological significance. While such an observation would be of great interest, the alteration could be secondary to another, hidden, process.

Interdependence of Systems

Most of the systems that we are interested in are *interdependent* with each other, and changes in one may lead to changes (either conpensatory or pathological) in another. This will be discussed in more detail later.

Inaccessibility of the Brain

We are unable to evaluate directly and quantify central nervous system acitivity controlling mood and behavior. Even assuming that we knew in which area of the brain to find a defect causing depression and mania, we have no way of directly measuring it. One interesting possibility is that the dysfunction in depression may be generalized, and not localized to the brain. This is a subject for future research.

Clinical studies, while of interest and value, must be interpreted with caution because of their indirect nature. Certainly results from indirect studies do not prove or disprove hypotheses. However, a confluence of findings from such studies is of potential importance.

Limitations of Study Methods

There are many compounds in the brain including glycine, glutamate, gamma-amino butyric acid and histamine, to name a few, which presumably play critical roles in central nervous system functioning. At present, there are very few studies of the function of these compounds and what, if any, their relationship may be to the pathogenesis of affective disorders. It would not be surprising, as techniques become available for better study of these compounds, to find that they are affected by many psychotropic drugs and that they also show altered function in some patients with affective disorders.

In spite of these and other difficulties, there has been considerable progress in developing models of the psychobiology of depression (Schildkraut, 1970; Mendels, 1974, 1975). It seems clear (see Chapter III) that there is a genetic predisposition to the development of certain types of affective disorders. Further, investigators have examined in some detail various aspects of biogenic amine function; electrolyte metabolism; cell membrane function; neuroendocrine function, including hypothalamic-pituitary activity; and electrophysiological activities, such as cortical evoked potential, electromyography and sleep electroencephalography.

In reviewing some of the evidence and findings in these areas, we will be considering them individually for reasons of convenience. However, it is important to remember that these systems all interact with each other in a complex fashion, and changes in one will probably lead to changes in others. Thus it is possible that some alteration in the interrelationships between several of these systems is far more important to the etiology of depression than a change in activity of an isolated system. Here, too, we have been slow to develop both theories and experiments. There are a few exceptions which will be noted later.

NEUROENDOCRINE STUDIES AND AFFECTIVE DISORDERS

There has been a longstanding interest in several aspects of neuroendocrine function in depressed and manic patients (Kraines, 1966; Rubin and Mandell, 1966; Whybrow et al., 1969; Davies et al., 1972; Sachar, 1973, 1975). This has recently been stimulated by the development of more advanced experimental strategies and the realization that the biogenic amines play an important role in the mediation of neuroendocrine function. Thus a systematic examination of aspects of endocrine function in depressed patients may provide indirect evidence of some aspect of aminergic function in the brain — or at least in the hypothalamus.

Some years ago Kraines (1966) suggested that there was an abnormality in hypothalamic function in patients with affective disorders. It is known that lesions in the hypothalamus may be associated with mood disturbance in man and that hypothalamic stimulation will produce intense affective responses. Furthermore, the regulation of appetite, sexual activities, menstruation and aggression, all of which may be disturbed in depressed patients, are mediated through the hypothalamus.

Hypothalamic-Pituitary-Adrenal Function

A relatively large number of studies of adrenal cortical function in depressed patients have been reported (Rubin and Mandell, 1966; Davies et al., 1972; Sachar, 1973). In summary, there is evidence of increased adrenocortical activity in many depressed patients. This includes: elevation in plasma cortisol; elevated urinary free cortisol; elevated cerebrospinal fluid free cortisol; elevated urinary 17-hydroxycorticosteroids; resistance to dexamethasone suppression; and a flattening of the normal diurnal curve for plasma cortisol with increased amplitude of the pulses of cortisol release.

Many of these findings are seen in patients with Cushing's Syndrome (hyperadrenalism). In fact, many patients with Cushing's Syndrome exhibit significant affective changes including both euphoria and depression. Likewise, therapeutic administration of adrenocortical hormones may be associated with mood change. Butler and Besser reported that a variety of tests of adrenal function did not distinguish between patients with Cushing's Syndrome and patients with severe depression.

Several suggestions have been made as to the significance of the increased adrenocortical activity seen in some depressed patients. While it may be the result of such nonspecific factors as the stress of the illness, concomitant anxiety, or hospitalization, this does not seem to provide an adequate explanation for several findings. Thus, Stokes, Carroll and others have reported that: schizophrenic patients with psychosis ratings equivalent to depressives do not have any abnormality in dexamethasone suppression whereas the depressed patients do (Carroll, 1975a); there is no consistent correlation between the elevated adrenocortical activity and manifest anxiety; the administration of anxiolytic drugs does not suppress the exaggerted adrenal cortical activity; and changes in adrenocortical acitivity tend to persist beyond the period of initial adaptation to hospital and are of a greater magnitude than those seen in other hospitalized patients.

The increased adrenocortical function may reflect an abnormality in the hypothalamic control of pituitary function and the subsequent release of ACTH. Hypothalamic biogenic amines are involved in the regulation of the release of corticotropin releasing factor (McCann and Porter, 1969; Ganong, 1970), and it has been suggested that there is a failure to inhibit the mechanism which normally stops the release of corticotropin releasing factor in depressed patients. There is evidence that noradrenergic neurons play an important role in this mechanism (Davies et al., 1972, p. 23). For example, procedures which increase norepinephrine content (e.g. monoamine oxidase inhibitors) will decrease ACTH release, while depletion of norepinephrine by FLA-63, a dopamine beta hydroxylase inhibitor, is associated with an increase in adrenocortical activity. Further, alpha-methyl-paratyrosine (AMPT), which inhibits norepinephrine synthesis, will enhance corticosteroid release.

Thus, it may be that the increased adrenocortical activity found in some depressed patients is a reflection of a reduction in activity of noradrenergic neurons which normally inhibit ACTH release. This would result in increased ACTH release and subsequent increased adrenocortical activity. If this explanation is correct, it would support the hypothesis of a norepinephrine deficit in depression (*infra vide*).

Thyroid Hormone

There have been several studies of thyroid function in depression, with no clear evidence of abnormal function emerging. Patients with thyroid disease do have significant psychiatric disturbance, with symptoms of depression common in those with hypothyroidism (Whybrow et al., 1969b). Of related interest are the reports by Prange and his associates (1969) that L-tri-iodothyronine (T_3) and thyroid stimulating hormone (TSH) will accelerate the antidepressant response to imipramine in female (but not male) depressed patients. A similar association with amitriptyline has been reported (Wheatley, 1972). Recently there has been considerable interest in reports that thyrotropic releasing factor (TRH), the hypothalamic polypeptide which stimulates the release of TSH from the pituitary, produces a temporary but significant symptomatic response in some depressed patients (Kastin et al., 1972; Prange et al., 1927). These reports have assumed additional interest in view of the finding that TRH is present throughout the brain. Several recent studies have failed to confirm the claim for an antidepressant effect for TRH (Hollister et al., 1974). It is possible that TRH may be useful only in a discrete subgroup of patients.

Sex Hormones

There is considerable evidence that factors associated with aspects of sex hormone functions may be of importance in our understanding of the development of depression (Janowksy et al., 1971). Thus depression is more common in females than in males, especially among unipolar depressives (this may be due to genetic rather than hormonal factors), and is more likely to occur at times of endocrine change—premenstrually, post-partum, at the menopause, or in association with oral contraceptive administration.

It is unlikely that we are dealing with a simple increase or decrease in the level of a particular hormone but rather with a more complex action. For example, there may be sex-related differences in the activity of monoamine oxidase (Belmaker et al., 1974) which could contribute to alterations in amine function. To date, little attention has been directed toward this issue, and there are a number of important lines of investigation which need to be developed.

Growth Hormone

A number of studies of growth hormone release in depressed patients have recently been completed (Sachar, 1975; Frazer, 1975), aimed in part at an evaluation of the functional integrity of the hypothalamic mechanisms (involving catecholaminergic and perhaps serotonergic neurons) regulating the release of this hormone. These studies have produced negative findings. For example, the growth hormone response to L-DOPA or apomorphine administration in depressed patients is no different from that of control subjects. Likewise, growth hormone release during sleep in normal in depressives when age and sex are controlled.

One possible exception to these negative findings is the report by Sachar (1974) that the growth hormone response to insulin-induced hypoglycemia is low in postmenopausal unipolar depressed females, as compared with other groups of depressed patients. Sachar has suggested that this is an indication of inadequate "endogenous" brain catecholamine reserves. One must also consider the possibility that the degree of hypoglycemia produced in the depressed patient may have been insufficient to cause adequate growth hormone release, as it has been suggested that depressed patients are relatively insensitive to insulin. An alternative explanation is suggested by the report that the serotonin receptor blocking agents cyproheptadine and methysergide inhibit the normal growth hormone response to hypoglycemia (Bivens et al., 1973). Thus the inadequate growth hormone response to hypoglycemia in some depressed patients may reflect impaired serotonin function.

ELECTROLYTE METABOLISM

Electrolytes play a central role in several critical aspects of neuronal function (Hodgkin, 1964; Katz, 1966; Molinoff and Axelrod, 1971). This includes their involvement in maintaining the normal resting potential of nerves; in carrying the current required for the action potential; in the synthesis, storage, release and inactivation of neurotransmitters; and in carrying the current responsible for depolarization of postsynaptic membranes. Depression and mania are presumably associated with an alteration in neuronal function, and it is therefore conceivable that an abnormality of electrolyte metabolism may be of importance in their development (Baer et al., 1970b; Durell, 1974; Mendels and Frazer, 1974a; 1975a).

Several investigators have shown that clincial depression is associated with a retention of sodium followed by an increased loss of sodium in the urine with clinical recovery. This has been observed with studies of 24-hour urinary sodium concentration; 24-hour exchangeable sodium; and sodium 22 retention.

Coppen and Shaw suggested that the sodium retained during clinical depression resulted in an increase in residual sodium—defined as the combination of intracellular and bone sodium. However, the methodology employed in their study is controversial, and further investigation of this possibility is needed. Two groups of investigators have measured intracellular (erythrocyte) sodium concentration in depressed patients. Naylor noted an elevation in the intraerythrocyte sodium concentration in psychotic depressives which returned to normal with clinical recovery. We have not been able to confirm this observation and have found no consistent significant differences in erythrocyte sodium concentration in male depressed patients and hospitalized control subjects matched for age and sex. It is possible that the different findings in these two sets of studies may be due to sex differences in the two groups of patients.

Calcium

Calcium plays an important role in several aspects of neuronal function. However, investigation of the distribution and concentration of this cation in depressed patients has been more limited than that of sodium because of methodological problems. There is a report of an increased calcium retention in a group of depressed patients who improved as compared with patients who did not improve (Flach, 1964). The patients who improved had a reduction in urinary calcium excretion. It has been suggested that there may be an alteration in calcitonin activity in depression. However, the more important studies of ionized plasma calcium with adequate control of diet and physical activity have yet to be conducted.

Magnesium

Magnesium plays an important role in nervous system activity with a direct effect on excitable membranes and by acting as a cofactor in several critical enzymatic reactions. Magnesium also shares some important physical properties with lithium (Williams, 1973), adding further interest to investigations of this cation. There are reports of alterations in plasma and erythrocyte magnesium concentration in depressives, but these have not been confirmed by others (Mendels, 1974, p. 504). Further studies with clearly defined patient groups and control of concomitant medications may resolve these contradictions. Furthermore, plasma magnesium is both protein-bound and free. To date, there has been only one study reported of the measurement of free magnesium levels in depressed patients and no significant differences from controls were found (Frizel et al., 1969).

Cell Membrane

Attention has been focused recently on the possibility that some depressed patients may have altered functioning of the processes responsible for cation distribution across the cell membrane (Mendels and Frazer, 1974a; Glen and Reading, 1973). Thus we have reported that depressed patients who respond to treatment with lithium have a different distribution of the cation across the erythrocyte membrane *in vivo* than do patients who do not respond to lithium.

This may be due to differences in either the entry of lithium into the cell or its transport from the cell. In subsequent experiments we have shown that the distribution of lithium across the erythrocyte membrane is under genetic control, both *in vitro* (Dorus, et al., 1974) and *in vivo* (Dorus, personal communication). Furthermore, in experiments using erythrocytes obtained from sheep, we found that intrinsic differences in cell membrane properties regulating cation distribution produce large changes in the distribution of lithium (Schless et al., 1975).

On the basis of these data, we have formulated a working hypothesis; namely, that there is a subgroup of depressed patients with a genetically determined abnormality in some aspect of cell membrane properties which regulate the movement of electrolytes across the plasma membrane. This subgroup of patients may partially overlap with the diagnostic group designated as having bipolar depressive illness.

Unfortunately, there are only a few reports in the literature dealing with cation transport in depressed patients. To our knowledge, only one group of investigators has examined sodium and potassium transport in erythrocytes obtained from depressed patients. Naylor and associates reported lower active transport of sodium in erythrocytes from eleven psychotically depressed women compared with erythrocytes from thirteen neurotically depressed patients. In both patient groups the active and the passive transfer of sodium (but not of potassium) increased significantly with recovery after treatment with electroconvulsive therapy. In a subsequent study these investigators reported that neither Na, K-activated adenosine triphosphatase (ATPase) activity nor ouabain-sensitive potassium flux was different in erythrocytes obtained from either psychotically or neurotically depressed women. Hokin-Neaverson and associates (1974) have reported a reduced transport of ^{22}Na from sodium-loaded erythrocytes obtained from patients with bipolar depressive illness. This report is in accordance with the initial observations of Naylor and associates. Recently, it has been reported that lithium treatment is associated with an increase in erythrocyte Na,K-activated ATPase activity (Naylor et al., 1974a). Further investigations of the cation transport systems in patients with affective illnesses are clearly indicated.

Glen and his colleagues used a different system to evaluate membrane transport characteristics in patients with manic-depressive or recurrent depressive illness. They measured sodium activity and pH in secreted salvia. The final composition of this fluid depends on the flow rate and the rates of selective reabsorption or secretion of ions across the collecting duct walls of the salivary glands. They found that depressed patients had significantly higher sodium activity and lower hydrogen ion activity than did healthy control subjects. These data indicate reduced reabsorption of sodium and of bicarbonate (measured as pH) in the depressed patients.

Another approach to evaluating electrolyte transfer has been the measurement of the rate of entry of ^{24}Na from plasma into lumbar spinal fluid. The underlying mechanisms of this transfer of sodium are not clear. Passive diffusion is certainly involved, but active processes appear to play a role as well. In a review of several studies, Carroll concluded that ^{24}Na transfer may be reduced in depressed patients. Unfortunately, the significance of this and its relationship to the transfer of electrolytes across the erythrocyte membrance is unclear.

There have been several investigations of the effect of lithium on action potentials, cation transfer, and sodium- and potassium-activated ATPase activity. Most investigators agree that lithium can substitute for sodium, at least initially, in carrying the current of the action potential. However, this effect is short-lived, probably because lithium is extruded from nerve cells at a much slower rate than sodium. This corresponds to the inability of lithium to substitute for sodium in stimulating Na,K-activated ATPase activity. Lithium does have some affinity for the external site of cation transport and Na,K-activated ATPase, but it is less potent than potassium in activating these processes.

In the presence of sodium ions, lithium does not appear to inhibit cation pump activity (Baker, 1965) and may actually enhance Na,K-activated ATPase activity (Tobin et al., 1974). In keeping with this latter observation, Glen (Glen et al., 1972) reported that relatively low concentrations of lithium (3 or 6 nM) stimulated the efflux of ^{22}Na from erythrocytes in the presence of 3 nM external potassium.

Lithium can influence sodium pump activity; it may alter neuronal excitability by changing the contribution of electrogenic pump potentials to either the resting membrane potential or the membrane potential following a tetanus (Thomas, 1972). Indeed, Ploeger and Hertog (1973) found that low concentrations of lithium caused a dose-dependent decrease in the amplitude of the potassium-activated response potential (a hyperpolarization due to the electrogenic nature of the sodium pump) in rat cervical vagi. In an extension of this study, Ploeger (1974) found that the inhibition produced by lithium is due to an action at both the external K site of the pump and the internal Na site of the carrier system. Evidence was also obtained that the inhibitory effect of lithium is most pronounced during periods of increased nervous activity, which supports the earlier observation of Giacobini and Stepita-Klauco (1970). Ploeger proposed a model in which lithium ions block pump activity practically irreversibly on the inside of the membrane, due to a very low dissociation and association constant of the lithium carrier complex at this site. According to this model, the concentration of intracellular lithium ions would be an important determinant of the pharmacological effectiveness of the cation, which is in keeping with our finding that erythrocyte lithium correlates with the clinical effectiveness of lithium whereas plasma measures do not.

In accord with this model, we have also recently reported that lithium administration is associated with an increase in erythrocyte sodium concentration (Mendels and Frazer, 1974a). Naylor (Naylor et al., 1974a) found this as well. Furthermore, the trend was for erythrocyte sodium to increase in those patients who improved clinically. This increase in erythrocyte sodium did not occur in those patients who received lithium and did not show clinical improvement. These findings are compatible with the observations by Aronoff (Aronoff et al., 1971) and Baer (Baer et al., 1970a) that patients who improved when treated with lithium had a significantly greater increase in twenty-four-hour exchangeable sodium than patients who failed to respond.

BIOGENIC AMINES

Following the discovery by Walter Cannon in 1915 that animals exposed to rage-inducing or fear-inducing situations secrete increased amounts of epinephrine (adrenalin), there has been an increasing interest in the association between emotional behavior and biogenic amines. A further spur to such investigations was the finding that some patients with hypertension who were treated with reserpine developed a syndrome thought by some to be similar to clinical depression, together with the observation that reserpine produced a depletion of brain norepinephrine, dopamine and serotonin. These investigations and subsequent pharmacological studies showing that most antidepressant drugs increase the amount of amine available at receptor sites (at least after acute administration of the drug) led to the formulation of the biogenic amine hypothesis of affective disorders (Pare and Sandler, 1959; Prange, 1964; Bunney and Davis, 1965; Schildkraut, 1965, 1973a; Coppen, 1967; Lapin and Oxenkrug, 1969, Ashcroft et al., 1972; Mendels and Stinnett, 1973b). In brief, this suggests that depression is associated with a functional deficiency of norepinephrine or serotonin at significant receptor sites in the brain, whereas mania is associated with an excess of the amine.

Physiology and Pharmacology of Biogenic amines

Before reviewing the clinical studies, a brief review of the physiology and pharmacology of the biogenic amines might be useful. The interested reader may consult available reviews and books for further details (Axelrod, 1971; Geffen and Livett, 1971; Blaschko and Muscholl, 1972; Shore, 1972; Frazer and Stinett, 1973; Costa et al., 1974; Hamon and Glowinski, 1974).

There is general agreement that compounds such as acetylcholine, norepinephrine, dopamine and 5-hydroxytryptamine (serotonin) function as transmitter substances in the central nervous system. Even though most of the individual synapses in the brain where these compounds serve as neurohumoral agents remain to be elucidated, there is compelling evidence linking them with a variety of complex functions including eating, drinking, sleep and reward systems.

Norepinephrine is synthesized from the amino acid L-tyrosine by a pathway first suggested in 1939 by Blaschko. Metabolic intermediates in this process are L-dihydroxyphenylalanine (L-DOPA) and dopamine. Serotonin is formed in the body by enzymatic conversion of L-tryptophan to 5-hydroxytryptophan (5HTP), which is then decarboxylated to serotonin. Neither norepinephrine nor serotonin penetrate into the brain from the vascular system at the pH of blood. However, both of the precursors of these amines, L-DOPA and tryptophan, can enter the brain and are taken up by neurons and converted enzymatically to catecholamines and serotonin, respectively. This train of events provides the rationale for the evaluation of these amino acids as antidepressant agents.

Several investigators have examined the behavioral consequences of relatively selective monoamine depletion with drugs which interfere with the biosynthesis of either catecholamines or serotonin. For example, alpha-methyl-paratyrosine (AMPT) depletes brain catecholamines by inhibiting the enzymatic reaction that is rate-limiting in their biosynthesis (Spector et al., 1965). In a similar manner, para-chlorophenylalanine (PCPA) depletes brain serotonin by inhibiting its synthesis (Koe and Weissman, 1966; Jequier et al., 1967). The behavioral effects of these synthesis inhibitors will be reviewed later.

In the neuron, norepinephrine exists not in a single homogenous state, but in functionally different states called "pools." Most neuronal norepinephrine is found in a bound or stored form within subcellular particles termed "granules" or "vesicles." An extra-granular pool of norepinephrine which is transported into the granule by a "pump" system requiring ATP and low concentrations of sodium ion may also exist. This "pump" is inhibited by reserpine providing the basis for the depletion of monoamines caused by this compound.

On stimulation, norepinephrine is released from the intraneuronal granules into the synaptic gap. There is evidence that newly synthesized or newly stored norepinephrine (which constitutes a small percentage of the total intraneuronal norepinephrine) is preferentially released by stimulation. Thus this may constitute the functionally active pool.

After release into the synapse, the physiological actions of norepinephrine are thought to be largely terminated by its uptake back into the presynaptic terminal. This uptake process is temperature-dependent, exhibits saturation kinetics, requires the presence of sodium ion in the external medium, and exhibits stereospecificity in favor of the naturally occurring L-isomer of norepinephrine. Inhibition of this uptake process results in a potentiation and prolongation of noradrenergic activity.

Serotonin is also stored in vesicles within neurons and, as with norepinephrine, there is an active uptake process into nerve terminals.

Tricyclic antidepressants, such as imipramine and desmethylimipramine, inhibit the uptake of serotonin and norepinephrine but do not seem to affect dopamine uptake (Carlsson et al., 1969a). There is evidence that tertiary amines such as imipramine are more potent in inhibiting the uptake of serotonin than that of norepinephrine, while the secondary amines such as desmethylimipramine are more potent in inhibiting norepinephrine uptake than that of serotonin. The possible importance of these differential effects of the tricyclic compounds on monoamine uptake will be discussed later.

Enzymatic degradation of dopamine and norepinephrine occurs by the action of two enzymes, catechol-3-0-methyl-transferase (COMT) and monoamine oxidase (MAO). The predominant metabolism of serotonin occurs by oxidative deamination catalyzed by MAO, to 5-hydroxyindoleacetic acid (5HIAA). In addition to metabolizing circulating monoamines, MAO regulates the intraneuronal level of endogenous monoamines. This is due to its intraneuronal location in the mitochondrial membrane, from which it comes into contact with axoplasmic amines. After treatment with MAO inhibitors such as tranylcypromine or phenelzine, the concentration of dopamine, norepinephrine and serotonin in the brain increases markedly (Bevan Jones et al., 1972). The 3-0-methylation of norepinephrine by COMT results in the formation of normetanephrine. COMT is thought to have, primarily, an extraneuronal localization, and it has been suggested that it has some functional relationship with adrenergic receptors (Axelrod, 1966). As a consequence, it has been suggested that the rate of formation of normetanephrine *may* serve as an index of adrenergic receptor activity.

MAO converts catecholamines to their corresponding aldehyde derivatives. In peripheral tissues, the end product of catecholamine metabolism is 3-methoxy-4-hydroxymandelic acid (VMA) formed by oxidation of the intermediate aldehyde. However, in the CNS it appears that the intermediate aldehyde product is reduced to an alcohol by an aldehyde reductase so that the main CNS metabolite of norepinephrine in several species is 3-methoxy-4-hydroxyphenylglycol (MHPG). Dopamine is metabolized by both COMT and MAO to 3-methoxy-4-hydroxyphenylacetic acid (homovanillic acid, HVA).

Antidepressant Drug Effects on Biogenic Amines

As was mentioned above, a major impetus for the development of the biogenic amine hypothesis of affective disorders was the finding that most antidepressant drugs have *acute* pharmacological actions that would tend to increase the activity of amines at postsynaptic receptors in the brain. The tricyclic compounds inhibit the reuptake of biogenic amines in both peripheral tissues and brain with a consequent potentiation of aminergic activity.

The monoamine oxidase inhibitors increase the intraneuronal concentration of the monamines, and it is presumed that this leads to an increased release of active transmitters onto the receptor site. However, conclusive evidence is lacking that they produce increased functional activity at central aminergic receptor sites.

Monoamine oxidase inhibitors may also inhibit amine reuptake. Thus Escobar (Escobar et al., 1974) found that the (-) isomer of tranylcypromine, which is a stronger inhibitor of amine reuptake but a weaker inhibitor of monoamine oxidase than the (+) isomer, is a more effective antidepressant. While this finding needs to be replicated, it suggests that the clinical efficacy of this MAO inhibitor may be due to effects other than the inhibition of MAO, perhaps to blockade of amine reuptake. It has been reported that several different MAO inhibitors will reduce amine uptake and that their clinical efficacy correlates with their ability to inhibit uptake (Hendley and Snyder, 1968).

Iprindole appears to be as effective an antidepressant as imipramine (Imlah et al., 1968), but has little or no ability to block the reuptake of serotonin or norepinephrine (Fann et al., 1972). This is of interest as iprindole is related chemically to the tricyclic compounds. Thus it is conceivable (but speculative) that the tricyclics might exert their antidepressant action through a mechanism other than inhibition of amine reuptake.

While an understanding of the pharmacological actions of antidepressant drugs may provide useful clues to the pathology of depression, these must be evaluated with caution. For one thing, as Carroll (1975b) has pointed out, it is a logical fallacy to reason backward from the presumed pharmacological action of the antidepressant in order to determine the etiology of depression. In other words, just because most antidepressant drugs appear to increase the amount of amine at synaptic sites does not necessarily mean that depression is due to an amine deficiency. The drugs may be activating amine systems which compensate for a defect in other systems.

Secondary and Tertiary Tricyclics

The tricyclic compounds are dibenzazepine derivatives and are either tertiary or secondary amines. The tertiary amines, such as imipramine, amitriptyline, chlorimipramine and doxepin, are, in general, potent inhibitors of serotonin uptake (Carlsson et al., 1969b; Todrick and Tait, 1969), but less effective in inhibiting norepinephrine uptake (Carlsson et al., 1969a; Salami et al., 1971). In contrast, secondary amines such as desipramine, nortriptyline and protriptyline are potent inhibitors of norepinephrine uptake (Carlsson et al., 1969a; Salami et al., 1971), but have less effect on the uptake of serotonin (Carlsson et al., 1969b; Todrick and Tait, 1969). This distinction presents the opportunity, then, to attempt to distinguish between the postulated roles of serotonin and norepinephrine in depression, by systematic examination and comparison of the clinical effects of representative drugs from each group. Thus it is possible to plan studies in which we would examine which features of the depressive syndrome were altered when the patients received a drug which had its main effect on blocking norepinephrine uptake in contast to a drug which had its main effect on blocking serotonin uptake. As will be discussed later, it *may* also be possible to identify patients, by biochemical measures, who are more responsive to tertiary amines and patients who are more responsive to secondary amines.

Studies of Chronic Administration of Antidepressants

Many of the studies of the basic pharmacological effects of drugs which are clinical antidepressants have been acute studies, often an examination of the effects of a single injection of the drug under investigation. In contrast, it is widely believed that these drugs often do not exert a significant clinical effect before seven to fourteen or even more days. Thus it is important to consider the possibility that late-developing pharmacological effects of these drugs may be important with regard to their clinical effectiveness.

Recent evidence suggests that compensatory changes occur which modify and attenuate the initial alterations in aminergic activity produced by the mood-altering drugs.

Carlsson and Lindqvist (1963) originally suggested that such alterations may reflect the activity in a feedback loop between the postsynaptic receptor and the presynaptic neuron. Antipsychotic phenothiazines and butyrophenones, which block dopamine receptors, increase the turnover of dopamine in the corpus striatum (Nyback et al., 1968; O'Keeffe et al., 1970). In contrast, tricyclic compounds slow neuronal amine turnover or radioactive amine disappearance (Glowinski and Axelrod, 1966; Schanberg et al., 1967; Corrodi and Fuxe, 1969; Schildkraut et al., 1969; Schubert et al., 1970). Such a mechanism might account for the fact that the unit firing rate of serotonergic neurons in midbrain raphe nuclei is depressed upon acute administration either of tricyclics (Sheard and Aghajanian, 1972) or MAO inhibitors (Aghajanian et al., 1970). As a consequence of such effects, the enhancement of aminergic activity caused by antidepressant drugs would be expected to be attenuated. Thus the degree to which central aminergic activity is enhanced by chronic treatment with antidepressants is unknown.

Several investigations of the effects of chronic administration of antidepressants and the lithium ion also indicate that processes develop over time which serve to counteract the acute pharmacological effects of these agents. For example, several short-term studies indicate that the lithium ion increases serotonin biosynthesis (Sheard and Aghajanian, 1970; Perez-Cruet et al., 1971; Knapp and Mandell, 1973). However, Knapp and Mandell (1973) have shown that two weeks of treatment with lithium resulted in decreased activity of the enzyme tryptophan hydroxylase in the striatum of rats. This in turn was associated with the initial increased rate of serotonin synthesis returning toward baseline values. Such observations are consistent with those of Ho (Ho et al., 1970), who found that treating rats for twenty-eight days with lithium chloride decreased serotonin levels in the brainstem and hypothalamus and decreased serotonin turnover in these areas.

Chronic treatment with tricyclic antidepressants lowers the brain concentration of norepinephrine or serotonin and their metabolites (Schildkraut et al., 1970; Alpers and Himwich, 1972; Ahtee and Kaariainen, 1973; Roffler-Tarlov et al., 1973) whereas acute treatment is without effect. The reason for this is unknown. Hulme (Hulme et al., 1974) was unable to find any effect from seven days of imipramine treatment on the activity of solubilized tyrosine hydroxylase or tryptophan hydroxylase in different brain areas of the rat. Schildkraut (Schildkraut et al., 1970) found that treatment of rats for twenty-one days with imipramine accelerated the disappearance of radioactive norepinephrine from brain. This could contribute to the reduced levels of amine seen with chronic imipramine administration.

In man, psychotropic drug administration also alters monoamine metabolism in a direction that is compensatory to the initial acute effects. Thus treatment with tricyclic compounds lowers both lumbar spinal fluid 5-hydroxyindoleacetic acid (5HIAA) concentrations (Bowers et al., 1969; Papeschi and McClure, 1971; Post et al., 1974) and the probenecid-induced increased in 5HIAA in lumbar spinal fluid (Post et al., 1974), suggesting a possible decrease in serotonin turnover. Bowers (Bowers, Jr., 1974b) has recently reported the results of a study in which tryptophan was administered to depressed patients after probenecid loading both before and during treatment with amitriptyline. In the six patients studied, administration of amitriptyline resulted in clinical improvement; in these subjects the tryptophan-induced increase in lumbar spinal fluid 5HIAA was significantly less during treatment with amitriptyline as compared to the pretreatment accumulation. This result is consistent with the idea that amitriptyline administration to patients reduces serotonin turnover.

In this regard, it is of interest that Post and Goodwin (1974) found that the longer patients were treated with tricyclic compounds, the smaller was the effect of the drugs in lowering the probenecid-induced accumulation of 5HIAA. If the turnover of brain serotonin (as measured by the probenecid-induced accumulation of 5HIAA) is inversely correlated with activity at central serotonin receptors, then this finding would indicate that some change occurs over time which lessens the stimulatory effect of these agents on serotonergic transmission. We would suggest that this change may be an *alteration in the sensitivity of postsynaptic receptors*.

Recent investigations demonstrate the development of receptor supersensitivity or subsensitivity (decreased sensitivity) upon chronic administration of psychotropic drugs. Agents which reduce adrenergic transmission cause the development of receptor "supersensitivity," whereas drugs which enhance adrenergic transmission produce, over time, "subsensitivity" of adrenergic receptors.

For example, neuroleptic agents produce adrenergic blockade. However, upon cessation of chronic neuroleptic administration, the response produced by adrenergic agonists is exaggerated (Christensen and Moller-Nielsen, 1974; Fjalland and Moller Nielsen, 1974; Gianutsos et al., 1974) due to the development of postsynaptic receptor "super-sensitivity" (Fjalland and Moller-Nielsen, 1974; Gianutsos et al., 1974). Indeed, Christensen and Moller-Nielsen (1974) have suggested that chronic neuroleptic administration to patients may result in either adrenergic blocking activity or increased sensitivity to adrenergic transmitters, depending on the dose of neuroleptic administered.

The converse phenomenon occurs with chronic administration of tricyclic compounds. While the acute effect of such compounds is usually the potentiation of aminergic responses, chronic administration either of desmethylimipramine or iprindol (Vetulani et al., 1974) or of imipramine (Frazer et al., 1974) has been shown to produce a *decrease* in the stimulatory effects of norepinephrine on brain adenosine $3',5'$ monophosphate (cyclic AMP) accumulation.

Futhermore, B. Carroll (personal communication) has found that *acute* imipramine administration to mice potentiates the stimulation of locomotor activity caused by morphine administration, whereas *chronic* imipramine administration blocks this morphine-induced effect. These changes may be due to the tricyclic compounds producing receptor subsensitivity.

These alterations may have functional consequences in man as suggested by the effects of psychotropic drugs on rapid eye movement (REM) sleep. Tricyclic antidepressants produce a characteristic effect on REM sleep (Dunleavy et al., 1972). Their initial effect is to sharply reduce REM sleep; with continued administration, the amount of REM sleep returns toward pretreatment values, although still remaining somewhat below normal levels, suggesting the possible development of tolerance. Upon cessation of drug administration, there is a "rebound" so that the amount of REM sleep markedly increases. Alterations in postsynaptic receptor sensitivity may contribute to the "tolerance" and "rebound" effects on REM sleep seen with these agents.

Clinical Studies

One of the methods frequently used to explore the relationship between biogenic amines and affective illness has been the measurement of the concentration of amine metabolites in the urine of depressed and manic patients (Robins and Hartman, 1972; Schildkraut, 1975). Unfortunately, no more than 5 percent of most urinary amine metabolites is of central origin, which makes it difficult to infer much about brain function from these studies. One possible exception to this is 3-methoxy-4-hydroxyphenylglycol (MHPG) (Maas and Landis, 1968). It is, of course, possible that changes in peripheral amine metabolism in affective illness parallel changes in the brain, but there is, at this time, little direct evidence to support this view. Moreover, even if it were true, such changes might well be masked by the effect of such variables as diet, activity, endocrine factors and anxiety levels which alter the excretion rate of amines and their metabolites. Thus it is not surprising that no consistent findings have emerged from the study of urinary amines and their metabolites.

Robins and Hartman (1972) have summarized the findings from nine urinary studies of both depressed and manic patients in which norepinephrine, epinephrine, dopamine, metanephrine, normetanephrine and VMA were measured. They concluded that the urinary findings were in general not consistent with the catecholamine hypothesis of depression, whereas the findings with manic patients were more consistent. The increased amine and metabolite excretion seen in manic patients of course could be secondary to increased activity.

Several investigators have reported decreased concentrations of MHPG in urnines collected from mixed groups of depressed patients, primary affective disorder patients, unipolar recurrent depressions, and bipolar depressive disorders, as compared with controls, secondary depression or chronic characterological depression. Not all investigators, however, have been able to replicate these findings. Furthermore, patients with schizoaffective disorder have been found to have low urinary MHPG concentrations. Three groups of investigators have followed several manic-depressive patients over time and found reduced urinary MHPG during depressive phases as compared with periods of mania or normothymia. The results of these studies have been interpreted by some as being compatible with the hypothesis of reduced central noradrenergic acitivity in depression (reflected in the lower urinary MHPG concentration) and an increased activity in mania (reflected in the higher urinary MHPG concentration). However, these findings and interpretations must be regarded as tentative at this time. Not only have some investigators reported urinary MHPG concentration to be normal in depression, but even investigators who find low values appear to have patients in their group with normal values, i.e., the group mean may be low, but the group variance is large. Here, too, anxiety and physical activity may have affected the values. Furthermore, not all investigators agree that urinary MHPG provides a useful index of brain norepinephrine turnover (Costa and Neff, 1970; Chase et al., 1971).

Even if urinary MHPG is not a reliable reflection of brain norepinephrine activity, it has been suggested that it may provide a basis for distinguishing between depressed patients who respond to imipramine and those who respond to amitriptyline. Thus it has been reported that patients with a favorable response to imipramine have *low* pretreatment urinary concentrations of MHPG (Maas et al., 1972; Beckman et al., 1974), whereas amitriptyline responders have normal or high levels of MHPG in the urine prior to treatment (Beckman et al., 1974; Schildkraut, 1973b). This distinction is blurred by the report that while urinary MHPG did predict response to imipramine and amitriptyline in *unipolar* depressives, it did not do so in a group of bipolar depressives, most of whom had a relatively low MHPG concentration (Goodwin, 1974).

From these and other data, Maas has postulated that there may be a group of depressed patients who respond to imipramine, have an acute relief of symptoms with d-amphetamine (Maas, 1974), have a low urinary MHPG concentration, and may be deficient in norepinephrine. In contrast, the amitriptyline responders will experience no relief from d-amphetamine, have normal or high excretion of MHPG, and may be deficient in serotonin.

While this is an attractive proposal, it is not immediately apparent why imipramine and amitriptyline should be effective in different groups of patients. As tertiary amines, both drugs are highly effective in inhibiting the reuptake of serotonin into brain and blood platelets (Carlsson et al., 1969b; Todrick and Tait, 1969) and only moderately effective in inhibiting the uptake of norepinephrine into brain (Carlsson et al., 1969a; Salami et al., 1971). One possible explanation is that the rate of conversion of these two tertiary amines into their demethylated secondary amine derivatives is different. Thus Maas (1974) suggests that patients given imipramine have proportionately much more desmethylimipramine (a potent blocker of norepinephrine uptake) in blood and tissues than amitriptyline patients will have of nortriptyline. This could account for a greater effect on noradrenergic systems in patients treated with imipramine than in patients treated with amitriptyline. It may be possible to produce a more clear-cut test of this hypothesis by comparing the response to chlorimipramine and nortriptyline. Chlorimipramine is a potent inhibitor of serotonin uptake with little or no effect on noradrenergic systems, whereas nortriptyline has converse effects.

An alternative explanation for the differential effectiveness of imipramine and amitriptyline may be in their relative sedative properties. Urinary MHPG levels may be altered by stress, anxiety or physical activity (Ebert et al., 1972), though there is disagreement about this (Goode et al., 1973). Thus agitated depressives may excrete more MHPG than retarded depressives. It is possible, therefore, that amitriptyline, being somewhat more sedative than imipramine, would be more effective in high-MHPG patients—those with more anxiety and less psychomotor retardation than patients with lower levels of MHPG.

Cerebrospinal Fluid Studies

A number of investigators have measured the concentrations of biogenic amine metabolites in the cerebrospinal fluid (CSF) of patients with affective illnesses (Bowers, Jr., 1972; Goodwin and Post, 1974). Interpretation of these results is complicated by several factors. For example, there is uncertainty about what percentage of the metabolites produced in the brain actually reach the lumbar fluid, as there is active transport of metabolites out of the CSF. Thus lumbar 5HIAA concentrations are reported to be only a third of those in the ventricles (Moir et al., 1970). Furthermore, a significant percentage of lumbar fluid 5HIAA is probably a product of spinal cord serotonin metabolism (Bulat and Zivkovic, 1971).

While some investigators have suggested that lumbar fluid homovanillic acid

(HVA) is derived exlusively from brain, others have pointed out that the HVA may reflect capillary dopamine metablism rather than neural tissue activity (Bartholini et al., 1971). Furthermore, since there is a concentration gradient for 5HIAA and HVA along with cerebrospinal space, variations in the amount of mixing of spinal fluid from different levels, as would occur with physical activity, might contribute to the variability of the results.

Another difficulty in the interpretation of reports arises from the fact that the lumbar concentration of a metabolite is a function not only of its rate of production and entry into the CSF but also of the rate of its outflow from the CSF. Thus an assumption is made when relating basal metabolite concentrations to amine production, namely, that the rate of loss of metabolite from the CSF is constant across time and individuals. Obviously, this may not be so. Therefore, it is difficult to obtain meaningful information about central amine activity from the measurement of basal lumbar fluid metabolite concentrations.

Evaluation of reports is also complicated by the fact that several of the fluorometric methods used to assay HVA and 5HIAA are not very reliable when used for the measurement of the low basal concentrations of these metabolites found in lumbar spinal fluid (Wilk and Green, 1972).

Studies of lumbar fluid HVA levels in depressed patients have yielded inconsistent results. There are reports of decreased concentrations in depressives which increase with clinical improvement and other reports of no differences from levels found in control subjects. Studies with manic patients have been similarly inconsistent, with either low or normal HVA concentrations being reported. Van Praag has suggested that a low lumbar spinal fluid HVA concentration is found in patients with psychomotor retardation and that L-DOPA will improve psychomotor activity but not mood in these patients.

The original report by Ashcroft and Sharman that depressed patients had significantly lower 5HIAA concentrations in lumbar fluid than neurological patients has been confirmed by some but not all investigators. There are also reports of low lumbar fluid 5HIAA in some schizophrenic patients (Bowers et al., 1969; Ashcroft et al., 1971). Of interest are the reports that some manic patients also have low 5HIAA concentrations (Dencker et al., 1966; Coppen et al., 1972b; Mendels et al., 1972a) and that there may be little change in the low 5HIAA values seen in some depressed and manic patients with treatment and clinical recovery.

These findings raise the possibility that the low lumbar spinal fluid 5HIAA values *may* reflect a trait rather than a state variable. These findings have also contributed to the so-called "permissive hypothesis" of depression (Kety, 1972). We have noted that 5HIAA concentrations in lumbar spinal fluid were lower in psychotic than in neurotic-depressives (Mendels et al., 1972a). Furthermore, psychotic-depressives may have less slow-wave sleep than neurotic depressives (Mendels and Hawkins, 1968). There is evidence that serotonin plays an important role in the mediation of slow-wave sleep (Jouvet, 1972). Thus it is possible to speculate that *reduced serotonergic activity may be associated with being psychotic*—whether depressive or schizophrenic.

MHPG concentrations in lumbar spinal fluid of depressives have been reported to be low by some (Gordon and Oliver, 1971) but not other (Shopsin et al., 1973a) investigators and may remain low after clinical recovery in some patients (Goodwin, 1974). Lumbar fluid MHPG concentration has been reported to be normal or elevated in both manic and acute schizophrenic patients (Shopsin et al., 1973a; Post et al., 1973). The variability between studies may be the result of differences in the procedure used to obtain spinal fluid, to variations in physical activity, or to varying reliability in the MHPG assay.

Probenecid Studies

In an attempt to obtain some consistent and meaningful data about brain amine metabolism, several investigators have studied the accumulation of the metabolites in lumbar fluid after the administration of probenecid (Van Praag et al., 1973; Sjostrom, 1974). Probenecid blocks the active transport of 5HIAA and HVA from spinal fluid. This serves to reduce several of the problems associated with the measurement of basal lumbar fluid metabolite levels. By increasing the concentration of 5HIAA or HVA in lumbar fluid, the probenecid procedure decreases the gradient between ventricular and lumbar levels, so that lumbar fluid 5HIAA and HVA concentration may provide a more accurate reflection of ventricular levels. The diminished gradient also reduces discrepancies due to variations in the amount of mixing between fluid from different levels. The inhibition of outflow from the CSF probably serves to make the rate of HVA or 5HIAA production the main parameter affecting the level of these compounds in the lumbar fluid. (There can be some transfer directly from plasma to the CSF, but by maintaining patients on a diet free of monoamines and performing lumbar punctures early in the morning after a fast, the contribution from this source is kept to a minimum.) Finally, by increasing the concentration of HVA or 5HIAA lumbar fluid, the probenecid technique increases the reliability of the fluorometric assay for these compounds.

Despite its advantages, there are some problems associated with this procedure. These include variations in probenecid absorption with consequent differences in CSF probenecid concentration and the degree of blockade of transport obtained (Sjostrom, 1974), and the possible effects of probenecid itself on brain tryptophan concentration and serotonin turnover.

However, studies using the probenecid technique have provided more consistent results than studies where basal values of metabolites were measured. Decreased lumbar fluid 5HIAA and HVA accumulations after probenecid in depression and mania have been reported. Bowers (Bowers, Jr., 1974a) reports a reduced

5HIAA and HVA accumulation in bipolar depressives as compared with unipolar depressives. The latter group had normal 5HIAA and increased HVA accumulation.

Recently, investigators have begun studying the correlations between pretreatment CSF 5HIAA concentrations or accumulation with probenecid administration and the therapeutic response to various antidepressants. There are preliminary reports that depressed patients with low 5HIAA levels are responsive to treatment with lithium carbonate (Goodwin and Post, 1974) and to 5-hydroxytryptophan (Van Praag et al., 1972), but are unlikely to respond to nortriptyline (Asberg et al., 1973). The latter finding suggests that there may be a subgroup of depressed patients with a serotonin deficiency who respond poorly to a tricyclic antidepressant that preferentially inhibits norepinephrine uptake, such as nortriptyline. In a more recent report, it has been suggested that patients with low 5HIAA accumulation respond well to treatment with chlorimipramine, which is more potent in blocking serotonin than norepinephrine reuptake. In contrast, patients with low lumbar fluid MHPG concentration responded to nortriptyline (Sjoqvist, 1974).

These studies of lumbar fluid amine metabolites in affective illness appear to indicate a decreased central turnover of both serotonin and dopamine in some depressed and manic patients, but provide no clear evidence of reduced norepinephrine turnover. There is some evidence that 5HIAA and HVA may also be reduced in some schizophrenic patients. Further, these values may stay low after treatment and clinical improvement. The findings may, of course, be incidental or secondary. It is also possible that the reduced lumbar fluid accumulation may not be a reflection of reduced amine activity but may be secondary to the development of increased activity at the postsynaptic receptor.

It has been postulated that a constitutional deficiency of central serotonin may predispose individuals to develop an affective illness—the permissive hypothesis—and that a subsequent decrease in norepinephrine activity would then be associated with the clinical depression while an increased noradrenergic activity would be associated with mania (Kety, 1972). This hypothesis requires further evaluation.

Tryptophan

Coppen (Coppen et al., 1972a) reported that the concentration of CSF tryptophan is low in both manic and depressed patients; Rafaelsen (personal communication) has not been able to confirm this finding. Coppen (Coppen et al., 1973) has also reported a reduction in free plasma tryptophan in female depressives. Aylward and Maddock (1973) have provided some support for this finding, and Rees (Rees et al., 1974) has reported a tendency for plasma tryptophan levels in regularly cycling manic-depressives to be elevated during periods of mania and reduced when the patients were depressed. A variety of dietary factors can affect plasma tryptophan levels, and the ratio of tryptophan to certain plasma amino acids is important in determining how much tryptophan crosses the blood-brain barrier.

Post-Mortem Studies

Shaw and Pare and their associates have reported decreased serotonin concentrations in the hindbrains of suicide victims compared to the hindbrains of persons who died of other causes. Bourne was unable to find any abnormality in brain serotonin levels but did report low concentrations of 5HIAA. He also found no abnormality in hypothalamic and hindbrain norepinephrine or in caudate dopamine concentrations. Lloyd (Lloyd et al., 1974), in a study of discrete brain areas, found that serotonin levels were reduced significantly in the raphe nuclei dorsalis and centralis inferior. He also studied higher brainstem and telencephalon, where he found normal concentrations of serotonin but possibly increased 5HIAA in the mammillary bodies. There are a large number of uncontrolled variables in any post-mortem study that make the results hard to evaluate. Nevertheless, the approach of Lloyd, with its emphasis on the study of discrete brain areas, may prove to be a useful strategy.

Amine Depletion Studies

The findings that some hypertensive patients treated with reserpine develop a syndrome resembling clinical depression and that a retarded behavioral state in rats similarly treated is associated with a depletion of brain biogenic amines played an important role in the formulation of the biogenic amine hypothesis of depression. We have recently reviewed the reports dealing with the behavioral effects of brain monoamine depletion (Mendels and Frazer, 1974b). The reserpine syndrome in humans may not be a good model for depressive illness. Probably no more than 6 percent of patients receiving reserpine over a long period of time develop this syndrome. The incidence may, in fact, be even lower than 6 percent since in the only prospective study of this question the investigators found no significant depression in fifty patients treated with reserpine for twelve to eighteen months. It appears that the main behavioral effects of reserpine treatment are some combination of sedation and psychomotor retardation. These changes may lead secondarily to the development of depression in vulnerable individuals with a previous history of depression. It is also important to note that the sedation seen in animals given reserpine appears to be due chiefly to dopamine depletion, and not to the effects of reserpine on norepinephrine or serotonin, as was originally emphasized in the development of the biogenic amine hypothesis. The increase of brain dopamine may in some depressives lead to an increase in psychomotor activity but does not, in itself, appear to alleviate depressed mood in the majority of depressed patients.

The multiple effects of reserpine on dopamine, norepinephrine, serotonin and acetylcholine make it a poor drug for elucidating the role of particular amines in the development of depression. A number of agents with more specific amine-depleting actions have been developed. One of these is 6-hydroxydopamine (60HDA) which, when injected intraventricularly in animals, produces destruction of catecholaminergic neurons with much less effect on serotonergic neurons. Animals treated with 60HDA show increased irritability and aggression, but no long-term behavioral changes resembling depression, despite the depletion of brain norepinephrine by 60 to 70 percent. The development of increased postsynaptic receptor sensitivity in these animals may minimize the effects of the amine depletion.

The effects of several relatively specific amine depletory drugs have been studied in humans. Alpha-methyl-paratyrosine (AMPT) depletes peripheral catecholamine and brain dopamine and norepinephrine through inhibition of the enzyme tyrosine hydroxylase. Lower animals treated with AMPT evidence sedation and decreased spontaneous motor activity but no behavioral changes suggestive of depression. In *Macaca speciosa* Redmond has reported that AMPT produces decreased motor activity, decreases in social initiatives and social interactions, and postural and facial changes suggestive of withdrawal. The monkeys continued to respond to the social initiatives of others, unlike most depressed patients, and did not show some of the characteristic biological signs and symptoms of depression such as sleep disturbance, decreased appetite and loss of weight and libido.

Medical and schizophrenic patients treated with doses of AMPT sufficient to produce significant inhibition of peripheral and presumably central catecholamine synthesis showed evidence of sedation and, in some cases, anxiety, but did not become depressed. In another study Brodie and colleagues found that AMPT produced improvement in five of seven manics; one became worse and three of the five apparent responders did not relapse when placebo was substituted for the AMPT. In the same study three depressed patients were treated with AMPT and showed some aggravation of symptoms. These patients had significant psychomotor retardation beforehand and may have been particularly vulnerable to the sedative effects of AMPT. A small number of depressed patients who improved when treated with imipramine did not show any return of symptoms when given AMPT (Shopsin et al., 1973b). It seems that AMPT will not induce depression in individuals who are not initially depressed. Its effects in persons with affective illness remain uncertain and need further exploration.

When AMPT is given, it depletes both dopamine and norepinephrine. In an attempt to focus more specifically on the role of norepinephrine in mania, Sack and Goodwin (1974) treated eight manic and hypomanic patients with fusaric acid, an inhibitor of dopamine-β-hydroxylase. This enzyme blocks the normal conversion of dopamine into norepinephrine. Fusaric acid produced a 25 percent decrease in lumbar fluid MHPG concentration and a significant increase in CSF

HVA and 5HIAA in the patients. The more severe manic patients became *worse* with fusaric acid, while the milder hypomanics showed no change or improved slightly.

Parachlorophenylalanine (PCPA), an inhibitor of tryptophan hydroxylase, produces significant depletion of peripheral and brain serotonin, along with much smaller reductions in catecholamines. In animals, PCPA frequently causes insomnia, increases in sexual and aggressive behavior, and an irritability and hyperreactivity to the environment that are, if anything, more suggestive of mania than depression.

PCPA has been given to normal volunteers, patients with carcinoid syndrome and migraine, and one addict receiving methadone, and appears to produce a number of nonspecific effects, such as tiredness, restlessness and anxiety, whereas at higher doses confusion, agitation and paranoid thinking have been noted.

There is an interesting preliminary report of a study in which PCPA was given to several depressed patients who had responded to imipramine and to one who had responded to tranylcypromine. Despite continuation of the antidepressant drugs, these patients all became depressed within forty-eight hours of PCPA administration and recovered on withdrawal of the drug (Shopsin et al., 1973b). This, of course, suggests a possible effect from serotonin depletion in certain vulnerable individuals.

The available data strongly suggest that the depletion of brain norepinephrine, dopamine or serotonin is in itself not sufficient to account for the development of clinical depression. Such depletion, even if severe and accompanied by a reduction in amine turnover, produces few *persistent* behavioral changes compatible with depressive symptomatology. In fact, when one considers how much amine reduction is necessary to produce behavioral deficits in animals, it seems unlikely that such severe depletion could occur in depressed patients and not be more readily detectable, unless it were sharply localized. In this regard, it should be noted that the extent of amine depletion (as measured by urinary and CSF metabolites) produced with synthesis inhibitor administration to normal subjects, who do not develop depressive reactions, is greater and more consistent than that reported in depressed patients. While these results do not rule out the possibility that amines play an important role in affect regulation, they do suggest the importance of other systems which may interact with changes in amine function to perhaps cause clinical depression or mania.

Administration of Monoamine Precursors

While serotonin and norepinephrine do not cross the blood-brain barrier, their amino acid precursors do, and a number of investigators have attempted to evaluate the effectiveness of these compounds in the treatment of depression (Carroll, 1971; Mendels and Frazer, 1975b). Probably much of the interest in this approach has stemmed from the successful use of L-DOPA in the treatment of Parkinson's disease.

Several investigators have given depressed patients large doses of L-DOPA, but there have been few reports of significant antidepressant activity. There have been reports of the development of hypomanic-like activity without actual relief of the depressive affect and of partial improvement in symptoms in patients with significant psychomotor retardation and low levels of lumbar fluid homovanillic acid. However, there is no consistent evidence of a significant antidepressant action from L-DOPA. The lack of antidepressant activity by L-DOPA does not invalidate the norepinephrine hypothesis since the administration of L-DOPA may not significantly increase brain norepinephrine concentration. Moreover, L-DOPA tends to decrease brain serotonergic activity, which might counteract any beneficial effects from the increased dopamine synthesis.

The studies of the effects of serotonin precursors fall into two groups: 5-hydroxytryptophan (5HTP), the immediate precursor of serotonin, and tryptophan, the precursor of 5-hydroxytryptophan.

The results with 5-hydroxytryptophan have been inconsistent, but in general indicate that it is not an effective antidepressant. There is an interesting preliminary report that a subgroup of depressed patients with low pretreatment accumulation of spinal fluid 5HIAA after probenecid showed a greater response to 5HTP than to placebo (Van Praag et al., 1972), suggesting the possibility that 5-hydroxytryptophan might have corrected a serotonin deficiency in these patients. There are several difficulties in evaluating findings obtained with 5-hydroxytryptophan. For example, exogenous 5-hydroxytryptophan is taken up not only into serotonergic but also into dopaminergic neurons, where it is decarboxylated to form serotonin which may serve as a false transmitter in these neurons.

Numerous studies have been conducted testing the antidepressant efficacy of L-tryptophan either alone or together with an inhibitor, a tricyclic antidepressant or L-DOPA. While Coppen and associates have suggested that L-tryptophan may be as effective as electroconvulsive therapy or imipramine, we, and other investigators, have not found tryptophan to be a useful antidepressant.

L-tryptophan has been consistently reported to potentiate the antidepressant effect of MAO inhibitors by several investigators, and it is of special interest to note two recent reports that L-tryptophan alone may have significant antimanic activity (Murphy et al., 1974a; Prange et al., 1974). These reports, if confirmed, raise important questions about the relationship between serotonin metabolism and abnormal mood state, and about the relationship between depression and mania (infra vide).

Adenylate Cyclase, Cyclic AMP and Receptor Sensitivity

The physiological effects produced by catecholamines and serotonin result from their interacting with specific "receptors" located on the plasma membrane of the target cell, e.g., postsynaptic neuron. Two types of adrenergic receptors were proposed by Ahlquist (1948): alpha (α) for most excitatory actions and beta (β) for the majority of inhibitory effects, and both types appear to be present in CNS. Ahlquist wisely cautioned that these two types of receptors cannot be classified simply as excitatory or inhibitory because each separate receptor can have either effect depending on where it is found. Blocking agents specific for each type of receptor (e.g., phentolamine for alpha receptors and propranolol for beta receptors) are available.

The receptors for dopamine and for serotonin have not been investigated as extensively as have those for norepinephrine. However, both dopamine receptor stimulating and blocking agents are available. For example, apomorphine can stimulate directly dopamine receptors (Anden et al., 1967; Ernst, 1967), whereas haloperidol blocks such receptors (Janssen, 1967). Various compounds, such as cyproheptadine and methysergide, have been suggested as being able to block serotonin receptors in the CNS (Gyermek, 1961; Boakes et al., 1970), and the claim has recently been made that quipazine stimulates serotonin receptors in the CNS (Hang et al., 1969).

It would be of considerable interest to investigate systematically the effects of receptor agonists and antagonists in depressed and manic patients.

The molecular nature of adrenergic receptors has been the subject of considerable study and speculation. Recently, evidence has been presented that some component of the enzyme adenylate cyclase serves as the adrenergic receptor (Robison et al., 1967). This enzyme catalyzes the formation of the compound adenosine 3',5'-monophosphate (cyclic AMP) from ATP. It is now established that the effects of several different hormones, as well as norepinephrine, are dependent upon the cellular concentration of cyclic AMP (Sutherland and Rall, 1960). The cyclic nucleotide, acting as an intracellular "second messenger," stimulates reactions so as to produce the effects caused by the hormone. Degradation of cyclic AMP to 5'-AMP is catalyzed by the enzyme phosphodiesterase, which is present in the brain in multiple forms (Uzunov and Weiss, 1972a; Uzunov et al., 1974).

There is considerable evidence that stimulation of adenylate cyclase by catecholamines results in a beta adrenergic response. This concept that adenylate cyclase acts as the receptor for catecholamines has been extended recently to include catecholamine effects mediated through alpha-receptors. In this case, adenylate cyclase is also involved, but responses due to alpha-receptor stimulation are thought to result from a decrease in the intracellular level of cyclic AMP (Robison et al., 1969). The decrease in cyclic AMP could result from a direct inhibition of adenylate cyclase or, perhaps, from a change in the supply of substrate for adenylate cyclase (Bloom and Goldman, 1966).

Recently, an adenylate cyclase preparation from the caudate nucleus of rat brain was shown to have features suggestive of its being a component of the receptor for dopamine (Kebabian et al., 1972).

Cyclic AMP: Animal and Patient Studies

In view of the involvement of cyclic AMP with adrenergic effects, several investigators have examined the excretion of cyclic AMP in patients with affective disorders. The urinary excretion of cyclic AMP has been reported to be low in depression and elevated in mania by some (Abdulla and Hamadah, 1970; Paul et al., 1971) but not all (Brown et al., 1972; Jenner et al., 1972) investigators. There are reports of reduced urinary excretion of cyclic AMP in depressives changing in the direction of normal values with clinical improvement (Abdulla and Hamadah, 1970; Paul et al., 1970; Naylor et al., 1974b). Further, a marked elevation in the urinary excretion of cyclic AMP was observed on the day of rapid switch from depression to mania (Paul et al., 1971).

The relationship of these observations to the disease process is unclear. A significant percentage of urinary cyclic AMP comes from the kidney (Broadus et al., 1970a) and the excretion of the cyclic nucleotide may be influenced by physical activity (Eccleston et al., 1970) and endocrine changes (Takahashi et al., 1966; Chase and Aurbach, 1967; Broadus et al., 1970b). Furthermore, most of the cyclic AMP in the plasma is reabsorbed by different tissues in the body and not excreted in the urine (Blonde et al., 1974; Wehmann et al., 1974).

Robison (Robison et al., 1970) found no difference in cyclic AMP concentration in lumbar spinal fluid obtained from either neurologic, epileptic, depressed or manic patients. This finding is difficult to evaluate because the cyclic AMP determinations were done on specimens or lumbar fluid which were *pooled* from each group of patients.

More recently, Cramer (Cramer et al., 1972) reported that the increase in lumbar spinal fluid cyclic AMP concentration following probenecid administration was significantly greater in two manic patients than in depressed or neurological patients. In this study, the baseline concentration of cyclic AMP in the lumbar spinal fluid was significantly higher in the depressed patients as compared with either the manic or neurological subjects. Further investigations of lumbar spinal fluid cyclic AMP concentrations in patients with affective diseases are indicated, with particular reference to nosologic subgroups and treatment response.

Since it is established that many psychotropic drugs alter adrenergic transmission, investigators have begun to examine the effects of these drugs on the system through which catecholamines are thought to work, namely, the adenylate cyclase, cyclic AMP, phosphodiesterase system. Not unexpectedly, positive results have been obtained. Phenothiazines (Kakuichi and Rall, 1968; Uzunov and Weiss, 1971; Palmer and Manian, 1974), butyrophenones (Uzunov and Weiss, 1972b; Clement-Cormier et al., 1974), tricyclic antidepressants (Palmer et al., 1972; Palmer, 1973; Frazer et al., 1974) and the lithium ion (Dousa and Hechter, 1970; Forn and Valdecasas, 1971; Walker, 1974; Wang et al., 1974a) have all been reported to modify the ability of catecholamines to stimulate adenylate cyclase. Inhibition of phosphodiesterase activity occurs with several phenothiazines (Honda and Imamura, 1968; Weiss et al., 1974) and tricyclic antidepressants (Roberts and Simonsen, 1970; Muschek and McNeill, 1971). Whether or not these pharmacological effects, which are observed *in vitro* and upon acute administration, are related to the therapeutic efficacy of the drugs is unknown but is an important subject for study.

It appears that some of lithium's clinical side effects may be a consequence of its inhibiting hormone-induced stimulation of adenylate cyclase. For example, the administration of lithium carbonate to man can produce polyuria (Lee et al., 1971; Ramsey et al., 1972) which is resistant to the administration of antidiuretic hormone (ADH) (Singer et al., 1972; Forrest et al., 1974). The antidiuretic effect of this hormone is thought to result from an increase in medullary adenosine $3',5'$ monophosphate (cyclic AMP) (Orloff and Handler, 1967). Since ADH activation of adenylate cyclase preparations from human renal medullary tissues is decreased by lithium ions (Dousa, 1972), the diuretic effect of lithium may be, in part, a consequence of this cellular effect of the ion. Recent evidence indicates that lithium may also interfere with the effects of ADH at a site distal to the formation of cyclic AMP (Forrest et al., 1974). In a similar manner, the antithyroid effects of lithium (Schou et al., 1968; Sedvall et al., 1969) may be related to an inhibition of the effect of thyroid-stimulating hormone (TSH) on thyroid adenylate cyclase (Burke, 1970; Wolff et al., 1970) in addition to effects in the thyroid gland at a site subsequent to cyclic AMP formation. The inhibitory effect of the lithium ion appears to be the consequence of its activity at an intracellular site (Frazer, 1975); extracellular Li^+ is ineffective in this regard.

Receptors and Depression

The postulated aminergic deficit in depression could arise by one of several different means. While, as reviewed above, most attention has been focused on alterations in presynaptic neuronal activity, suggestions have been made recently of a postsynaptic monoamine receptor abnormality in certain depressed patients (Frazer, 1975; Ashcroft et al., 1972). Such an idea can be evaluated by measurement of amine-induced or amine precursor responses in depression. However, there have been relatively few investigations of this type in depressed patients.

The dearth of investigations measuring amine responses may be caused, in part, by the difficulty in quantifying central nervous system responses evoked by monoamines. Yet it is important to attempt to evaluate monoamine-induced responses in patients with affective disorders, as the type of information gained from studies of amines or their metabolite concentration per se is somewhat limited. There need not necessarily be a correlation between amine concentrations and their functional effects. A rise in amine or metabolite concentrations or an increase in amine "turnover" can occur as a consequence of receptor blockade. This would be accompanied by a diminished postsynaptic effect of the amine.

Prange examined the systolic blood pressure rise produced by an infusion of norepinephrine in thirty-eight depressed patients. They reported that depressed patients upon improvement, regardless of the type of treatment, had a greater systolic blood pressure response to norepinephrine than when ill. As a nondepressed control group was not included in this study, it could not be concluded, as the authors themselves emphasize, that depressive illness per se was associated with decreased reactivity to norepinephrine.

We have recently completed two studies concerned with the issue of a receptor, or, more properly, a response abnormality in depression. In one study (Wang et al., 1974b), a peripheral adrenergic response elicited by NE was evaluated. The norepinephrine-induced decrease in cyclic AMP was measured *in vitro* in platelets obtained from male depressed patients. The results obtained provide no evidence that the response elicited was abnormal in depressives. In a similar experiment in which female as well as male patients were studied, Murphy (Murphy et al., 1974b) has confirmed and extended this observation.

In the second study (Frazer, 1975), the growth hormone response induced *in vivo* by a single dose of the direct-acting dopamine receptor-stimulating agent apomorphine was assessed in depressive and in hypomanic patients. Although the number of patients studied to date is small, the results obtained do not suggest any consistent abnormality in patients with affective illnesses. Our data, then, do not support the idea of a *generalized* amine receptor or response abnormality in depression.

Negative data, however, must be interpreted cautiously. These results certainly do not eliminate the possibility of an amine receptor defect in affective disease. It may be that the receptors mediating growth hormone release are functioning normally in depressives, whereas amine receptors activating other responses (e.g., pleasure, anger, motor activity) are not. Attention must be focused on responses mediated by limbic system activation, for example. To do this, clearer understanding of the ways in which amines modify such responses is needed, as are improved techniques to quantify such behaviors in man.

In addition, examination should be made of responses elicited by endogenously released amines (caused, for example, by physiological and psychological stresses and stimuli) as opposed to those caused by exogenous agonists. If, indeed, there is an abnormality of amine systems in depression, proper evaluation must be made of the functional consequences of such abnormalities. This can only be done, ultimately, by evaluating the responses produced by activation of these systems. Further research, then, should be directed to this end.

Acetylcholine

Relatively little research has been conducted into possible abnormalities of central cholinergic function in depression. In a recent study, Janowsky (Janowsky et al., 1973a) found that he could produce rapid, though temporary, remission of manic symptoms by the intravenous administration of physostigmine, a centrally active acetylcholinesterase inhibitor. He also reported that in some of these patients physostigmine produced feelings of hopelessness along with psychomotor retardation and other signs and symptoms of depression. He suggests that the affective state may be determined by a balance between cholinergic and noradrenergic activity, with mania a condition of relative adrenergic predominance and depression a state in which cholinergic systems are preponderant. We (Carroll et al., 1973) have attempted to replicate these findings and have found that while physostigmine did alter behavior by decreasing activity, rate of speech, and aggressiveness, the patients continued to evidence an elevated mood and signs of manic thought disorder. There was no evidence of depression. It seemed that physostigmine reduced the hyperactivity of mania without affecting the accompanying disorder of thinking or mood state.

Clearly, further research into the possible relationship between cholinergic function and mood is indicated.

INTERACTIONS BETWEEN BIOCHEMICAL SYSTEMS

From the preceding discussions, it is obvious that investigators are starting to recognize that the different monoamine systems in the brain interact with each other. Biological theories of affective disorders have arisen concerning the balance between serotonin and norepinephrine systems (Kety, 1972) and between acetylcholine and norepinephrine systems (Janowsky et al., 1972). Such an idea is not new; it was, perhaps, first formally stated some twenty years ago by Brodie and Shore (1957), who suggested that norepinephrine and serotonin were the transmitters for systems mediating opposing central nervous system effects. Recent investigators have expanded and refined this idea. As noted above, Janowsky suggested that cholinergic predominance favors depression whereas adrenergic excess leads to mania. In keeping with this idea, these investigators (Janowsky et al., 1973b) reported that the central acting anticholinesterase inhibitor, physostigmine, and the sympathomimetic agent, methylphenidate, produced opposite behavioral effects when given alone to manic and to schizophrenic patients. In general, physostigmine caused the schizophrenics to become more lethargic and hypoactive and also decreased manic behavior. Methylphenidate activated the schizophrenics and intensified certain manic behaviors. When given to the same patient, the behavioral effects of one drug were antagonized by the other compound.

The different monoamine systems may produce certain similar effects in addition to having antagonistic actions as just described. For example, it seems clear that increased dopaminergic activity can lead to release of pituitary growth hormone (Martin, 1973). However, the observation that serotonin antagonists inhibit growth hormone release due to hypoglycemia (Bivens et al., 1973) suggests a role for serotonin in mediating such release. Thus, both dopaminergic and serotonergic systems may mediate growth hormone release, albeit to different stimuli.

In addition to the interactions between the different monoamine systems, electrolytes and steroid hormones can influence aminergic activity (Maas, 1972). Cations such as sodium, calcium and magnesium play key roles in the synthesis, storage, release and reuptake of monoamines. Similarly, steroid-hormone administration can alter both monoamine synthesis and monoamine-induced responses. It seems possible, then, that disturbances in electrolyte metabolism or steroid hormone regulation would modify monoamine function. Alterations in central monoamine activity not only may cause disturbances in other systems but may, in fact, be the result of such disturbances. If subsequent research supports this idea, it suggests that cycles may be established in patients with affective disorders due to consecutive disturbances in multiple systems.

MANIA-DEPRESSION RELATIONSHIP

Some of the prevalent biological theories of affective disorders are clearly based on the view that depression and mania are polar opposites—a view that is apparently supported by aspects of manifest symptomatology. However, a number of clinical, biochemical and neurophysiological observations suggest that mania and depression may have a number of biological changes in common; these observations, which have led to alternative ways of conceptualizing the relationship between the two affective states (Mendels, 1970; Court, 1968; Whybrow and Mendels, 1969a), include the following:

(1) Transitory periods of dysphoric mood, lasting for hours or even days, occur frequently during episodes of mania; in fact, many manic patients consistently have ratable symptoms of depression. Manic episodes are also frequently, but not invariably, preceded and/or followed by periods of depression. Mixed states, such as pressure of speech and grandiose ideas along with depression and suicidal ideation, are also commonly seen.

(2) Lithium carbonate is effective in the treatment of both manic and selected depressed patients.

(3) Some manic patients have been reported to respond to imipramine, which is usually viewed as an antidepressant.

(4) Manics and some depressives have been reported to have decreased levels of platelet MAO.

(5) Some manic and depressed patients have reduced erythrocyte concentrations of catechol-3-O-methyl-transferase.

(6) Depressed and manic patients both have decreased accumulation of spinal fluid homovanillic acid and 5HIAA after probenecid administration.

(7) CSF tryptophan concentration is low in both depression and mania.

(8) Manics and bipolar depressives demonstrate an increase in the amplitude of the average evoked response—a measure of the cortical potential produced by sensory stimulation—with increasing light intensity.

(9) Sleep changes in hypomanic and depressed patients have many features in common.

(10) Residual sodium, which consists of intracellular sodium and a small amount of bone sodium, has been reported to be increased in both depression and mania.

(11) The rate of transfer of sodium into the CSF has been reported to be decreased in both depressed and manic patients.

These observations are not always consistent and clearly need to be replicated. They should be compared to measurements made of the relevant parameters in patients with schizophrenia, to be sure that the abnormalities are not merely secondary to severe psychiatric illness. However, these findings do suggest that mania and depression, particularly biphasic depression, have many important features in common, as well as the obvious dissimilarities. This fact should be borne in mind in our efforts to conceptualize the biochemistry of affective disorders (Mendels, 1975).

ACKNOWLEDGMENTS

Preparation of this manuscript was supported in part by funds from the Veterans Administration and NIMH Grant #MH25433. Alicia Teichman prepared the bibliography and Phyllis Palascak and Sandra Koch patiently typed several drafts of the manuscript.

COMMENTARIES

DR. LIPTON: Dr. Mendels has offered us an excellent and thorough review of the manifold investigations that have been under way for the past decade on the biology of affective disorders. He has addressed himself to the difficulties associated with such studies, and these include the heterogeneity of the illnesses, the accessibility of tissues, and the problems of microanalysis of drugs and neurotransmitters. He has also summarized the contributions from therapeutics, as well as from the study of the biochemistry and endocrinology of the disturbed affective states. He has given us a superb "state of the art" paper. Where does it leave us?

Obviously things are much more complicated than we saw them less than a decade ago. At that time there was the catecholamine hypothesis, which tended to relate the affective state to the quantity of central catecholamines. If they were high, there was mania; if they were low, there was depression. This hypothesis was uniquely American, but in England a similar hypothesis involving serotonin was proposed by Coppen. Now Dr. Mendels has presented evidence that both serotonin and the catecholamines, as well as acetylcholine and perhaps other transmitters, may all be involved in affective disorders, and that the ratios of these may be crucial in determining the biological substrates of affective states. I suspect strongly that he is correct.

Despite the increased sophistication of our methods and the advances which follow their diligent application, there are several important questions to which we have no answers and, indeed, which we seem to forget to ask as often as we should. First, why are depressions self-limiting in duration? Barring suicide and other misadventures, depressed patients will recover spontaneously and will have periods of sound health without medication. Bipolar depressions will have variable but often prolonged normal periods between the depressed and manic periods. Unipolars may go on for many months between depressive attacks. What in our biological hypotheses can account for these spontaneous remissions?

A second and related question is: Why do patients with affective illness not need medication continuously? Perhaps for optimum management, including prevention of relapses, they should receive it for prolonged periods. But with lithium and the other drugs for affective illness, there is not a precipitous resumption of the illness when medication is discontinued. It is not like the diabetic relapse when insulin is discontinued but rather like the gradual intensification of symptoms of essential hypertension when medication is stopped. And in many cases the resumption of symptoms may be delayed for months or years.

A related question is: Why do all psychotropic drugs take so long to act? Significant clinical response within a week is very rare; usually, clinical effectiveness requires closer to a month. This time course is quite different from that encountered in the therapeutics of other branches of medicine. Antibiotics, nutrients, antihypertensives, digitalis, etc., usually act much more rapidly. The delayed action of psychotropic drugs can hardly be attributed to the time required to achieve an adequate blood or tissue level because side effects occur quickly, while therapeutic effects occur slowly. Dr. Mendels has effectively shown us several examples where hypotheses relating to mechanism of drug action have proved to be in error because they were based on evidence derived from acute animal experiments. Later experiments involving chronic administration have yielded quite different results. Since we employ the drugs chronically, it will be mandatory to study their pharmacological effects under chronic conditions.

In general, maximum clinical therapeutic effects occur when the acute pharmacological effects are markedly diminished. Thus the acute effects of lithium on serotonin turnover and of imipramine on the reuptake of norepinephrine are much smaller in the chronic state. These are difficult but highly relevant questions which require answers if we are to understand the pathogenesis of the affective disorders and the mechanism of action of the drugs we employ. For years I had thought the delay in drug action meant merely that we had poor drugs and that we would ultimately develop more rapid ones. More recently I have wondered whether this is so or if we may not be looking at the wrong model of illness. Mental illness may not fit the model of toxic or deficient states which respond rapidly to appropriate antibiotics or nutrients. For many reasons, they may be viewed as the result of chronic stress and maladaptation in genetically susceptible individuals. Illnesses resulting from stress or tissue injury respond to medication over about the same time course as do mental illnesses. No one expects a burn, a peptic ulcer or a damaged liver to restore itself in a few days; clinical recovery takes weeks just as it does when psychotropic drugs are used with mental illness. The analogy with tissue injury is weakened, of course, by the fact that no one has ever found microscopic structural injury in the major mental illnesses. Yet damage may occur at a submicroscopic level and be detectable only by chemical means. Alterations in the quantity of the enzymes required for the synthesis of neurotransmitters and alterations in the sensitivity of the postsynaptic receptors on which they act may well occur in the course of the illness. Restoration of these alterations involves synthesis and transport of new protein to the appropriate sites. These processes involve substantial periods of time and may account for the delay in therapeutic response to psychopharmacologic drug administration.

I have no answer to the question of why affective disorders remit spontaneously, or why patients do not require medication constantly. It is worth recalling that the onset of depression is usually slow and that it is associated with withdrawal from environmental stimuli. Similarly, the recovery is associated with reentry into social and interpersonal transactions. It would appear that, in some fashion which we do not understand, the affective environment acts neurobiologically to continue the same events that we initiated with antidepressant drugs. Conceptually, this is not unreasonable, but the anatomy, physiology and biochemistry of such events are clearly not worked out.

Finally, I should comment on our continued use of a very simplistic model of neuronal connections. We know that a single neuron may synapse with a hundred or more other neurons. While a single presynaptic neuron has only one transmitter, it is likely that the postsynaptic neuron has receptors for the many neurotransmitters offered it by the many neurons which impinge upon it synaptically. The fate of the postsynaptic neuron in terms of firing or not firing may therefore depend upon its input from many presynaptic neurons which may offer it a mix of transmitters such as serotonin, acetylcholine, GABA, other amino acids, and perhaps even polypeptides. If to this blend we add the various hormones which are known also to localize in neurons and which probably affect their responsiveness to different inputs, we end up with a most complex system of inhibitory and excitatory regulations. These are likely disturbed in mental illness, and the task is to restore and stabilize them. It would appear that our psychotropic drugs initiate such processes, but precisely how we cannot yet say.

DR. GALLANT: I agree with Dr. Mendels' statement that depression is a heterogeneous condition and "that it is unlikely that there is a single cause for all its forms." However, the same statement can be made for the majority of disease or syndrome complexes. No one disputes the fact that multiple causes are associated with most depressive reactions and that depression expresses itself in several different forms. However, it is still not unreasonable to suggest that the depressive reaction is a final common metabolic pathway that can express itself in several different types of clinical forms, according to the environmental variables that affected the subject prior to the reaction. Dr. Mendels suggested this possibility when he expressed the opinion that depression and mania may share a number of important biochemical features.

With the administration of antidepressant agents, the delay of onset of therapeutic activity may be explained if the intracellular as well as extracellular changes are more intensively evaluated. The demonstration of the efficacy of lithium in the treatment of recurrent depression is not fully explained by the catecholamine hypothesis of affective disorders (e.g., specific antidepressant activity is primarily due to an increase of biogenic amines at specific brain receptor sites, and the converse would be true for those drugs that cause depression or are effective in mania) and leads us back to the more basic pharmacodynamic concepts involving relative quantitative distribution, lipid solubility, hydrophilism, basicity, and cell and intracellular membrane permeability. Thus one may then attempt to explain the apparent paradoxical efficacy of lithium in both depression and mania by concluding that lithium causes ion-induced and enzyme alterations in cellular and intracellular membrane excitability resulting in stabilization effects at the receptor level, perhaps having a greater effect in the limbic and hypothalamic areas. Thus the catecholamine changes could be secondary to the alterations in cell membrane permeability. This concept, which has been mentioned by Mendels (Mendels and Frazer, 1974a), may best explain the therapeutic effect of lithium in bipolar and unipolar depression as well as the effects of hydrazine, tricyclic and tetracyclic antidepressant drugs in the therapy of unipolar depression. It may be that the efficacious antidepressant compounds show more affinity for deposition in the limbic and hypothalamic areas (where the concentration of norepinephrine is highest) than in the corpus striatum (where tricyclic agents do not block reuptake of norepinephrine) and other brain areas. If the relationship between efficacy and relative quantitative distribution were proved valid, it would tend to support the cellular and intracellular membrane concept. These findings would lead to the conclusion that a greater quantitative deposition of antidepressant agents in the limbic and hypothalamic areas interfere with biogenic amine reuptake and/or electrolyte transfer processes in these areas to a greater extent than in other areas of the brain, thus making a greater amount of intracellular sodium and/or norepinephrine available for decreasing depressive symptomatology. A similar explanation of cell membrane permeability suggests a theoretical concept for antipsychotic drug activity except for the differences in brain area deposition. A gross example of the importance of relative quantitative distribution of a drug is thiethylperazine, a phenothiazine that meets all of the required structural and pharmacological properties for an antipsychotic agent (as specified by Dr. Janssen, Dr. S. Snyder, and others), but possesses only antiemetic and antivertigo properties. This medication deposits mainly in the vermis and paraflocculus areas and cannot be detected in the highly vascular hypothalamic area or in areas associated with antipsychotic drug effect such as the median forebrain bundle, septal area, etc. (Guth, 1964).

For the sake of closure, I should mention the phenylethylamine hypothesis of affective disorders. In one study, free and/or conjugated 2-phenethylamine (PEA) was lower in the urine of 71 percent of depressed patients than the lowest values in control subjects (Sabelli and Mossmain, 1974). PEA can cause alertness and excitement, and may decrease the course of depression, and the effects are enhanced by MAO inhibitors. Another interesting fact about PEA is that it readily crosses the blood-brain barrier and is increased by antidepressant agents. While urinary PEA is not modified by diet, it can be affected by posture and activity, which may account for some of the laboratory differences noted in the measurement of this compound in depressed patients.

In regard to the neuroendocrine studies, the findings are not clear. Prange and his associates administered 600 μg of TRH in single injections to unipolar depressed females who were euthyroid, in a double-blind comparison with i.v. saline as the control agent in a crossover study (Prange et al., 1972). The findings were inconclusive; the use of i.v. saline added to the confusion since saline can facilitate norepinephrine reuptake, which may result in depressive symptomatology. Prange expressed the opinion that the hypothalamus, the area of greater norepinephrine concentration, is "underactive in depression" and that "TRH may potentiate DOPA, thus decreasing depression." However, Hollister and his associates (1974), using doses of 600 μg injections, found a lack of efficacy and no major side effects. These placebo-like findings indicate that TRH has no therapeutic value in depression.

A number of clinicians familiar with the administration of L-DOPA have been more impressed by the increase of psychomotor activity in the subjects and less impressed with the alleviation of depression which some observers believed was not significantly affected. It should also be noted that AMPT decreases mania. These two observations suggest the possibility that the catecholamine abnormality may only be secondary to a more basic change in cellular and intracellular membrane permeability.

An additional important factor which may help to explain the final clinical action of the drug is the stereochemical property of the molecule, and I should like to ask Dr. Wilhelm to comment, during his discussion today, about this particular property of psychopharmacologic agents since he has written extensively on the subject.

DR. WILHELM: Dr. Mendels' discussion of the various biomolecular hypotheses indicates clearly that a new area of research in affective disorders has begun. After decades of an empirical approach to psychopharmacology with its serendipitous discoveries, we have entered a period of research that might be typified as analytical. The attempts to associate symptomatological changes with drug-induced biochemical phenomena proved the existence of definite correlations between the phenomenological and molecular aspects of mental diseases. Although we are still far from fully recognizing the impact of the various neurochemical, enzymatic and endocrinological factors upon human behavior, emotions and perception, there is little doubt that in the near future we shall be able to classify some affective disorders by specific biochemical criteria (Schildkraut, 1974). The most urgent tasks for biological research will be to establish a uniform classification of depression and to provide the wherewithal for causal therapy based on biological principles.

Biological classification and, subsequently, objective analysis of affective disorders represent the immediate diagnostic goal of research. The therapeutic goal has to be a biochemical characterization of the agents which interfere with and regulate pathologic biochemical processes of the CNS. It can be anticipated that therapy based on a diagnosis that takes into account the biochemical relationship of symptoms and medication will finally result in a more specific treatment of the various manifestations of depressive disorders than the present palliative approach.

Stereochemical Classification of Antidepressants

The first comprehensive effort to classify the antidepressants associated their structure with a triple-component activity profile consisting of a depression-relieving, drive-enhancing and anxiety-reducing factor (Kielholz, 1971). A more penetrating biomolecular analysis of the drug-receptor interactions as well as of the drug-neurotransmitter interferences, effecting these behavior and mood changes, reveals common stereochemical characteristics of those agents that demonstrate similar biological effects, and hence suggest a stereochemical classification of antidepressants (Wilhelm, 1974).

If we confine ourselves in these structure-activity considerations to drugs that display definable antidepressant effects, then only a few groups of substances need to be considered: the bicyclics and polycyclics and the MAO-inhibitors. Among the former, the antidepressants of the dibenzazepine, the dibenzocycloheptadiene, the dibenzoxepine and the dibenzo-bicyclo-octadiene types are the most important from both the practical and the theoretical standpoint. All these compounds share the same structural elements; they consist of a bicyclic or tricyclic skeleton, usually an aliphatic side chain and a basic substituent (Table I, below). Depending on the way these various elements are put together, the molecule, as a whole, exhibits a particular type of steric configuration which apparently determines its site of action and hence its properties.

In an attempt to correlate the spatial structure with clinical effects, steric

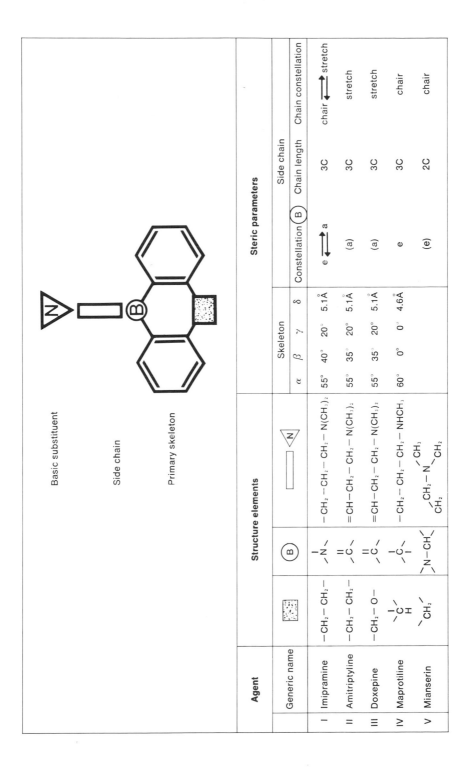

Basic substituent

Side chain

Primary skeleton

Agent	Structure elements			Steric parameters						
Generic name	▨	Ⓑ	▷N / ▭	Skeleton α	β	γ	δ	Constellation Ⓑ	Side chain Chain length	Chain constellation
I Imipramine	−CH₂−CH₂−	−N<	−CH₂−CH₂−CH₂−N(CH₃)₂	55°	40°	20°	5.1 Å	e ⇄ a	3C	chair ⇄ stretch
II Amitriptyline	−CH₂−CH₂−	=C<	=CH−CH₂−CH₂−N(CH₃)₂	55°	35°	20°	5.1 Å	(a)	3C	stretch
III Doxepine	−CH₂−O−	=C<	=CH−CH₂−CH₂−N(CH₃)₂	55°	35°	20°	5.1 Å	(a)	3C	stretch
IV Maprotiline	>C< H	−C<	−CH₂−CH₂−CH₂−NHCH₃	60°	0°	0°	4.6 Å	e	3C	chair
V Mianserin	>N−CH< / CH₂	>N−CH<	−CH₂−N< (CH₃, CH₂)					(e)	2C	chair

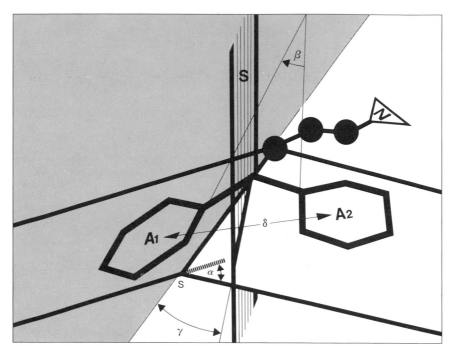

FIG. 1.   Stereochemical Parameters: angle of flexion α, angle of annelation β, angle of torsion γ, Distance δ.

parameters of polycyclic antidepressants defining their three-dimensional topography have been proposed (Wilhelm and Kuhn, 1970). These are the angle of flexion α, the angle of annelation β, the angle of torsion γ and the distance δ (Fig. 1). Their average value has been estimated to be $\alpha = 60° \pm 10°$, $\beta = 0° \pm 40°$, $\gamma = 0° \pm 10°$ and $\delta = 5.0 \pm 0.3 A$.

While the shape of the primary skeleton appears to be a decisive factor for an agent's capacity to interact with a neurotransmitter system, the distance between the skeleton and the basic center as well as their position in relation to each other, represent additional selective factors which determine a drug's potential to interfere specifically with one of the neurohormones. This latter stereochemical relationship is determined by both the structure of the side chain and the basic substituent. It can be described by definition of three steric parameters of the side chain: (a) constellation at bridgehead B, (b) chain length, and (c) constellation of the side chain (Fig. 2).

The constellation at bridgehead B describes the substitution pattern of the side chain relative to the fundamental skeleton. A "quasi-equatorial" and a "quasi-axial" constellation are the theoretical alternatives (Fig. 2). Due to the flexibility of the molecule, most of the tricyclic antidepressants are likely to adopt

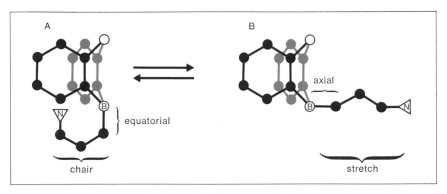

FIG. 2.   Side chain constellations.

both these configurations. The ratio between the two is affected by the nature of the substituents at the aromatic rings and by the structure of the basic group. Imipramine (I) preferentially assumes a quasi equatorial constellation (Fig. 2, A). A substitution in position 3 of the skeleton effects a shift of the equilibrium toward the quasi-axial constellation, as is found with clomipramine (Fig. 2, B).

Addition of another ring system to the tricyclic skeleton may restrict the flexibility of the parent skeleton and therefore yield agents with fixed, nonvariable parameters. Maprotiline (V) is representative of a series of dibenzo-bicyclo-octadiene derivatives where stereochemical parameters are well defined due to the rigid structure (Fig. 3).

The second side chain parameter, the chain length, is self-explanatory. Experience suggests that unbranched, three-membered carbon chains give rise to the most specific antidepressive effects.

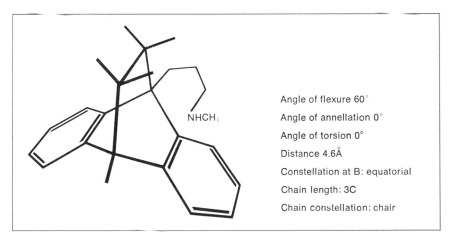

FIG. 3.   Structure and steric parameters of maprotiline.

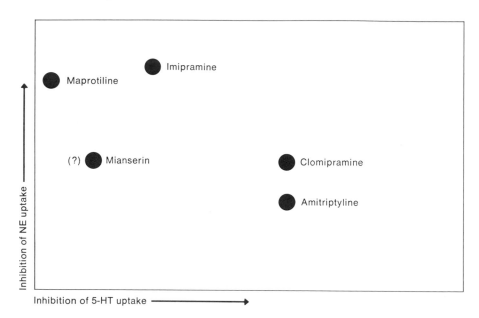

FIG. 4.   Biochemical classification of antidepressants.

The third parameter, the side chain configuration, limits the number of different constellations the side chain can adopt. The theoretical possibilities are reduced to a reasonable figure if one assumes that the side chain is most likely to adopt a thermodynamically favorable constellation at its site of action. In the case of an unbranched, three-membered side chain, the favored spacial arrangement is either a "quasi-chain configuration" in connection with a quasi-equatorial bridge-head substitution, or a "stretch" chain configuration providing a quasi-axial bridgehead attachment of the side chain. Table I summarizes the seven steric parameters of the most representative chemical classes of antidepressants.

Biochemical Classification of Antidepressants

Before relating steric characteristics to an antidepressant's activity profile, the latter has to be uniformly defined. Accepting the interaction of the polycyclics with the neurotransmitters as the biochemical trigger for the therapeutic effect occurring at some point in the mechanism of action of the amine pump, it becomes reasonable to consider neurochemical effects as the crucial parameters. Fig. 4 represents an effort to tabulate the inhibitory effects of antidepressants on the uptake of norepinephrine and serotonin into brain synaptosomes; this mechanism of action is considered essential for the psychomotor and mood-elevating effects of antidepressants (Carlsson et al., 1969a). The dibenzazepines, imipramine and clomipramine, show a twofold effect in this respect (Lindbrink et al., 1971). They

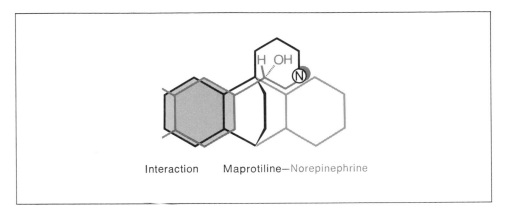

Interaction   Maprotiline—Norepinephrine

FIG. 5.   Interaction Maprotiline-Norepinephrine.

inhibit the uptake of both norepinephrine and serotonin, the ratio between the two depending on the substitution at the aromatic rings. The reports on biochemical effects of amitriptyline are somewhat contradictory but there is evidence that this agent interferes preferentially with the serotonergic system (Carlsson et al., 1969b; Schubert et al., 1970). Maprotiline, in contrast to hitherto known agents, specifically inhibits the uptake of norepinephrine (Maitre et al., 1970). The biochemical profile of mianserin (V) remains to be fully revealed; however, experimental facts do indicate that this agent has impact upon the adrenergic system and is a competitive inhibitor of central noradrenergic neurones (Goodlet and Sugrue, 1974).

Structure-Activity Correlations of Antidepressants

An extremely accurate correlation can be recognized between the biochemical characteristics and the stereochemical parameters of polycyclic antidepressants. A bent primary skeleton in combination with a quasi-equatorial substituted side chain adopting a chair constellation is associated with an interaction with norepinephrine, whereas a skeleton quasi-axially substituted by a stretched side chain interferes with the serotonergic system.

This hypothesis is supported by experimental facts as well as by theoretical considerations. Antidepressants in accord with this hypothesis are members of the dibenzazepine, dibenzocyclo-octadiene, dibenzoxepine and dibenzo[b.e.]bicyclo [2.2.2.] octadiene series. Prothiaden, iprinolol, dibenzepine and the experimental compound C-21024 (Gabriel et al., 1974) are also representative of chemical groups of anti-depressants that fulfill the above postulated steric requirements.

Further support of our structure-activity hypothesis is afforded by the biochemical theories of depression and experimental findings cited in Mendels paper. Assuming a direct competition of an antidepressant with either norepinephrine or serotonin at some unknown point in the amine pump system, we may

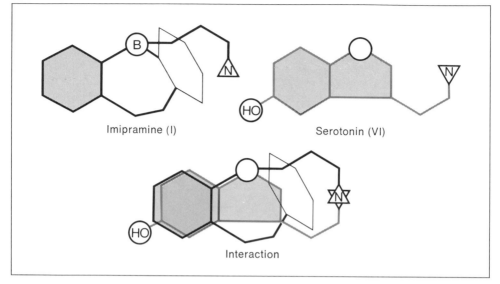

Imipramine (I)   Serotonin (VI)

Interaction

FIG. 6.   Interaction Imipramine-Serotonin.

hypothesize that this sort of competitive reaction is particularly influenced by an agent whose stereochemical structure and constellation share common features with those of either the transmitter or the receptor. Fig. 5 illustrates such a spacial correlation between maprotiline and norepinephrine. A similar steric conformity can be drawn between serotonin and a tricyclic antidepressant with a three-carbon side chain substituent adapting quasi-axial configuration (Fig. 6). A configurational change of the skeleton or the side chain would impair such conformity.

Stereochemical and biochemical parameters represent some aspects that are essential for a better understanding of the mechanism of action of antidepressants. A classification of therapeutics by means of these parameters is now feasible.

Impact of Antidepressants on Enzyme Systems

Other mechanisms of action than interference with biogenic amines are conceivable in new types of antidepressants. Dr. Mendels discussed the potential role of adenyl cyclase and of endocrine functions in the development of abnormal mood states in man. Prostaglandin E_2 opposes the release of norepinephrine at the prejunctional site (Hedquist, 1973; Stjarne, 1972). Inhibitors of prostaglandin synthetase (Lee, 1974) might consequently interrupt this negative feedback and indirectly increase release of norepinephrine into the synaptic cleft.

DR. PERRIS: I have one brief comment about the biogenic amine hypothesis. We have been investigating the relationship of CSF biogenic amines with depression.

Now we know that these findings proved to be quite nonspecific because almost the same results have been found in normals as in depression. Moreover, similar results have been obtained in a series of other conditions: the major psychotic states, senile patients, multiple sclerosis, parkinson subjects, etc. As Dr. Lipton said, we have to try to identify what is common to all these disorders in order to find the real meaning behind our findings concerning biogenic amines and their metabolites.

DR. KLEIN: I would like to add to Dr. Lipton's list of difficult questions. The question is why all of these extremely potent agents do practically nothing to normal human beings? If you give a normal human lithium, MAO-inhibitors, tricyclics, just about nothing happens except sedation. You may be affecting all these biochemical and physiological mechanisms in exactly the same way as in depressed people, but in terms of affecting manifest mood or behavior they produce very few changes. This type of observation supports the idea that these agents are effective in restoring a disordered control system to normal and that they are not affecting the central nervous system the way a rheostat does, as the catecholamine and indoleamine theories imply.

DR. MENDELS: I think that these drugs do have some effect on normal subjects—an effect which has perhaps not received sufficient attention in the literature. However, I'm not sure how relevant it is to the theories. Lithium and some of the tricyclics have a fairly profound sedative effect in many normal subjects; at least that has been our experience. We did one study in which we had a group of eight normals take lithium. Only four of them were able to tolerate 1,200 milligrams a day with relatively moderate plasma levels for a 10-day study period; the remaining subjects became too weak and tired. It is true that lithium and the tricyclics do not seem to have much effect on mood in normals, but we must remember that these evaluations have usually involved relatively small amounts of drug for brief periods of time and may not constitute an adequate test.

The other side of this coin is the question of why the amine-depleting compounds such as AMPT or PCPA have so little effect on mood in normal people. My impression from the literature is that you can give a fairly high dose of these compounds with subsequent profound depletion of serotonin and norepinephrine and in most instances not produce a syndrome that looks like depression. The one interesting exception, which I think speaks directly to Dr. Klein's point, is the recent study by Shopsin and Gershon. They gave imipramine to depressed patients and, when these patients improved, gave them either AMPT or PCPA in moderate doses—doses that were no bigger than those given to normals in previous evaluations. The recovered depressives who were given PCPA became depressed within a short period of time and, when the PCPA was withdrawn, recovered fairly rapidly. Those who were given AMPT did not manifest any particular mood change; there are arguments as to whether or not they received enough AMPT. What is interesting is that a drug which does not have a significant effect on mood in normals may, like PCPA, have a fairly profound effect on mood in people who are vulnerable. Likewise, with reserpine, the people who developed the reserpine-induced syndrome that is called depression are in most instances people who have had a previous history of depression. Again this implies some vulnerability in individuals, which makes their response different.

One final comment: to my way of thinking, one of the useful strategies available to us at this time rests on the fact that not all tricyclics are the same. Sorting out what the different tricyclics are doing in different patients (and to different biochemical systems) may help to clear the air and remove some of the large variance that has occurred in most studies to date.

DR. SIMPSON: It seems to me that the studies in normals fall into the same trap as those investigations by the animal pharmacologists, who seem to have taken nearly twenty years to realize that if you give a drug chronically it has different effects from those resulting if you give it acutely. The usual normal studies evaluate acute dosages, and having given somebody 50 milligrams of amitriptyline with resultant profound sedation I would say that these large single dosages can produce very pronounced effects in some normal people.

REFERENCES

Abdulla, Y. H., and Hamadah, K. (1970). 3',5' cyclic adenosine monophosphate in depression and mania *Lancet* 1:378–81.

Aghajanian, G. K., Graham, A. W., and Sheard, M. H. (1970). Serotonin-containing neurons in brain: depression of firing by monoamine oxidase inhibitors. *Science* 169:1100–02.

Ahlquist, R. P. (1948). A study of the adrenotropic receptors. *Am. J. Physiol.* 153:586–600.

Ahtee, L., and Kaariainen, I. (1973). 5-hydroxytryptamine in platelets and brain of rabbits treated chronically with imipramine, morphine or methadone. *N.S. Arch. Pharmacol.* 277:429–36.

Alpers, H. S., and Himwich, H. E. (1972). The effects of chronic imipramine administration on rat brain levels of serotonin, 5-hydroxyindoleacetic acid, norepinephrine and dopamine. *J. Pharmacol. Exp. Ther.* 180:531–38.

Anden, N. E., Rubensson, A., Fuxe, K., et al. (1967). Evidence for dopamine receptor stimulation by apomorphine. *J. Pharm. Pharmacol.* 19:627–29.

Aronoff, M. S., Evens, R. G., and Durell, J. (1971). Effect of lithium salts on electrolyte metabolism. *J. Psychiat. Res.* 8:139–59.

Asberg, M., Bertilsson, L., Tuck, D., et al. (1973). Indoleamine metabolites in cerebrospinal fluid of depressed patients before and during treatment with nortriptyline. *Clin. Pharm. Ther.* 14:277–86.

Ashcroft, G. W., Brooks, P. W., Cundall, R. L., et al. (1971). Changes in the glycol metabolites of noradrenaline in affective illness. Presented at 5th World Congress of Psychiatry, Mexico City.

———, Eccleston, D., Murray, L. G., et al. (1972). Modified amine hypothesis for the aetiology of affective illness. *Lancet* 2:573–77.

Axelrod, J. (1966). Methylation reactions in the formation and metabolism of catecholamines and other biogenic amines. *Pharm. Rev.* 18:95–113.

——— (1971). Noradrenaline: fate and control of its biosynthesis. *Science* 173:598–606.

Aylward, M., and Maddock, J. (1973). Plasma-tryptophan levels in depression. *Lancet* 1:936.

Baer, L., Durell, J., Bunney, W. E., Jr., et al. (1970a). Sodium balance and distribution in lithium carbonate therapy. *Arch. Gen. Psychiat.* 22:40–44.

————, Platman, S. R., and Fieve, R. R. (1970b). The role of electrolytes in affective disorders. *Arch. Gen. Psychiat.* 22:108–13.

Baker, P. F. (1965). Phosphorus metabolism of intact crab nerve and its relation to the active transport of ions. *J. Physiol.* (London) 180:383–423.

Bartholini, G., Tissot, R., and Pletscher, A. (1971). Brain capillaries as a source of homovanillic acid in cerebrospinal fluid. *Brain Res.* 27:163–68.

Becker, J. (1974). *Depression: Theory and Research.* Washington: Winston.

Beckman, H., Jones, C. C., and Goodwin, F. K. (1974). Urinary MHPG and response to anti-depressant drugs. Presented at American Psychiatric Association Meeting.

Belmaker, R. H., Murphy, D. L., Wyatt, R. J., et al. (1974). Human platelet monoamine oxidase changes during the menstrual cycle. *Arch. Gen. Psychiat.* 31:553–56.

Bevan Jones, A. B., Pare, C. M. B., Nicholson, W. J., et al. (1972). Brain amine concentrations after monoamine oxidase inhibitor administration. *Br. Med. J.* 1:17–19.

Bivens, C. H., Lebovitz, H. E., and Feldman, J. M. (1973). Inhibition of hypoglycemia-induced growth hormone secretion by the serotonin antagonists cyproheptadine and methysergide. *N. Eng. J. Med.* 289:236–39. *Blaschko, H. and Muscholl, E. (1972). Eds., Catecholamines.* New York: Springer-Verlag.

Blonde, L., Wehmann, R. E., Steiner, A. L. (1974). Plasma clearance rates and renal clearance of ^{3}H-labeled cyclic AMP and ^{3}H-labeled cyclic GMP in the dog. *J. Clin. Invest.* 53:163–72.

Bloom, B. M., and Goldman, I. M. (1966). The nature of catecholamine-adenine mononucleotide interactions in adrenergic mechanisms. *Adv. Drug. Res.* 3:121–69.

Boakes, R. J., Bradley, P. B., Briggs, I., et al. (1970). Effects of lysergic acid derivatives on 5-hydroxytryptamine excitation of brain stem neurones. *Br. J. Pharmacol.* 453P–54P.

Bowers, M. B., Heninger, G. R., and Gerbode, F. (1969). Cerebrospinal fluid 5-hydroxyindoleacetic acid and homovanillic acid in psychiatric patients. *Intl. J. Neuropharmacol.* 8:255–62.

Bowers, M. B., Jr. (1972). Clinical measurements of central dopamine and 5-hydroxytryptamine metabolism: reliability and interpretation of cerebrospinal fluid acid monoamine metabolite measures. *Neuropharmacol.* 11:101–11.

———— (1974a). Lumbar CSF 5-hydroxyindoleacetic acid and homovanillic acid in affective syndrome. *J. Nerv. Ment. Dis.* 158:325–30.

———— (1974b). Amitriptyline in man: decreased formation of central 5-hydroxyindoleacetic acid. *Clin. Pharmacol. Ther.* 15:167–70.

Broadus, A. E., Kaminsky, N. I., Hardman, J. G., et al. (1970a). Kinetic parameters and renal clearances of plasma adenosine 3′,5′-monophosphate and guanosine 3′,5′-monophosphate in man. *J. Clin. Invest.* 49:2222–36.

————, Kaminsky, N. I., Northcutt, R. C., et al. (1970b). Effects of glucagon on adenosine 3′,5′-monophosphate and guanosine 3′,5′-monophosphate in human plasma and urine. *J. Clin. Invest.* 49:2237–45.

Brodie, B. B., and Shore, P. A. (1957). A concept for a role of serotonin and norepinephrine. *Ann. N.Y. Acad. Sci.* 66:631–42.

Brown, B. L., Salway, J. G., Albano, J. D. M., et al. (1972). Urinary excretion of cyclic AMP and manic-depressive psychosis. *Br. J. Psychiat.* 120:405–08.

Bulat, M., and Zivkovic, B. (1971). Origin of 5-hydroxyindoleacetic acid in the spinal fluid. *Science* 173:738–40.

Bunney, W. E., Jr., and Davis, J. M. (1965). Norepinephrine in depressive reactions: a review. *Arch. Gen. Psychiat.* 13:483–94.

Burke, G. (1970). Effects of cations and ouabain on thyroid adenyl cyclase. *Biochim. Biophys. Acta* 220:30–41.

Carlsson, A., and Lindqvist, M. (1963). Effect of chlorpromazine or haloperidol on formation of 3-methoxytyramine and normetanephrine in mouse brain. *Acta Pharmacol.* (Copenhagen) 20:140–144.

————, Corrodi, H., Fuxe, K., et al. (1969a). Effects of some antidepressant drugs on the depletion of intraneuronal brain catecholamine stores caused by 4,α-dimethyl-meta-tyramine. *Eur. J. Pharmacol.* 5:367–73.

————, Corrodi, H., Fuxe, K., et al. (1969b). Effect of antidepressant drugs on the depletion of intraneuronal brain 5-hydroxytryptamine stores caused by 4-methyl-α-ethyl-meta-tyramine. *Eur. J. Pharmacol.* 5:357–66.

Carroll, B. J. (1971). Monoamine precursors in the treatment of depression. *Clin. Pharmacol. Ther.* 12:743–61.

———— (1975a, in press). Limbic system–adrenal cortex regulation in depression and schizophrenia. *Psychosom. Med.*

———— (1975b, in press). Review of clinical research strategies in affective illness. In J. Mendels, ed., *Psychobiology of Depression.* New York: Spectrum Publications, Inc.

————, Frazer, A., Schless, A. P., and Mendels, J. (1973). Cholinergic reversal of manic symptoms: letter. *Lancet* 1:427–28.

Chase, L. R., and Aurbach, G. D. (1967). Parathyroid function and the renal excretion of 3′,5′-adenylic acid. *Proc. Natl. Acad. Sci.* 58:518–25.

Chase, T. N., Breese, G. R., Gordon, E. K., et al. (1971). Catecholamine metabolism in the dog: comparison of intravenously and intraventricularly administered (^{14}C) dopamine and (^{3}H) norepinephrine. *J. Neurochem.* 18:135–40.

Christensen, A. V., and Moller-Nielsen, I. (1974). Influence of flupenthixol and flupenthixol-decanoate on methylphenidate and apomorphine-induced compulsive gnawing in mice. *Psychopharmacol.* 34:119–26.

Clement-Cormier, Y. C., Kebabian, J. W., Petzold, G. L., et al. (1974). Dopamine-sensitive adenylate cyclase in mammalian brain: a possible site of action of antipsychotic drugs. *Proc. Natl. Acad. Sci.* 71:1113–16.

Coppen, A. (1967). The biochemistry of affective disorders. *Br. J. Psychiat.* 113:1237–64.

————, Brooksbank, B. W. L., and Peet, M. (1972a). Tryptophan concentration in the cerebrospinal fluid of depressive patients. *Lancet* 1:1393.

————, Eccleston, E. G., and Peet, M. (1973). Total and free tryptophan concentration in the plasma of depressive patients. *Lancet* 2:60–63.

————, Prange, A. J., Jr., Whybrow, P. C., et al. (1972b). Abnormalities of indoleamines in affective disorders. *Arch. Gen. Psychiat.* 26:474–78.

Corrodi, H., and Fuxe, K. (1969). Decreased turnover in central 5-HT nerve terminals induced by antidepressant drugs of the imipramine type. *Eur. J. Pharmacol.* 7:56–59.

Costa, E., and Neff, N. H. (1970). Estimation of turnover rates to study the metabolic regulation of the steady-state level of neuronal monoamines. In A. Lajtha, ed., *Handbook of Neurochemistry.* New York: Plenum Press.

————, Gessa, G. L., and Sandler, M. (1974). Eds., *Serotonin—New Vistas.* New York: Raven Press.

Court, J. H. (1968). Manic-depressive psychosis: an alternative conceptual model. *Br. J. Psychiat.* 114:1523–30.

Cramer, H., Goodwin, F. K., Post, R. M., et al. (1972). Effects of probenecid and exercise on cerebrospinal-fluid cyclic AMP in affective illness. *Lancet* 1:1346–47.

Davies, B., Carroll, B. J., and Mowbray, R. M. (1972). *Depressive Illness: Some Research Studies.* Springfield: Charles C. Thomas.

Dencker, S. J., Malm, U., Roos, B. E., et al. (1966). Acid monoamine metabolites of cerebrospinal fluid in mental depression and mania. *J. Neurochem.* 13:1545–48.

Dorus, E., Pandey, G. N., Frazer, A., and Mendels, J. (1974). Genetic determinant of lithium ion distribution. I. An *in vitro* monozygotic-dizygotic twin study. *Arch. Gen. Psychiat.* 31:463–65.

Dousa, T., and Hechter, O. (1970). Lithium and brain adenyl cyclase. *Lancet* 1:834–35.

Dousa, T. P. (1972). 5th International Congress of Nephrology, Mexico City, Abstr. 79.

Dunleavy, D. L., Brezinova, V., Oswald, I., et al. (1972). Changes during weeks in effects of tricyclic drugs on the human sleeping brain. *Br. J. Psychiat.* 120:663–72.

Durell, J. (1974). Sodium and potassium metabolism. Lithium salts and affective disorders. In N. S. Kline, ed., *Factors in Depression*. New York; Raven Press, pp. 67–96.

Ebert, M. H., Post, R. M., and Goodwin, F. K. (1972). Effect of physical activity on urinary MHPG excretion in depressed patients. *Lancet* 2:766.

Eccleston, D., Loose, R., Pullar, I. A., et al. (1970). Exercise and urinary excretion of cyclic AMP. *Lancet* 2:612–13.

Ernst, A. M. (1967). Mode of action of apomorphine and dexamphetamine on gnawing compulsion in rats. *Psychopharmacol.* (Berlin) 10:316–23.

Escobar, J. I., Schiele, B. C., and Zimmermann, R. (1974). The tranylcypromine isomer: a controlled clinical trial. *Am. J. Psychiat.* 131:1025–26.

Fann, W. E., Davis, J. M., Janowsky, D. S., et al. (1972). Effect of iprindole on amine uptake in man. *Arch. Gen. Psychiat.* 26:158–62.

Fjalland, B., and Moller Nielsen, I. (1974). Enhancement of methylphenidate-induced stereotypes by repeated administration of neuroleptics. *Psychopharmacol.* 34:105–09.

Flach, F. F. (1964). Calcium metabolism in states of depression. *Br. J. Psychiat.* 110:588–93.

Forn, J., and Valdecasas, F. G. (1971). Effects of lithium on brain adenyl cyclase activity. *Biochem. Pharmacol.* 20:2773–79.

Forrest, J. N., Jr., Cohen, A. D., Torretti, J., et al. (1974). On the mechanism of lithium-induced diabetes insipidus in man and the rat. *J. Clin. Invest.* 53:1115–23.

Frazer, A. (1975, in press). Adrenergic response in depression: implications for a receptor defect. In J. Mendels ed., *Psychobiology of Depression*. New York: Spectrum Publications.

———— and Stinnett, J. L. (1973). Distribution and metabolism of norepinephrine and serotonin in the central nervous system. In J. Mendels, ed., *Biological Psychiatry*. New York: John Wiley & Sons, pp. 35–64.

————, Haugaard, E. S., Mendels, J., et al. (1975, in press). The effects of intracellular lithium on epinephrine-induced accumulation of cyclic AMP in skeletal muscle. *Biochem. Pharmacol.*

————, Pandey, G., Mendels, J., et al. (1974). The effect of tri-iodothyronine in combination with imipramine on (^{3}H)-cyclic AMP production in slices of rat cerebral cortex. *Neuropharmacol.* 13:1131–40.

Frizel, D., Coppen, A., and Marks, V. (1969). Plasma magnesium and calcium in depression. *Br. J. Psychiat.* 115:1375–77.

Gabriel, E., Muller, E., Presslich, O., and Schuster P. (1974). Experimental-psychologische und psychophysiologische fangsschnittuntersuchungen an depressiven patienten unter thymoleptischer medikation. *Arzneimittel-forschung* 24:1131–33.

Ganong, W. F. (1970). Control of adrenocorticotropin and melancocyte-stimulating hormone secretion. In L. Martini, M. Motta and F. Fraschini, eds., *The Hypothalamus*. New York: Academic Press, p. 313.

Geffen, L. B., and Livett, B. G. (1971). Synaptic vesicles in sympathetic neurons. *Physiol. Rev.* 51:98–157.

Giacobini, E., and Stepita-Klauco, M. (1970). Studies on the mechanism of action of lithium ions. I. The effect of lithium ions on the impulse activity of the crayfish stretch receptor neuron. *Acta Physiol. Scand.* 80:519–27.

Gianutsos, G., Drawbaugh, R. B., Hynes, M. D., et al. (1974). Behavioral evidence for dopaminergic supersensitivity after chronic haloperidol. *Life Sci.* 14:887–98.

Glen, A. I. M., and Reading, H. W. (1973). Regulatory action of lithium in manic-depressive illness. *Lancet* 2:1239–41.

————, Bradbury, M. W. B., and Wilson, J. (1972). Stimulation of the sodium pump in the red blood cell by lithium and potassium. *Nature* 239:399–401.

Glowinski, J., and Axelrod, J. (1966). Effects of drugs on the disposition of H-3-norepinephrine in the rat brain. *Pharmacol. Rev.* 18:775–85.

Goode, D. J., Dekirmenjian, H., Meltzer, H. Y., et al. (1973). Reaction of exercise to MHPG excretion in normal subjects. *Arch. Gen. Psychiat.* 29:391–96.

Goodlet, I., and Sugrue, M. F. (1974). The effect of a new antidepressant, ORG GB94, on amine uptake mechanism. *Br. J. Pharmacol.* 52:431P.

Goodwin, F. K. (1974). Biological subgroups of affective illness: evidence from studies of CSF metabolites. Presented at World Psychiatric Association Meeting, Munich.

———— and Post, R. M. (1974). Brain serotonin, affective illness, and antidepressant drugs: cerebro spinal fluid studies with probenccid. *Adv. Biochem. Pharmacol.* 11:341–55.

Gordon, E. K., and Oliver, J. (1971). 3-methoxy-4-hydroxyphenylethylene glycol in human cerebrospinal fluid. *Clin, Chim. Acta* 35:145–50.

Guth, P.S.: The Mode of Action of Chlorpromazine: A Review. *Bull. Tul. Univ. Med. Facul.* 24:35–42, 1964.

Gyermek, L. (1961). 5-hydroxytryptamine antagonists. *Pharmacol. Rev.* 13:399–439.

Hamon, M., and Glowinski, J. (1974). Regulation of serotonin synthesis. *Life Sci.* 15:1533–48.

Hang, E., Sancilo, L. F., Vargas, R., et al. (1969). Similarities between the pharmacological actions of quipazine and serotonin. *Eur. J. Pharmacol.* 6:274–80.

Hedquist, P. (1973). Prostaglandin as a tool for local control of transmitter release from sympathetic nerves. *Brain Res.* 62:483–88.

Hendley, E. D., and Snyder, S. H. (1968). Relationship between the action of monoamine oxidase inhibitors on the noradrenaline uptake system and their antidepressant efficacy. *Nature* 220:1330–31.

Ho, A. K. S., Loh, H. H., Craves, F., et al. (1970). The effect of prolonged lithium treatment on the synthesis rate and turnover of monoamines in brain regions of rats. *Eur. J. Pharmacol.* 10:72–78.

Hodgkin, A. L. (1964). *The Conduction of the Nervous Impulse.* Springfield: Charles C. Thomas.

Hokin-Neaverson, M., Spiegel, D. A., and Lewis, W. C. (1974). Deficiency of erythrocyte sodium pump activity in bipolar manic-depressive psychosis. *Life Sci.* 15:1739–48.

Hollister, L. E., Berger, P., Ogle, F. L., et al. (1974). Protirelin (TRH) in depression. *Arch. Gen. Psychiat.* 31:468–70.

Honda, F., and Imamura, H. (1968). Inhibition of cyclic 3′,5′-nucleotide phosphodiesterase by phenothiazine and reserpine derivatives. *Biochim. Biophys. Acta* 161:267–69.

Hulme, E. C., Hill, R., North, M., et al. (1974). Effects of chronic administration of drugs which modify neurotransmitter reuptake, storage and turnover on levels of tyrosine and tryptophan hydroxylase in rat brain. *Biochem. Pharmacol.* 23:1393–1404.

Imlah, N. W., Murphy, K. P., and Mellor, C. S. (1968). The treatment of depression: a controlled comparison between iprindole (Prondol) and imipramine. *Clin. Trials J.* 5:927–31.

Janowsky, D. S., El-Yousef, M. K., Davis, J. M., et al. (1972). A cholinergic-adrenergic hypothesis of mania and depression. *Lancet* 2:632–35.

————, El-Yousef, M. K., Davis, J. M., et al. (1973a). Parasympathetic suppression of manic symptoms by physostigmine. *Arch. Gen. Psychiat.* 28:542–47.

————, El-Yousef, M. K., Davis, J. M., et al. (1973b). Antagonistic effects of physostigmine and methylphenidate in man. *Am. J. Psychiat.* 130:1370–76.

————, Fann, W. E., and Davis, J. M. (1971). Monoamines and ovarian hormone-linked sexual and emotional changes: a review. *Arch. Sexual Behavior* 1:205–18.

Janssen, P. A. J. (1967). The pharmacology of haloperidol. *Intl. J. Neuropsychiat.* 3 (Suppl. 1):10–18.

Jenner, F. A., Sampson, G. A., Thompson, E. A., et al. (1972). Manic-depressive psychosis and urinary excretion of cyclic AMP. *Br. J. Psychiat.* 121:236–37.

Jequier, E., Lovenberg, W., and Sjoerdsma, A. (1967). Tryptophan hydroxylase inhibition: the mechanism by which p-chlorophenylalanine depletes rat brain serotonin. *Mol. Pharmacol.* 3:274–78.

Jouvet, M. (1972). The role of monoamines and acetylcholine-containing neurons in the regulation of the sleep-waking cycle. In R. H. Adrian, E. Helmreich, H. Holzer, et al., eds., *Reviews of Physiology.* Berlin: Springer-Verlag, pp. 166–307.

Kakuichi, S., and Rall, T. W. (1968). The influence of chemical agents on the accumulation of adenosine 3′,5′-phosphate in slices of rabbit cerebellum. *Mol. Pharmacol.* 4:367–78.

Kastin, A. J., Schalch, D. S., Ehrensing, R. H., et al. (1972). Improvement in mental depression with decreased thyrotropin response after administration of thyrotropin-releasing hormone. *Lancet* 2:740–42.

Katz, B. (1966). *Nerve, Muscle, and Synapse*. New York: McGraw-Hill Book Co.

Kebabian, J. W., Petzold, G. L., and Greengard, P. (1972). Dopamine-sensitive adenylate cyclase in caudate nucleus of rat brain, and its similarity to the "dopamine receptor." *Proc. Natl. Acad. Sci.* 69:2145–49.

Kety, S. (1972). Brain amines and affective disorders. In B. T. Ho and W. M. McIsaac, eds., *Brain Chemicstry in Mental Disease*. New York: Plenum Press, pp. 237–44.

Kielholz, P. (1971). *Diagnose und Therapie der Depressionen furt den Prakiker*. Munich: Lehmanns.

Klein, D. F. (1974). Endogenomorphic depression. *Arch. Gen. Psychiat.* 31:447–54.

Klerman, G. L. (1971). Clinical research in depression. *Arch. Gen. Psychiat.* 24:305–19.

Knapp, S., and Mandell, A. J. (1973). Short- and long-term lithium administration: effects on the brain's serotonergic biosynthetic systems. *Science* 180:645–47.

Koe, B. K., and Weissman, A. (1966). P-chlorophenylalanine: a specific depletion of brain serotonin. *J. Pharmacol. Exp. Ther.* 154:499–516.

Kraines, S. H. (1966). Manic-depressive syndrome: a physiologic disease. *Dis. Nerv. Syst.* 27:3–19.

Lapin, I. P., and Oxenkrug, G. F. (1969). Intensification of the central serotoninergic processes as a possible determinant of the thymoleptic effect. *Lancet* 1:132–36.

Lee, R. E. (1974). The influence of psychotropic drugs on prostaglandin biosynthesis. *Prostaglandins* 5:63.

Lee, R. V., Jampol, L. M., and Brown, W. V. (1971). Nephrogenic diabetes insipidus and lithium intoxication—complications of lithium carbonate therapy. *N. Eng. J. Med.* 284.93–94.

Lindbrink, P., Jonsson, G., and Fuxe, K. (1971). The effect of imipramine-like drugs and anti-histamine drugs on uptake mechanisms in the central noradrenaline and 5-hydroxyhyptamine neurons. *Neuropharmacol.* 10:521–36.

Lloyd, K. G., Farley, I. J., Deck, J. H. N., et al. (1974). Serotonin and 5-hydroxyindoleacetic acid in discrete areas of the brainstems of suicide victims and control patients. *Adv. Biochem. Psychopharmacol.* 11:387–97.

Maas, J. W. (1972). Adrenocortical steroid hormones, electrolytes, and the disposition of the catecholamines with particular reference to depressive states. *J. Psychiat. Res.* 9:227–41.

——— (1974). Clinical, biochemical, and pharmacological identification of depressed patients having an alteration in norepinephrine metabolism and/or disposition integral to their illness. Presented at World Psychiatric Association Meeting, Munich.

——— and Landis, D. H. (1968). *In vivo* studies of the metabolism of norepinephrine in the central nervous system. *J. Pharmacol. Exp. Ther.* 163:147–62.

———, Fawcett, J. A., and Dekirmenjian, H. (1972). Catecholamine metabolism, depressive illness, and drug response. *Arch. Gen. Psychiat.* 26:252–62.

McCann, S. M., and Porter, J. C. (1969) Hypothalamic pituitary stimulating and inhibiting hormones. *Physiol. Rev.* 49:240–84.

Maitre, L., Staehelin, M., and Bein, H. (1970). Blockade of noradrenaline uptake by 34276 Ba, a new antidepressant drug. *Biochem. Pharmacol.* 20:2169–86.

Martin, J. B. (1973). Neural regulation of growth hormone secretion. *N. Eng. J. Med.* 288:1384–93.

Mendels, J. (1970). *Concepts of Depression*. New York: John Wiley & Sons.

——— (1974). Biological aspects of affective illness. In S. Arieti, ed., *American Handbook of Psychiatry*. New York: Basic Books, pp. 448–79.

——— (1975). *Psychobiology of Depression*. New York: Spectrum Publications.

——— and Frazer, A. (1973). Intracellular lithium concentration and clinical response—towards a membrane theory of depression. *J. Psychiat. Res.* 10:9–18.

——— and Frazer, A. (1974a). Alterations in cell membrane activity in depression. *Am. J. Psychiat.* 131:1240–46.

————— and Frazer, A. (1974b). Brain biogenic amine depletion and mood. *Arch. Gen. Psychiat.* 30:447–51.

————— and Frazer, A. (1975a, in press). Lithium distribution in depressed patients: implications for an alteration in cell membrane function in depression. In J. Mendels, ed., *Psychobiology of Depression.* New York: Spectrum Publications.

————— and Frazer, A. (1975b, in press). Reduced central serotonergic activity in mania: implications for the relationship between depression and mania. *Br. J. Psychiat.*

————— and Hawkins, D. R. (1968). Sleep and depression: further considerations. *Arch. Gen. Psychiat.* 19:445–52.

————— and Stinnett, J. (1973). Biogenic amine metabolism, depression and mania. In J. Mendels, ed., *Biological Psychiatry.* New York: John Wiley & Sons, pp. 99–131.

—————, Frazer, A., Fitzgerald, R. G., et al. (1972a). Biogenic amine metabolites in cerebrospinal fluid of depressed and manic patients. *Science* 175:1380–82.

—————, Secunda, S. K., and Dyson, W. L. (1972b). A controlled study of the antidepressant effects of lithium. *Arch. Gen. Psychiat.* 26:154–57.

—————, Stinnett, J., Burns, D., et al. (1975). Amine Precursors and depression. *Arch. Gen. Psychiat.* 32:22–30.

Moir, A. T. B., Ashcroft, G. W., Crawford, T. B. B., et al. (1970). Central metabolites in cerebrospinal fluid as a biochemical approach to the brain. *Brain* 93:357–68.

Molinoff, P. B., and Axelrod, J. (1971). Biochemistry of catecholamines. *Ann. Rev. Biochem.* 40:465–500.

Murphy, D. L., Baker, M., Goodwin, F. K., et al. (1974a). L-tryptophan in affective disorders: indoleamine changes and differential clinical effects. *Psychopharmacol.* 34:11–20.

—————, Donnelly, C., and Moskowitz, J. (1974b). Catecholamine receptor function in depressed patients. *Am. J. Psychiat.* 131:1389–91.

Muschek, L. D., and McNeill, J. H. (1971). The effect of tricyclic antidepressants and promethazine on 3′,5′-cyclic AMP phosphodiesterase from rat brain. *Fed. Proc.* 30:330.

Naylor, G. J., Dick, D. A. T., Dick, E. G., et al. (1974a). Lithium therapy and erythrocyte membrane cation carrier. *Psychopharmacol.* 37:81–86.

—————, Stansfield, D. A., Whyte, S. F., et al. (1974b). Urinary excretion of adenosine 3′,5′-cyclic monophosphate in depressive illness. *Br. J. Psychiat.* 125:275–79.

Nyback, H., Borzechi, Z., and Sedvall, G. (1968). Accumulation and disappearance of catecholamines formed from tyrosine-^{14}C in mouse brain: effect of some psychotropic drugs. *Eur. J. Pharmacol.* 4:395–403.

O'Keeffe, R., Sharman, D. F., and Vogt, M. (1970). Effect of drugs used in psychoses on cerebral dopamine metabolism. *Br. J. Pharmacol.* 38:387–04.

Orloff, J., and Handler, J. (1967). The role of adenosine 3′,5′-phosphate in the action of antidiuretic hormone. *Am. J. Med.* 42:757–68.

Palmer, G. C. (1973). Influence of amphetamines, protriptyline and pargyline on the time course of the norepinephrine-induced accumulation of cyclic AMP in the rat brain. *Life Sci.* 12:345–55.

————— and Manian, A. A. (1974). Effects of phenothiazines and phenothiazine metabolites on adenyl cyclase and the cyclic AMP response in the rat brain. In I. S. Forrest, C. J. Carr and E. Usdin, eds., *The Phenothiazines and Structurally Related Drugs.* New York: Raven Press, pp. 749–67.

—————, Robison, G. A., Manian, A. A., et al. (1972). Modification by psychotropic drugs of the cyclic AMP response to norepinephrine in the rat brain *in vitro. Psychopharmacol.* (Berlin) 23:201–11.

Papeschi, R., and McClure, D. J. (1971). Homovanillic and 5-hydroxyindoleacetic acid in cerebrospinal fluid of depressed patients. *Arch. Gen. Psychiat.* 25:354–58.

Pare, C. M. B., and Sandler, M. (1959). A clinical and biochemical study of a trial of iproniazid in the treatment of depression. *J. Neurol. Neurosurg. Psychiat.* 22:247–51.

Paul, M. I., Cramer, H., and Goodwin, F. K. (1971). Urinary cyclic AMP excretion in depression and mania. *Arch. Gen. Psychiat.* 24:327–33.

————, Ditzion, B. R., and Janowsky, D. S. (1970). Affective illness and cyclic-AMP excretion. *Lancet* 1:88.

Perez-Cruet, J., Tagliamonte, A., Tagliamonte, P., et al. (1971). Stimulation of serotonin synthesis by lithium. *J. Pharmacol. Exp. Ther.* 178:325–30.

Ploeger, E. J. (1974). The effects of lithium on excitable cell membranes. On the mechanism of inhibition of the sodium pump of non-myelinated nerve fibres of the rat. *Eur. J. Pharmacol.* 25:316–21.

———— and Den Hertog, A. (1973). The effects of lithium on excitable cell membranes. II. The effect on the electrogenic sodium pump of non-myelinated nerve fibres of the rat. *Eur. J. Pharmacol.* 21:24–29.

Post, R. M., and Goodwin, F. K. (1974). Effects of amitriptyline and imipramine on amine metabolites in the cerebrospinal fluid of depressed patients. *Arch. Gen. Psychiat.* 30:234–39.

———— and Goodwin, F. K. (1975, in press). Studies of cerebrospinal fluid amine metabolites in depressed patients: conceptual problems and theoretical implications. In J. Mendels, ed., *Psychobiology of Depression.* New York: Spectrum Publications.

————, Gordon, E. K., Goodwin, F. K., et al. (1973). Central norepinephrine metabolism in affective illness: MHPG in the cerebrospinal fluid *Science* 179:1002–03.

Prange, A. J., Jr. (1964). The pharmacology and biochemistry of depression. *Dis. Nerv. Syst.* 25:217–21.

————, Wilson, I. C., Lara, P. P., et al. (1972). Effects of thyrotropin-releasing hormone in depression. *Lancet* 2:999–1002.

————, Wilson, I. C., Lynn, C. W., et al. (1974). L-tryptophan in mania. *Arch. Gen. Psychiat.* 30:56–62.

————, Wilson, I. C., Rabon, A. M., et al. (1969). Enhancement of imipramine antidepressant activity by thyroid hormone. *Am. J. Psychiat.* 126:457–69.

Ramsey, T. A., Mendels, J., Stokes, J. W., et al. (1972). Lithium carbonate and kidney function. A failure in renal concentrating ability. *JAMA* 219:1446–49.

Rees, J. R., Allsopp, M. N. E., and Hullin, R. P. (1974). Plasma concentration of tryptophan and other amino acids in manic-depressive patients. *Psychol. Med.* 4:334–37.

Roberts, E., and Simonsen, D. G. (1970). Some properties of cyclic 3',5'-nucleotide phosphodiesterase of mouse brain: effects of imidazole-4-acetic acid, chlorpromazine, cyclic 3',5'-GMP, and other substances. *Brain Res.* 24:91–111.

Robins, E., and Guze, S. (1972). Classification of affective disorders: the primary-secondary, the endogenous-reactive, and the neurotic-psychotic concepts. In T. A. Williams, M. M. Katz, J. A. Shield, eds., *Recent Advances in the Psychobiology of the Depressive Illnesses.* DHEW Publication #70-9053, pp. 283–93.

———— and Hartman, B. K. (1972). Some chemical theories of mental disorders. In R. W. Albers, G. J. Siegel, R. Katzman, et al., eds., *Basic Neurochemistry.* Boston; Little, Brown pp. 607–44.

Robison, G. A., Butcher, R. W., and Sutherland, E. W. (1967). Adenyl cyclase as an adrenergic receptor. *Ann. N.Y. Acad. Sci.* 139:703–23.

————, Butcher, R. W., and Sutherland, E. W. (1969). On the relation of hormone receptors to adenyl cyclase. In J. F. Danielli, J. F. Moran and D. J. Triggle, eds., *Fundamental Concepts in Drug-Receptor Interactions.* New York: Academic Press, pp. 59–81.

————, Coppen, A. J., Whybrow, P. G., et al. (1970). Affective disorders. *Lancet* 2:1028–29.

Roffler-Tarlov, S., Schildkraut, J. J., and Draskoczy, P. R. (1973). Effects of acute and chronic administration of desmethylimipramine on the content of norepinephrine and other monoamines in the rat brain. *Biochem. Pharmacol.* 22:2923–26.

Rubin, R. T., and Mandell, A. J. (1966). Adrenal cortical activity in pathological emotional states: a review. *Am. J. Psychiat.* 123:387–400.

Sabelli, H. C., and Mossmain, A. V. (1974). Phenethylamine hypothesis of affective behavior. *Am. J. Psychiat.* 131:695–99.

Sachar, E. J. (1973). Endocrine factors in psychopathological states. In J. Mendels, ed., *Biological Psychiatry*. New York: John Wiley & Sons.

—— (1974). A letter. *Am. J. Psychiat.* 131:608–09.

—— (1975, in press). A neuroendocrine strategy in the psychobiological study of depressive illness. In J. Mendels, ed., *Psychobiology of Depression*. New York: *Spectrum Publications*.

Sack, R. L., and Goodwin, F. K. (1974). Inhibition of dopamine-β-hydroxylase in manic patients: a clinical trial with fusaric acid. *Arch. Gen. Psychiat.* 31:649–54.

Salami, A. I., Insalaco, J. R., and Maxwell, R. A. (1971). Concerning the molecular requirements for the inhibition of racemic ^{3}H-norepinephrine into rat cerebral cortex slices by tricyclic antidepressants and related compounds. *J. Pharmacol. Exp. Therap.* 178:474–81.

Schanberg, S. M., Schildkraut, J. J., and Kopin, I. J. (1967). The effects of psychoactive drugs on norepinephrine-3-H metabolism in brain. *Biochem. Pharmacol.* 16:393–99.

Schildkraut, J. J. (1965). The catecholamine hypothesis of affective disorders: a review of supporting evidence. *Am. J. Psychiat.* 122:509–22.

—— (1970). *Neuropsychopharmacology and the Affective Disorders*. Boston: Little, Brown.

—— (1937a). Neuropharmacology of the affective disorders. *Ann. Rev. Pharmacol.* 13:427–54.

—— (1973b). Norepinephrine metabolites as biochemical criteria for classifying depressive disorders and predicting response to treatment: preliminary findings. *Am. J. Psychiat.* 130:695–99.

—— (1974). Biochemical criteria for classifying depressive disorders and predicting responses to pharmacotherapy. *Pharmakophyschiat.* 7:98.

—— (1975, in press). Depressions and biogenic amines. In S. Arieti, ed., *American Handbook of Psychiatry*. New York: Basic Books.

——, Schanberg, S. M., Breese, G. R., et al. (1969). Effects of psychotropic drugs on the metabolism of intracisternally administered serotonin in rat brain. *Biochem. Pharmacol.* 18:1971–78.

——, Winokur, A., and Applegate, C. W. (1970). Norepinephrine turnover and metabolism in rat brain after long-term administration of imipramine. *Science* 168:867–69.

Schless, A. P., Frazer, A., Mendels, J., et al. (1975, in press). Genetic determinants of lithium metabolism. II. An *in vivo* study of lithium distribution across erythrocyte membranes. *Arch. Gen. Psychiat.*

Schou, M., Amdisen, A., Jensen, S. E., et al. (1968). Occurrence of goitre during lithium treatment. *Br. Med. J.* 3:710–13.

Schubert, J., Nyback, H., and Sedvall, G. (1970). Effect of antidepressant drugs on accumulation and disappearance of monoamines formed *in vivo* from labeled precursors in mouse brain. *J. Pharm. Pharmacol.* 22:136–39.

Sedvall, G., Jonsson, B., and Petterson, U. (1969). Evidence of an altered thyroid function in man during treatment with lithium carbonate. *Acta Psychiat. Scand.* 207(Suppl.) 59–67.

Sheard, M. H., and Aghajanian, G. K. (1970). Neuronally activated metabolism of brain serotonin: effect of lithium. *Life Sci.* 9:285–90.

——, Zolovick, A., and Aghajanian, G. K. (1972). Raphe neurons: effect of tricyclic antidepressant drugs. *Brain Res.* 43:690–94.

Shopsin, B., Wilk, S., Gershon, S., et al. (1973a). Cerebrospinal fluid MHPG: an assessment of norepinephrine metabolism in affective disorders. *Arch. Gen. Psychiat.* 28:230–33.

——, Wilk, S., Goldstein, M., et al. (1973b). The use of imipramine, AMPT and PCPA in hospitalized depressives. Presented at 12th Annual Meeting, American College of Neuropharmacology, Palm Springs.

Shore, P. A. (1972). Transport and storage of biogenic amines. *Ann. Rev. Pharmacol.* 12:209–26.

Singer, I., Rotenberg, D., and Puschett, J. B. (1972). Lithium-induced nephrogenic diabetes insipidus: *in vivo* and *in vitro* studies. *J. Clin. Invest.* 51:1081–91.

Sjoqvist, F. (1974). On the mechanisms behind marked interindividual variations in steady-state plasma concentrations of antidepressants—mass fragmentographic studies suggesting differential effects of nortriptyline and chlorimipramine on noradrenaline and serotonin neurons in man (effects on MHPG and 5HIAA in CSF). Presented at World Psychiatric Association Meeting, Munich.

Sjostrom, R. (1974). Diagnosis of manic-depressive psychosis from cerebrospinal fluid concentration of 5-hydroxyindoleacetic acid. *Adv. Biochem. Psychopharmacol.* 11:369–75.

Spector, S., Sjoerdsma, A., and Udenfriend, S. (1965). Blockade of endogenous norepinephrine synthesis by α-methyl tyrosine, an inhibitor of tyrosine hydroxylase. *J. Pharmacol. Exp. Ther.* 147:86–95.

Stjarne, L. (1972). Enhancement by indomethacin of cold-induced hypersecretion of noradrenaline in the rat *in vivo* by suppression of PGE mediated feedback control. *Acta Physiol. Scand.* 86:388–97.

Sutherland, E. W., and Rall, T. W. (1960). The relation of adenosine-3′,5′-phosphate and phosphorylase to the actions of catecholamines and other hormones. *Pharmacol. Rev.* 12:265–99.

Takahashi, K., Kamimura, M., Shinko, T., et al. (1966). Effects of vasopressin and waterload on urinary adenosine 3′,5′-cyclic monophosphate. *Lancet* 2:967.

Thomas, R. C. (1972). Electrogenic sodium pump in nerve and muscle cells. *Physiol. Rev.* 52:563–94.

Tobin, T., Akera, T., Han, C. S., et al. (1974). Lithium and rubidium interactions with sodium- and potassium-dependent adenosine triphosphatase: a molecular basis for the pharmacological actions of these ions. *Mol. Pharmacol.* 10:501–08.

Todrick, A., and Tait, A. C. (1969). The inhibition of human platelet 5-hydroxytryptamine uptake by tricyclic antidepressive drugs. The relationship between structure and potency. *J. Pharm. Pharmacol.* 31:751–62.

Uzunov, P., and Weiss, B. (1971). Effects of phenothiazine tranquilizers on the cyclic 3′,5′-adenosine monophosphate system of rat brain. *Neuropharmacol.* 10:697–708.

——— and Weiss, B. (1972a). Separation of multiple molecular forms of cyclic adenosine-3′,5′-monophosphate phosphodiesterase in rat cerebellum by polyacrylamide gel electrophoresis. *Biochim. Biophys. Acta* 284:220–26.

——— and Weiss, B. (1972b). Psychopharmacological agents and the cyclic AMP system of rat brain. *Adv. Cyclic Nucleotide Res.* 1:435–53.

———, Shein, H. M., and Weiss, B. (1974). Multiple forms of cyclic 3′,5′-AMP phosphodiesterase of rat cerebrum and cloned astrocytoma and neuroblastoma cells. *Neuropharmacol.* 13:377–91.

Van Praag, H. M., Korf, J., Dols, L. C. W., et al. (1972). A pilot study of the predictive value of the probenecid test in application of 5-hydroxytryptophan as an antidepressant. *Psychopharmacol.* 25:14–21.

———, Korf, J., and Schut, D. (1973). Cerebral monoamines and depression. *Arch. Gen. Psychiat.* 28:827–31.

Vetulani, J., Dingell, J. V., and Sulser, F. (1974). Effect of chronic treatment with desipramine (DMI) and iprindole (IP) on the norepinephrine (NE) sensitive adenylate cyclase system in slices of the rat limbic forebrain (LFS). *Pharmacol.* 16:287.

Walker, J. B. (1974). The effect of lithium on hormone-sensitive adenylate cyclase from various regions of the rat brain. *Biol. Psychiat.* 8:245–51.

Wang, Y. C., Pandey, G. N., Mendels, J., et al. (1974a). The effect of lithium on prostaglandin E_1-stimulated adenylate cyclase activity of human platelets. *Biochem. Pharmacol.* 23:845–55.

———, Pandey, G. N., Mendels, J., et al. (1974b). Platelet adenylate cyclase responses in depression: implications for a receptor defect. *Psychopharmacol.* 36:291–300.

Wehmann, R. E., Blonde, L., and Steiner, A. L. (1974). Sources of cyclic nucleotides in plasma. *J. Clin. Inv.* 53:173–79.

Weiss, B., Fertel, R., Figlin, R., et al. (1974). Selective alteration of the activity of the multiple forms of adenosine 3′,5′-monophosphate phosphodiesterase of rat cerebrum. *Mol. Pharmacol.* 10:615–25.

Wheatley, D. (1972). Potentiation of amitriptyline by thyroid hormone. *Arch. Gen. Psychiat.* 26:229–33.

Whybrow, P. C., and Mendels, J. (1969a). Toward a biology of depression: some suggestions from neurophysiology. *Am. J. Psychiat.* 125:1491–500.

———, Prange, A., and Treadway, C. (1969b). Mental changes accompanying thyroid gland dysfunction. *Arch. Gen. Psychiat.* 20:48–63.

Wilhelm, M. (1974). La chimie des psychotropes polycycliques, jeu de hasard ou systématique? *Act. Chimie Thérapeutique* 2:33–46.

——— and Kuhn, R. (1970). Versuch einer stereochemisch-strukturellen klassifizierung der trizyklus-psychopharmaka mit einschluss der dibenzo-bicyclooctadiene. *Pharmakopsychiat.* 3:317–32.

Wilk, S., and Green, J. P. (1972). On the measurement of 5-hydroxyindoleacetic acid in cerebrospinal fluid. *J. Neurochem.* 19:2893–95.

Williams, R. J. P. (1973). The chemistry and biochemistry of lithium. In S. Gershon and B. Shopsin, eds., *Lithium: Its Role in Psychiatric Research and Treatment.* New York: Plenum Press, pp. 15–31.

Wolff, J., Berens, S. C., and Jones, A. B. (1970). Inhibition of thyrotropin-stimulated adenyl cyclase activity of beef thyroid membranes by low concentration of lithium ion. *Biochem. Biophys. Res. Commun.* 39:77–82.

CHAPTER III

Frequency and Hereditary Aspects of Depression

C. Perris

Both areas under investigation in this review imply very complex methodological problems, and it is a difficult task to summarize them within the limits of a short report. However, since recent reviews are available concerning both epidemiological (Rawnsley, 1968; Silverman, 1968; Lehman, 1971) and genetic studies (Winokur et al., 1969; Becker, 1974; Perris, 1973b; Zerbin-Rüdin, 1971), I can concentrate on a few highlights.

Concerning the first part of my presentation, an appropriate subtitle would be *How little we know about the real frequency of depression in the general population.*

There has been a general impression that the morbidity rates of affective disorders have been rising in European countries and declining in the United States, but we have only indirect and somewhat controversial evidence to support such assumptions (Rawnsley, 1968; Silverman, 1968). Even more uncertain are figures concerning developing countries where both patient care and epidemiological research are strongly influenced by cultural factors.

Determination of the frequency of a psychic disorder in the general population may serve widely different purposes (Table I). Accordingly, different techniques may be used. Broadly speaking, it is very hazardous to use findings obtained with a specific technique for purposes other than those for which the adopted technique was selected. According to Hanna (1965), the existence of a higher frequency of a given disorder among relatives of a proband compared to the general population would support the hypothesis that there is a genetic transmission of the disorder under scrutiny. Thus knowledge of morbidity rates in the general population is a necessary condition for clinical genetic investigations.

Table I
Some of the main objectives of epidemiological studies

---

1) To elucidate etiologic factors.
2) To facilitate the development of preventive measures.
3) To determine the availability and utilization of services
   for treatment.

DEFINING TERMS AND METHODOLOGICAL ASPECTS

Current assessments of the frequency of a given abnormality are a question of the determination of either "incidence," "prevalence" or "disease expectancy" ("morbidity risk") of the abnormality concerned. Since these terms are sometimes used improperly, it is worthwhile to remember (Table II) that "incidence" is understood to mean the relative frequency within a specified population of new instances of a disorder in a specified limited period. By "prevalence" we mean the percentage of the population with the abnormality (both new and old cases) at a given moment. The time limits in prevalence studies range from one day ("one day point prevalence") to several years ("period prevalence"). "Disease expectancy" means the probability of an individual manifesting the abnormality at some time in his life, provided that he lives through the whole period when he will be exposed to the risk. Thus an adequate knowledge of the age limits within which the abnormality can manifest itself is a necessary prerequisite for an exact calculation of disease expectancy. For research purposes, methods have been developed for correcting results with respect to the "risk period" variable (Weinberg, 1920; Strömgren, 1935).

A primary condition for epidemiological research is an accurate case identification. Unfortunately, depending on the multiple shades of meaning given to the term "depression," the most crucial point in epidemiological studies of this disorder has been the lack of consensus on reliable, objective case criteria. Moreover, since depression as a symptom is ubiquitous and transient in pathological as well as in normal conditions, research focused on depression as a symptom would be almost meaningless.

Most of the epidemiological research work carried out in the field of affective disorders has been focused upon frequency estimates of depression, intended as a consistent syndrome or a definite disease entity. Since the classification of affective disorders is still controversial, and no definitive agreement exists concerning subgroups of depressive disorders, results from different sources are scarcely consistent and hardly comparable. This lack of reliability is an important source of error not only in comparisons between results in different countries, but also in

Table II
Different techniques in assessing the frequency of an abnormality in the population

---

A definition of terms currently used

Prevalence: the percentage of the population with the abnormality at a given moment (point or period prevalence).

Incidence (morbidity): percentage risk within a specified population of manifesting the abnormality within a specified limited period.

Disease Expectancy (morbidity risk): probability of the individual manifesting the abnormality at some time of his life provided that he lives through the whole risk period.

Risk Period: the age limits for the possible onset of the disorder under scrutiny.

---

comparisons between results obtained in the same country by different investigators. Mediocre diagnostic reliability very likely accounts for apparent discrepancies between epidemiological findings derived from studies of admission rates in different parts of the world (Rawnsley, 1968; Silverman, 1968; Becker, 1974). Another important source of variation in epidemiological studies is the fact that depression as a syndrome seems to change its form of expression both in different time periods and with respect to different cultural settings (Lungerhausen, 1973; Perris, 1973a; Asuni, 1973; Chaudhry, 1973; Alouso-Fernández, 1973).

A survey of the approaches used in epidemiological studies of affective disorders is given in Table III. Studies of admission rates, usually incidence assessment, may be of interest for many purposes but hardly as a basis for genetical studies, since many sources of error, as indicated in Table IV, might influence the results.

Main Findings in Epidemiological Studies

In order to illustrate some of the discrepancies in different studies carried out according to different techniques, I have summarized some of the main findings obtained with different methods of estimation in Tables V through VIII. Most of these discrepancies depend mainly upon differences in the definition of the unit of research. Whereas some authors take into account only narrowly defined cases of

Table III
Different approaches in epidemiological studies of psychic disorders

1) Estimation of first admission rates.
2) Estimation of the frequency among psychiatric outpatients or in general practice.
3) Studies of samples or total populations within geographically defined areas.
4) Studies of particular communities.
5) Estimation of the disease expectancy among relatives of healthy individuals.
6) Studies in relation to different sociodemographic variables.

manic-depressive psychosis (MDP), others consider all the psychotic depressive conditions or all forms of depression independently of their severity. Some of the factors usually assumed to influence the frequency distribution of affective disorders and the direction of such assumptions are presented in Table IX. Concerning these factors, however, the results are quite inconsistent, as has been demonstrated, for example, by transcultural studies (Tonks et al., 1970; Fernando, 1966).

My view about epidemiological information concerning affective disorders is rather pessimistic, but it does not mean that I want to disregard the body of knowledge built up so far. One cannot pretend that the available findings give us a definitive picture of the frequency in the population of all affective disorders, but they do give us a few clues about the frequency of the major psychotic conditions. As a matter of fact, in this last respect, there seems to be a little more consistency among population estimates of disease expectancy. Accordingly, an assumed disease expectancy in the general population ranging from 0.9 to 1.8 percent in males and 1.2 to 2.8 percent in females may serve as a basis for comparison with estimates obtained from studies of families of probands.

Table IV
Factors which limit the reliability of data emerging from studies of admission rates

Inter- and intra-observer inconsistency.
Relative age distribution in the population and at hospital.
Availability of psychiatric services outside the hospital.
Distance to the psychiatric hospital (or psychiatric service).
Attitude in the population towards psychiatric care in general and with regard to the specific disorder in particular.
Expansion of preventive measures.

Table V
Affective disorders: One-day Point Prevalence Estimates in selected community surveys (per 1,000 population)

	Psychotic	Neurotic
U.S.A. (Roth and Luton, 1943)	0.7	1.4
Sweden (Sjogren, 1948)	0.5	(only MDP)
Sweden (Book, 1953)	0.2	
Sweden (Essen-Moller, 1956)	2.0	5.8
Iceland (Helgason, 1961)	10.4	25.5
Denmark (Sorensen et al., 1961)	7.8	26.5
Czechoslovakia (Ivanys et al., 1964)	1.3	

From that point on, we can start to analyze the evidence in support of a genetic predisposition for affective disorders.

Genetic Predisposition to Affective Disorders and the Impact of an Ambiguous Terminology

Concerning behavioral disorders, several approaches are possible in investigating the relative importance of genetic factors. The main aspects of these approaches are summarized in Table X. In the field of affective disorders, clinical studies are far more numerous than biological investigations with the exception of adoptive genetic studies which are still lacking. I will try to summarize the main findings that have emerged from these studies and to add a few comments about perspectives for future investigations. Genetic investigations of affective disorders

Table VI
Affective disorders: Period prevalence estimates in selected community surveys (per 1,000 population)

	Psychotic	Neurotic
U.S.A. (Cohen and Fairbank, 1938	0.8	
U.S.A. (Lemkau et al., 1941)	0.9	0.3
Hutterites Communities (Eaton and Keil, 1955)	0.9	
Canada (Leighton et al., 1963)	3.0	72.0
Formosa (Lin, 1953)	0.4	

Table VII
Affective disorders: period prevalence estimates in general practice (per 1,000 population)

	Psychotic	Neurotic
(Crombie, 1957)	6.0	3.0
(Shepherd et al., 1966)	2.4	
(Watts, 1966)	5.0	10.0

Table VIII
Affective disorders: lifetime disease expectancy rates according to different methods of assessment (per 1,000 population)

Population studies:	Male	Female
Denmark (Fremming, 1951)	10.2	22.4
Sweden (Larsson and Sjogren, 1954)	9.0	12.0 (only MDP)
Iceland (Helgason, 1964)	18.0	24.6
Sweden (Essen-Moller, 1956)	17.0	28.0
First admission studies:		
Norway (Odegaard, 1962)	4.2	6.2
London (Norris, 1959)	8.0	14.4
New Zealand (James and Chapman, 1975)	2.0	2.7
Prospective studies:		
Sweden (Essen-Moller and Haguell, 1961)	85.0	177.0 (all kinds of depression)

have been mainly concerned with those conditions which are labeled as "endogenous" or "primary" or "major" psychotic affective disorders, i.e., those disorders for which the influence of external precipitating factors or other somatic conditions is regarded as less probable. Moreover, very few investigations have been concerned with disorders of mood judged as neurotic or reactive.

A critical analysis of current labels frequently attached to affective disorders would easily reveal many ambiguities, but this problem cannot be discussed on this occasion. However, a few historical notes are necessary for a better under-

Table IX
Factors assumed to influence the frequency distribution of affective disorders

Factor	Assumption
Age	Increase with increasing age
Sex	More frequent in women
Race/Religion	Less frequent in blacks, more frequent among Jewish, etc.
Socioeconomic Status	Different M/F ratios in the lower classes
Cultural Frame	Different mania/depression ratios in different cultures, etc.

Table X
Some of the main approaches used to investigate the possible importance of genetic factors in the transmission of affective disorders

Level of investigation	Kind of studies
Clinical	Family studies (assessment of the morbidity risk among relatives as compared with the population)
	Twins studies (assessment of concordance and discordance rates)
	Adoptee studies (comparison of morbidity rates among biological and adoptive families)
Biological	Association studies (in relation to known genetic markers whose distribution in the general population is well known)
	Linkage studies (to assess a possible linkage between the abnormality and a known genetic marker whose chromosomal position is known)
	Chromosome studies (to provide evidence of possible aberrations)

standing of most of the older genetic studies. There is little doubt that our present conception of "primary" affective disorders in general, and MDP in particular, is still influenced by Kraepelin's ideas. For this reason, it may be useful to recall Kraepelin's definition of MDP. According to him, the label MDP included "the whole domain of the so-called periodic or circular insanities, the simple mania, a greater part of the morbid states termed melancholia, and also, a not inconsiderable number of cases of amentia." Kraepelin later expanded the concept to include under the same heading "all cases of affective excess, also at a personality level," and later even "involutional melancholia" — a disorder that he had regarded at the very beginning as a separate nosological entity. Since Kraepelin strongly believed in the hereditary etiology of "nonorganic" psychotic disorders, he maintained that the main etiology of MDP was hereditary in at least 80 percent of his MDP patients (Kraepelin, 1910).

The influence of Kraepelin's diagnostic scheme was very great, and for the next fifty years research reports on MDP rarely distinguished between the different component varieties. As a consequence, attempts aimed at investigating a possible hereditary disposition in affective disorders has focused until a few years ago on MDP and has centered on Kraepelin's definition. Since this definition was extremely broad, these studies have consequently comprised very heterogeneous patient series.

I have already mentioned the ambiguity of some labels frequently attached o affective disorders. Now I would like to make a few comments about one of the most common among them: the term "endogenous." This term was introduced by Möbius (Möbius, 1910) and later was adopted by Kraepelin to refer to illnesses which he assumed to be caused by degenerative or hereditary disorders (Kraepelin, 1913). Afterwards the term "endogenous" was given different meanings, as indicated in Table XI. This table shows one of the most important sources of error in genetic studies starting with probands labeled "endogenous depressives": the fact that the presence of a hereditary taint (to be demonstrated) has mainly influenced the selection of the series to be investigated.

Turning to family studies of MDP, an attempt has been made in a few of them (Slater, 1938; Stenstedt, 1952; Kinkelin, 1954; Asano, 1960) to identify subgroups of probands according to different phenomenological parameters. Unfortunately, such a differentiation has not been subsequently applied to the secondary cases among relatives.

MAIN FINDINGS IN FAMILY STUDIES OF PROBANDS LABELED MDP

Estimations of morbidity risk among relatives of patients with MDP have shown wide variations (Table XII), a fact which is hardly surprising if the above-mentioned sources of error are taken into account. Furthermore, differ-

Table XI
A semantic analysis of the term "endogenous" as an attribute of a
depressive syndrome

The term is used to indicate that the syndrome is:

a) of internal origin
b) hereditary
c) of unknown origin
d) of a psychotic dimension
e) characterized by a particular symptomatology
    (depression + retardation + diurnal rhythm + early awakening in the morning)
f) the depressive phase of a manic-depressive (bipolar) psychosis

---

(A similar semantic confusion occurs with regard to other attributes commonly
used in defining depression.)

ences in the composition of the series, in methodology, and in statistical analysis
have also occurred. However, wide as the variation may be, the minimum percentage for each first-degree category is considerably above the median for the general
population (0.7 percent). Moreover, the morbidity rates for more distant relatives
sharing less than half the proband's genes, such as half-sibs, aunts, uncles, etc.,
are at least double the population median (Table XIII).

In a division of proband groups into those showing typical symptomatology,
several or few episodes do not appear to influence the morbidity rates among
first-degree relatives.

The evidence produced by these earlier family studies seems to give strong
support in favor of a genetic predisposition, but it has some limitations beside those
produced by diagnostic uncertainties. First of all, it could be suspected that
morbidity rates in the general population from which the probands come may be
higher than in other populations whose figures are used for a comparison. I do not
believe that this is a serious source of error when family investigations are carried
out in the same country and under similar circumstances as epidemiological
studies. However, if probands come from isolates or belong to special communities, then a control group would be desirable since the morbidity rates in
such populations may be much higher than assumed. Secondly, the most readily
accessible probands for research tend to be quite unrepresentative of the patient
population as a whole. As Becker (1974) has pointed out, these are usually hospitalized patients who are more severely ill than typical patients. Such patients are
likely to come from families with a greater number of virulent or pathological
genes. It has not yet been ascertained whether or not the selection of these types

Table XII
Morbidity risk (%) for relatives of patients labeled as
"Manic-Depressive"

	Morbidity risk %		
	Mean values	Range	Median
Parents	10 – 15	3.4 – 23.4	7.6
Children	10 – 15	6.0 – 24.1	8.1
Sibs	10 – 15	2.7 – 22.7	11.2
DZ twins	20	0 – 38	
MZ twins	70	25 – 92	

of patients is an important source of error. However, taking into account the increasing development of outpatient facilities, it could be assumed that the impact of such possible source of error may be greater in future research. Thirdly, knowledge of the diagnosis of the proband and of the hypotheses to be tested may affect the investigator's diagnosis of the proband's relatives. This source of error could be minimized by the use of independent observers, but it would raise noticeable difficulties in large field investigations. Finally, attention must be paid to the possible occurrence of consanguineous marriages and assortative mating (Gershon et al., 1971).

FAMILY STUDIES OF PROBANDS LABELED AS OTHER THAN MDP

Several family studies have focused mainly on patients who have suffered from depressive syndromes and, among other things, have considered the age variable. These studies are in part linked with Kraepelin's original assumption that nosologically the so-called involutional melancholia occupies a special position in relation to MDP.

The most comprehensive investigation in this field was carried out in Sweden by Stenstedt (1959) and concerned a study of 307 patients with a hospital diagnosis of involutional melancholia. Stenstedt found the morbidity risk percent (MR%) among parents was 1.6 for involutional melancholia, 0.6 for MDP, and 3.8 for "endogenous depression." Among sibs the corresponding percentages were 3.0, 1.7 and 2.4. Stenstedt's conclusion from the investigation was that involutional melancholia could scarcely be regarded as a uniform nosological entity.

Table XIII
Morbidity risk % for MDP among other than first-degree relatives of
MDP probands*

	Morbidity risk %
Half-sibs	1.4 – 47.6**
Uncles – aunts	4.2
Cousins	0.4 – 1.3
Grandchildren	1.9 – 3.3
Nieces and nephews	1.3 – 2.3

*Constructed from the data by Angst, 1971, and Zerbin-Rudin, 1967, only certain secondary cases.

**The highest value refers to half-sibs born from the ill parent.

Even if the conclusion is correct, the study has some limitations. In fact, no definite diagnostic criteria were given, nor was any definite age at the first attack specified. It seems, however, that the average age at the first onset of illness for the whole series was 57.5 ± .4 years. Kishima (1967) reported the results of a clinical genetic study of mental disorders in the aged with special reference to involutional depression. Seventy-five of his 161 psychotics were included in a "depression group," whereas the others were diagnosed either as "schizophrenic" or "organic." No age of onset was given, nor were diagnostic criteria specified for the depressive group. Among relatives in the depression group, a very high hereditary loading for MDP has been found with an MR% of 7.5 both among parents and sibs and also an MR% for schizophrenia of 1.4 among parents, and 7.6 among sibs. Kishima remarks that his figures are higher than those obtained by other investigators, but gives no explanation for the difference.

In a British study (Hopinkson, 1964), one hundred depressed patients were divided according to age at onset. Thirty-nine patients had suffered from attacks before the age of fifty (early-onset group), while sixty-one had initial attacks after this age (late-onset group). The MR% for "affective psychosis" of the early and late onset groups, respectively, were 25.5 and 10.0 for parents, 17.2 and 6.8 for sibs, and 23.5 and 12.8 for children. Quite recently, Winokur and his group (1971) have been especially concerned with possible interrelationships between sex, age at onset, and the degree of hereditary loading. As expected, they show that relatives of early-onset probands have a greater risk for depression than do the relatives of late-onset probands of both sexes. In addition they found that "more female relatives are depressed than male relatives of early onset male probands."

Since the whole series comprises no more than one hundred depressive probands, the importance of these findings is difficult to evaluate, considering the small number of probands in each subgroup.

The only family study specifically concerned with a family investigation of patients with defined "neurotic depression" comes from Sweden (Stenstedt, 1966). In this series, involving 176 patients, the MR% for "affective disorders" among first-degree relatives was 4.8. Among secondary cases, instances of both MDP and neurotic depression were found. This study, however, cannot be considered an exhaustive investigation of the question of hereditary taint within families of patients classified as neurotic-depressive in a hospital. This unanswered question is most likely a result of the difficulties encountered in clearly defining this undoubtedly greatly heterogenous patient group.

NEW APPROACHES: THE UNIPOLAR-BIPOLAR DICHOTOMY

It is well known that constructive criticism of Kraepelin's classification of "endogenous psychoses" has been put forward by Kleist and his pupils—in particular Leonhard (Leonhard, 1957-69). The latter has for the last few decades been developing Kleist's suggested classification and has presented his own classification of "endogenous" psychoses, which not only includes the two classical groups, MDP and schizophrenia, but is divided into four large groups (Table XIV): "affective psychoses," "cycloid psychoses," "systematic schizophrenia" and "nonsystematic schizophrenia." Furthermore, the "affective psychoses" group has been divided by Leonhard into "bipolar" (i.e., MDP in the strict sense with recurring phases of mania and depression) and "monopolar" (when changes of mood recur in a consistently depressive or manic direction without any occurrence of episodes of opposite polarity). Leonhard has discussed the dissimilarities in the two affective psychoses subgroups, dealing partly with the "cumulative hereditary taint with "endogenous psychoses" and partly with some clinical and personality variables. The most recent genetic study utilizing Leonhard's classification was published by von Trostorff (1968). For bipolar patients, the cumulative MR% is 9.5 in parents and 10.6 in siblings. For the monopolar probands, the corresponding MR% are 5.3 and 4.6. A higher hereditary loading in patients with circular (bipolar) psychosis, as compared with patients with isolated or recurrent depressive episodes, was also reported by Kinkelin (1954) and Asano (1960).

In the middle of the Sixties, Perris and d'Elia (Leonhard, 1957-69) presented some preliminary findings of a large investigation aimed at verifying Leonhard's hypothesis about the possible heterogeneity of MDP. In this very preliminary paper, support was found for the hypothesis that a possible specific hereditary loading could occur in Leonhard's subgroups of affective psychoses. It is in this

Table XIV
Leonhard's classification of "endogenous" psychoses

| Affective psychoses | | Cycloid psychoses | Nonsystemic schizophrenic psychoses | Systemic schizophrenic psychoses |
Bipolar type	Monopolar types			
Manic-depressive	Pure depressive with several p subgroups	Anxiety-happiness psychosis	Affect-laden paraphrenia	Paranoid type
	Pure manic with several subgroups	Confusion psychosis	Cataphasia	Hebephrenic type
		Motility psychosis	Periodic catatonia	Catatonic type each with several subgroups

Table XV
Diagnostical differentiation of secondary cases (parents and siblings)

	Bipolar or manic	Unipolar depressive	Other depressive and suicide cases
Bipolar probands			
Angst	3.7 ± 1.5	11.2 ± 2.5	3.1 ± 1.4*
Perris	10.8 ± 1.4	0.58 ± 0.03	8.6 ± 1.2
Unipolar probands			
Angst	0.29 ± 0.03	9.1 ± 1.6	2.3 ± 0.8*
Perris	0.35 ± 0.02	7.4 ± 1.1	6.8 ± 1.0

*Only suicide.

early paper that the label "unipolar" was used for the first time as preferable to "monopolar" for semantic reasons.

The investigation of 277 probands and 2,396 relatives was completed in 1966 (Perris, 1966) and resulted in a monograph in which the differences between narrowly defined series of bipolar and unipolar patients were documented by means of a multifactor approach. By a strange coincidence, a similar study was published independently in the same year by Angst (1966).

Since the results of these two surprisingly similar studies have been compared (Angst, 1971) and reviewed on several previous occasions (Becker, 1974; Perris, 1968, 1969, 1973c, d; Zerbin-Rudin, 1971; Price, 1968; Mayer-Gross et al., 1969), I will concentrate at this juncture on the main point which emerged from them, that is, that a generic as well as a specific predisposition to a defined kind of affective disorder can be inherited. The results presented in Table XV show, in fact, that there is strong evidence for bipolar subjects to have first-degree bipolar relatives and for unipolar subjects to have first-degree relatives with unipolar disorders. There was no excess of bipolar bases in the families of the unipolar probands or vice versa, although the MR for the homologous type of disorder increased far above the level for the general population. Differences between Angst's and my results concerning the distribution of secondary cases within families of bipolar probands are mainly due to differences in the definition of a "unipolar disorder," for which I require the occurrence of at least three separate episodes. More recent studies in New Zealand (James, 1975) and in Sweden (Petterson, 1974) indicate that an increase of depressive secondary cases can occur in bipolar families. However, even in these studies, differences in the definition of the patients may account for part of the variation. At almost the same

Table XVI
Sex distribution of secondary cases among parents and siblings

	Secondary cases of affective disorders (%)	
	Male relatives	Female relatives
Bipolar		
Angst	14.8 ± 3.9	15.0 ± 4.0
Perris	10.2 ± 2.0[a]	11.6 ± 2.0*
Unipolar		
Angst	2.8 ± 1.2	16.4 ± 2.9
Perris	5.6 ± 1.4[b]	8.8 ± 1.6**

*Only bipolar secondary cases.

**Only unipolar secondary cases (i.e., patients with at least three separate depressive episodes).

time, another group of research workers in St. Louis led by Winokur, adopting a similar approach, reached almost the same conclusion regarding a separation of the bipolar MDP form of illness from unipolar recurrent depressive psychosis on the basis of heredofamilial findings (Winokur et al., 1969).

In the light of these findings, some older investigations have been re-evaluated. The family histories reported by Slater (1938) have been reanalyzed (Price, 1968) and found to be in accordance with this dichotomy.

Another finding of interest for genetic considerations common to both Angst's and Perris' studies concerns the sex distribution for bipolar and for unipolar psychosis (Table XVI). Both authors found that the sex distribution is symmetrical for bipolar psychosis when all cases (not only hospitalized ones) are taken into account, while for unipolar depressive psychoses there is a clear female predominance.

OTHER APPROACHES

Attempts have been made (Angst, 1961, 1964; Pare et al., 1962; Pare and Mack, 1971) to identify genetic factors in affective disorders through a study of possible similarities in response to antidepressive therapies in members of the same family, and some challenging results have been presented. However, be-

Table XVII
MZ twins reared apart: concordance for "affective disorder"*

Author	Case no.	Age of separation	Concordance
Rosanoff et al.	1	6 months	Yes
Stenstedt	106	1 year	Yes
Shields and Slater	Sf3	13 months	Yes
	Sf5	from birth	Mild depressives
	Sf11	8 years	Yes
	Sf14	3 months	Neurotic depressives
	Sf19	4 years	Yes
	Sf21	from birth to 12 years	
	Sf26	6 months	Yes
Juel-Nielsen	4	from 1 to 7 years	Yes
	6	3 years	Neurotic depressives
	8	3 weeks	Yes

*All kinds of "affective disorders." Constructed from the case reports
 published by Price, 1968.

cause of methodological uncertainties, the findings of these studies are more
suggestive of possibilities for future research than they are conclusive. Instead of
studies concerned with clinical response to treatment, biological investigations of
possible similarities or differences among relatives of the same family in their
capacity to metabolize different drugs may furnish some clues for the identification of a genetically determined biological substratum in individuals suffering
from affective disorders.

Twin Studies

Several series of twins have been thoroughly investigated with special regard
to the concordance or discordance of affective disorders. Because monozygotic
(MZ) twins have identical genes, a very high concordance rate would be expected
in the case of a genetically determined abnormality. Hanna's (1965) second criterion for genetic transmission is that MZ twins have a higher concordance rate than
dizygotic (DZ) twins.

Since earlier studies in twins have been recently reviewed in detail (Price,

1968; Zerbin-Rüdin, 1969; Diebold, 1972), it is sufficient to remember at this point that concordance rates for MZ twins range from 50 to 100 percent and for DZ twins from 0.0 to 38.5 percent. Although concordance is four to five times higher in MZ twins as compared to DZ twins, it is still far below the expected 100 percent that would favor certain genetic predispositions. Different sources of error are likely to have influenced twins studies and may account for the variations in different series. Among the most serious methodological problems, the difficulties in collecting an unbiased series should be mentioned, as well as the fact that it has seldom been possible to follow up pairs of twins through the whole risk period for affective disorders. Moreover, it is still possible that a high concordance in MZ twins is due to the fact that environmental influences tend to be more similar for MZ than for DZ twins. So far, no acceptable studies of twins reared apart are available in the field of affective disorders. The few cases described in the literature have been reviewed by Price (1968). Table XVII has been constructed from his case reports.

Twin data on nonendogenous (Shapiro, 1970) or neurotic depression (Shields and Slater, 1966), although concerned with small series, tend to suggest that neurotic depression is not a specific genetic entity.

Of some interest has been a retrospective study of published twins series in order to see if there is any support for the bipolar-unipolar dichotomy. Such an analysis was performed by Zerbin-Rüdin (1969), the results of which are shown in Table XVIII. Of eighty-three pairs on whom information was sufficiently comprehensive, 70 percent were concordant; that is, both twins had suffered from an affective disorder. When these 70 percent were studied with regard to the type of affective disorder, there emerged a predominance of concordant twins with a similar form of illness, and 81 percent of these are concordant for the type of course of the depression. Zerbin-Rüdin considers that if there is a 30 percent discordance in the total material, it cannot be expected that there will be complete correspondence regarding the type of depression in the concordant pairs. One factor is that the observation period for some of the pairs was very short. It is to be assumed that a hereditary disposition for a depressive psychosis would not then manifest itself. Twin data seem, if anything, to provide support for the hypothesis that bipolar and unipolar depressive psychoses are two genetically separate illnesses.

Summing Up Clinical Genetic Studies

The findings of the clinical studies reviewed so far have well documented the familial occurrence of affective disorders, especially those characterized by a more severe, psychotic dimension. The great difference in relation to the frequency of the abnormality in the general population and all the findings concerning twins supports the hypothesis that a genetic predisposition is important for the occurrence of affective disorders. The more recent findings related to the bipolar-uni-

Table XVIII
Diagnostical differentiation in MZ twins
(Data collected by E. Zerbin-Rudin, 1969)

Kind of pair	No. of pair	Percent	
Both unipolar depressive	22	26.5	
Both bipolar	16	19.3	
Both unipolar manic	5	6.0	
Total	43	80.6	
1 unipolar – 1 bipolar	5	6.0	
1 manic – 1 depressive	2	2.4	
Total certain concordant for affective psychosis	50	60.2	
Probably concordant	9	10.8	
			71.1
Discordant	24	28.9	
Total	83	99.9	

polar dichotomy suggest, moreover, that this predisposition might be specific for specific disorders. Several points, however, still remain obscure, and many sources of error might have influenced the results of many investigations. Further research work is still needed to ascertain the relative importance of both genetic and nongenetic factors. Future research should be characterized, in my opinion, by a critical and narrow definition of the series to be investigated in order to diminish the variation due to heterogeneity in the proband's population. The bipolar-unipolar dichotomy represents, in this respect, one major advance toward a closer definition of the patients in question.

BIOLOGICAL STUDIES

To my knowledge, only one study has been concerned with an investigation of possible chromosomal abnormalities in affective disorders (Ebaugh et al., 1968). No deviance whatsoever was found.

Table XIX
S system: distribution percent

	Controls n = 287	Pat.s total n = 87	Unipolar n = 40	Bipolar n = 26	Cycloid n = 21
SS	18	25*	18	42**	19
Ss	46	38	40	27	48
ss	36	37	42	31	33

*p < .05
**p < .01

Several authors (Parker et al., 1961; Masters, 1967; Tanna and Winokur, 1968; Grof et al., 1971; Lange, 1970) have been concerned with disease-association studies on the assumption that the association of an illness with a well-known genetic trait establishes that the illness is genetically determined. The attention of scholars so far has been mainly focused on the possible association between affective disorders and blood groups. The findings obtained have apparently proved to be inconsistent, but some trends are emerging which are a challenge to further study. An increased association between type 0 blood group and MDP (Parker et al., 1961) seems to occur, and there is a decrease in the frequency of N in bipolar psychosis (Grof et al., 1971). Moreover, statistically significant differences between bipolar and unipolar patients have been obtained in a study (Lange, 1970) of hereditary postalbumin groups in the serum proteino-grams of patients with affective disorders.

At present we are carrying out a comprehensive study of the possible association between affective disorders and some thirty genetic markers. For the purpose of this meeting, I have made some preliminary calculations about a few of them. Besides many other trends in the Rh, ABO and MN systems, some striking differences have already emerged in the S and in the Lewis system (Tables XIX, XX). In our opinion, the most important finding concerns the intergroup differences and especially the difference between the bipolar group and the group here labeled "cycloid" which broadly corresponds to the American diagnosis "schizoaffective disorder." These groups are still too small to allow any conclusion, but we hope to be able to present more comprehensive results in the near future.

Some recently published linkage studies (Winokur, 1969; Fieve and Mendlewicz, 1973) seem to support the hypothesis that bipolar MDP could be linked both with the genes for color blindness and with the locus of the XG blood group. Since both these loci are on the short arm of the X chromosome, such a linkage would favor an X-linked type of transmission for bipolar MDP. However, an X-linked transmission would imply that no instances of father-to-son transmission

Table XX
Distribution (%) of the blood groups of the Lewis system among different patient groups and healthy controls

Blood group	Unipolar N = 39	Bipolar N = 26	Cycloid N = 21	Controls N = 265
Le (a$^+$ b$^-$)	2.6	26.9	14.3	21.1
Le (a$^-$ b$^+$)	71.8	57.7	61.9	67.2
Le (a$^-$ b$^-$)	25.6	15.4	23.8	11.7

Bipolar vs Unipolar chi-square 8.75 p < .02 df 2 (Yates corr.)
Bipolar vs Cycloid chi-square 1.34 p n.s.
Bipolar vs Controls chi-square 0.95 p n.s.
Unipolar vs Cycloid chi-cquare 3.03 p n.s.
Unipolar vs Controls chi-square 11.26 p < .01
Cycloid vs Controls chi-square 2.79 p n.s.

should occur. These instances are probably not frequent, but they do exist. Further cases have been recently added to those already reported in the literature (Mendlewicz, 1971) (Table XXI). Moreover, contrasting findings have been claimed on separate occasions by the same author (Fieve and Mendlewicz, 1973). Linkage studies present many difficulties, especially when the risk period for the disease under scrutiny is very long. Thus it is quite difficult to collect an acceptable number of relatives who have passed the risk limits. However, this is a challenging field of investigation, and further studies are required.

REMARKS ABOUT THE POSSIBLE MODE OF TRANSMISSION OF AFFECTIVE DISORDERS

Mentioning linkage studies and the implications contained in the results of these studies, I have come to the final point in my presentation. This concerns the question: How are affective disorders transmitted?

In past decades several hypotheses have been put forward, but none of them is completely satisfactory. The fact that in earlier studies of MDP a distinction between bipolar and unipolar families was not taken into account makes previous hypotheses even more uncertain. Besides the X-linked two genes theory defended by Winokur, which is quite similar to the earlier one presented by Rüdin (1923), two other modalities have been mainly discussed. One of these assumes the

Table XXI
Parent — child pairs in different series

	Slater (MDP)	Stenstedt (MDP)	Winokur (Manics)	Perris (BIP)	Perris (UNIP)	James (BIP)
Ill father — ill daughter	18	8	13	22	17	5
Ill father — ill son	14	5	0	13	9	5
Ill mother — ill daughter	32	21	17	8	6	14
Ill mother — ill son	11	14	17	2	10	9

possibility of an autosomal dominant type of transmission (Slater, 1938; Stenstedt, 1952), while the other stresses a possible polygenic inheritance.

Arguments could be presented for and against both hypotheses. Since a critical discussion of these hypotheses is available in many sources (Becker, 1974; Perris, 1973b; Zerbin-Rüdin, 1971; Price, 1968), it will not be repeated here. In this regard, I would conclude that further studies of well-defined patient groups combined with biological investigations of significant enzyme systems are necessary to elucidate this problem further.

CONCLUSION

The combined results of clinical and biological genetic studies of affective disorders support the hypothesis that genetic factors are of some importance for the occurrence of at least some subgroups of these disorders. Diagnostic uncertainties and methodological inaccuracies have partly hampered progress in this field of investigation. I would say, however, that we have reached a more stable ground from which to start searching for answers to genetic questions. Moreover, we have the advantage of having more sophisticated and adequate research techniques. It is, therefore, not improbable that if we learn to manage adequately the research tools at our disposal, we shall then be able to solve the problems which have been raised in this paper.

COMMENTARIES

DR. RASKIN: Dr. Perris concluded his excellent review of hereditary aspects of depression with the comment, "The combined results of clinical and biological genetic studies of affective disorders support the hypothesis that genetic factors are of some importance for the occurrence of at least some subgroups of these disorders." By qualifying the importance of genetic factors, Dr. Perris implied that nongenetic factors also play an important role in the genesis of some depressive illnesses. As a social scientist, I would like to elaborate on this point.

Dr. Perris noted that the lifetime morbidity risk for the depressive illnesses is higher for females than for males. Studies of the rate of first admissions to hospitals in this country, in England, and in the Scandinavian countries generally show a 1:2 or 1:3 male-to-female ratio (Lehmann, 1971; Essen-Möller and Haguell, 1961). These figures have been used by some investigators to support a genetic basis for depression. For example, Winokur and associates (1969) cited this sex ratio to support their X-linked dominant inheritance pattern for manic-depressive illness where mothers can transmit to sons and daughters but fathers can only transmit to daughters. In another study, Winokur (1971) also used a genetic paradigm to separate two prototypes of unipolar affective illness. In depressive spectrum disease, there was a marked preponderance of females, and they tended to be seen in families with a marked deficit of depressed male patients.

Although genetics may play a role in the higher incidence and prevalence of depression in females than in males, nongenetic factors can also affect this sex ratio. When survey data on the incidence of depression by sex is broken down further by treatment setting, the greatest discrepancy occurs in patients seen in outpatient rather than inpatient settings. The number of females seeking treatment for depression in outpatient settings is far greater than the number of males (Taylor and Chaves, 1964). Diagnostic differences also play a significant role in the ratio of male to female depressed patients. In order of decreasing magnitude, the ratio of males to females is approximately 1:1.5 for manic-depressive reaction, depressive type, 1:2 for psychotic-depressive reaction, 1:3 for involutional psychotic reaction, and anywhere from 1:3 to 1:11 for neurotic-depressive reaction. Consequently, the greatest discrepancy occurs in patients seen in outpatient settings and diagnosed neurotic-depressive reaction. These findings are consistent with survey data that indicate women are seen more frequently than men by private psychiatrists and general practitioners for treatment of psychological or functional disorders (Balter, 1969).

The sex ratio for affective illnesses also seems to differ as a function of social class. Schwab and associates (1967) noted that among depressed inpatients, depression was especially prevalent among middle- and upper-class females and that the typical sex ratio was reversed for the lower class, where male depressives outnumbered females.

A number of reports also suggest the sex ratio may vary in different cultures. Lamont (1951) reported that the mean annual incidence of manic-depressive psychosis and involutional melancholia per 100,000 population for Europeans in South Africa was 5.7 for males and 4.6 for females. Rao (1970) reported that the sex ratio for depression in India was 64 percent for males and only 36 percent for females.

Age is another factor that affects the sex ratio for affective disorders. Kielholz (1959) found that the peak ages for reactive depression are twenty-six to forty years for females, and thirty-six to forty years for males. Watts (1964) reported that the peak ages for endogenous depression in females are forty-five to fifty years, while the peak for males is reached after sixty years. Kendell (Beck, 1971) reviewed numerous statistical reports on depression and concluded that after age sixty-five depressive illnesses are almost as common in men as in women. Therefore, the sex ratio for depression varies at different age periods and tends toward equality as age increases.

Race may also be a factor that influences this sex ratio. Although blacks as a group are thought to show less depressive illness than whites, the ratio of female to male depression in blacks appears to be greater than for whites (Raskin et al., 1970).

Although the meaning of these findings is not always clear, the widely accepted sex ratio for depression is not constant, but seems to vary as a function of age, social class, type of depressive disorder, country of birth, and race. Hence, if genetic inheritance is primarily responsible for this sex ratio, its effects can be significantly enhanced or diminished by nongenetic or environmental factors.

Age of onset of depressive disorder is another variable that has been associated with genetically distinct depression subtypes. Reference was previously made to Winokur's (Winokur et al., 1971) genetic classification of two subtypes of unipolar depressive illness. In addition to an excess of women, depressive spectrum disease was further characterized by an early onset of depression and the presence of depressive equivalents such as alcoholism and sociopathy. In this group, the depressive equivalents were most prevalent among the depressed males. Pure depressive disease was characterized by a late onset of the disorder and the absence of depressive equivalents.

A number of additional hypotheses can be derived from the Winokur (Winokur et al., 1969) genetic paradigm. First, one would assume there would be a high correlation between the age of onset of depressive disorder in the patient and in a parent with a prior history of depressive illness. This prediction is based on the premise that age of onset of depressive illness is genetically determined and transmitted from parent to child. Hence, early-onset patients should have early-onset parents, and vice versa. Second, one would hypothesize that genetic factors, such as a history of depression or depressive equivalents, in a patient's mother or father would be more highly correlated with age of onset of depression in the patient than would nongenetic or environmental factors.

Joseph Galdi, a graduate student in psychology at George Washington University, decided to test these hypotheses, utilizing data from the National Institutes of Mental Health collaborative depression studies (Raskin et al., 1974). Ninety patients were selected from a pool of 800 who showed significant signs of depression on admission, had no history of mania, hypomania or schizophrenia and in whom there was a history of unipolar depression in at least one parent. For parents the diagnosis of depression was based on reports from a close family informant, usually an immediate relative of the patient's. Age of onset was defined as the earliest age at which the patient (or parent) revealed affective symptoms or a depressive episode irrespective of whether or not hospitalization occurred.

The correlation between age of onset of depressive symptoms in patients and their parents was .24, which was close to the .05 level of significance (d.f. = 55). However, this is not an impressive correlation, especially in view of the fact that the shared variance between age of onset in patients and in their parents is only 6 percent.

At least square regression analysis was undertaken to assess the relative importance of genetic and nongenetic factors in age of onset of depressive symptoms in the patients. The three genetic factors included in this analysis were onset of depression, alcoholism or sociopathy in the patient's mother prior to the patient's sixteenth birthday, onset in the patient's father, and sex of the patient. The nongenetic factors consisted of eight variables which assessed the adequacy of the maternal and paternal role fulfilled by the patient's parents, the patient's school and the psychological adjustment in childhood and adolescence and social class of origin.

The combination of genetic and nongenetic factors accounted for 51 percent of the total variance, which is generally considered quite good. However, 34 percent of the explainable variance was attributable to nongenetic factors and only 14 percent was attributable to the genetic variables. Consequently, age of onset of depressive illness is another example of a variable that appears to have both genetic and nongenetic determinants.

These findings show that although the course and manifestations of a depressive illness may be genetically predetermined, nongenetic or environmental factors can significantly alter such effects and should not be overlooked.

DR. WEISSMAN: First, I'd like to commend Dr. Perris' attention to the definition of incidence, prevalence, and morbidity rates. The confusion of these simple concepts in population studies plagues interpretation of studies and makes comparisons between them difficult.

Second, I'd like to take issue with the point that morbidity rates for depression are declining in the United States. While hospitalization for depression has declined in the United States, I believe that there has been an increase in ambulatory depressives; for example, studies of admissions to the Yale–New Haven Outpatient Services between 1960 and 1970 conducted by Drs. Zonana and

Henisz (Zonana et al., 1973) found an increase in all diagnostic categories which was greatest in the diagnosis of depression. In 1970, depression was the single most utilized diagnosis, whereas in 1960 schizophrenia and alcoholism had been. There was a fourfold increase in the diagnosis of depression over the decade.

In a separate study of suicide attempters conducted at Yale and covering a fifteen-year period, 1955 to 1970, we found an 1100 percent increase in suicide attempters (Weissman et al., 1973; Weissman, 1974). These attempters were primarily young (under thirty) depressed females. Neither study could explain the increases as due primarily to population or service changes. Undoubtedly, some of the increase in depression has to do with the fact that more treatments and more outpatient treatment facilities are available; therefore, more people are coming for treatment who might not have come before, and more are coming earlier in their illnesses—lithium clinics, for instance, are now common in major medical centers.

While it is possible that the patterns of care for depression have changed more than the total numbers of persons who are depressed, both treated and untreated, we have no evidence for a decrease and all our evidence is in the direction of an increase.

Finally, I'd like to comment briefly on the discrepancies we've observed between treated and untreated depressions and on the past and future direction of population studies.

Dr. Perris noted that studies of admission rates are not suitable for genetic studies because many sources of errors may influence results. Our experiences in New Haven indicate that a similar caveat can be used for all studies which include only treated cases, whether hospitalized or ambulatory. A population survey conducted in New Haven, Connecticut, in 1967 by Jerome Myers found that 11 percent of the population displayed moderate to severe depressive disorders, but only a fraction of those depressed (10 percent) had received psychiatric treatment of any kind either in the past year or ever (Myers et al., 1972, 1974).

We compared the untreated depressives in the community with depressives coming for treatment, both as inpatients and outpatients, during the same period, using data from an epidemiologic study undertaken by Drs. Klerman and Paykel, and Mrs. Prusoff (Klerman and Paykel, 1970). We found that the untreated cases were older, included more males and more persons from the lower social classes, and more blacks. Therefore, any study of depression based only on persons in treatment, any treatment, probably represents a biased sample of the population of depressives.

This observation makes good population studies most important. However, a major flaw in the population survey is the absence of diagnostic criteria. Population surveys in the United States have frequently been undertaken by persons interested in deviance rather than disease, so that detailed diagnostic criteria have not been used. Generally, surveys are designed for screening, i.e., determining high-risk groups, and not for making diagnoses. These screening tests sort out apparently well persons who have a disease from those who probably don't, but these tests do not tell us too much about the disease itself.

Dr. Perris commented that his talk could be subtitled *How little we know about the frequency of depression in the general population.* We could extend that to *How little we know about the frequency of depression in the general population, using the same diagnostic criteria we've applied to studies of treated depressives.* In the future we need to make population studies more than screening surveys. This is a problem we are confronted with now in New Haven as Dr. Myers and I plan a community study of depression. The research tool that we feel has the most promise in this regard is an instrument developed by Drs. Spitzer and Endicott, appropriately called the SADS (Schedule for Affective Disorders and Schizophrenia). The SADS is a detailed structured interview which can be used to assess the subject's current and past history and psychopathology. Information derived from this interview is then used to establish diagnoses which are precisely defined in an accompanying manual called *Research Diagnostic Criteria* (RDC). The RDC was developed by Drs. Spitzer, Endicott and Robins. Both the SADS and the RDC are currently being tested. The advantage is that both the diagnostic criteria and the method of obtaining the data to make the judgment about diagnoses are precisely laid out. We are planning to incorporate the SADS and the RDC in our community survey.

Optimistically, Dr. Perris pointed out that we are on stable ground to begin searching for answers to the genetic questions in depression. Collaborations between geneticists and epidemiologists may help to provide the baselines for this work. In order for this collaboration to bear fruit, however, we must apply the same precise thinking to our epidemiologic studies that has characterized the work described by Dr. Perris and his group today.

DR. VARGA: Six years ago, in 1968, when Dr. Perris discussed the genetic transmission of depressive psychoses, he wrote that "no clear answers are available." Today his opening statement is *How little we know about the real frequency of the affective disorder,* and the main reason is because of inaccuracy of the case identification. I would add to his statement that depression, as a symptom, or even as a syndrome, is a part of the normal psychic life; everyone is depressed, more or less, at sometime throughout his life. We must mention that the main problem in case identification is neurotic depression since the dichotomy between neurotic and endogenous depression is debatable.

When Dr. Perris reaches his conclusions, he reduces the main findings to a very small group of statements: the reports agree, from the time of Kraepelin to the German, Swiss, Scandinavian, British and American researchers, that there is a hereditary loading in the affective disorders, probably less in involutional melancholia and greater in the bipolar affective disorders. So, accepting the fact that genetic predisposition is important for the occurrence of the affective disorders, we might add that there is a specificity for the unipolar and bipolar depressions.

Knowing all this, I am still skeptical since I do not know if anyone has investigated normal probands who passed their risk period (their whole life) without having affective disorder.

DR. GALLANT: The methodological faults and somewhat inconsistent results of epidemiologic studies of affective disorders have been thoroughly reviewed by Dr. Perris and reemphasized by Drs. Raskin and Weissman. There is no doubt that the inconsistency of diagnostic criteria has contributed to the difficulties in comparing the results in various genetic studies. Coexistence of thought and mood disorders has contributed to this nosologic confusion in the area of depression, but data from family studies do suggest that schizoaffective illness, or what Dr. Perris refers to as cycloid, is more closely related to the affective disorders than to schizophrenia (Ianzito et al., 1974; Cohen et al., 1972). I should like to cite the important study by Cohen and his associates, who evaluated more than 15,000 twin pairs from the U.S. Armed Forces Service records. Four hundred and twenty cases had a history of psychiatric disorder, and the monozygotic concordance rate of 40 to 50 percent for schizoaffective disorder was not significantly different from that of manic-depressive illness, but was twice that of schizophrenia. Monozygotic twins who were concordant for the syndrome of schizoaffective disorder had affective symptoms equal to those of manic-depressive twins and schizophrenic symptoms equal to those of schizophrenic twins. Seven of the twenty-one monozygotic index schizoaffective twins committed suicide, as opposed to none of eight manic-depressive cases and only three of one hundred index schizophrenic twins. The average age of onset of the schizoaffective cases was approximately twenty years; for manic-depressive illness, twenty-six years; for schizophrenia, twenty-two years. The dizygotic concordance rate for manic-depressive illness was 1 percent; for schizoaffective illness, 0 percent; for schizophrenia, 5 percent. Thus these concordance rates for the dizygotic twins were not significantly different. For the clinician in practice, Cohen and his associates used the following criteria in an attempt to separate schizophrenia from the manic-depressive illness, recurrent depressive episodes, and schizoaffective reactions. The last three groups of patients were more self-critical, as opposed to perceiving their delusions from an external source, and their remissions were relatively complete. In the schizoaffective group, the age of onset was earlier; family history of an associated disorder was more frequent; intensity of mood disorder was more apparent; suicide was definitely more prevalent. In clinically homogeneous schizophrenia, the affect was quite flat; the patients were definitely more severely autistic during their remissions; the illness was more chronic, with social and mental deterioration noted in those patients who had the disease process for a longer period of time.

Clayton and his associates (1967) confirmed some of the findings by Cohen's group. In a one- and two-year follow-up of thirty schizoaffective patients, Clayton found that 85 percent were either well or mainly suffering from an affective disorder, but not displaying symptomatology of schizophrenia. Thus schizophrenic deterioration is not a usual result of schizoaffective illness; this finding correlates with those observations described by Cohen and his associates. In addition, the schizoaffective patient is more likely to have a family history of affective disorder than a family history of schizophrenia; Clayton and his associates also concluded that schizoaffective disorder was simply a severe clinical variant of affective illness. They evaluated 1,000 patient admissions; one hundred of these patients were schizophrenics and thirty-nine were schizoaffective subjects. A positive family history of affective disorder had a high correlation with a greater incidence of manic symptoms among the schizoaffective subjects. This group of schizoaffective individuals with a relatively good prognosis may be compared to a group of patients described by Vaillant in 1964 as "good prognosis" schizophrenic patients. The "good prognosis" in Vaillant's (1964) evaluation showed the following attributes: (1) family history of an affective illness; (2) a good precipitating reason for the psychotic reaction; (3) relatively healthy premorbid personality between the psychotic episodes; (4) relatively good affect between psychotic episodes; (5) depression as the major symptomatology at time of admission; (6) preoccupation with suicide at time of admission; (7) relatively poor memory of the psychotic episode. In addition, there was rarely a family history of schizophrenia. It is my opinion that the supposedly "good prognosis" schizophrenic patients were actually those patients we now call schizoaffective and in some cases manic-depressive, an illness which was underdiagnosed in this country during earlier years when it was probably being more accurately diagnosed in the European countries.

There is a need to explore more extensively the effects of environmental variables upon similar genetic substrates to understand the final development of the depressive syndrome. The importance of environmental factors was recently emphasized in an article by Allen (Allen et al., 1974) who found that 67 percent of 117 monozygotic twins were discordant for *all* types of depression; he also confirmed previous genetic evidence that unipolar and bipolar illness are separate entities.

In addition to utilizing the genetic aspects to help in the prevention, diagnosis and treatment of affective illness, we should also be able to understand the genetic vulnerability to experiential deprivation. Genetic susceptibility may be of major importance in those individuals who more readily develop endogenous depressions when they are exposed to minor environmental stresses.

Dr. Perris has reviewed the studies by Winokur and his associates (1973), who coined the term "depressive spectrum disease" in those families that displayed symptomatology of depression, alcoholism, and/or sociopathy. These observations may be quite significant for the treatment of those patients with symptomatic alcoholism or antisocial behavior who have a family history of depression and/or alcoholism. The potential value of lithium and of the antidepressant agents in certain alcoholism subgroups and sociopathic subgroups, who may have underlying symptomatology of depression and a family history of the "depressive spectrum," should be fully explored in controlled studies.

DR. PERRIS: I agree that we have many unsolved problems, and I would say that some of the questions raised by Dr. Raskin have already been answered by Dr. Weissman: namely, that we cannot rely on the admission rates or rate derived from the primary patient population. We have to look at the families, the population, and investigate all of the relatives. If we do that, we may find that these differences between sexes are artifacts depending upon cultural factors, type of care, etc. In regard to Dr. Varga's concern, I would say that if one doesn't know the risk for the general population in the place where the investigation is made, then a control group would be a necessity to eliminate the possibility that the rate on hereditary loading found in the proband material may be quite higher than the rate in the general population. I don't think that instances of this kind have been found to date. Another point I would make is that the unipolar group is not a homogeneous one but quite heterogeneous. I feel that it is a necessity to have some very narrow definition of the unipolar group to be investigated just to see if we can identify some indicators. I require at least three separate episodes to label a patient as a unipolar, and in many of the recent studies the label unipolar has been attached to patients after their first episode.

I found that if we use at least three separate episodes, the risk of becoming bipolar is about 16 percent. If we have four separate episodes, the risk is only 4 percent to change to mania. I guess we have to specify a cutoff point, and three seems quite acceptable; if we choose four episodes, we then have too small a group of patients for investigation.

REFERENCES

Allen, M. G., Cohen, S., Pollin, W., and Greenspan, S. I. (1974). *Am. J. Psychiat* 131:1234–39.

Alonso-Fernández, F. (1973). Aspectos transhistóricos de las distintas modalidades de depresión. In M. Lader and R. Garcia, eds., *Aspects of Depression*. Publ. by authority of WPA, pp. 133–48.

Angst, J. (1961). A clinical analysis of the effects of Tofranil in depression. Longitudinal and follow up studies. Treatment of blood relations. *Psychopharmacologia* 2:381–407.

———— (1964). Antidepressiver effekt und genetische faktoren. *Arzneimittel Forsch* 14:496–500.

———— (1966). *Zur Ätiologie and Nosologie Endogener Depressiver Psychosen*. Berlin, Heidelberg, New York: Springer.

———— (1971). Zur nosologie endogener depressionen. Vergleich der ergebniss zweier untersuchungen. *Arch. Psychiat. Zschr. Neurol.* 210:373–82. Repr. *Intl. J. Mental Health*, 1971.

Asano, N. (1960). Clinico-genetic study of manic-depressive psychoses. *Jap. J. Human Genet.* 5:224–53.

Asuni, T. (1973). Diagnostic aspects of depression from a transcultural point of view. In M. Lader and R. Garcia, eds., *Aspects of Depression*. Publ. by authority of WPA, pp. 123–26.

Balter, M. (1969). The use of drugs in contemporary society. *Highlights of the Fourteenth Annual Conference, Veterans Administration Cooperative Studies in Psychiatry*, pp. 55–63.

Beck, A. T. (1971). *Depression: Clinical, Experimental, and Theoretical Aspects.* New York: Harper & Row.

Becker, J. (1974). *Depression, Theory and Research.* Washington, D.C.: V. H. Winston & Sons.

Böök, J. A. (1953). A genetic and neuropsychiatric investigation of a north Swedish population with special regard to schizophrenia and mental deficiency. *Acta Genet. Stat. Med.* 4:1–100.

Chaudhry, M. R. (1973). Transcultural aspects of depression in Pakistan. In M. Lader and R. Garcia, eds., *Aspects of Depression.* Publ. by authority of WPA, pp. 127–32.

Clayton, P. G., Rodin, L. R., and Winokur, G. (1967). Family history studies: schizoaffective disorder, clinical and genetic factors including a one to two year follow up. *Compr. Psychiat.* 9:31–49.

Cohen, B. M., and Fairbank, R. E. (1938). Statistical contributions from the mental hygiene study of the Eastern Health District of Baltimore. *Am. J. Psychiat.* 94:1153–61, 1377–95.

Cohen, S. M., Allan, M. G., Pollin, W., and Hrubec, Z. (1972). Relationship of schizoaffective psychosis to manic depressive psychosis and schizophrenia. *Arch. Gen. Psychiat.* 26:539–46.

Crombie, D. L. (1957). *Coll. Gen. Pract. Res. Newsletter* 16:218.

Diebold, K. (1972). Aspekte der erb- und umweltbedingtheit endogener psychosen. *Nervenarzt* 43:69–76.

Eaton, J. W., and Keil, R. J. (1955). *Culture and Mental Disorders: A Comparative Study of the Hutterites and Other Populations.* New York: Free Press.

Ebaugh, I., Freiman, M., Woolf, R., et al. (1968). Chromosome studies in patients with affective disorders. *Arch. Gen. Psychiat.* 19:751–58.

Essen-Möller, E. (1956). Individual traits and morbidity in a Swedish rural population. *Acta Psychiat. Neurol. Scand.* Suppl. 100.

——— and Haguell, O. (1961). The frequency and risk of depression within a rural population group in Scandinavia. *Acta Psychiat. Scand.* Suppl. 162:28–32.

Fernando, S. J. M. (1966). Depressive illness in Jews and non-Jews. *Br. J. Psychiat.* 112:991–96.

Fieve, R. R., and Mendlewicz, J. (1973). New evidence for X-linkage in manic-depressive illness. In M. Lader and R. Garcia, eds., *Aspects of Depression.* Publ. by authority of WPA, pp. 171–78.

Fremming, G. H. (1951). The expectation of mental infirmity in a sample of the Danish population. *Occasional Papers on Eugen.* London: Eugen Soc., 7.

Gershon, E. S., Duncer, D. L., Sturt, L., et al. (1971). Assortative mating in the affective disorders. Meeting of APA, Washington.

Grof, P., MacCrimmon, D., Blaichman, M., et al. (1971). MN blood groups and affective disorders. 1st World Congr. Biol. Psychiat., Buenos Aires.

Hanna, B. L. (1965). Genetic studies of family units. In *Genetics and the Epidemiology of Chronic Diseases.* Washington, D. C.: DHEW.

Helgason, T. (1961). The frequency of depressive states in Iceland as compared with the other Scandinavian countries. *Acta Psychiat. Scand.* Suppl. 162:81–90.

——— (1964). Epidemiology of mental disorders in Iceland. *Acta Psychiat. Scand.* Suppl. 173.

Hopinkson, G. (1964). A genetic study of affective illness in patients over 50. *Br. J. Psychiat.* 110:244–54.

Ianzito, B. M., Cadoret, R. J., and Pugh, D. P. (1974). Thought disorders in depression. *Am. J. Psychiat.* 131:703–07.

Ivanys, E., Dzdkova, S., and Vana, J. (1964). Prevalence of psychoses recorded among psychiatric patients in a part of the urban population. *Psychiat.* (Cesko) 60:152–63.

James, N., and Chapman, C. J. (1975, in press). A genetic study of bipolar affective disorders. *Br. J. Psychiat.*

Kielholz, P. (1959). Acta Psychotherapeutics et Psychosomatics, North American Ser.

Kinkelin, M. (1954). Verlauf und prognose des manisch depressiven irreseins. *Schwiz. Arch. Neurol. Psychiat.* 73:100–46.

Kishima, C. (1967). Clinico-genetic study of mental disorders in the aged with special reference to involutional depression. *Bull. Osaka Med. School* Suppl. XII:276–87.

Klerman, G. L., and Paykel, E. S. (1970). Depressive pattern, social background and hospitalization. *J. Nerv. Mental Dis.* 150:466–78.

Kraepelin, E. (1910). *Trattato di Psichiatria,* 4th ed. Italian transl. by G. Guidi. Milan: Vallardi.
────── (1913). *Lectures on Clinical Psychiatry.* New York: Hafner. Repr., 1968.
Lamont, A. (1951). Affective types of psychotic reaction in Cape colored persons. *S. Afr. Med. J.* 25:40–42.
Lange, V. (1970). Die verteilung erblicher serumgruppen bei manisch-depressiver krankheit. *Intl. J. Pharmacopsychiat.* 4:1–29.
Larsson, T., and Sjögren, T. (1954). A methodological, psychiatric and statistical study of a large Swedish rural population. *Acta Psychiat. Neurol. Scand.* Suppl. 89.
Lehmann, H. E. (1971). Epidemiology of depressive disorders. In R. R. Fieve, ed., *Depression in the 1970's: Modern Theory and Research.* Princeton, N. J.: Excerpta Medica, pp. 21–31.
Leighton, D. C., Harding, J. S., Macklin, D. B., et al. (1963). *The Character of Danger: Psychiatric Symptoms in Selected Communities.* New York: Basic Books.
Lemkau, P. V., Tietze, C., and Cooper, M. (1941). Mental hygiene problems in an urban district. *Mental Hyg.* 25:624–46.
Leonhard, K. (1957–69). *Aufteilung der endogenen psychosen,* 1st–4th eds. Berlin: Akademieverlag.
Lin, T. (1953). A study of the incidence of mental disorders in Chinese and other cultures. *Psychiatry* 16:313–36.
Lungerhausen, E. (1973). Überlegungen zum problem des gestaltwandels zyklothymer depressionen. In J. Glatzel, ed., *Gestaltwandel Psychiatrischer Krankheitsbilder.* Stuttgart, New York: Schattaner Verl., pp. 179–94.
Masters, A. B. (1967). The distribution of blood groups in psychiatric illness. *Br. J. Psychiat.* 113:1309–15.
Mayer-Gross, W., Slater, E. T. O., and Roth, M. (1969). *Clinical Psychiatry,* 3rd ed. London: Bailliere, Tindal and Cassel.
Mendlewicz, J. (1971). *Discussion in Depression, 1970.* R. Fieve, ed. Excerpta Med. Intl. Congr. Series 239:44.
Möbius: Quoted by Kraepelin (1910). In *Trattato di Psichiatria,* 4th ed. Italian transl. by C. Guidi. Milan: Vallardi.
Myers, J., Lindenthal, J. J., and Pepper, M. P (1974). Social class, life events, psychiatric symptoms: a longitudinal study. In B. S. Dohrenwend and B. T. Dohrenwend, eds., *Stress and Life Events: Their Nature and Effect.* New York: John Wiley & Sons, pp. 191–206.
──────, Lindenthal, J. J., Pepper, M. P., and Ostlander, D. (1972). Life events and mental status: a longitudinal study. *J. Health & Soc. Behav.* 13:398–406.
Norris, V. (1959). *Mental Illness in London.* London: Maudsley Monographs, No. 6.
Ödegaard, Ö. (1962). The epidemiology of depressive psychoses. *Acta Psychiat. Scand.* Suppl. 162:33–38.
Pare, C. M. B., and Mack, J. W. (1971). Differentiation of two genetically specific types of depression by the response to antidepressant drugs. *J. Med. Genet.* 8:306–09.
──────, Rees, L., and Sainsbury, M. J. (1962). Differentiation of two genetically specific types of depression by the response to antidepressants. *Lancet* 2:1340–43.
Perris, C. (1966). A study of bipolar (manic-depressive) and unipolar recurrent depressive psychoses. *Acta Psychiat. Scand.* Suppl. 194:42.
────── (1968). Il concetto di plaritá e la nosologia delle psicosi depressive. *Arch. Psicol. Neurol. Psychiat.* 29:111–28.
────── (1969). The separation of bipolar from unipolar recurrent depressive psychoses. *Behav. Neuropsychiat.* 1:14–24.
────── (1973a). Das chronische cotardsche syndrom "délire de négation" ein syndrom, das verschwindet? In J. Glatzel, ed., *Gestaltwandel Psychiatrischer Krankheitsbilder.* Stuttgart, New York: Schattaner Verl., pp. 145–58.
────── (1973b). The genetics of affective disorders. In J. Mendels, ed., *Biological Psychiatry.* New York, London, Sidney, Toronto: J. Wiley & Sons, pp. 385–415.
────── (1973c). New approaches to the classification of affective disorders. In M. Lader and R. Garcia, eds., *Aspects of Depression.* Publ. by authority of WPA, pp. 95–107.

———— (1973d, in press). The heuristic value of a distinction between bipolar and unipolar affective disorders. Symposium on Classification and Prediction of Outcome of Depression, Erbach am Rhein, BRD.

————, and dElia, G. (1964). Pathoplastic significance of the premorbid situation in depressive psychoses. *Acta Psychiat. Scand.* Suppl. 180:87–100.

Parker, J. B., Theile, A., and Spielberger, C. D. (1961). Frequency of blood types in a homogeneous group of manic depressive patients. *J. Mental Sci.* 107:936–43.

Petterson, V. (1974). Manisk-depressiv sjukdom. In *Klinisk, Social Genetisk Undersökning.* Stockholm: M. D. thesis.

Price, J. (1968). The genetics of depressive behavior. In A. Coppen and A. Walk, eds., *Recent Developments in Affective Disorders. Br. J. Psychiat.* Spec. Publ. No. 2:27–36.

Rainer, J. D. (1966). Genetic aspects of depression. *Can. Psychiat. Assn. J.* 11:29–33.

Rao, A. V. (1970). A study of depression as prevalent in South India. *Transcult. Psychiat. Res. Rev.* 7:166–67.

Raskin, A., Schulterbrandt, J. G., et al. (1970). Differential response to chlorpromazine, imipramine and placebo: a study of subgroups of hospitalized depressed patients. *Arch. Gen. Psychiat.* 23:164–73.

————, Schulterbrandt, J. G., et al. (1974). Depression subtypes and response to phenelzine, diazepam, and a placebo: results of a nine hospital collaborative study. *Arch. Gen. Psychiat.* 30:66–75.

Rawnsley, K. (1968). Epidemiology of affective disorders. In A. Coppen and A. Walk, eds., *Recent Developments in Affective Disorders.* Ashford, Kent: Headly & Brothers Ltd, pp. 27–36.

Roth, W. F., and Luton, F. H. (1943). Mental health program in Tennessee. *Am. J. Psychiat.* 99:662–75.

Rüdin, E. (1923). Über vererbung geistiger störungen. *Z. ges. Neurol. Psychiat.* 81:459–96.

Schwab, J., Bialow, M., et al. (1967). Sociocultural aspects of depression in medical patients. II. Symptomatology and class. *Arch. Gen. Psychiat.* 17:539–43.

Shapiro, R. W. (1970). A twin study of nonendogenous depression. *Acta Jutlandica* XLII:2.

Shepherd, M., Cooper, B., Brown, A. C., et al. (1966). *Psychiatric Illness in General Practice.* Oxford: Oxford Univ. Press.

Shields, J., and Slater, E. T. O. (1966). La similarité du diagnostic chez les jumeaux et le problème de la spécificité biologique dans les néuroses et les troubles de la personalité. *Evol. Psychiat.* 2:441–51.

Silverman, C. (1968). *The Epidemiology of Depression.* Baltimore: John Hopkins Press.

Sjögren, T. (1948). Genetic-statistical and psychiatric investigations of a west Swedish population. *Acta Psychiat. & Néurol. Scand.* Suppl. 52.

Slater, E. T. O. (1938). Zur erbpathologie des manisch-depressiven irreseins. *Z. ges. Neurol. Psychiat.* 163:1–147.

Sorensen, A., and Strömgren, E. (1961). Frequency of depressive states within geographically delimited population groups. *Acta Psychiat. Scand.* Suppl. 162:62–68.

Stenstedt, A. (1952). A study in manic-depressive psychosis. *Acta Psychiat. Scand.* Suppl. 79.

———— (1959). Involutional melancholia. *Acta Psychiat. Neurol. Scand.* Suppl. 127.

———— (1966). Genetics of neurotic depression. *Acta Psychiat. Scand.* Suppl. 42:392–409.

Strömgren, E. (1935). Zum ersatz des weinbergschen "abgekürzten verfahrens." Zugleich ein beitrag zur frage von der erblichkeit des erkrankungsalters bei der schizophrenic. *Z. ges. Neurol. Psychiat.* 153:484–497.

Tanna, V., and Winokur, G. (1968). A study of association and linkage of ABO blood types and primary affective disorder. *Br. J. Psychiat.* 114:1175–81.

Taylor, L., and Chaves, S. (1964). *Mental Health and Environment.* London: Longmans, Green & Co.

Tonks, C. M., Paykel, E. S. and Klerman, G. L. (1970). Clinical depressions among Negroes. *Am. J. Psychiat.* 127:329–35.

Vaillant, G. E. (1964). Prospective prediction of schizophrenic remission. *Arch. Gen. Psychiat.* 11:509–18.

Von Greiff, H., McHugh, P. R., and Stokes, P. (1973). The family history in sixteen males with bipolar manic depressive disorder. 3rd annual meeting, Am. Psychopathol. Assn., New York.

von Trostorff, Z. (1968). Über die hereditäre belastung bei den bipolaren und monopolaren phasischen psychosen. *Schweiz. Arch. Neurol. Psychiat.* 102:235–43.

Watts, C. (1964). *Discussion Two in Depression: A Cambridge Postgraduate Medical Course.* E. B. Davies, ed. London: Cambridge University Press, p. 55.

———— (1966). *Depressive Disorders in the Community.* Bristol: Blackwell.

Weinberg, W. (1920). Methodologische gesichtspunkte für die statische untersuchung der vererbung bei dementia praecox. *Z. ges. Neurol. Psychiat.* 59:39–50.

Weissman, M. M. (1974). The epidemiology of suicide attempts, 1960 to 1971. *Arch. Gen. Psychiat.* 30:737–46.

————, Paykel, E. S., French, N., Mark, H., Fox, K., and Prusoff, B. A. (1973). Suicide attempts in an urban community, 1955 and 1970. *Soc. Psychiat.* 8:82–91.

Winokur, G. (1973). Genetic aspects of depression. In G. P. Scott and E. C. Senay, eds., *Separation and Depression.* Washington, D. C.: AAAS Pub. No. 94.

————, Cadoret, R. J., Dorzab, J., et al. (1971). Depressive disease: a genetic study. *Arch. Gen. Psychiat.* 24:135–44.

————, Clayton, P. J., et al. (1969). *Manic Depressive Illness.* St. Louis: C. U. Mosby Co.

Zerbin-Rüdin, E. (1967). Endogene psychosen. In P. E. Becker, ed., *Humangenetik, Ein Kurzes Handbuch infünf Bänden.* Stuttgart: Thieme, Bd v/2:446–577.

———— (1969). Zur genetik der depressiven erkrankungen. In H. Hippius and H. Šelbach, eds., *Das Depressive Syndrom.* Munich, Berlin, Vienna: Urban & Schwarzenberg, pp. 37–56.

———— (1971). Genetische aspekte der endogenen psychosen. *Fortschr. Neurol. Psychiat.* 39:459–94.

Zonana, H., Henisz, J., and Levine, M. (1973). Psychiatric emergency service a decade later. *Psychiat. in Med.* 4:273–89.

CHAPTER IV

Recent Advances in Blood Levels of Antidepressant Agents: Assay Procedures, Reliability and Relationship to Therapeutic Outcome and Side Effects

G. M. Simpson,
T. B. Cooper and
J. H. Lee

The introduction of the antidepressants created an immediate interest in the pharmacology and metabolism of these drugs. In 1964, Brodie suggested that biological effects of a drug are much more closely related to the plasma or tissue level than to the dose. It was soon found that there were very marked individual differences in plasma levels of these drugs both in animals and in man. This led to attempts to define the plasma level ranges from the viewpoint of when improvement occurs and when side effects develop—currently the focus of intensive research. While this at first appeared to be an easy task, it has turned out to be an extremely difficult one.

The careful monitoring of plasma levels suggested that there were marked "interindividual" differences not only in the steady-state levels, but also in the time required to reach steady state. (Steady state is defined as the condition where there is no longer an accumulation of drug; i.e., input and output are equal.) The

109

marked "interindividual" differences in steady-state levels of tricyclic antidepressants were first demonstrated by Hammer (Hammer et al., 1966), who found a thirty-six-fold difference between the lowest and highest steady-state levels of patients receiving the same dosage of desmethylimipramine. Similar individual differences were later shown for nortriptyline (Hammer and Sjoqvist, 1967) and also for the parent compounds, imipramine and amitriptyline. In terms of the time required to reach steady state, Hammer and Sjoqvist (1967) claimed that, in general, steady-state levels in the plasma were constant within one week of administration. However, there were exceptional subjects with whom it took longer than two weeks.

In addition to the problem of individual differences, there was also the issue of the equivalence of the parent compounds and their metabolites. Thus imipramine and amitriptyline have been studied together with their metabolites, desmethylimipramine and nortriptyline, and while imipramine and amitriptyline are chemically similar there is the possibility they might not behave the same in a therapeutic context. No clinical evidence is available to support this; however, from a pharmacological point of view, it is certainly possible.

There were also technical or methodological difficulties. Thus, even when people studied the same drug, the methods they used to evaluate it were different, and frequently it was not possible to reproduce the previous finding.

It was not until 1970 that a correlation was shown between the plasma levels of nortriptyline and side effects (Asberg et al., 1970). Another year was to pass before the important question of the relationship between blood levels and therapeutic outcome was examined. Asberg (Asberg et al., 1971a) studied thirty-two inpatients diagnosed as endogenous depressions who received 75 to 225 mg of nortriptyline daily after having received a placebo for four to seven days. Barbiturates or glutethimide were given when required, and "occasional dosages of diazepam" were administered. Plasma concentrations of nortriptyline were determined twice weekly during treatment, and an amelioration score (the difference between the placebo and the active treatment rating) was used to estimate therapeutic effect. Three patients became hypomanic during the treatment and were excluded from the study, though it seemed that they might have been included. Therefore, twenty-nine patients were available for analysis. The range of plasma levels was 32–164 ng/ml. They claimed a curvilinear relationship between nortriptyline plasma level and therapeutic effect. Thus both low and very high levels of nortriptyline were associated with slight or no improvement, whereas intermediate concentrations were associated with improvement. There was a significant difference in plasma concentration between men and women, with the women having a higher mean value than men although this was determined to be related to the dosage and body weight. When these latter were controlled, there was no difference between males and females. However, there is evidence that even when these variables are controlled women have higher mean levels than men (Sjoqvist et al., 1968). It is possible to criticize this study on the

Table 1
Blood Sample Time Collection

Investigator		Time after last dose	Regimen
Hammer	1967	7 hours	TID
Alexandersen	1969	5-7 hours	TID
Burrows	1972	6-7 hours	TID
Asberg	1971	7 hours	TID
Kragh-Sorensen	1974	11 hours	TID
Braithwaite	1972	19 hours	TID

basis that the sample size was small and that a two-week period is not adequate for a full therapeutic trial of an antidepressant. The addition of other drugs could also have affected the levels and the clinical response.

Braithwaite (Braithwaite et al., 1972) in a study of amitriptyline and nortriptyline plasma levels found a linear correlation between the combined parent and metabolite plasma levels and clinical response, but these investigators collected bloods at markedly different intervals from others. Table I shows the time intervals for collection of six investigators, and it is clear that Braithwaite collected samples at much longer intervals than in other studies.

In that same year, Burrows (Burrows et al., 1972) administered a fixed dosage of 150 mg of nortriptyline daily to a group of thirty-two depressed patients. In this study, after a week's observation on an inpatient unit (drug-free) those who had not remitted entered the trial, but the severely ill received electroconvulsive therapy (ECT). Thus the group was restricted and not representative of depressives but consisted of patients regarded as not ill enough to require ECT. At four weeks, 59 percent of the patients had demonstrated improvement, after six weeks, 79 percent. However, no correlation between plasma level and clinical response was noted at either four or six weeks. It should be noted that the mean plasma levels were higher in this study than in the studies by Braithwaite and by Asberg and a different time sampling procedure was used. The authors felt that the daily administration of 150 mg of nortriptyline would be satisfactory in the initial treatment of depressive illness and were quite pessimistic about the value of plasma levels. Yet these same authors noted that increasing the dosage in some patients produced a better response and also that there did seem to be a correlation between increasing and decreasing the dosage and therapeutic effect and loss of therapeutic effect in some patients. Furthermore, this would contradict the work of Wharton (Wharton et al., 1971), who showed that the administration of methylphenidate increased the plasma levels of imipramine and that this increase appeared to be associated with clinical improvement in treatment-resistant pa-

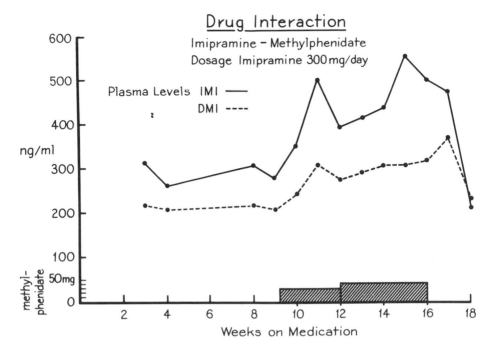

FIG. 1.   Drug Interaction.

tients. This was an open study, but still the results were impressive. Fig. 1 details work from our unit confirming these findings. These data could be interpretated as a direct effect of methylphenidate; however, an interaction would seem more probable.

Our own findings in a double-blind, controlled study of 150 mg of imipramine vs. 300 mg indicated that the higher-dosage group showed a significantly better response, together with a higher plasma level, than the lower dosage group (Simpson, 1973).

Kragh-Sorensen and associates (1973a) criticized their own earlier work as well as that of Burrows (Burrows et al., 1972) and Asberg (Asberg et al., 1971a). In the Kragh-Sorensen study, thirty-seven patients were given 150 mg of nortriptyline daily. Within the first week of treatment, all but three patients reached a plateau value which remained constant throughout the remainder of the study. In only one patient did the plasma level continue to rise over the course of treatment. The levels ranged from 48 to 238 ng/ml, significantly higher than in the previous study done by Asberg (Asberg et al., 1971a). There was a positive correlation between plasma levels and depression at the fourth week and a negative correlation for those with plasma concentrations above 170 ng/ml. No concomitant medication was used, and this may be one of the reasons why the plasma concentrations were higher in this study than in their previous studies; another reason may be that two different methods of assaying nortriptyline were used. An interesting

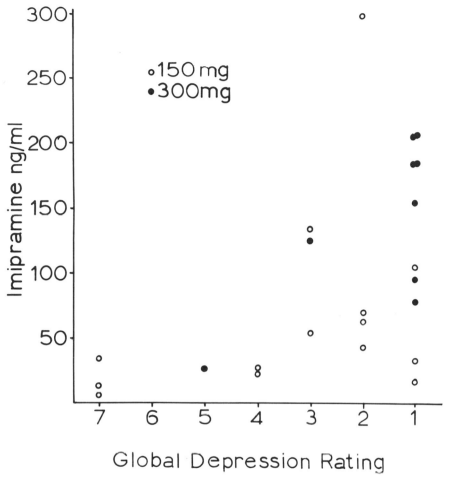

FIG. 2.   Global Depression Rating Scale (9 point scale — 8 & 9 = Very Much Worse Not included. 5 = no change. 1 = Very much improved)

observation was that of seven nonresponders with a plasma nortriptyline concent-ration above 170 ng/ml, five were well and discharged from the hospital within a week after reduction of dosage.

The question of drug interactions has already been mentioned and certainly should be borne in mind in interpreting any results. The question of plasma binding is another source of variation. The Scandinavian investigators (Borga et al., 1969) feel that there is no great range in plasma binding, whereas work from New York (Glassman et al., 1973b) suggests that there is a considerable range in the proportion of bound tricyclic antidepressants from subject to subject and point out that these differences are present in Borga's own data. If this is so, unless we know the amount of free tricyclics and if it is the free moiety which correlates with efficacy, then measuring this bound/free ratio would be more meaningful. This could be a possible explanation for some of the discrepancies.

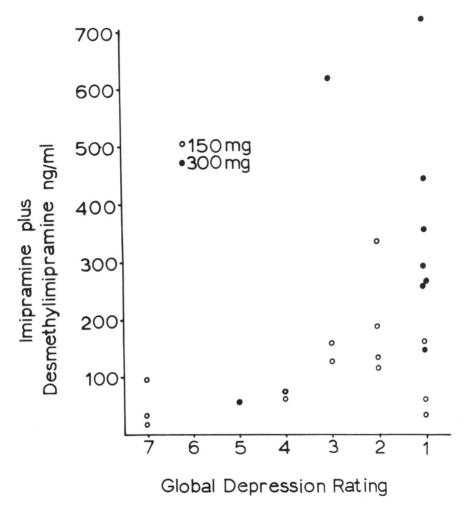

FIG. 3.   Global Depression Rating Scale. (9 point scale — 8 & 9 = Very Much Worse Not included. 5 =no change. 1 = Very much improved)

The technical problems of measuring nanogram quantities of drugs in biological fluids and tissues are not easily overcome. Methodologies vary—fluorescence, isotope derivative techniques, thin-layer chromatography, gas chromatography, gas chromatography linked with a mass spectrometer, mass fragmentography—and while these techniques are quite widely used little attempt has been made to compare them in the same samples or in the same lab.

One investigator who made comparisons of methods was Kragh-Sorensen (Kragh-Sorensen et al., 1973b). He and his associates analyzed some of their data using gas chromatography as well as the original isotope derivative procedure and found a small difference (10 percent) in the two methods. The small difference

Table 2
Desmethyl Doxepin
Method Comparison

Pat.	Isotope Derivative Technique ng/ml	GLC ng/ml
1	25	29
2	27	33
3	24	29
4	45	50
5	50	60
6	65	87
7	78	91
8	50	57
9	60	47
	mean = 53.6	mean = 47.1
	S.D. = 23.1	S.D. = 10.9

Correlation coefficient = 0.92
Paired t test — no significant difference

could have been ascribed to the didesmethyl compound, which is not differentiated by the isotope derivative procedure. In our own lab, we have compared GLC methods and isotope derivative methods for DMI and desmethyl doxepine and found little difference (Table II). Additional evidence to support the correlation between methods is that plasma levels are, in general, at approximately the same level no matter which technique is used in the various centers.

At this stage, one can characterize the results of work on blood levels of the tricyclic antidepressants as conflicting. The methodology would seem to have been refined to usable levels. Some of the possible reasons for differences have been elucidated, the main ones being genetic and environmental; additional variations such as drug interaction and plasma binding must also be considered.

Of paramount importance in this whole area is the classification of depression. It would seem unlikely that hospitalized patients who may represent something in the order of 5 percent of the total population of depressives would be typical. It is possible that the research psychiatrists are dealing with the hard-core, atypical group of patients with a probable poorer response rate to any type of treatment; therefore, it will be difficult to obtain positive results and to generalize from this group. In addition, the sample sizes in all of these studies were very small. It would seem valuable to include outpatients in these studies, which admittedly leads to a study of milder depressions but to a group who, although more fluctuating in character, are more treatment-responsive. A correlation of blood levels and clinical response in this group of patients would include a lot of noise from patients who are getting better for non-drug-related reasons, but it is still worthwhile to begin attempting to extend the samples tested. This could be another reason for Burrows' (Burrows et al., 1972) conflicting results, in that he used less severely ill patients. In general, the consensus would probably be that there is a correlation between blood levels and therapeutic outcome but it is not an easy relationship to demonstrate.

When we come to examine the monoamine oxidase inhibitors, despite their more checkered career, their less widespread use and their questioned value in depression, the picture would seem to be more optimistic in terms of the relationship between their metabolism and clinical response. The initial studies on the efficacy of these drugs were plagued by many of the problems mentioned above, but most of all by dosage and diagnosis. It has been suggested for some time that neurotic or atypical depressions respond better to these drugs than do endogenous depressions, and yet the former were the patients who were excluded from the MRC trial in 1965 (one of the largest MAO inhibitor efficacy studies, whose discouraging results probably contributed to the decreased interest in monoamine oxidase inhibitors).

More recent work has shown that there is a genetic control of platelet and plasma monoamine oxidase activity (Nies et al., 1973) and also that MAO activity is higher in platelets in depressed patients than in normals (Nies et al., 1971). At the same time, these investigators have shown that platelet MAO activity correlates with brain MAO activity and that there is an increase in MAO with age possibly paralleling the increased likelihood of depression. Thus MAO activity in the hindbrain is higher in the elderly, who are more prone to depression, and also higher in the platelets of depressed patients. Futhermore, phenelzine, a commonly used monoamine oxidase inhibitor, is metabolized by acetylation, and it has been shown that there is a genetic control of acetylation (Evans et al., 1965). Thus people can be divided into fast or slow acetylators.

Johnstone and Marsh (1973) were able to show, in outpatient depressives, that the clinical response of fast acetylators to MAO inhibitors did not differ from those receiving placebo, but the slow acetylators did significantly better than those on placebo.

Of even greater importance has been the work of Robinson and Nies (Robinson et al., 1973), who, in treating outpatient depressives with phenelzine, increased the dosage until 80 percent MAO inhibition occurred. A double-blind design was preserved by making upward dosage adjustments in both placebo- and phenelzine-treated patients. Sixty patients completed six weeks of treatment, thirty-three on phenelzine and twenty-seven on placebo. The groups were very well matched for their monoamine platelet and plasma MAO activity, and also for depression. The mean improvement in the phenelzine group exceeded that for placebo in eighteen of nineteen items. The response to phenelzine was speedier than with placebo in each of the five composite scales: total depression, total anxiety, somatic anxiety, hypochondriasis-agitation, and psychomotor change. Phenelzine was superior in all five composite scales at a statistically significant level and also was superior in nine of ten individual symptom measures.

This same group of workers (Nies et al., 1974) in a second study used a protocol similar to the first except that there were three groups (phenelzine, 60 mg per day; phenelzine, 30 mg per day; placebo), each treated at a fixed dosage so that platelet MAO inhibition and clinical change could be examined in relation to dosage. They also looked at the question of atypical depression in this study and demonstrated that the presence of atypical symptoms were predictive of a positive response to phenelzine. In terms of dosage, they found that 60 mg of phenelzine daily was superior to placebo, thus replicating their original findings, with an additional finding that 30 mg per day was shown to be no better than placebo. They point out that many of the studies in the literature used an intermediate dose (45 mg per day), which their data would suggest is suboptimal. These authors next stratified the patients according to percentage of platelet MAO inhibition and response to therapy and showed that there was a good chance for a favorable outcome if greater than 80 percent inhibition of platelet MAO activity was achieved, whereas with less than 80 percent the patients did no better than with placebo. Thus, in the area of depressives suitable for treatment with monoamine oxidase inhibitors, it would appear that plasma or platelet monitoring of monoamine oxidase is a suitable technique for achieving optimal results.

SUMMARY

The relationship among acetylator status, MAO inhibition and clinical response seems reasonably clear at the moment. Greater than 80 percent inhibition is associated with clinical improvement and the response of patients with lower levels cannot be distinguished from placebo. Yet it should be noted that these investigations have all come from one laboratory, and independent verification would be valuable. The results, however, of investigations with the tricyclics attempting to relate blood levels and response are much less consistent. The Scandinavian investigators (Asberg et al., 1970; 1971a; Sjoqvist et al., 1968; Kragh-Sorensen et al., 1973b) report a curvilinear relationship with improvement occurring at moderate levels. The American (Glassman et al., 1973b; Simpson, 1973) and English (Braithwaite et al., 1972) groups find a positive correlation, with higher levels associated with improvement and lower levels with no improvement, while the Australian investigators (Burrows et al., 1972; 1974a) find no relationship at all. It is important to note that higher dosages of antidepressants produce a better clinical response than lower dosages (Simpson, 1973; Blashki et al., 1971), and while the relationship is positive if not substantial between dosage and blood levels this may presage the ultimate resolution.

COMMENTARIES

DR. MENDELS: There is a study that addresses itself specifically to one of the questions raised to Dr. Simpson's paper; Braithwaite recently reported a significant correlation (0.75) between plasma nortriptyline level and the extent of block of norepinephrine uptake. This is an example of the kind of investigation which people will have to pay more attention to in the evaluation of these drugs.

I have been impressed by the findings of a thirty- or forty-fold variability in the plasma levels of these drugs and, given that there are the further differences in protein binding, etc., the possibility of a variability of fifty- or one hundredfold. However, the therapeutic range for these drugs is in a two- to threefold range. Thus, it may be that there are other modifying influences that serve to reduce this variability in a very substantial manner.

In regard to the issue of correlation or relationship between plasma amitriptyline levels and therapeutic response, I believe that Braithwaite has confirmed this relationship in a study of enuretic children who were given amitriptyline. Apparently the results were similar to Kragh-Sorensen's findings. They found that nortriptyline levels above 170 nanograms were mainly associated with therapeutic failures and that reducing the plasma levels of nortriptyline below 170 ng was associated with a therapeutic response in five out of seven cases. In another study, they administered nortriptyline to a series of patients and studied kinetic and steady-state levels. They found that their results correlated very highly, suggesting some sort of polygenetic factor that regulated tricyclic metabolism. The Burrows study, which differs the most, should be put aside for the moment, since there were a number of differences between their methodology and that of the other groups. In addition to the differences that Dr. Simpson mentioned, there is also considerable variability in their steady-state levels, which does raise questions about the reliability of their assays. It is really up to the Burrows group to demonstrate that their assays are as reliable as those being used by other investigators. The assay issue is, as Dr. Simpson indicated, really a critical one; everyone is using somewhat different, if not very different, techniques. Dr. Simpson showed some data here for doxepin indicating that he obtained a good correlation between two different assays. That is most encouraging.

In regard to the comments about MAO inhibition, I would remind the group of the study published by Oswald's group. Their results suggested that their depressed patients did not get better with MAO inhibitor treatment unless and until they received a sufficient dose of the MAO inhibitors to totally eliminate all REM sleep. This is an interesting observation that ought to be evaluated in future studies and perhaps looked at in relation to the degree of MAO inhibition and therapeutic response.

DR. SIMPSON: The investigational group mentioned by Dr. Mendels, in another study (Burrows et al., 1974b), treated people at specified levels between 49 and

140 nanograms and a sequential analysis didn't show significant differences. The trouble is, one could say that their method is invalidated by the lack of correlation, or that it confirms the Scandanavian data.

In regard to REM sleep changes, the data available at this time are insufficient for any definitive comments relating REM sleep to blood levels and therapeutic response.

DR. KLEIN: The notion of a therapeutic window, as Dr. Simpson phrased it, is a stimulating one because it implies that a patient who is refractory to an antidepressant may respond to a dosage adjustment. The patient may be receiving too little or perhaps too much medication.

When I was first getting involved with tricyclics, I made considerable dose adjustments with patients who were refractory to 300 mg daily, pushing the dosage up or down. My recollection is that if the patient had been refractory to this substantial dose for the last two weeks of a five-week period, no amount of dosage "juggling" would be of help to the patient. I agree that 300 mg is often better than 150 mg. Also, there has been no properly designed study that clinically demonstrates the therapeutic window. The study of Sorensen, for instance, showed that in some seven patients who had been refractory to antidepressant therapy over a four-week period, changing the dosage during the fifth week so that the blood level moved into the therapeutic window produced excellent results in five of the seven cases. Now, that was a good hypothesis which generated results, but it was not a good design because the observed improvement might have occurred just by chance over that period of time. A more valid study in a group of people who are apparently refractory to tricyclics for a period of time—say, five weeks—would be to measure their blood levels and randomly assign half of them to dosage adjustments to get their levels in the therapeutic window. This type of study would then contain a control group for comparison of the results. Unless one does this sort of study, the whole notion of a therapeutic window remains an unsubstantiated although promising notion.

All the studies relating blood level to amelioration of symptoms have used a global measure of improvement. It is quite possible that blood level may relate to some specific aspect of the syndrome's amelioration. There was a study presented by Angst in which he correlated blood level with a variety of syndromal aspects and showed that only improvement in retardation correlated with blood level, all the other aspects of a depressive syndrome showing no correlation. I find it a very challenging and interesting notion that only retardation would correlate, since that does seem to be a core symptom for a certain subgroup of the depressive disorders. We need not only better methods for determination of blood levels and all of the metabolites, but also better calibrated methods with regard to the kinds of clinical improvement that we are talking about. Dr. Simpson's data about the relationship of IMI (imipramine) and DMI (desmethylimipramine) to improvement are considerably more striking than Glassman and Perel's data. They do make the interesting point—which again indicates the complexity of the problem—that if one takes out depressives with psychotic symptomatology the relationship between blood level and improvement becomes quite good. In the depressives with psychotic delusional symptomatology, the relationship was zero.

One more small point, relating to the idea that methylphenidate administered with tricyclics may enhance the clinical benefit of the tricyclic agent: whether or not the benefit is due to increase in blood levels is dubious. For one thing, I had obtained exactly the same increase in therapeutic benefits with dextroamphetamine. As far as I know, no one has ever studied how the addition of dextroamphetamine affects imipramine blood levels. I would find it surprising to learn that two unrelated sympathomimetic compounds, methylphenidate and dextroamphetamine, interfere with imipramine metabolism in the same manner.

DR. GALLANT: As Dr. Simpson stated in the original manuscript, individual genetic variability has a most significant effect on the absorption and metabolism of all drugs that are metabolized by the microsomal enzymes in combination with the cytochrome P-450 reductase system in the smooth endoplasmic reticulum of the liver. As Dr. Simpson has demonstrated and Drs. Mendels and Klein have reemphasized, the utilization of plasma concentrations of drug as a guide for therapy is limited at the present time. This statement particularly holds true for those drugs which exert their main therapeutic effects in body "compartments" kinetically distinct from plasma, since rapid changes in the relationship between excretion and plasma concentration may result in compartmental drug redistribution (Perrier and Gibaldi, 1974).

The gross importance of the individual genetic factors is emphasized by these general facts. Most lipid soluble drugs (such as the tricyclic agents) are metabolized by nonspecific enzymes to metabolites of increasing polarity until they become sufficiently water-soluble to be excreted by the kidney. For most drugs, absorption, distribution and excretion are the result of simple diffusion through lipoid membranes. The diffusion depends upon two related factors: one is the lipid solubility of the unionized form of the drug (or the polarity of the drug) and the second is the ratio of ionized to unionized drug in the pH environment of the different cellular compartments. All membranes are basically lipoid membranes, and thus for the tricyclic agent imipramine only the original parent chemical structure and its metabolite desmethylimipramine, both lipid-soluble, can adequately penetrate the blood-brain barrier and be reabsorbed from both the kidney tubules and small bowel. In contrast, the hydroxylated hydrophilic phenolic metabolites and their glucuronides are water-soluble and readily excreted. Thus the rate at which imipramine and desmethylimipramine are excreted from the body depends upon the hydroxylation rate, which in turn depends upon the liver microsomal cytochrome P-450 reductase system. These varieties of biochemical processes reinforce the concept of the importance of individual genetically determined metabolic variability as the major factor affecting the plasma level of various pharmacologic preparations.

Concerning the interaction of other compounds with antidepressant agents, it appears that the benzodiazepines do not significantly alter the metabolism of tricyclics in man. Therefore, for sleep disturbances the clinician may use a benzodiazepine agent, which may be more appropriate than the standard hypnotic agents, when the patient is already receiving an antidepressant drug. However, the absence of pharmacokinetic interaction does not exclude pharmacodynamic interaction at the receptor sites. After reading Dr. Simpson's manuscript, every practicing physician should have a clear understanding of the reasons for various patients requiring such great differences in dosages of all medications in order to obtain similar therapeutic effects. It should be quite obvious that there is a definite need for the development of long-acting intramuscular antidepressant agents, which would prove to be of great benefit to those patients who are relatively poor gastrointestinal absorbers or rapid drug-metabolizers, and who require prolonged maintenance drug therapy.

DR. PERRIS: We have heard that the problem of correlation between blood levels and therapeutic effect is still quite controversial. Our results have also been somewhat inconsistent. We collaborated in a multicenter investigation of a new imipramine derivative vs. imipramine in a double-blind trial. Blood assay levels of DMI in fifty-one depressed outpatients showed no correlation between blood levels and therapeutic results. Another point that Dr. Simpson touched was the interaction of tricyclics with other drugs. We were interested to see if the addition of barbiturates or hypnotics might influence the blood levels. What we found out was that if barbiturates are used for only a very short period of time at the beginning of tricyclic treatment, significant changes in the plasma level concentrations are not obtained.

DR. SIMPSON: In reply to Dr. Klein, I would say that the reason we did the study is that we have seen over and over again patients who have been getting 150 mg of imipramine without a therapeutic response. If the dosage is doubled, they get better in a few days. This observation holds true for inpatient and outpatient settings. When we were doing the study, we observed a significant difference between 150 mg and 300 mg. There was a differential response to varying doses of imipramine in our study, whereas the Scandinavians were using nortriptyline, so the differences in results might be attributed to the drugs utilized.

I have very deliberately adopted a simplistic approach to the problem from a "rough" therapeutic window as well as global improvement. When our techniques are refined enough, we might look at symptoms. Glassman and Perel's data involve only some ten delusional patients. Perhaps this is a subgroup, but it might also suggest that *severe* depressions do not respond to tricyclics.

DR. WILHELM: Dr. Simpson's review may lead to the conclusion that there is little correlation between blood level and therapeutic efficacy of tricyclic antidepressants. Our own studies on imipramine, clomipramine and maprotiline seem to confirm this apparently disappointing statement. An analysis of the metabolic pattern of maprotiline (Riess et al., 1972) may help explain some of the phenomena discussed by Dr. Simpson.

The bioavailability of maprotiline in humans is essentially 100 percent after oral administration. Single doses of 150 mg show peaks of 100 ± 20 ng/ml after eight hours. A half-life of thirty-nine hours has been calculated with individual values varying from twenty-eight to fifty-seven hours. Mean blood levels one hour after a 50 mg i.v. dose were 38 ng/ml. Assuming an average blood volume of 5 liters, a concentration of 10 μg/ml should have been obtained. The data thus show that within an hour more than 99 percent of the administered maprotiline left circulation and was concentrated extravascularly. Such a disposition pattern is not unique for maprotiline; it is common for many lipophilic organic bases such as amitriptyline and other tricyclics.

Based on these data obtained in experiments with a single dose regimen, it was possible to design a computer model which simulates the absorption kinetic of the drug and which allows one to predict the concentration pattern to be expected after a multiple dosing schedule. The model consisting of three compartments corresponding to the gastrointestinal tract as well as central and peripheral compartments was compared with experimental results. Calculations based on this pharmacokinetic model showed that the blood level resulting from repeated daily doses of 150 mg maprotiline should reach a steady-state level varying between 250 and 350 ng/ml within two weeks of medication.

The actual experiment partially confirmed these predictions. Steady-state level was reached after two weeks; however, the variability between patients was larger than the computer simulated differences (180 ng/ml to 450 ng/ml).

Several factors might contribute to these individual differences of steady-state levels. The high values of apparent volume of distribution indicate that only a very small fraction of maprotiline present in the body is in the blood. A similar pattern of distribution has been reported for chlorpromazine (Salzman and Brodie, 1956; Gouzon et al., 1956), thioridazine (Degkowitz, 1967) and amitriptyline (Eschenhof and Rieder, 1968). It is therefore conceivable that minor differences of the drug concentration in tissues between individuals should lead to several-fold differences in blood levels, although in absolute terms these levels correspond to less than 1 to 2 percent of total body content of the drug being in the blood.

Alternatively, the individual differences in blood levels might be traced to differences in half-lives. In an experiment where the daily 150 mg dose was given in single or divided doses, the decline of blood levels was measured after the termination of the third dosing regimen (days 43 to 47). The data, obtained in eight healthy subjects, appear to indicate distinct differences in half-lives.

A third factor that might markedly affect steady-state blood levels is the variability in the metabolism in maprotiline during its first pass through the liver after an oral dose. Large differences in first-pass effect have been seen with propranolol (Shand et al., 1970) and other drugs.

To sum up, we can conclude that blood level measurements give little information about the concentration of uptake inhibitors at the receptor site. This might be a major factor responsible for the inconclusive and variable results observed in the attempts to correlate blood levels of a polycyclic antidepressant with its therapeutic efficacy. A second factor could be the heterogeneity of biochemical disease patterns within the groups of patients randomly selected for the studies. The therapeutic response of such a nonhomogeneous population to unspecific uptake inhibitors—maprotiline being the exception—must be expected to be variable. Future studies aiming at a blood level-activity relationship should, therefore, require an exact biological definition and classification of the pathologic disease pattern and a subsequent treatment with specific agents.

DR. SIMPSON: I agree that it is hard to conduct a flawless study. However, if we attempted to control all of the variables, we would never initiate a study.

DR. MENDELS: My understanding, Dr. Wilhelm, is that your model was based on a single dose. Yet in order to get a real estimate of the steady state, a single dose of most of these antidepressant drugs is not sufficient. If you use a single dose even in a good computer model, the question is what is the relevance of that model to the steady state.

DR. WILHELM: Based on the single dose in the computer model, we calculated these constants and then extrapolated to the multiple dose.

DR. MENDELS: Then the single-dose values are not the same as steady-state values and your study could be misleading. While you have a valid computer model, the question is whether or not that model is relevant to the clinical state and the steady-state levels.

In other words, twenty-four hours after a single dose of imipramine you can just detect DMI. But in steady-state studies, you have very high levels of DMI at that period of time so that there are new metabolic processes going on if you give a drug on a chronic basis.

DR. SIMPSON: I would like to conclude with a positive statement that reiterates that most of the data suggest a correlation between clinical outcome and plasma blood level. The seven cases of Kragh-Sorensen are very convincing. All the groups discussed have at least some positive data and so we need not be pessimistic.

REFERENCES

Asberg, M., Cronholm, B., Sjoqvist, F., and Tuck, D. (1970). Correlation of subjective side effects with plasma concentrations of nortriptyline. Br. Med. J. 4:18–21.

———, Cronholm, B., Sjoqvist, F., and Tuck, D. (1971a). Relationship between plasma levels and therapeutic effect of nortriptyline. *Br. Med. J.* 3:331–34.

———, Evans, D. A. P., and Sjoqvist, F. (1971b). Genetic control of nortriptyline kinetics in man: a study of relative of propositi with high plasma concentrations. *J. Med. Gen.* 8:129–35.

Blashki, T. G., Mowbray, R., and Davies, B. (1971). Controlled trial of amitriptyline in general practice. *Br. Med. J.* 1:133–38.

Borga, O., Azarnoff, D. L., Plyma Forshell, G., and Sjoqvist, F. (1969). Plasma protein binding of tricyclic antidepressants in man. *Biochem. Pharmacol.* 18:2135–43.

Braithwaite, R. A., Goulding, R., Theano, G., Bailey, J., and Coppen, A. (1972). Plasma concentration of amitriptyline and clinical response. *Lancet* 1:1297–300.

Brodie, B. J. (1964). In T. B. Binne, ed., *Absorption and Distribution of Drugs.* London. Livingstone Ltd., pp. 199–251.

Burrows, G. D., Davies, B., and Scoggins, B. A. (1972). Plasma concentration of nortriptyline and clinical response in depressive illness. *Lancet* 2:619–23.

———, Scoggins, B. A., Turecek, L. R., and Davies, B. (1974a). Plasma nortriptyline and clinical response. *Clin. Pharm. & Ther.* 16:639–44.

———, Turecek, L. R., Davies, B., Mowbray, R., and Scoggins, B. A. (1974b). A sequential trial comparing two plasma levels of nortriptyline. *Austral. & New Z. J. Psychiat.* 8:21–23.

Degkowitz, R. (1967). Leitfaden der psychopharmakologie. Wissenschaftl. Verlagsges. Stuttgart:

Eschenhof, E., and Rieder, J. (1968). On the metabolism of the antidepressant amitriptyline in rat and man. 2nd Intl. Symp. Pharmacol. Chem., Münster, Germany, Abstr. p. 43.

Evans, D. A. P., Davison, K., Garratt, R. G. (1965). The influence of acetylator phenotype on the effects of treating depression with phenelzine. *Clin. Pharmacol. & Ther.* 6:430–35.

Glassman, A. H., and Perel, J. M. (1973a). The clinical pharmacology of imipramine. *Arch. Gen. Psychiat.* 28:649–53.

———, Hurwic, M. J., and Perel, J. M. (1973b). Plasma binding of imipramine and clinical outcome. *Am. J. Psychiat.* 130(12):1367–69.

Gouzon, B., Prunneyre, A., and Donnet, V. (1956). Concentrations of chlorpromazine in different tissues. *C. R. Soc. Biol.* (Paris) 148:2039.

Hammer, W., and Sjoqvist, F. (1967). Plasma levels of monomethylated tricyclic antidepressants during treatment with imipramine-like compounds. *Life Sci.* 6:1895–1903.

———, Iderström, C. M., and Sjoqvist, F. (1966). Chemical control of antidepressant drug therapy. *Proceedings of the 1st International Symposium on Antidepressant Drugs.* S. Garattini and M. N. G. Dukes, eds., Excerpta Medica Intl. Cong. Ser. No. 122:301–10.

Johnstone, E. C., and Marsh, W. (1973). Acetylator status and response to phenelzine in depressed patients. *Lancet* 1:567.

Kragh-Sorensen, P., Asberg, M., and Eggert-Hansen, C. (1973a). Plasma-nortriptyline levels in endogenous depression. *Lancet* 1:113–15.

———, Hanse, C. E., and Asberg, M. (1973b). Plasma levels of nortriptyline in the treatment of endogenous depression. *Acta Psychiat. Scand.* 49:444–56.

Medical Research Council (1965). Clinical psychiatry committee: clinical trial of the treatment of depressive illness. *Br. Med. J.* 1:881–86.

Nies, A., Robinson, D. S., Lamborn, K. R., and Lampert, R. P. (1973). Genetic control of platelet and plasma monoamine oxidase activity. *Arch. Gen. Psychiat.* 28:834–38.

———, Robinson, D. S., Lamborn, K., Ravaris, C. L., and Ives, J. O. (1974). The efficacy of the MAO inhibitor phenelzine: dose effects and prediction of response. *Present Status in Research and Clinical Use of MAO Inhibitors.* IX Cong. Collegium International Neuropsychopharmacologicum, Symposium No. 11, Paris.

———, Robinson, D. S., Ravaris, C.L., and Davis, J. M. (1971). Amines and monoamine oxidase in relation to aging and depression in man. *Psychosomat. Med.* 33:470.

Perrier, D., and Gibaldi, M. (1974). Drug concentrations in the plasma as an index of pharmacologic effect. *J. Clin. Pharm.* 16:415–17.

Riess, W., Rajagopalan, T. G., and Keberle, H. (1972). The metabolism and pharmacokinetics of Ludiomil (maprotiline). In P. Kielholz, ed., *Depressive Illness.* Bern: Hans Huber Publishers, p. 140.

Robinson, D. S., Nies, A., Ravaris, C. L., and Lamborn, K. (1973). The monoamine oxidase inhibitor, phenelzine, in the treatment of depressive-anxiety states. *Arch. Gen. Psychiat.* 29:407–13.

Salzman, N. P., and Brodie, B. B. (1956). Physiological disposition and fate of chlorpromazine and a method for its estimation in biological material. *J. Pharmacol. Exp. Ther.* 118:46.

Shand, D. G., Nuckolls, E. M., Oates, J. A. (1970). Plasma propranolol levels in adults with observations in four children. *Clin. Pharmacol. Ther.* 11:112–20.

Simpson, G. M. (1973). Classification and prediction of outcome of depression. Symposium Medicum Hoechst 8, Germany.

Sjoqvist, F., Hammer, W., Ideström, C. M., Lind, M., Tuck, D., and Asberg, M. (1968). Plasma level of monomethylated tricyclic antidepressants and side effects in man. *Proc. Eur. Soc. Study Drug Tox.* 9:246.

Wharton, R. N., Perel, J. M., Dayton, P. G., and Malitz, S. (1971). A potential clinical use for methylphenidate with tricyclic antidepressants. *Am. J. Psychiat.* 127(12):1619–25.

CHAPTER V

Differential Diagnosis and Treatment of the Dysphorias

D. F. Klein

DSM-II suffers from numerous drawbacks related to lack of diagnostic reliability. It confuses etiological and behavioral descriptions, gives inexact composite portraits of dubious reliability as a basis for diagnosis, and fails to offer exact classificatory decision rules. All of these faults are open to change through exact definition and decision rule stipulation. An APA Task Force on Nomenclature is endeavoring to remedy this problem.

However, a more basic problem than reliability (which can be improved by an academic exercise) is validity, which requires research demonstration. The validity of a class can only be established if it is shown that assigning an individual to a class tells you *more* about that individual than the fact that he has the characteristics that entitle him to the class label.

In psychiatry, as in medicine, we would hope that our diagnostic classification would validly predict etiology, pathophysiology, prognosis, familial tendencies and response to treatment. This, DSM-II has not succeeded in doing.

I will focus on differential indications for treatment as a categorical validation procedure, well recognizing that other validation procedures are possible (e.g., genetics). Hopefully, growing knowledge will allow us to develop categories that will have multiple simultaneous validations.

The first major distinction made by DSM-II is the classification of major affective disorders, i.e., affective psychoses (296). This is defined as a non-precipitated, dominating mood disturbance which is responsible for any loss of environmental contact. The category comprises involutional melancholia, manic-depressive illness, and other major affective disorder.

The term "psychosis" is used in DSM-II as a synonym for "severe." There is no implication that the patient must suffer from loss of contact with reality, delusions, hallucinations, etc.

Therefore, affective psychosis, as defined by DSM-II, is simply a severe endogenous mood disorder. As I will discuss below, this group of patients is usually responsive to somatic interventions. However, the category does not give any guidance concerning the relative utility of antipsychotics and antidepressants among its members.

Further, the treatment implication, erroneously accepted by many clinicians, is that if you do not have an affective psychosis, as in the major alternative category, Neuroses, Depressive (300.4), somatic interventions are contraindicated. Depressive neurosis is defined as an excessive reaction of depression due to an internal conflict or identifiable event.

This definition needlessly asserts an etiological hypothesis (internal conflict) which is always an inference and often undemonstrable. Further, the only qualitative difference from the affective psychoses is the precipitant, which may be irrelevant to somatic treatment.

Also, the DSM-II definition of depressive neurosis thoroughly confounds chronic recurrent dysphoria secondary to a whole variety of characterological inadequacies and malformations with the acute dysphoric reaction to a severe disappointment that may occur in normal personalities (reactive depression).

It has been convincingly shown (Covi et al., 1974) that many neurotic depressions, i.e., mild depressions, respond to antidepressants, although not as uniformly as the affective psychoses. Therefore, this distinction is oblique to prediction of somatic intervention; it predicts well at the psychotic pole but offers no guidance concerning the neurotic pole, except by a misleading implication of lack of somatic treatment effectiveness.

Similarly, the endogenous-precipitated contrast predicts well for the endogenous group but offers no guidance for the precipitated group.

Confusion reaches its height with the psychotic depressive reaction (298.0) which is both psychotic (severe) and precipitated. Such a category offers no guidance concerning treatment, since this heterogenous group would include both severe precipitated retarded depressions and precipitated incapacitating dysphorias in inadequate personalities. Therefore, it is no surprise that group membership conveys little treatment relevant information.

More recent work has emphasized a number of other distinctions that are actually treatment-relevant: unipolar vs. bipolar, primary vs. secondary, qualitatively defined psychotic signs, the importance of defects in pleasure and interest, retardation vs. agitation, depression vs. dysphoria vs. demoralization vs. akinesia, and severity defined with regard to both symptomatology and social incapacitation. A useful treatment-relevant categorization should reflect these considerations.

Such an outline is presented and each subset's appropriate psychopharmacological treatment is discussed.

Dysphoric Disorders

I. Primary
   A. Endogenomorphic Depression
   B. Reactive or Situational Dysphorias
   C. Schizoaffective Illness.
II. Secondary
   A. Secondary to Schizophrenia and Schizoid States
   B. Secondary to Personality Disorders and Neuroses
      1. Endogenomorphic
         a. Phobic-Anxious
         b. Obsessive compulsive neurosis
         c. Passive dependent and antisocial personality
      2. Dysphorias
         a. Hysteroid dysphoria
         b. Emotionally unstable character disorder
         c. Histrionic character disorder
         d. Inadequate and hypochondriacal personality (demoralized)
   C. Dysphorias Secondary to Organic and Toxic Illness
      1. Chronic brain syndrome
      2. Temporal lobe epilepsy
      3. Hypothyroidism or "low normal" thyroid
      4. Covert alcohol and/or drug abuse
      5. Antipsychotic akinesia
      6. Others

DYSPHORIC DISORDERS

These illnesses are characterized by the phasic appearance of a difficult to bear (dysphoric) mood, i.e., depressed, sad, blue, hopeless and/or a decreased ability to respond to pleasurable or interesting stimuli, i.e., apathy and anhedonia. Anxious states may fairly be called dysphoric but are not relevant to this presentation.

I. Primary (No Diagnosable Preexisting Psychiatric or Relevant Somatic Illness)

A. Endogenomorphic Depression (Klein, 1973; 1974)

The term endogenous has suffered from at least two conflicting usages. Some authors emphasize the lack of precipitants as a central defining feature of endogenous depression, which at least has the merit of etymological consistency. Others equate endogenous with "autonomous" and emphasize the lack of reactivity of the symptoms once established without regard to precipitation. Factually, it has been shown that the symptom pattern characteristic of endogenous depression possesses only a small, though significant, correlation with lack of precipitant.

What I am suggesting is the use of the easily definable severe endogenous (nonprecipitated) depressions as the criterion group that most clearly discloses a coherent symptom pattern. All patients (regardless of precipitation) with such a pattern are "endogenomorphic." Plainly, the endogenomorphic depressions are conceptually divided into endogenous depressions and precipitated endogenomorphic depressions. The endogenomorphic depression, which may or may not be precipitated and may or may not require hospitalization, regularly results in a sharp, unreactive, pervasive impairment of the capacity to experience pleasure or to respond affectively to the anticipation of pleasure. This key inhibition of the pleasure mechanism results in a profound lack of interest and investment in the environment, often associated with inability to enjoy food, sex or hobbies. Studies of intracerebral self-stimulation indicate that stimulation of certain areas of the brain results in repeated self-stimulation. Other areas lead to the abrupt termination of self-stimulation. These findings have led to the hypothesis that certain brain mechanisms deal with evaluation of sensory input as either pleasurable or painful, and a direct stimulation of these areas is then experienced subjectively as pleasure or pain. By "pleasure center" we do not specify a delimited anatomic location, but rather point to a distinct vulnerable functional organization that may be impaired by the pathophysiology of particular depressive states. In a certain proportion of these patients, the inhibition of this hypothesized pleasure center seems accompanied by disinhibition of an equally hypothetical pain evaluation center, resulting in severe fearful anticipation and agitation.

It is postulated that if the pleasure mechanism becomes unresponsive, one cannot experience pleasure either from current sensory input or via the method of anticipatory or recollective imagery. The person with a normal pleasure mechanism, when thinking of a future pleasurable situation, experiences an anticipatory glow. If the pleasure center is malfunctioning, however, this glow does not occur, and the person simply has a cold experience of anticipating a situation that does not evoke any warm affective response.

Associated with this core disorder are more inconstant features that confirm the diagnosis, but are not required. However, their appearance diminishes the likelihood of a false positive misdiagnosis, and they may even dominate the symptom picture. If one wishes to be relatively certain of the diagnosis, as in research studies, a stipulated minimum number of these ancillary characteristics would serve (as in the Renard Hospital group's approach). Clinicians, however, must often act on provisional diagnoses. Their relaxation of criteria incurs fewer false-negative but more false-positive misdiagnoses.

These confirmatory characteristics are:

Psychomotor (includes gross motor action, speech and thinking)

Vegetative
  Hypo- or hypersomnic
  Hypo- or hyperphagic
  Loss of energy

Self-critical
  Guilt
  Shame
  Suicidal concern or impulse

Psychotic mood congruent delusions
  Poverty
  Somatic illness
  Guilty responsibility
  Ideas of reference

Historical course

Unipolar—only depressive episodes. (Again for research purposes one may want to stipulate a minimum number of depressive episodes but this is not a clinical necessity.)

Bipolar—at least one episode of mania. (Some researchers also stipulate a separate class of bipolar illnesses where only an episode of hypomania has occurred, but the clinical significance of this category is as yet obscure.)

Once the diagnosis of primary endogenomorphic depressive illness is made, the frequent utility of somatic intervention is clear. These episodes are usually self-limiting; however, proper treatment spares much needless pain, social disruption, and the possibility of suicide. Treating such illness without appropriate somatic intervention is outmoded. The relevant interventions are ECT, lithium, tricyclic antidepressants, MAO inhibitors and the antipsychotics. The relative merits of these therapeutic procedures in depression will be considered below, although considerable controversy exists.

Evidence indicates that ECT is slightly superior to the antidepressants in the regularity of good to excellent short-term antidepressant effect. However, other reported advantages of ECT, such as increased rapidity of remission and aid in the prevention of suicide, have not been clearly demonstrated.

There are also certain disadvantages to ECT. Relapse may be more frequent following ECT than during treatment with maintenance antidepressants. Convulsive therapy is regularly attended by some degree of confusion, amnesia and recent memory loss, secondary to the production of an organic mental syndrome. It is not clear whether the degree of cerebral dysfunction manifested in the organic mental syndrome has permanent structural residual deficit associated with it. Frequently, no decrement is shown on cognitive tests given before and after shock treatment. But this is also true after major destructive procedures, such as prefrontal lobotomy, and attests more to the inadequacy of cognitive test procedures than to a lack of cerebral deficit due to convulsive therapy. We have personally seen several patients with histories of excellent educational attainments who had IQ's in the 70's after multiple courses of ECT. Clinical experience demonstrates that patients who have received multiple courses of convulsive therapy often present abnormal rigidity of character, perseverative trends and an inability to learn flexibly—all strongly reminiscent of organic brain disease. However, it is possible that these characteristics were present prior to ECT.

The confusion produced by convulsive therapy requires family member involvement in shepherding the outpatient to and from treatment. This inconvenience is not necessary with pharmacotherapy. Also, the confused states often require the patient to interrupt his work, whereas pharmacotherapy allows many depressed patients to continue working. The residual memory defect and amnesia produced by ECT cause frequent socially embarrassing situations, especially to patients who feel convulsive therapy carries a stigma.

Pilot reports indicate that unilateral application of electrodes to the nondominant hemisphere during convulsive therapy produces less of an organic mental syndrome with equivalent therapeutic effectiveness. If this is borne out by further work, a major drawback to ECT will have been overcome. Long-term follow-up studies of residual amnesia have not been done. The value of chemical convulsants also bears further investigation.

Other disadvantages of convulsive therapy include occasional vertebral and long bone fractures. These complications can largely be avoided through adequate prophylactic use of muscle relaxants (e.g., succinylcholine). Unfortunately, the use of muscle relaxants incurs its own dangers and requires the presence of a medical team equipped to do artificial pulmonary ventilation and perhaps endotracheal intubation. Other drawbacks are the aversion most patients have for this procedure and its relatively high cost in relation to pharmacotherapy.

To sum up, we recommend the use of ECT only after the failure of pharmacotherapy. However, one should not be hesitant in this case. The use of maintenance ECT for the prevention of relapsing depression also has its adherents, although its value has not been clearly demonstrated.

For the treatment of depression, the specific role of lithium is not yet firmly established. This is not the case for its prophylactic use, which will be discussed by Dr. Schou in this volume, nor for its use in the chronically disturbed emotionally unstable character disorder, described below.

The differential indications for tricyclics, MAO inhibitors and antipsychotics require discussion in terms of the above descriptors. First, it should be made clear that little is known on a scientific comparative study basis concerning the relevant differential indicators. Several comparative studies have been done (Klein, 1967; Greenblatt et al., 1964; Overall et al., 1964; Raskin et al., 1970), but a good deal remains to be resolved. Klein and Davis (1969) review much of this literature.

My personal beliefs are as follows: The MAO inhibitors are generally less effective than the tricyclics. Nonetheless, patients who do not respond to tricyclics may respond to MAO inhibition. Therefore, following four weeks of ineffective, maximum-dosage tricyclic therapy, the patient should receive either an MAO inhibitor or ECT. The choice is usually determined by social practicalities rather than purely psychopharmacological considerations. If the family and patient can put up with the possibility of yet another course of ineffective treatment, and if an MAO inhibitor has not been previously shown to be ineffective, I would usually opt for an MAO inhibitor rather than ECT. The only case where MAO inhibition may be the treatment choice, preferable to tricyclics, is in those atypical endogenomorphic depressions characterized by hypersomnia and hyperphagia, often associated with personality characteristics of a histrionic and rejection-sensitive nature.

The utility of antipsychotics is restricted to those patients with marked agitation and psychotic delusional or referential features. Phenothiazines will produce quick control of agitation and insomnia; mood elevations do not occur until the usual two to three weeks. The patient may appear somewhat subdued and lethargic at this point, and shifting to a tricyclic may produce beneficial results.

Interestingly, many agitated and/or psychotic patients will do well in two to four weeks on tricyclics alone, if combined with proper supervision. The question has been raised whether treating such patients with antipsychotics does not needlessly expose them to the risk of persistent tardive dyskinesia, even if the antipsychotics are used for only four to six weeks. More data are necessary to resolve this issue, but the possibility seems slight. For many agitated and/or psychotic patients, the use of antipsychotics often allows outpatient treatment that would not be possible with tricyclics.

Suicidal risk is often used as an indication for ECT. I believe clear suicidal risk is an indication for hospitalization under close supervision, and that there is no convincing evidence that under these circumstances ECT is superior in rapidity or effectiveness to the tricyclics.

A bipolar history is troublesome since such depressives may react to antidepressants with a manic swing. Such patients require close monitoring, with family cooperation, substituting antipsychotic for antidepressant treatment if mania occurs. The use of maintenance lithium therapy for this condition will be discussed by Dr. Schou in his presentation. Simple antidepressant discontinuation is insufficient.

The possibility that combined MAO inhibitors and tricyclics, or antidepressant with lithium therapy, may prove advantageous awaits convincing demonstration.

B. Reactive or Situational Dysphorias (Disappointment Dysphorias)

These are primary difficulties (i.e., no previous relevant psychiatric or physical illness), secondary to a clear precipitant, that are not endogenomorphic.

A reactive depression is unhappiness following severe disappointment in an apparently normal personality. It is often associated with anxiety, resentment, anger and a tendency to blame others. It is generally agreed that reactive depressions remit within a two-month period. Winokur and Pitts (1964) have shown that, in almost all of a carefully studied series of hospitalized patients initially diagnosed as suffering from reactive depression, other more specific diagnoses were possible. They suggest that the term is superfluous. We agree and would hypothesize that the remaining, usually nonhospitalized patients with reactive depression (self-limiting unhappiness upon severe disappointment in a normal personality) were having a normal emotional reaction that received a discrete disease label from psychiatrists habituated to considering all emotional distress as reflective of a pathological state. We wish to emphasize that this sort of error is the exception rather than the rule. We believe that most emotional states considered pathological by psychiatrists are due to pathological derangements. The fact that an occasional normal although extreme emotional experience may lead to a psychiatric diagnosis does not mean that all psychiatric diagnoses are based on a mechanistic misperception of the richness of life experience. Each syndrome requires specific study to determine whether or not it should be considered pathological. Transient emotional states that remit promptly do not require therapeutic intervention, are psychologically comprehensible, occur in normal personalities and should not be labeled pathological. The symptomatology closely resembles mourning, with tearfulness, brooding preoccupation with the loss, feelings of tension and inability to shift attentive focus from the inciting situation. Loss of appetite and insomnia are common.

Nonetheless, the patient maintains the reactive capacity for pleasure and interests and can be distracted from his brooding focus, as at a wake. Further, his affective status is not fixed and a change in life circumstances (the friend calls again, etc.) may instantly relieve his distress.

It is often not diagnostically certain whether or not one is dealing with an uncomplicated reactive depression. However, since these depressions, better called disappointment dysphorias, are self-limiting and usually remit within a two-month period under any nontoxic treatment regimen, regular case contact allows possible diagnostic revision. This follow-up procedure protects the patient in case an endogenomorphic depression supervenes. Otherwise, the patient requires little psychotherapeutic help except for temporary support and the maintenance of perspective.

Patients often do not accept continued, purely diagnostically oriented case contact because their primary interest is symptom relief. For this reason it is sensible to prescribe small doses of a safe minor tranquilizer (e.g., 5 mg chlordiazepoxide t.i.d.). The patient's expectations of help are thereby mobilized, albeit by placebo effect. These drugs are preferable to actual placebos because the patient may research the agent he is taking. Small doses should be used since the sedative and toxic qualities of these agents may outweigh their beneficial effects. They will not prevent the development of an agitated or retarded depression. Therefore, a downhill course during such treatment calls for immediate diagnostic reevaluation. The use of d-amphetamine may have a place in the treatment of these problems, but this is controversial.

Major antidepressants of the imipramine-like or MAO inhibitor class are unwarranted for reactive dysphorias and often have therapeutically adverse effects.

Some diagnosticians include states labeled "pathological grief" under the rubric of situational depression. This is an error. Mourning and grief are severe situational dysphorias. On occasion such dysphorias shift symptomatology and become qualitatively distinct pathological states, most often endogenomorphic depressions, which require appropriate treatment (Klein and Davis, 1969). Freud's distinction between mourning and melancholia (Freud, 1957) is still useful diagnostically. In mourning, the world is empty, with the patient focused on his loss. In melancholia, the ego is empty, with the patient focused on his own incapacities and distress.

C. SchizoAffective Illness

Some patients present as an endogenomorphic depression with a mood congruent psychotic delusional overlay. Such patients have an endogenomorphic depression with psychosis. However, other such patients also have a variety of features reminiscent of schizophrenia, such as nonmood congruent delusions, i.e., thought broadcasting, hallucinations, thought disorder, communicative incompetence, and flatness or inappropriateness of affect, without preexisting illness or marked personality deviation. In fact, most American diagnosticians are so struck by the schizophrenic traits that the affective disorder is ignored. Plainly, the distinction between an endogenomorphic depression with qualitatively psychotic characteristics and a schizoaffective depression may not be very clear phenomenologically. Further, it is possible that this distinction is not relevant to choice of treatment. Klein (1964, 1970a) has discussed the possibility that these categories reflect different stages along a dimension of primary activation dyscontrol, complicated by different secondary cognitive dysfunctions.

The treatment of choice is antipsychotic medication. Some clinicians believe that the piperazine phenothiazines are more stimulating than the aliphatic phenothiazines and therefore more appropriate for the retarded, perplexed, inactive schizoaffective. There is considerable evidence that this is not true. However, at the end of the resolving phase of the psychosis, the piperazine phenothiazines may be less sedative in effect and therefore more appropriate for a period of social reintegration. There are data to support the usefulness of lithium in schizoaffective disorders (Prien, 1974).

Some patients respond slowly to antipsychotics. Adjunctive ECT is often very useful in shortening the period of illness, since such patients can be severe suicidal risks without it being obvious or communicated.

Following a period of antipsychotic medication, the patient may be improved yet maintain a mild lowering of spirits, inactivity, apathy and lack of spontaneity. There is a difficult differential diagnosis here between a residual depression and an iatrogenic extrapyramidal syndrome—akinesia.

Often this distinction is not possible on neurological or behavioral phenomenological grounds, although akinetic patients can enjoy themselves more than those with residual depression. Discontinuation of the antipsychotic medication would demonstrate whether the condition is secondary to medication or part of the course of the illness; however, this is rarely feasible for fear of relapse.

If the patient is not receiving an antiparkinson agent, a few days' trial may show a sudden rise in spontaneity and participation, indicating an akinesia. Other patients may not respond to an antiparkinson agent but will respond dramatically to an adjunctive tricyclic, often within several days.

Some clinicians are concerned that an antidepressant may exacerbate schizophrenia and are loath to use it in such patients. In my experience, this does not occur in primary schizoaffectives, but may occur in patients with secondary affective disorders consequent to a preexisting process schizophrenia or severely schizoid personality. Antidepressants are usually worthless for the apathy of chronic "burned-out" schizophrenics.

II. Secondary

A. Secondary to Schizophrenia and Schizoid States

Clear-cut schizophrenias may develop secondary dysphoric states. It is often difficult to determine if this is due to an iatrogenic parkinsonian akinesia, a true supervening endogenomorphic depression, a residual social-cognitive defect state, or demoralization.

Often the only feasible therapeutic procedure is to try first an antiparkinson agent and a lower dose of antipsychotic. If this does not work, an adjunctive tricyclic antidepressant is recommended by some physicians. Unfortunately, antidepressant treatment, especially in schizophrenics with childhood asociality, may first cause an euphoric expansiveness followed, in a week or two, by a psychotic disorganization (Klein, 1962b; Pollack et al., 1964). Frequently, the clinician has been favorably impressed by the initial mood elevation and therefore has irreversibly classified the antidepressant as a "good" intervention. The subsequent psychotic exacerbation is attributed to other factors (often pre-Oedipal) so that the toxic agent is erroneously continued.

Finally, some schizophrenic patients seem to develop chronic defect states that are refractory to all known interventions.

Patients who have profound, chronic, self-isolating, withdrawn, schizoid behavior patterns may develop a depressive syncrome, without manifest schizophrenia. Their treatment is not clear. Probably antipsychotic agents are the treatment of choice with the possibility of carefully monitored adjunctive antidepressant agents.

B. Secondary to Personality Disorders and Neuroses

1. Endogenomorphic

These disorders have the same symptomatic core disorders as primary endogenomorphic syndromes. However, since they occur in certain predisposed pathological groups, there is a complex overlay to salient symptoms and character traits that may mislead and confuse the diagnostician. The treatment is similar to that for primary endogenomorphic illness.

a. Phobic Anxious. About 15 to 20 percent of patients characterized by spontaneous panic attacks and phobic-dependent manipulations develop endogenomorphic depressions at some time during their life. Such patients may be unusually sensitive to tricyclic agents, manifesting an overstimulated, irritable insomniac syndrome. This may lead to patient rejection of the medication but can be simply handled by reducing the dosage, sometimes to as low as 10 mg imipramine daily.

b. Obsessive Compulsive Neurosis. Patients with frank obsessive compulsive neuroses often develop secondary depression, usually severely agitated in character. The depressive disorder may be obscured by the marked exacerbation of rituals and obsessions. With remission of the depression, the obsessive compulsive symptomatology slowly returns to baseline.

c. Passive Dependent and Antisocial Personality. Both of these groups are characterized by their chronic high level of manipulativeness and extractiveness. When they become depressed, usually in a retarded fashion, it is easy to misinterpret their complaints as being entirely coercive and parasitic in origin. Relief of their depression reinstates their usual difficult personality.

2. Dysphorias

These are nonendogenomorphic dysphorias that are characteristic of certain distinct personality patterns.

a. Hysteroid Dysphoria (Klein and Davis, 1969). These predominantly female patients are flamboyant, histrionic, man-centered, contrectation-minded and inordinately rejection-sensitive. Normally, they are expansive and energetic.

Consequent to a rejection, especially from a boyfriend, their mood abruptly crashes, producing an intense dysphoria, feelings of futility and hostility, a tendency to oversleep and overeat, and a leaden lethargy.

MAO inhibitors chronically taken for prophylaxis modify the abruptness and frequency of their crashes. Stimulants will immediately improve their mood during a crash. The possibility of addictive behavior is real, and therefore stimulants are not recommended.

b. Emotionally Unstable Character Disorder (Rifkin et al., 1972a). These predominantly female adolescents have extraordinary mood lability, changing drastically several times daily. Their self-presentation is primarily dysphoric, emphasizing their bad self-image and feelings of futility. To detect their high periods may require a knowledgeable informant.

When down they are hostile and reproachful, and tend to withdraw, uttering suicidal threats. When up they are overactive and hedonistic, lack frustration tolerance and are unable to accept rules and structure. They are frequently involved with drug abuse and promiscuity. Phenothiazines (Klein and Fink, 1962a; Klein, 1967) and lithium (Rifkin et al., 1972c) normalize both poles of these patients' lability. The patients find lithium more acceptable than the phenothiazines, probably because of their intolerance for akinesia.

c. Histrionic Character Disorder. These patients are characterized by self-dramatization and a craving for stage center. They often inordinately vain but, at the same time, are continually disappointed that they are not much more than they actually are. Therefore, their lives are replete with disappointment dysphorias often self-treated with alcohol and sedatives with resulting habituation.

Such patients show markedly negative somatizing responses to all of the standard major psychotropic agents. Because of their addictive potential, the use of drugs of the stimulant-sedative axis is unwise. They are an unsolved psychotherapeutic and pharmacotherapeutic problem. Various magical interventions, e.g., megavitamins, mescaline and mandalas, may drastically change symptomatology for the short run.

d. Inadequate and Hypochondrical Personality (Demoralized). A wide range of chronic dysphoric complaints occur in what are often called "chronic characterological" or "neurotic" disorders. These patients often seem to aspire to the security of the sick role. This class of patient is probably the final common pathway for a host of life defeats, stemming from social deprivation, affective and cognitive dysregulation, recurrent trauma, inadequate intellect or energy, etc. Such patients' symptomatology may simply be chronic demoralization. Medication seems of little value and often exacerbates somatic complaints.

One misunderstood aspect of psychiatric illness is demoralization—the belief in one's ineffectiveness, engendered by a severe life defeat. It is a change in self-image (the complex of attitudes and evaluations toward the self) in the direction of helplessness. While any life defeat is discouraging, depression is particularly demoralizing since a feature of the pathological depressive mood is the profound conviction of one's incompetence. This self-denigrating belief seems validated by the person's catastrophic life experience. Even after the pathological mood has remitted so that the enjoyment is possible, the ability to anticipate and plan competent activity may be severely diminished because of the persistent change in self-image. Such a state of attitudinal despair does not respond to antidepressant medication because it is not the concurrent manifestation of a pathological mood; rather, it is the secondary, but not functionally autonomous, residue of a past affective state.

Demoralized patients are unable to engage spontaneously in even normal life tasks since they view themselves as unequal to the effort involved. Therefore, they remain restricted in their activities, thus confirming their incapability. This self-fulfilling prophecy is also a frequent consequence of other psychotic disorders.

The differential diagnosis of demoralization and depression is relatively simple when the central role of pathological depressive mood is recalled. The demoralized person can enjoy himself in a setting in which no demands are made upon him. His appetites are not inhibited and his sleep pattern is normal.

It is demoralization, as a ubiquitous psychiatric phenomenon, that lies behind the misnamed "nonspecific" effectiveness of many therapeutic interventions, including placebos and supportive psychotherapy. We consider the idea of nonspecific therapeutic factors invalid; the effectivensss of therapy depends on demoralization, a specifiable state. Demoralization is nonspecific in the sense that it can be the secondary consequence of a wide variety of life defeats, and will respond to a wide variety of encouraging measures.

The benzodiazepines occasionally moderate the pain of anticipated failure, with some decrease in social paralysis. One problem is that an occasional phenomenologically indistinguishable patient shows marked benefit from either an imipramine-like drug or an MAO inhibitor. Therefore, it makes clinical sense to try the major antidepressants because benefit by only a minority of such drug-treated patients would be a clinical advance. Thus, in the treatment of such chronic dysphorics, a four-week trial of imipramine, reaching a minimum dosage of 200 mg per day during the fourth week and followed by a one-week drying-out period, and then a four-week trial of phenelzine at a dosage of 45 to 75 mg per day, is probably an adequate test of the clinical responsiveness of such patients to the major antidepressants. Some doctors may prefer to reverse this sequence.

This period of pharmacotherapy should be accompanied by an intensive effort to engage the patient in an appropriate form of psychotherapy. Certain psychotherapists object to this procedure on the basis that it focuses the patient upon the omnipotence of somatic therapies, rather than underlining the psychogenic origin of his disorder. Exactly the reverse is true in our experience. These patients are in marked psychic distress and are frequently childishly demanding. If after methodical testing, the doctor has not found an appropriate agent to ameliorate the distress, his case that the patient's disorder requires intensive psychological handling is far more persuasive than if he simply arbitrarily declared that medications would be ineffective. Also, some patients will benefit markedly from drugs, and they should not be denied this opportunity. Group directive and supportive therapy, assertion training, role modeling, and structured incremental activities seem useful. Sargant and Slater (1972) recommend a combination of amitriptyline and a MAO inhibitor in the treatment of atypical mixed symptomatic pictures. Controlled studies in this area seem overdue.

c. Dysphorias Secondary to Organic and Toxic Illness

A wide variety of toxic agents and somatic illnesses may be complicated by dysphoric states. The general approach follows the medical model exactly: first, diagnose and, if possible, alleviate the underlying condition. If this is not possible, because of chronic organic brain syndrome, for example, treat symptomatically. The closer the complicating dysphoria resembles one of the cryptogenic "functional" syndromes, the more likely it will respond similarly to pharmacotherapeutic interventions.

I will not list all the possible organic and toxic antecedents of dysphoria. I would like to emphasize the following, often ignored possibilities to be considered in every differential diagnosis:
1. Chronic brain syndrome
2. Temporal lobe epilepsy
3. Hypothyroidism or "low normal"thyroid function (Fader and Struve, 1972)
4. Covert alcohol and/or drug abuse
5. Antipsychotic akinesia (Rifkin et al., 1975)

A major difficulty in the evaluation of treatment is the reliance of the office practitioner on the testimony and appearance of only the patient when estimating his progress. When an antidepressant is beneficial, the initial change is frequently so subtle that it is not reported by the patient nor obvious to the interviewer. Many patients develop a more self-assertive, outgoing, extroverted manner without realizing it, although it may be obvious to friends and relatives. Frequently such patients complain that their psychic distress is unrelieved, although they may realize that they are more socially effective. Therefore, it is important to check the patient's functioning by interviewing friends and relatives. Often they will report that the patient is undoubtedly enjoying himself more, although the patient cannot recognize or admit this. The patient's increased self-assertiveness may lead to difficulties with superiors, colleagues, therapists, relatives and spouses, who are accustomed to dealing with the patient as a passively compliant individual. This assertiveness may take the form of refusing medication on the grounds that drugs do not really treat the main problem. The patient may report that since taking medication he is in even more life difficulty. This may eventually be distinctly to the patient's self-assertive advantage, especially if he can learn to handle this new capacity in a socially skillful fashion. However, lowering the dose of medication may be necessary when undue irascibility and temper tantrums occur.

The adjustment of dosage demands careful attention. It should be recognized that the effective major psychotropic agents act over long periods of time. Therefore, minor shifts in timing and dosage are rarely of any consequence. Having set as an initial goal the determination of the greatest tolerable dose, one should not deviate from this course prior to the achievement of the maximum clinical improvement considered likely. The attempt to titrate symptomatology by continually altering the dosage from interview to interview is an expression of the therapist's anxiety and overcompliance rather than rational procedure. A patient's clinical condition fluctuates, and it is the long-term trend rather than the short-term perturbation with which we are ultimately concerned. Patients will often pressure for minor changes, but it is usually not wise to make these adjustments simply to placate the patient; one must believe that the changes are otherwise warranted. Placation carries the message that the patient knows more than the doctor. Of course, if the patient's suggestion is valid, one should not hesitate to accept it and acknowledge the patient's good sense.

An even greater danger than therapeutic tinkering is therapeutic rigidity and inertia. Continued complaints of social or personal ineffectiveness may indicate either that treatment has not as yet proved effective but should be maintained as promising, or that some innovation is required. Far too often patients are maintained on ineffective programs with the rationalization that they are "working it through," without evidence that they are doing anything but suffering. We believe that four weeks without discernible progress usually indicates a need for review of treatment and possible innovation. The touchstone for evaluation of treatment progress is the patient's range of interests and ability to enjoy himself. To determine this often requires a reliable informant.

CONCLUSION

The current DSM-II is deficient for treatment guidance. Its organizing principles with regard to dysphoric disorders are only obliquely related to the problem of differential treatment. This paper reviews the other treatment-relevant aspects and attempts to coordinate them into an overall treatment outline, allowing specific treatment recommendations for each subset.

Much research remains to be done. The logistics of developing sufficiently large samples to allow definitive comparative studies are daunting. Multicenter collaborative studies are one approach to this problem; however, the development of good-sized programmatic research hospitals would represent a far superior means of generating the requisite knowledge. As I have discussed elsewhere (Klein, 1970b), to develop such facilities would require a sharp change in the current philosophy of small multicenter research support and the problematic interdigitation of research with clinical services.

COMMENTARIES

DR. PERRIS: There should be no difficulty in agreeing with Dr. Klein that current classifications of mental disorders are unsatisfactory. This is true both for the DSM-II and for the WHO's classification. Attempts to avoid some of the inconsistencies in current systems have been made in many quarters, and I would be pleased to present our own approach (Ottosson and Perris, 1973) during the course of the meeting.

Broadly speaking, I agree with Dr. Klein that response to treatment would be a very useful criterion to validate our diagnoses and that such a validation would give a practical meaning to our classifications. However, after some twenty-five years of psychiatric practice and research work, I am still not yet prepared to accept the view that the somatic therapies currently available for the treatment of depression are so rationally grounded and so specific that a therapeutic response can be taken as a validating criterion.

After having agreed that there is a need for critical revision of our current classifications, we should discuss whether or not Dr. Klein's approach offers a substantial improvement. Broadly speaking, it could be said that Dr. Klein's classification represents an advance in comparison with the DSM-II. However, I am afraid that many of the old critical concepts have been reissued in new clothes without losing too much of their ambiguity, and new ones have been introduced with the risk of adding confusion to an already confused terminology.

Most controversial, in my opinion, is the use of the term "endogenomorphic." As a matter of fact, Dr. Klein starts with a critical view of the term "endogenous" quite similar to that presented in my own paper, but later he seems to accept the same old criteria in defining an "endogenomorphic" disorder. Thus he includes in this concept an etiological meaning (i.e., precipitated/nonprecipitated, cryptogenic), a severity factor ("severe depressions"), a course factor (autonomy), and an alleged "coherent pattern of symptoms." Unfortunately, none of these variables has ever proved to be an exclusive characteristic of an "endogenous depression." Among the characteristics of his "endogenomorphic" group, Dr. Klein takes the historical course quite adequately into account. However, I would not agree that the "stipulation of a minimum number of depressive episodes is not a clinical necessity." If the bipolar/unipolar dichotomy has to be tested with regard to its possible prognostic value, then it is necessary to agree about the minimum requirements for labeling a depressed patient as "unipolar" (Perris, 1973, 1975). Dr. Klein's use of the terms "primary" and "secondary" is also a bit disturbing, for example, in the case of his group of "reactive or situational dysphorias." In this regard, the possible impact of personality characteristics should be more closely examined. Moreover, I wonder where depressive reactions to severe somatic illnesses are to be considered if they are not included under the heading "reactive depression."

Under the heading devoted to disorders secondary to personality disorders and neuroses, Dr. Klein lists a series of conditions very likely to occur in subjects with a neurotic personality structure. However, also in this case, the distinctions appear to be somewhat arbitrary and inconsistent. Furthermore, I fear that in overemphasizing personality patterns as criteria for differentiation, some questionable assumptions are made about the premorbid personality of depressed patients of the "endogenomorphic" type. In the light of the most recent studies concerning personality patterns in unipolar depressed patients (Perris, 1966, 1971; Tellenbach, 1961; von Zerssen et al., 1968), I would be very careful from a differential diagnostic point of view, before attributing too much value to personality characteristics in the development of the disorder.

Dr. Klein reminded us of an important problem in therapy: the risk of diagnostic misinterpretation of akinetic reactions to neuroleptic treatment. I would like to stress the point that it is even more important to remember the possible occurrence of severe depressive reactions, with a very high suicide risk, that may occur during the course of long-term neuroleptic treatment, especially with the long-acting agents. In these cases, a change to antidepressants is vitally necessary, and it is not sufficient merely to add antiparkinson agents or discontinue neuroleptic medication.

Neither MAO inhibitors nor amphetamines are available in Sweden. It is possible that the use of MAO inhibitors should be reconsidered, at least for some patients, but I would not suggest treating depressed patients of any kind with amphetamines.

Finally, I would like to comment very briefly on Dr. Klein's assumptions concerning ECT; here, cultural differences in health care are most evident. Since I cannot touch upon all the critical points, I will confine myself to a few issues. First, concerning the long term follow-up of memory impairment following conventional ECT, there are studies of this issue (Cronholm, 1969) which demonstrate that memory disturbances are no longer a problem as early as about one month after a series of traditional bilateral ECT (Table I).

Second, I cannot share Dr. Klein's opinion that studies of unilateral ECT are still to be regarded as "pilot studies." Such a statement may have been valid when first formulated in 1969 (Klein, 1969b), but the evidence today of the efficacy of unilateral ECT and of the significantly lesser degree of transient intellectual impairment is substantial enough (d'Elia, 1970, 1974; d'Elia and Laurell, 1972) not to be regarded as "pilot" results. Since I have been especially concerned with

Table I
"Retention" in percent as compared with scores before treatment,
at different time points after bilateral ECT. In brackets, no. of
ECT applications

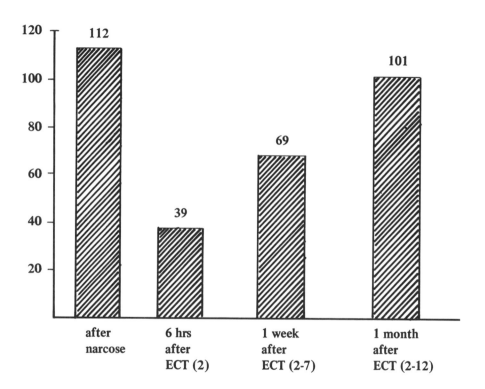

the schizoaffective (cycloid) patients (Perris, 1974), I would like to add that I do not agree that a differentiation of this group of "endogenomorphic depressive" patients is irrelevant to the choice of treatment. Furthermore, I am not sure that it is quite correct to state that ECT is only "slightly" superior to antidepressants when used in well-defined patient series of the kind labeled here as endogenomorphic. Finally, I would say that a course of ECT, even in an outpatient setting, would be no more expensive in Sweden than any other treatment and that our patients are very seldom shepherded to ECT treatments.

To summarize, I think that Dr. Klein's paper represents a sincere effort toward a methodological advance in the definition of different types of depressed patients and a serious attempt toward a validation of our diagnoses. However, attempts at verifying his assumptions would be plagued by problems that have persistently hampered previous classification attempts, namely, the difficulty of giving clear-cut definitions of labels, acceptance of subgroups which are probably not mutually exclusive, and use of different criteria of classification to define subgroups. It must be added that current somatic therapies for affective disorders are still based more on empirical than on rational or specific grounds. Moreover, much of our knowledge derived from old drug trials should perhaps be reconsidered, since many assumptions were formulated in a period when our methodological skills in this field were still very primitive.

DR. SIMPSON: Dr. Perris, I wonder if you could give us more details about the premorbid personality factors in unipolar patients.

DR. PERRIS: Yes. Many of these patients have a personality pattern characterized by obsessive-compulsive (anancastic) traits. It could be said that they had some kind of personality disorder, but these characteristics are quite common in just this kind of patient which Dr. Klein would call endogenomorphic. I would like to reemphasize that the diagnostic labels, such as "endogenous," "reactive," "neurotic," etc., given to depressive syndromes are quite controversial and are often used inconsistently. To avoid the confusion which might arise from an improper use of diagnostic labels, we have introduced in our department (Ottosson and Perris, 1973) a multifactorial model to describe our patients. This model comprises four independent factors as follows:

    a. *Main symptomatology:* i.e., three or more symptoms which characterized the patient under scrutiny.

    b. *Severity:* i.e., psychotic or nonpsychotic. The label "psychotic" is based upon disturbed reality evaluation.

    c. *Course:*

       1) within the episode: i.e., day fluctuations, reactive to changes in milieu, autonomous.

       2) anamnestic: i.e., single episode, recurrent (bipolar, unipolar, of different coloring), habitual or chronic.

    d. *Supposed etiology:*

       1) biological (e.g., heredity, histogenic, chemogenic, or toxic)

       2) sociopsychological (e.g., characterogenic, sociogenic, or reactive, neurasthenic)

       3) cryptogenic: i.e., unknown. Possible combinations may occur.

Example:

a. Depression, anxiety, inhibition, sleep disturbances

b. Occasionally psychotic

c.1) Day fluctuations, autonomous

c.2) Recurrent, unipolar, 4th episode

d. Probably hereditary

This model, comprising a code for each variable, is very easy to use and offers a comprehensible description of each patient in terms which are easily understood. In our opinion, patients in research projects should be described in this way to allow the replication of the study in similar patient populations in different geographical areas.

DR. CONNERS: The first thing that struck me about Dr. Klein's schema is that it seems to be a mixture of several levels of observation. For example, he eschews internal conflict as an example of a method of classification, surely one that the traditional psychoanalyst would rely upon a great deal. But in turn he substitutes other, what seem to me, equally inferential kinds of characteristics such as "loss of pleasure." Now, what I would like to see is a classification scheme which differentiates between different levels of observation. For example, he includes antecedents to the disorder, the mood state, the severity, cognitive factors, the history of the patient; all of these things are combined and shuffled into a complex schema. He starts off by saying that the purpose of a classification scheme is to predict something that we didn't know before, but of course if we take everything and shuffle it around so that it is a kind of mental factor analysis, it has to come out accounting for everything. This is rather opposite, it seems to me, to the approach to classification which is taken in biological science. In botany or zoology or anthropology, one tries to take a small number of characteristics which seem to be key dimensions of basic biological processes and show that this small number of characteristics accounts for the diversity of phenomena. For example, with animals, taking the number of teeth, the length of the tail, the color of the skin, the density of the fur, observable behavioral characteristics, in other words, one attempts to establish a classification system which then accounts for a number of things such as blood types or other physiological characteristics, genetic factors, phylogenetic developmental factors, and so on. One could, of course, approach the classification from a quite different point of view but, it seems to me, that in psychiatric classification one is stumbling because we don't know which of the several levels of observation are most fruitful. It would be interesting to ask how much more such a classification system offers than one that simply takes the question of is there or is there not a history of mood disturbance in the family, or, is there a reactive event, is there a clearly definable event in the history, etc. How much more is actually added by this kind of schema which mixes up moods, cognition, motor behavior, and response to treatment? Response to treatment seems to be the real animus of Dr. Klein's system, but, looking at the schema, an amazingly complex number of "somatic therapies" are lumped together under the endogenomorphic classification. I don't know how this classification tells us much more about which drugs to use than that we should use a drug. I think this comes back to Dr. Perris' point that the classification problem is ultimately still an empirical issue. I think what Dr. Klein has done is a rational factor analysis. I wonder if it may not be wiser to start with a smaller number of variables and try to account for the data, rather than take such a large number of disparate levels and try to organize the data in that fashion.

Another thing that strikes me is the mixture of etiological versus behavioral elements. As a behaviorist, I would be much more interested in a simple scheme based entirely on observable behavior, a classification which would probably come out in two or three dimensions (since we seem to only think in that number), and then see if many of these other characteristics, etiological factors, would be explained.

DR. POST: Dr. Klein has spoken from a background of considerable practical experience, tempered with scientific testing. He outlined a very sound program for the assessment and management of patients presenting with so-called depression, and I do not wish to raise any matters of detail with which one might disagree, except one.

I fear that his use of the term "psychotic" and "antipsychotic drugs" might lead psychiatrists in training and other neophytes into imprecise ways of thinking. I think we would all agree that many depressives could or even should be called "psychotic" on account of their beliefs, their psychomotor states and occasionally in relation to their perceptual disorders. When these abnormal beliefs and experiences are present, they can usually be derived from the mood of sadness, emptiness, perplexity or anxiety. They take their content from guilt, self-belittlement, hypochondriacal ideation, or fear of punishment. These psychotic phenomena usually yield to one or the other kind of antidepressant therapy. Occasionally, apparently or possibly depressed patients exhibit symptoms which closely resemble or seem identical with those seen in confirmed schizophrenics. As suggested by Klein, these may be removed by drugs which he calls "antipsychotic," but which I submit should be called not even "antischizophrenic" but simply what they are: major tranquilizers. Personally, I think that patients of this kind belong to the diagnostically and therapeutically very difficult schizoaffective group.

Turning to more important matters, I fully agree with the points made by Dr. Klein in his onslaught on DSM-II, and through it on the International Classification of Diseases, Injuries, and Causes of Death. However, I wonder whether his fire is not misdirected. I believe that the International Classification was not intended to enshrine a system of etiology, symptomatology, response to treatment, and prognosis. It merely presents an attempt to describe and define disorders in such a way as to facilitate international studies by ensuring that identical labels will be attached to similar psychiatric conditions, the world over. In my opinion, the classification is far too detailed and complex for this. I suspect that this is partially due to a reluctance on the part of various psychiatric establishment figures to give up their own or their country's pet diagnoses. I wonder (to refer to a condition mentioned by Dr. Klein) whether the collection under "298: Other psychoses," and especially "298.0: Reactive depressive psychosis," was not put in under pressure from the countries using these concepts, e.g., Scandinavia. The British won't have any of it, and the relevant item in the glossary prepared by the Registrar General's Advisory Committee ends as follows: "Psychiatrists who do not recognize this category include this condition under 296.2." (296.2 is, of course, the code number for depressed type of manic-depressive psychosis, including endogenous depression.)

Dr. Klein's aim in proposing his classification is far more ambitious, and his is a very creditable attempt at linking clinical picture with response to one or the other type of therapy. Patients with endogenomorphic dysphorias tend to respond to electroshock therapy, tricyclic antidepressants and, with less certainty, MAO inhibitors or lithium salts. These conditions may be found in pure culture not necessarily related to certain psychological events. They can also occur, as he puts it, "secondary to" (I would prefer to say "associated with") certain neuroses and personality disorders. I should be much more skeptical of his concept of nonendogenomorphic dysphoria. Dr. Klein himself quotes Winokur and Pitts as having shown that almost all patients with reactive or situational dysphorias were finally diagnosed differently. He himself suggests that patients with an initial diagnosis of one of the nonendogenomorphic dysphorias should be watched carefully for the emergence of an endogenomorphic picture, and he has reported favorably on the treatment with lithium of the dysphorias seen in female adolescents with emotionally unstable character disorders. And yet one would not expect lithium to act in any condition which was not in some way related to what used to be called "manic-depressive," and thus endogenomorphic.

I am myself very much afraid that the time is not yet ripe in terms of our knowledge for classifying so-called functional psychiatric disorder except for purely operational purposes. Research in this area should, however, proceed in the usual way, by putting up and then demolishing a succession of hypotheses. Mine would be that all depressions sufficiently long-lasting and severe to reach the physician or psychiatrist are endogenous, by which I do not mean cryptogenic or necessarily unrelated to environmental impacts, but somewhere and somehow related to biological dysfunctioning. The severity of depressions and their symptomatology is a product of the severity of endogenous dysfunctioning of each patient's personality and of his sociocultural setting.

DR. GALLANT: No one could disagree with Dr. Klein's opinion that the diagnosis should predict genetic tendencies and response to treatment. The genetic history of the patient may help to guide the therapist in the selection of the specific treatment modality. Pitts and Winokur have reported that male first-degree relatives of unipolar depressed patients showed five times the prevalence of alcoholism than relatives of a control group, and that affective disorder *may sometimes* manifest itself as symptomatic alcoholism (Pitts and Winokur, 1966). An inference from these data is that affective disorders may be related to alcoholism or drug abuse, and environmental variables such as socioeconomic class, culture, age of onset, sex, and individual life experiences may be major determinants of the final symptomatic expression of the affective disorder. Although atypical features of depression may lower the response of a patient to prophylactic lithium treatment, there is a possible subgroup of alcoholics and drug addicts which may respond well to either tricyclic agents or lithium if they receive the medication over a sufficient period of time.

During this discussion, I would like to hear some opinions concerning the use of lithium and neuroleptics in schizoaffective disorders, particularly since the publication of Prien's report in May of this year, which stated that lithium is as effective as chlorpromazine in reducing schizophrenic behavior in the "mildly active" schizoaffective patient (Prien, 1974). I personally have strong reservations about combination therapy or polypharmacy, but the indications are that some controlled studies of a neuroleptic plus lithium compared to either one of these drugs alone should be initiated in the schizoaffective population. Most of us are still dissatisfied with the clinical results in the treatment of this serious disorder which produces a very high suicide rate.

DR. MCKINNEY: I was disappointed to learn that DSM-III is keeping the whole concept of endogenous and reactive depression. It seems to me that there is so much confusion about these terms that we should really think about dropping them from the vocabulary as they are completely misleading terms. No matter how carefully one chooses to define endogenomorphic, or whatever terms, these carry so many connotations in so many people's minds that I wonder what use they are serving. Why not have a category called primary dysphoric disorders or primary affective disorders, and why does one have to get into the endogenous reactions?

DR. KLEIN: As a matter of fact, that particular categorization will probably not be in DSM-III.

DR. HAMILTON: I think we should abandon "psychotic vs. neurotic," which doesn't mean anything, and "schizoaffective," which is just a way of pretending we know what we are talking about when we do not. May I recommend that diagnosis in military medicine (which is not used often enough): "NYD"—Not Yet Diagnosed.

Dr. Klein has raised one or two points on which I would like to comment. Concerning ECT, he exaggerates the confusion that this produces in patients, in a manner common in American psychiatric literature. I see very little of it; I remember particularly one patient, a schoolteacher, who used to come for ECT in the morning and return to teach his children in the afternoon.

As for spinal fractures complicating ECT, I have not seen ECT given without muscle relaxants since 1952, so I cannot understand why there should be a problem.

I am concerned by the suggestion that amphetamines might be prescribed to the patients who have obviously disturbed personalities. It is true that the physician will stop prescribing after three or four weeks, but the patient will not necessarily stop taking them. As for the suggestion that amphetamines should be combined with sedatives such as the benzodiazepines, we know that such a combination is extremely addicting, particularly for patients with unstable personalities. Such prescribing is just asking for trouble. I myself have not prescribed amphetamines since 1959.

DR. KLEIN: Dr. Perris states that he does not accept the view that the somatic therapies currently available are so rationally grounded and so specific that therapeutic response can be taken as a validating criterion.

If by rationally grounded he means grounded in a firm understanding of therapeutic mechanism, I agree with him. We are clearly at the level of crass empiricism. If by rationally grounded, he means that there is no empirical evidence that these treatments work, I would have to differ. Further, whether or not treatments are so specific that therapeutic response can be taken as a validating criterion of a diagnostic schema is an empirical question. If the system presented by me does not aid in the selection of correct treatments, it has at best aesthetic value of a somewhat rococo nature.

Dr. Perris feels that my term "endogenomorphic" simply incorporates the same old criteria as the term "endogenous." I would presume that my paper was not sufficiently clear. I specifically exclude the notion of precipitation as being relevant to the diagnosis of "endogenomorphic" state. I also exclude severity, since there exist mild "endogenomorphic" states. I do utilize the concept of autonomy associated with a coherent symptom pattern. This too is an empirical question.

Dr. Perris objects to my statement that stipulation of a minimum number of depressive episodes is not a clinical necessity, since it is required to test out the bipolar/unipolar distinction with regard to possible prognostic value. I agree with him, but this is a research rather than a clinical necessity. In trying to demonstrate the correlates of a class distinction, it is important that the class be as homogeneous as possible. Establishing a minimum number of depressive episodes for inclusion in the unipolar category is a sensible way of increasing class homogeneity. It decreases false positives. Unfortunately, for clinical purposes it also increases false negatives. Since the clinician often has to act in an obscure situation, he may well want to use the category of unipolar depression, even for patients who have had only one episode.

Dr. Perris is concerned that when I use the term "primary" I may be neglecting the possible impact of anancastic personality characteristics as an antecedent to illness. Here, I think a distinction is necessary between personality traits, e.g., meticulous, perfectionistic, histrionic, etc., and personality disorders. It is certainly possible that many patients with primary affective illness have a distinguishable group of antecedent personality traits which are insufficient to incur dysfunction or suffering. Such people simply have a distinctive personality, so their affective disorder would properly be referred to as primary. I did discuss disorders secondary to actual personality disorders.

Dr. Perris alerts us to the possibility of severe depressive reactions during the course of long-term neuroleptic treatment, especially with long-acting agents. In our experience, all such apparent severe depressive reactions are actually manifestations of a severe parkinsonian akinesia. However, Dr. Perris may well be right since it will require a very broad experience with the long-acting neuroleptics before all possible secondary effects are understood.

Dr. Perris states that he would not suggest treating depressive patients of any kind with amphetamines. I can well sympathize with his cautious approach in view of the very major problem of habituation and chronic amphetamine toxicity. Nonetheless, I have seen a number of patients with good personalities and no history of addictive behavior who have been severely upset by a major life disappointment. Their upset did not in any way resemble endogenomorphic depression but was much closer to a state of mourning. They showed excellent responses to dextroamphetamine and were easily able to stop the use of medication within a few weeks.

Dr. Hamilton is also concerned about the possible use of minor tranquilizers, especially in combination with amphetamines, as being an addicting drug combination. The combination may be unwise, and it was not my intent to recommend the combined use of these agents. Those patients for whom dextroamphetamines may be useful are suffering from a leaden inertia as an aspect of their mourning state, and I would not see the advisability of minor tranquilizers for such patients, in any case.

Both Dr. Perris and Dr. Hamilton take me to task as unduly cautious concerning ECT and exaggerating the amount of confusion incurred. The work quoted by Dr. Perris indicates that on certain psychological memory tests there is a return to normal functioning within a month after the termination of ECT. The problem here is whether or not these tests can be considered an adequate representative of the entire range of memory functions that may be affected by ECT. It is also possible that only the unusual patient will respond to ECT by a persistent amnestic syndrome. If 5 percent of ECT patients were to show such a syndrome, it is unlikely that the studies quoted would detect an experimental effect of such minor magnitude (although of major importance for the individuals concerned).

Nonetheless, I concur with both Dr. Perris and Dr. Hamilton that most depressive patients derive major benefit at little cost from ECT. Our only real point of difference is how often ECT should be used as a primary mode of treatment.

Dr. Perris' "model" seems to me an admirable attempt to bring systematization into patient description by insisting that a statement be made about four key aspects of any patient. It is not a substantive model however, as it does not stipulate any particular typological subdivisions or validating correlates. Perhaps Dr. Perris feels that such substantive models are premature.

Dr. Conners believes that internal conflict is no more inferential than loss of pleasure. I find it hard to believe that observers would not find it far easier to agree as to whether or not a patient is showing a loss of pleasure response than to agree as to whether or not a patient has a specified internal conflict.

He also states that the classification scheme requires different levels of observation. To this I plead guilty. The question is whether the complexity of the scheme is required by the complexity of the phenomena with which it is dealing. The real question is whether or not the scheme can be validated. My claim is that the scheme's complexity allows for sufficiently defined differential predictions so that validation becomes possible.

Dr. Conners has mistaken my purpose when he points out that under the endogenomorphic classification a large number of somatic therapies are applicable. My point is that if the patient is not endogenomorphic very few therapies are available. My claim is that the endogenomorphic vs. nonendogenomorphic distinction enables us to make this treatment prediction better than the endogenous vs. nonendogenous distinction or the psychotic vs. neurotic distinction. Dr. Conners further states he would be much more interested in a simple scheme based entirely on observable behavior. I prefer useful complexity to aesthetic simplicity.

Dr. Hamilton suggests greater use of the term "Not Yet Diagnosed." This is optimistic since it presumes that a diagnosis will eventually be made. The phrase "undiagnosed psychiatric disorder" seems worthy of greater currency. If such a diagnostic practice could be combined with a therapeutic regimen of watchful waiting, much good might come about and not a little harm prevented.

Dr. Post feels that the term major tranquilizer is preferable to the term antipsychotic. In particular he submits that these drugs should not even be called antischizophrenic but rather major tranquilizers. I can't accept this since antipsychotic drugs are of such significant benefit to the retarded, perplexed, quiet, thought-disordered schizophrenic. To refer to these drugs' action on this sort of patient as major tranquilization seems to miss the mark.

Dr. Post correctly states that my classification is more ambitious than the International Classification of Diseases. No attempt is made by the ICD or DSM-II to develop categories tied to treatment response. However, the ICD and DSM-II have also failed if their purpose is to facilitate international studies by ensuring that identical labels will be attached to similar psychiatric conditions the world over. The high degree of diagnostic unreliability that results when psychiatrists attempt to utilize these categories is notorious. Hopefully, DSM-III will include explicit operationally definable categories, even if these are not tied to treatment response.

REFERENCES

Covi, L., Lipman, R. S., Derogatis, L. R., Smith, J. E., and Pattison, J. H. (1974). Drugs and group psychotherapy in neurotic depression. *Am. J. Psychiat.* 131:191–98.

Cronholm, B. (1969). Post ECT amnesias. In G. A. Talland and N. C. Waugh, eds., *The Pathology of Memory.* New York: Academic Press.

d'Elia, G. (1970). Unilateral electroconvulsive therapy. *Acta Psychiat. Scand.* Suppl. 215.

——— (1974). Unilateral electroconvulsive therapy. In M. Fink, S. Kety, W. McGaugh and T. A. Williams, eds., *Psychobiology of Convulsive Therapy.* Washington, D.C.: Winston & Sons, pp. 21–34.

——— and Laurell, B. (1972). Ger "elektrochock" hjärnskada? *Läkartidn* 69:853–56.

Fader, B. W., and Struve, F. A. (1972). A possible value of the EEG in detecting subclinical hypothyroidism associated with agitated depression. *Clin. EEG.* 3:94–101.

Freud, S. (1957). *Mourning and Melancholia,* Standard Edition. J. Strachey, ed. Hogarth Press.

Greenblatt, M., Grosser, G. H., and Wechsler, H. (1964). Differential response of hospitalized depressed patients to somatic therapy. *Am. J. Psychiat.* 70:935–43.

Klein, D. F. (1964). Behavioral effects of imipramine and phenothiazines: implications for a psychiatric pathogenetic theory and theory of drug action. *Rec. Adv. Biol. Psychiat.* 7:273–87.

——— (1967). Importance of psychiatric diagnosis and prediction of clinical drug effects. *Arch. Gen. Psychiat.* 16:118–26.

——— (1969). Psychopharmacological treatment of bereavement and its complications. In A. H. Kutscher, ed., *Death and Bereavement.* Springfield, Ill.: Charles C. Thomas, pp. 299–304.

——— (1970a). Psychotropic drugs and the regulation of behavioral activation in psychiatric illness. In W. L. Smith, ed., *Drugs and Cerebral Function.* Springfield, Ill.: Charles C. Thomas, pp. 69–81.

——— (1970b). Non-scientific constraints on psychiatric treatment research produced by the organization of clinical services. In S. Merlis, ed., *Non-Scientific Constraints on Medical Research.* New York: Raven Press, pp. 69–90.

——— (1973). Drug therapy as a means of syndromal identification and nosological revision. In J. O. Cole, A. M. Freedman, and A. J. Friedhoff, eds., *Psychopathology and Psychopharmacology.* Baltimore, Md.: John Hopkins University Press, pp. 143–60.

——— (1974). Endogenomorphic depression: a conceptual and terminological revision. *Arch. Gen. Psychiat.* 31:447–54.

——— and Davis, J. M. (1969). *Diagnosis and Drug Treatment of Psychiatric Disorders.* Baltimore, Md.: Williams & Wilkins.

——— and Fink, M. (1962a). Behavioral reaction patterns with phenothiazines. *Arch. Gen. Psychiat.* 7:449–59.

——— and Fink, M. (1962b). Psychiatric reaction patterns to imipramine. *Am. J. Psychiat.* 119:432–38.

Ottosson, J. O., and Perris, C. (1973). Multidimensional classification of mental disorders. *Psychol. Med.* 3:238–43.

Overall, J. E., et al. (1964). Imipramine and thioridazine in depressed and schizophrenic patients. *JAMA* 189:605–08.

Perris, C. (1966). A study of bipolar (manic-depressive) and unipolar recurrent depressive psychoses. *Acta Psychiat. Scand.* Suppl. 194.

——— (1971). Personality patterns with affective disorders, J. O. Ottosson, ed. *Acta Psychiat. Scand.* Suppl. 221:43–51.

——— (1973, in press). The heuristic value of a distinction between bipolar and unipolar affective disorders. Symposium on Classification and Prediction of Outcome of Depression. Erbach am Rhein, BRD.

——— (1974). A study of cycloid psychoses. *Acta Psychiat. Scand.* Suppl. 253.

———— (1975, in press). The bipolar-unipolar dichotomy and the need for a consistent terminology. *Neuropsychobiol.*

Pitts, F. N., and Winokur, G. (1966). Affective disorder. VII. Alcoholism and affective disorders. *J. Psychiat. Res.* 4:37–50.

Pollack, M., Klein, D. F., Willner, A., Blumberg, A. G., and Fink, M. (1964). Imipramine-induced behavioral disorganization in schizophrenic patients: physiological and psychological correlates. *Rec. Adv. Biol. Psychiat.* 7:53–61.

Prien, R. F. (1974). The clinical effectiveness of lithium: comparisons with other drugs. VA Admin., Cent. Neuropsychiat. Res. Lab., Res. Rep. No. 97, pp. 1–19.

Raskin, A., et al. (1970). Differential response to chlorpromazine, imipramine and placebo. *Arch. Gen. Psychiat.* 23:64–173.

Rifkin, A., Levitan, S. J., Galewski, J., and Klein, D. F. (1972a). Emotionally unstable character disorder: a follow-up study. I. Description of patients and outcome. *J. Biol. Psychiat.* 4:65–79.

———, Levitan, S. J., Galewski, J., and Klein, D. F. (1972b). Emotionally unstable character disorder: a follow-up study. II. Prediction of outcome. *J. Biol. Psychiat.* 4:81–88.

———, Quitkin, F., Carrillo, C., Blumberg, A. G., and Klein, D. F. (1972c). Lithium in emotionally unstable character disorders. *Arch. Gen. Psychiat.* 27:519–23.

———, Quitkin, F., and Klein, D. F. (1975, in press). Akinesia, a poorly recognized extrapyramidal syndrome. *Arch. Gen. Psychiat.*

Sargant, W., and Slater, E. (1972). *An Introduction to Physical Methods of Treatment in Psychiatry.* New York: Science House.

Tellenbach, H. (1961). *Melancholie.* Berlin, Göttingen, Heidelberg: Springer Verlag.

von Zerssen, D., Koeller, D. M., and Rey, E. R. (1968). Objektivierende untersuchungen zur prämorbiden persönlichkeit endogen-depressiver. In H. Hippius, H. Selbach, eds., *Das Depressive Syndrom.* Munich, Berlin, Vienna, Urban & Schwarzenberg, pp. 183–205.

Winokur, G., and Pitts, F. N., Jr. (1964). Affective disorder: is reactive depression an entity? *J. Nerv. Ment. Dis.* 138:541–47.

CHAPTER VI

Clinical Evaluation of Depressions: Clinical Criteria and Rating Scales, Including a Guttman Scale

M. Hamilton

The last decade has seen the rapid development of biochemical researches in the depressions, and this has given rise to the hope that in the near future we may see biochemical tests for the diagnosis and evaluation of the depressive disorders. Unfortunately, this is as yet only a hope and the diagnosis and evaluation of depressive disorders are still based on clinical evaluation. This is not particularly difficult in practice, although current controversies might give a contrary impression. The trouble with these controversies is that they are befogged by theoretical preconceptions, for which there is little or no backing evidence. I refer particularly to psychoanalytical and sociological theories. Depression is a common and normal human reaction to deprivation and loss, but there is plenty of evidence to indicate that there is also a pathological condition which is quite distinct, although its manifestations overlap the normal.

CLINICAL EVALUATION

Clinical evaluation is usually considered to be concerned with the assessment of clinical state, but it also has other purposes: the making of a diagnosis, the estimation of prognosis and selection for treatment. The efficacy and sophistication of the first compares favorably with that of the last three. In the case of diagnosis, the difficulties arise from the confusion concerning diagnostic categories. Even a superficial examination of official lists of diagnoses will show this. The WHO list is bad enough but the American list is even worse. It is inconceivable that a clinician could use these lists unless he develops a method of what might best be called modified random selection. In consequence, attempts to use psychometric statistical techniques for the making of diagnoses within the depressive disorders have not been successful. There are also technical reasons for the lack of success. Most statistical techniques depend upon the linear model, and this is patently inapplicable in the making of diagnoses. When it is difficult to decide, on the basis of symptoms and history, whether a patient should be diagnosed as suffering from anxiety state or depressive illness, then a family history of depressive illness, suicide or even alcoholism will lead to a diagnosis of the latter condition. This implies that the weights given to the clinical features are a function of the family history.

Prognosis cannot be separated nowadays from the problem of predicting the results of treatment. Several prognostic indices have now been produced, but it cannot be said that these are at all satisfactory, in the sense of being obviously better than ordinary clinical experience and judgment. This is partly due to the inherent difficulty of the problem (prognosis in all branches of medicine still tends to be in terms of general categories) but also because insufficient attention has been paid to the problem of selection of cases. A predictive index is derived from data obtained from a sample of some sort of "population." It is of value only within that population, which therefore must be clearly defined. Furthermore, when this index is to be used for predicting the results of treatment for a given patient, a method must be available for determining if this patient is indeed a member of that population. Finally, little progress has been made toward clarifying the criteria for selection of treatments. Progress on this problem depends on the demonstration that some kinds of patients respond to one treatment and not to another and vice versa for other kinds. In technical terms, this means finding an interaction between drug and type. Regrettably, this has not yet been achieved.

Rating scales for the evaluation of clinical state are slowly being introduced into hospital practice in association with the storage of data on computers. Full clinical information is difficult to store unless the volume of the data can be reduced, and the simplest method of doing so is to use rating scales. This brings in standardization and the advantages of this will be obvious to anybody who has had to search through case records, for standardization also means completeness. Nevertheless, only a beginning has been made in this sort of work, and further progress will depend very much on the development of a system which is universally acceptable.

USE OF RATING SCALES

The chief use of rating scales is in research, and many scales are now available, particularly in the field of research on depressions, for the assessment of clinical state. This is to the benefit of the researcher, because he is in a position to choose those scales which are most suited for his purposes. In the present state of the art, different scales are required for different kinds of patients and for different circumstances. Nevertheless, the existence of so many scales suggests that insufficient work has been done to compare them and to evaluate them properly.

It is sometimes considered that scales give rise to objective data which could then be used for resolving some of the major controversies in psychiatry. Unfortunately, they can be of only limited use in this way. The construction of a scale requires a theoretical background, not only in psychometrics but in relation to the phenomena studied. The most obvious is that concerning what might be called the field of discourse. Most scales are concerned with symptoms but many also include such data as the length and course of illness, background variables such as sex and social class and even family history. It would be perfectly feasible to construct a scale which would be concerned solely with psychodynamics. A Jungian could construct a scale which would record the development of individuation during the course of psychotherapy. A Freudian could construct a scale concerned with the development of transference during psychotherapy. It is not at all obvious that either of these scales would help to resolve the theoretical problems concerning what goes on during psychotherapy. It is true that scales have been devised which, it is claimed, are able to tackle the problem of whether "endogenous" and "neurotic" depressions are extremes of a range of symptomatology or distinct disorders. The fact that completely opposite results have been obtained by the protagonists of the two different schools of opinion illustrates the difficulties. In this particular case, insufficient attention has been paid to the problem of the criteria by which the patients are selected. It is these criteria which lie at the route of the controversy. A rating scale is, in a sense, an end product of the development of psychiatry. When the phenomena to be studied have been completely defined in nature and range, then it is possible to construct a scale to evaluate them. A scale should be constructed with a particular purpose in mind and then validated to demonstrate that it fulfills that purpose. If it is to be used for other purposes, then it must be validated for them separately.

TYPES OF RATING SCALES

Scales can be classified in many different ways, but the most important of them is that which distinguishes between scales to be used by an observer, whether skilled, semiskilled or unskilled, and those which are used for self-rating by the patient himself. On theoretical grounds the former have most of the advantages, but the latter are often more useful in practice and can be shown to be about as effective under appropriate circumstances. A skilled observer can evaluate the intensity of any one symptom by comparing it against the background of experience which he has. Patients have many reasons for minimizing or emphasizing their symptoms, but a skilled observer can penetrate the mask which the patient holds up, whether deliberately or unintentionally. An observer can rate and assess certain manifestations of illness which the patient would find impossible or extremely difficult to do. For example, a patient cannot be expected to assess loss of insight, and he would find it extremely difficult to assess such symptoms as mild retardation, agitation, hypochondriasis and delusions. An observer can rate all grades of severity of illness, from the mildest to the most severe, whereas a patient can be too ill to be able to complete a questionnaire. Finally, self-ratings require that the patient should have sufficient concentration, be sufficiently literate, and understand the vocabulary. The last point is particularly important because patients and psychiatrists do not interpret words in the same way. This may give rise to some difficulties during an interview but it is almost insuperable with self-rating scales. Pinard and Tetreault (1974) found that patients tended not to distinguish clearly between sadness, fatigue and anxiety, because they experienced them simultaneously. Terms which connoted aggression to psychiatrists were interpreted as meaning anxiety by the patients.

When all these points are taken into consideration, together with the high reliability and validity of observer-ratings, it would seem that there is little value in using self-ratings. However, at their best, they require the use of skilled and experienced raters, and there are not enough such persons. Furthermore, they also take up much time, though too much should not be made of this. Psychiatrists should spend time with their patients, and an adequate interview which forms part of the essential basis of the doctor-patient relationship should give all the information required to fill in a rating scale. The difficulty arises when assessments have to be repeated frequently. It is then that self-rating comes into its own.

The two most important properties of scales are validity and reliability. With regard to the latter, it is of particular interest that rating scales compare favorably with physiological and biochemical measurements, despite popular belief to the contrary. As for validity, the ultimate criterion in mental disorder is that of clinical judgment. If and when we have biochemical tests for the diagnosis and evaluation of mental illness, they will have to be validated against the clinical phenomena.

VALIDITY

There are many different ways of defining validity, but for present purposes it is sufficient to say that it signifies that the scores on a rating scale accurately reflect the grades of severity of the phenomena measured. There are different ways of measuring validity, and the two most important give what are known as construct and concurrent validity. There are two ways of measuring the former: by group differentiation and by measuring the effects of experimental factors. Group differentiation is demonstrated by showing that a scale clearly differentiates between two groups of subjects known to differ in the particular characteristic which is being measured.

Snaith (Snaith et al., 1971) tested the Wakefield SADS on a group of "normal" subjects and a group of depressive patients and showed that there was very little overlap in the scores obtained by these two groups. Only 3 percent of patients and 7.5 percent of normals were misclassified by a cut-off score. Kerekjarto and Lienert (1970) did the same with the Hamburg inventory and obtained a biserial correlation coefficient of .72. Schwab (Schwab et al., 1967) tested the Hamilton Rating Scale (HRS) on medical patients and depressives and found a bimodal distribution of scores. Downing and Rickels (1972) used the Zung SDS and the Popoff Depression Inventory on a group of depressive patients and compared them with nondepressive psychiatric patients. They found no significant difference in the scores between these two groups. This finding is perhaps not particularly relevant as it could be argued that it demonstrates merely that scales designed for the assessment of severity of depressive symptoms are not necessarily of any value in diagnosis.

To identify the groups to be used for making such comparisons, it is first necessary to make a clinical decision about them, i.e., that they are suffering from a depressive illness or are "normal." Such clinical judgment can be refined by grading groups of depressive patients as suffering from different degrees of severity of illness. The scores of such groups on a scale can then be compared. In other words, the scales are validated against a "global" judgment of severity. Zealley and Aitken (1969) attempted to validate the HRS in this way and obtained a correlation of .90 for patients when admitted to hospital, but this decreased to .55 when they were discharged. It may well be that this decrease in validity reflects a decrease in the range of symptoms. They found that the Visual Analogue Scale gave a correlation of .78 for patients on admission which decreased to .13 when they were discharged. Beck (Beck et al., 1974) obtained a correlation of .84 for the HRS and .77 for the Beck scale against global judgments. Metcalfe and Goldman (1965) obtained a correlation of .62 with the Beck scale.

Validities for self-assessment inventories tend to be lower. Downing and Rickels (1972) found that the Popoff scale had a validity coefficient of .36 for GP patients and .28 for psychiatric patients. They found that the Zung SDS gave corresponding figures of .45 and .22.

Another way of determining construct validity is to show that the scores on rating scales change in response to the effects of experimental factors. The commonest of such factors is the effect of treatment, and the extensive literature on drug trials demonstrates that the majority of scales in current use satisfy this criterion. However, a few published papers reported that Zung SDS is somewhat lacking in sensitivity in this respect.

CONCURRENT VALIDITY

Concurrent validity connotes the agreement between different scales, usually measured as a correlation. It might be argued that it is of little importance, on the grounds that however many people believe that the earth is flat doesn't make it so. Such a comment would be beside the point. Concurrent validity is concerned not with facts but with judgments and therefore indicates that two different ways of making judgments are or are not in good agreement. Full information on concurrent validity requires the preparation of a complete matrix of intercorrelations among all scales, and this is obviously out of the question. A fair amount of work has been accomplished, but it is in this field particularly that more needs to be done and also replicated.

It would appear that most investigators have compared rating scales against the HRS, which has thereby almost become a sort of standard. Schwab (Schwab et al., 1967) found that it correlated .74 with the Beck scale, and this compares with the correlation of .72 found by Beck (Beck et al., 1974). Tan (1969) obtained a distinctly lower value of .51. Brown and Zung (1972) obtained a correlation of .79 with the Zung SDS. Zealley and Aitken (1969) obtained the same figure with the Visual Analogue Scale (VAS), but when the patients were discharged the correlation was only .06. On the basis of these figures it would appear that if the HRS and the VAS were used to evaluate a treatment, the results found might be very different. If so, what would that signify? Further work obviously needs to be done here. Concurrent validity of self-assessment scales with the HRS is low. Tan (1969) obtained a correlation of only .25 with the MMPI depression scale. This figure may be compared with that of Garside (Garside et al., 1970), who obtained a correlation of .49 with the MMPI neuroticism scale. It is surprising that the neuroticism scale should have a higher correlation with the HRS than a depression scale.

The next most common "standard" is the Beck Depression Inventory. Lubin (1965) found that it correlated with the Lubin Adjective Check List .40 to .66 for various groups of patients. Tan (1969) obtained a correlation with the MMPI Depression Scale of .53. A few other scales have also been correlated. Lubin (1965) compared his Adjective Check List with the MMPI depression scale and obtained correlations ranging from .31 to .53 for different groups of patients. Downing and Rickels (1972) obtained correlations between the Zung SDS and the

Popoff scale of .71 for GP patients and .65 with psychiatric patients. Zung (1972) found that his Depression Status Inventory and the SDS correlated .87. In general, it would appear that self-assessment scales tend to have a lower concurrent validity among themselves, with some few exceptions, than do observer-rating scales.

RELIABILITY

One way of defining reliability is that it is a measure of the amount by which random error interferes with the measurement. The greater the error, the less reliability. This is not a good definition, but it does indicate that repeated measurements will not correspond exactly. The two most important forms of reliability are inter-rater and test-retest reliability. The second is usually lower than the first because the function measured may undergo some change from test to retest and this will diminish the correlation between them. The literature contains comparatively little information on the reliability of rating scales. When the HRS was first described, it was stated to have an inter-rater reliability of .90. Since then a number of papers have reported findings which range from .88 to .98. Bojanovsky and Chloupkova (1966) found that the Bojanovsky Scale had an inter-rater reliability of .92. Wechsler (Wechsler et al., 1963) found that the Wechsler Scale had a reliability of .88 when the raters interviewed the patients simultaneously, but when the two raters interviewed the patients a week apart the reliability fell to .78. There has been even less interest in examining the reliability of global judgments, but Beck (Beck et al., 1974) reported a reliability of .88.

GLOBAL JUDGMENT

The traditional method of clinical evaluation is that of "global judgment." Such judgments usually have three grades: mild, moderate and severe. This becomes a four-point scale if one includes an additional grade for "well" or "recovered." More grades are possible but these are very rarely used. Because such judgments are in accordance with traditional clinical practice, they have been regarded as the ultimate criterion by which to evaluate rating scales. The mean scores on rating scales of groups of patients should have the same rank order as the global judgments, and it is desirable that there should be little overlap of the scores given to members of the different groups.

Now that experience is accumulating with the use of rating scales, it can be seen that the precedence given to global judgments rests purely on tradition. The clinician who makes a global judgment or uses a rating scale is in fact using the same information for both procedures. The way in which the information is converted into a score on a scale is clearly defined, but this is not so for the way in which a global judgment is reached. It is likely that the weights given to different symptoms vary considerably and they may not even be constant. There is a fruitful field of research available along these lines. On the assumption that the weights given by the clinicians are constant, it would be possible to determine their value by the use of multiple regression, the independent variables being the ratings on scale items and the dependent variable being the global judgment. An even better technique would be to use multiple discriminant functions as this would give a quantification of the grades of global judgment. It would also be useful to examine the relative merits of these two methods of assessment in drug trials.

The efficacy of a weighting system raises a point concerning current statistical techniques in drug trials in which rating scales have been used for assessment. It is customary to use total scores on the rating scales as the data for statistical analysis to test whether the effects of different treatments differ significantly. A total score is an equally weighted sum of crude scores of items, which is equivalent to an unequally weighted sum of standardized scores, the unequal weights being chosen so as to make the weights of the crude scores equal. It cannot really be said that such a choice, designed to make the arithmetic easier, has an adequate basis. An obviously better one would be that set of weights which maximizes the difference between treatments. If only two treatments are being compared, this could be achieved by the method of multiple regression, but for several treatments it would be necessary to use multiple discriminant functions. Although work in other fields has shown that a differential weighted system has only limited advantages over equal weights, it would still be worth exploring such a system.

NEW METHODS OF ASSESSMENT

Current methods of evaluation of treatments in psychopharmacology usually depend upon measuring the reduction of symptoms. Although there are scales for measuring behavior in the ward, used in studying schizophrenia, their number is few. There is also a great lack of scales for measuring occupational and social adjustment, though a good start has been made. In the depressive disorders, which are fluctuating and recurrent, these methods are insufficient. Until the last few years, therapeutic trials for the depressions have been concerned with short-term effects. Long-term studies need to be concerned not only with disturbances in subjective well-being, i.e., symptoms, but also with disturbances of personal and social relations. A good start has been made as in the scale devised by Paykel (Paykel et al., 1971) and the evaluation of chronic illness by Coppen (Coppen et al., 1971). Much more work will have to be done along these lines.

PSYCHOMETRICS OF RATING SCALES

Clinicians and nonpsychometric statisticians are dissatisfied with certain aspects of the practical use of rating scales. The former are disturbed by the practice of summing scores on different symptoms. They argue that to add scores on variables which are qualitatively different, e.g., depression, insomnia and loss of weight, gives a total score which has no meaning. Such objections are due to a misapprehension of the meaning of a total score on a scale. An answer to these doubts which is both simple and adequate is to point to the evidence of construct validity, as described above.

The evidence of clinical practice is always better if it is backed by some appropriate theory. When a complex phenomenon is split into a number of variables (items on the scale), the relationship between these can be shown by means of a dispersion matrix. The total dispersion can be partitioned into a number of orthogonal components (the number being equal to the number of variables), each component corresponding to a latent root of the dispersion matrix. Provided that the variables are all measured in an appropriate direction and the variance of the subjects on the individual variables is sufficiently large, i.e., selection has not diminished the variance of the largest latent root, then the first component, which is made up of a weighted sum of all the variables, has all its weights positive. Scores on this component are such that they give the greatest separation between individuals of the group rated. When the group is reasonably homogeneous with respect to the pattern of symptoms, then this separation is in terms of severity. In a sense, it is components of variance which are being summed. In practice, a straightforward unweighted sum of crude scores of the variables is very highly correlated with this first component. In consequence, very little is gained by the use of differential weights.

Of course, such a total score does not give as much information about an individual or about the group as do the scores on individual variables, and the loss of information can be seen by comparing the variance of the first latent root with the total variance. More information can be retained by taking into account the scores on the second, third and other components; finally, all the information will be retained by taking into account the scores on as many components as there are variables. In actual practice, several of the components correspond to latent roots which have a very small variance and make little contribution to the total. Such scores can therefore be ignored with only trivial loss of information, and this may be of use in reducing the number of variables to be considered and to make comprehension easier. The great advantage of using component scores instead of the original scores is that the former are uncorrelated. Even this will not be true if the weights obtained from one series are used for calculating component scores in a new series, and especially if the new series was obtained under different conditions of sampling.

Component scores (called factor scores in psychology) may sometimes be of interest, though it is usually difficult to interpret more than two or three. In depression rating scales, the first component is almost invariably one which measures severity of illness. The second component usually distinguishes between the anxious group of symptoms and the depressive group. Insofar as the components distinguish between groups of symptoms, they also classify them and, indirectly, classify patients in the same way.

Table I

	Severe	Moderate	Mild
Loss of Weight	+		
Vomiting	+	+	
Pain	+	+	+

Table II

Symptoms	P	Q	R
Group 1	+	+	+
Group 2		+	
Group 3		+	+

Table III

Symptoms	Q	R	P
Group 1	+	+	+
Group 3	+	+	
Group 2	+		

Table IV

Symptoms	P	Q	R	S	etc.
	+	+	+		
		+	+	+	
		+	+	+	+

Statisticians point out that when a variable is categorized into grades of severity, e.g., depression is rated as absent, mild, moderate or severe, such grades constitute a nominal scale. To allocate the numbers 0, 1, 2 and 3 to them in order to use these numbers as if they were true measurements implies that the grades constitute a difference scale, i.e., that the difference between absent and mild is equal to the difference between mild and moderate and the difference between moderate and severe. Furthermore, when such data are used in the ordinary metrical statistical tests, it implies that they constitute a true ratio scale, i.e., that "moderate" is twice as severe as "mild" and that "severe" is three times as much. They therefore conclude that only nonparametric statistical tests are appropriate for such data. This is perfectly true. One solution to this difficulty would be to replace the usual simple scores by scores which are based on the assumption that the frequency distribution of these grades is derived from a normal distribution. This is equivalent to giving a differential weighting system to the grades of the variables. It has already been pointed out that little is to be gained from using a differential weighting system for the variables and even less would be gained by using such a system for the grades of variables; the greater the number of items in a scale the less would be gained.

POSTSCRIPT: A GUTTMAN SCALE FOR DEPRESSION

One type of scale which has been largely ignored in psychiatry is the Guttman Scale (1944). The essential point of this type of scale is that the items have an order and this order is determined by the pattern of responses to the items. The pattern is such that when the items are placed in the correct order, then a positive response to any one item presupposes a positive response to all items below it and a negative response to all those above. A grossly oversimplified example will help to make the principle clear. All patients suffering from active duodenal ulcer will complain of pain, even the mildest cases. Patients who also suffer from vomiting will be regarded as more ill and the most severe cases will also complain of loss of weight. (Loss of weight may occur without vomiting, but as this is relatively uncommon it will be ignored). Table I puts the foregoing statements into succinct form.

All patients who have loss of weight also suffer from vomiting and pain; all who vomit also have pain; it is this relationship between the symptoms that produces the triangular pattern in the table.

Consider now three symptoms found in a group of patients. The patients can be sorted out into three groups such that the first consists of patients who have all three symptoms, the second have only one, and the third have two symptoms.

The symptoms and groups of patients can be rearranged as follows:

The triangular pattern shows clearly that all patients who show P also show Q and R, and all who show R also show Q. The symptoms show an *order*, which in this case has been assumed to be related to severity, but could be related to some other property. The order may show itself in another way, e.g., as a disease progresses the symptoms pertaining to the earlier stages may disappear, or the more severe cases may not show the symptoms of the milder form of the disease. In this case the table will show a parallelogram instead of a triangle:

Such patterns are the characteristic of a Guttman Scale, and the items which constitute such a scale have two important properties: they have an order and they are unidimensional; i.e., they are related to or measure one variable.

The correct method of construcing a Guttman Scale, which depends solely on the relation between the items, was not used here. Instead, a more simple device was used, because the patients were rated for intensity of symptoms at the same time as the items in the check list were checked off. The items of the check list could therefore be related to the severity of the symptom, i.e., to an external criterion.

ANALYSIS OF ITEMS IN "DEPRESSIVE MOOD"

Only the items concerned with Depressed Mood will be considered here. The first stage is shown in Fig. 1.

On the left of the figure is a list of items and on the right is the number of patients for whom these items were checked. At the bottom is shown the rating of the patients. It will be seen that no patients received a rating of less than 2 points for depressed mood. The figure shows that, for example, twelve patients compained that they wept frequently, and of these one was rated at 2 points for depressed mood, one at 5 points, nine were given a rating of 6 points, and one was given 8 points. The number of patients who were given ratings of 5 and 8 is very few and none were given ratings of 7; for this reason it is convenient to group the patients together, and this is shown in Fig. 2.

It is evident that there is a triangular pattern beginning to appear. This diagram is simple and easy to interpret but it is unsatisfactory, partly because it is unsuitable for a large number of cases (because all the squares would be filled in), but chiefly because the order of the items is determined by their frequency. The item at the top was checked seven times, the frequency increasing until the item at the bottom which was checked forty-two times.

The layout in Fig. 3 gives more information but it is less clear.

The bottom line shows that of the forty-eight men recorded in Fig. 3 eight received a rating of 2 points for depression, six of 3 points, nineteen of 4 points, and fifteen of 5–8 points. The figures on the right of the diagram show the mean rating of all the patients for whom the item on the left was checked as being present. For example, for the item "Feels depressed obviously," all the patients (100%) who scored 5–8 points had this item checked off. This is also true for all those who scored 3 points on this rating. Almost all the patients who scored 2

Depression (0-8)

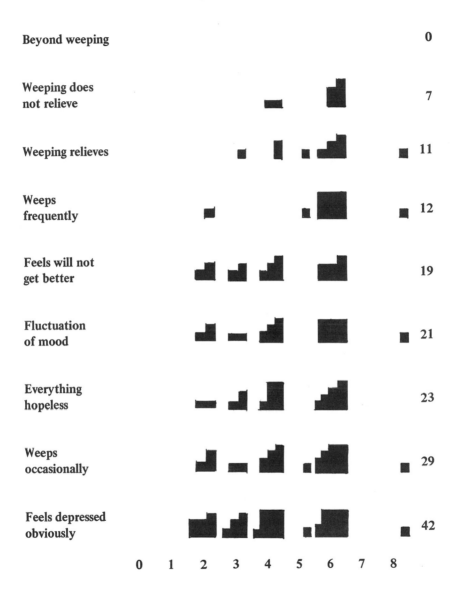

Fig. 1

Depression (0-8)

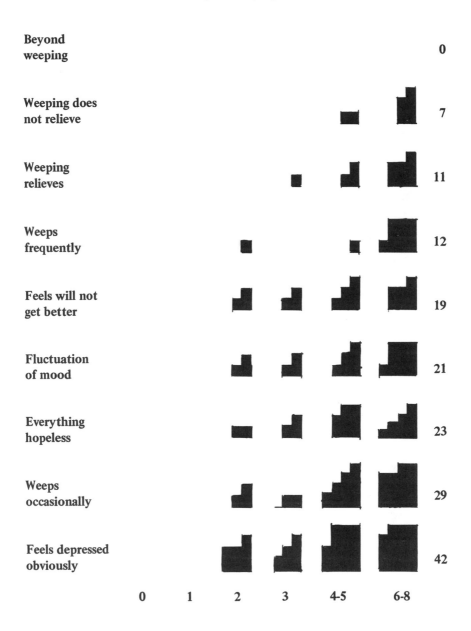

Fig. 2

Depression % (48 Men)
In order of Mean rating

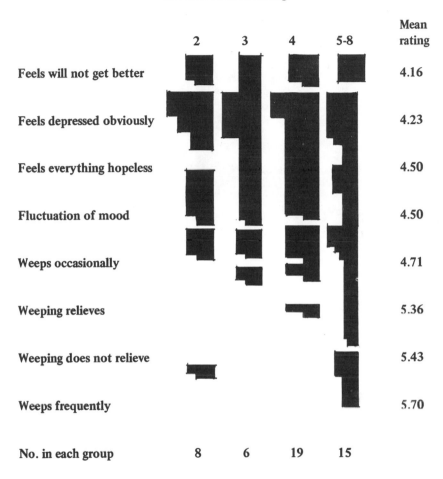

Fig. 3

points were checked off and not quite so many of those who scored 4 points. The mean rating of all the patients who complained of feeling obviously depressed was 4.23. Similarly for the item "Weeping does not relieve depression," nearly half of the patients who scored 5–8 said that weeping did not relieve their feelings; about an eighth of those who scored 4 said the same; and no patients who rated 3 points or 2 points said that this item applied to them. The average rating for the patients who said that weeping did not relieve their feelings was 5.43. It is clear that a fair approximation to a triangular pattern has been achieved.

Depression % (93 Women)
In order of Mean rating

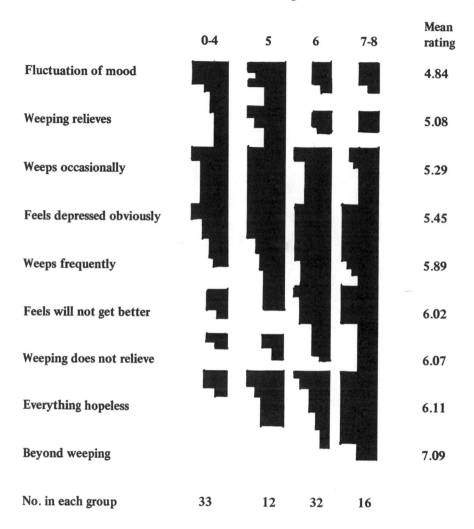

	0-4	5	6	7-8	Mean rating
Fluctuation of mood					4.84
Weeping relieves					5.08
Weeps occasionally					5.29
Feels depressed obviously					5.45
Weeps frequently					5.89
Feels will not get better					6.02
Weeping does not relieve					6.07
Everything hopeless					6.11
Beyond weeping					7.09
No. in each group	33	12	32	16	

Fig. 4

Table V

48 Men		93 Women	
Item	Mean rating	Item	Mean rating
Beyond weeping	—	Beyond weeping	7.1
Weeps frequently	5.7	Feels everything hopeless	6.1
Weeping does not relieve	5.4	Weeping does not relieve	6.1
Weeping relieves	5.4	Feels will not get better	6.0
Weeps occasionally	4.7	Weeps frequently	5.9
Fluctuation of mood	4.5	Feels depressed obviously	5.5
Feels everything hopeless	4.5	Weeps occasionally	5.3
Feels depressed obviously	4.2	Weeping relieves	5.1
Feels will not get better	4.2	Fluctuation of mood	4.8

Fig. 4 corresponds to Fig. 3 but is derived from the results obtained from ninety-three female patients.

Even a cursory glance shows that the pattern here is not so much a triangle as a parallelogram. Looking back at Fig. 3, it would appear that there is just a slight suggestion that this may be true for the men as well. It is a point of interest that the women have obtained higher scores on depression than the men.

COMPARISON BETWEEN MEN AND WOMEN

Table V gives the items placed in order of mean rating for the men and the women. It is very obvious that the women tend to score higher than the men, but it would be a great mistake to assume that this meant that the women were more depressed than the men. It may well be that the assessors, being men, were more sympathetic toward the female patients, or that women manifest their depressed mood more easily or more detectably.

Difference between the sexes in the symptoms of depression are shown by the relative positions of items. Thus the appearance of a pessimistic outlook signifies a greater severity of depression in women than in men; in the former those who feel everything is hopeless or who believe they will not get better have a mean rating of 6.1 and 6.0, whereas in the latter the means are 4.5 and 4.2. What is more to the point is that these items come second and fourth in women but seventh and ninth in men. The reverse is shown in the items concerning weeping: in men frequent weeping comes second and occasional weeping fifth, whereas in women these items come fifth and seventh. This may be a manifestation of the different cultural pressures on men and women with respect to weeping. Nowadays, girls are about as much discouraged as boys from weeping when upset, but this was certainly not true when these middle-aged patients were young. The table gives more information on many other matters of interest which could well serve as starting points for research. This is one of the great assets of the Guttman scale, that it permits of a more subtle analysis of the clinical phenomena than is possible with other methods.

COMMENTARIES

DR. RASKIN: Professor Hamilton has cited a number of important deficiencies in the rating scales now in use for assessing psychopathology in depressed patients. I find myself in agreement with most of his comments and suggestions and would therefore like to elaborate on his remarks rather than raise objections to them.

Professor Hamilton noted the popularity of global assessments of illness or improvement among clinicians because these judgments are in accordance with clinical practice. However, he went on to state that the meaning of these ratings is often obscure, as raters differ in the weights they assign to certain symptoms in making these ratings. He also made a brief reference to a variant of these global judgments, i.e., a total pathology score, which I would like to discuss in greater detail.

An approach that is very popular these days for assessing drug efficacy in depression is to derive a total pathology score from an instrument such as the Brief Psychiatric Rating Scale (BPRS) or Hamilton Depression Scale (HDS). Generally, this is done by a simple summation of the scale values for the items in the rating instrument. Unfortunately, a number of brief depression inventories contain a series of items sampling one aspect of depression and ignore other aspects of the illness. Consequently, it is not only conceivable but highly likely that a patient could get a higher total pathology score on one rating instrument than on another, depending on the emphasis given to his particular symptoms in the two depression inventories.

These differences among instruments can have a significant impact in evaluating drug effects and in the type of patient admitted to a study when a total pathology score is used as either an outcome measure or as a criterion for entry into a study. Suppose a rating instrument contains fifteen items and three of these items sample various forms of sleep disturbance, i.e., initial insomnia, middle insomnia and late insomnia. Evidence from the National Institutes of Mental Health collaborative depression studies (Raskin et al., 1967, 1969; Schulterbrandt et al., 1974) indicated that for most patients there was a high correlation among these forms of sleep disturbance and many patients with initial insomnia also experienced middle and late insomnia. Consequently, a patient with sleep disturbances is likely to attain a high total pathology score on this inventory. As a criterion or outcome measure, this pathology score is likely to be especially sensitive to drugs with marked sedative-hypnotic effects, and drugs with these effects will show a greater reduction in the total pathology score than drugs with mild or no sedative-hypnotic effects. This total pathology score would therefore work to the advantage of sedative-hypnotic drugs and against drugs with activating or energizing effects.

When these total pathology scores are used as an entry criterion, it is to ensure that patients admitted to the study have at least a specified minimum amount of quantifiable depression. If we again use the example cited above of an instrument that gives undue weight to one aspect of depression such as sleep disturbances, then there is a good chance of including a disproportionate number of patients with sleep disturbances in the study. Unfortunately, sleep disturbances occur more often in older than in younger patients, which would add a further biasing effect to the study results.

Instead of using a total pathology score for evaluating drug effects, I prefer to rely either on a series of global items or on derived factor scores which sample the ten or fifteen major dimensions of depression such as depressed mood, anxiety-tension, guilt-worthlessness, sleep disturbances, etc. Drugs have different pharmacological profiles and clinical effects which are often masked by the use of a total pathology score. The use of separate scores for the various symptoms of depression permits one to identify differential drug effects.

I am not opposed to the use of a quantified index or amount of depression as a criterion for entry into a study evaluating treatment effects. In fact, I favor this approach, as it provides a direct means for comparing patient samples across studies, which may have a bearing on reported differences in treatment effects. What is needed, however, is a measure of severity of depression that does not give undue weight to one or two of the major symptoms of depression. In the collaborative depression studies we used an approach which partially overcame this problem. After interviewing the patient, two psychiatrists or a psychiatrist and psychologist independently rated the patient on three 5-point scales measuring amount of depression in the patient's verbal reports, his behavior, and the secondary symptoms of depression. Cues were provided for evaluating each of these three global items. For example, the cues for rating the verbal report item were: "Says he feels blue," "Talks of feeling helpless, hopeless, or worthless," "Complains of loss of interest," "May wish he were dead," and "Reports crying spells." To be admitted to the study, the patient had to attain a total score of at least 9 on these three items. As each item was rated on a 5-point scale, this meant that a patient could not get into the study solely on the basis of appearing depressed, or of complaints of feeling blue, or of reports of secondary symptoms of depression such as insomnia and G.I. complaints.

Professor Hamilton also indicated there was a tendency for the inter-rater reliability of rating scales to decrease at the later evaluation periods when the patient was over the acute phase of his illness. This is a well-known phenomenon and is generally due to the fact that the total variance in the instrument declines dramatically as patients improve and small differences between raters are therefore magnified in computing the reliability estimates. The variance declines because these instruments generally are heavily loaded with items that sample severe forms of psychopathology, and as patients improve these symptoms disappear. Instruments are needed that sample mild and moderate forms of psychopathology as well as the more severe aspects of a depressive illness. In addition to increasing inter-rater reliability, these instruments would also be especially useful in follow-up studies.

Professor Hamilton rightfully pointed up some important deficiencies with patient self-report inventories. However, there is one area of psychopathology in depression in which I feel the patient is the most reliable source of information. I am referring to the mood or affective component of depression. Rationally, the patient would appear to be the best source for rating his inner states and mood. This impression was confirmed in the NIMH collaborative depression studies in which a mood scale completed by the study patients was one of the best instruments for discerning statistically significant treatment effects (Raskin et al., 1970).

Finally, I would like to conclude by commending Professor Hamilton on his efforts to devise a rating scale for depression that utilizes a Guttman scale. As he indicates, a Guttman scale avoids a number of statistical criticisms that have been leveled at frequency of occurrence ("seldom," "occasionally," "quite often") and intensity scales ("a little," "moderately," "quite a bit"). Frequency of occurrence and intensity scales assume equal intervals between scale points which is often not the case, i.e., that "moderately" is twice as much as "a little." However, I do not envy Professor Hamilton's task of devising test items that meet the criteria of a Guttman scale. I feel the psychopathology manifest in depressive illness does not generally lend itself to this approach. For example, how would one order symptoms such as "crying spells," "thoughts of death and dying," and "difficulty in falling asleep." Although these symptoms occur in some patients, they do not necessarily order themselves on a severity of illness or diagnostic dimension so that the presence of one of these symptoms automatically presumes the presence or absence of the other two.

DR. CONNERS: It is very encouraging to see psychiatrists beginning to pay some attention to this kind of methodological issue. I know of the successful use of the Guttman scale in a few cases, for example in Schutz's scale, which is very carefully constructed to develop three dimensions having to do with interpersonal distance based on the Guttman scale. It is truly far superior to many other forms of scaling in that area. I have a few random thoughts that occurred to me as Dr. Hamilton was speaking. First, in the issue of the global judgment vs. the use of a scale, these are in fact two forms of scaling. A global judgment is a form of category scale. In a category scale, there are only two points on the scale, zero and one. It is a question then of utility, of whether or not one could make finer discriminations than presence or absence. Let us consider the frequency distribution of scales, such as adjective check lists. If one takes an adjective check list and makes it a 5-point scale instead of a yes or no, one may find that virtually all of the information given by the respondent can be captured by simply dividing the response on a 2-point scale instead of on a 5-point scale. This is a question of the discriminative power of the observer, and presumably as a psychiatrist or clinician becomes more skilled in making subtle distinctions, he ought to have a scale which reflects that. The fact that as one increases the number of steps on a scale one doesn't necessarily add information means that it is an empirical question and a practical matter, whether one uses a global judgment or not. I would refer to a study that Bob Sprague did with children in which he took my 39-item scale and compared it with a scale in which the teacher simply said "better" or "worse"; the correlation was very high. In that case it was just as well for the teacher to say "It was better" or "It was worse" as it was to use this complex scale.

There is another issue which I think is perhaps more important in treatment studies than reliability or validity, and that is sensitivity. There is a form of validity, I suppose, but one could have a highly reliable and valid scale for distinguishing between different states of the disease which is absolutely insensitive to treatments. In Raymond Cattell's work on scaling, he always makes the distinction between a *state* and a personality *trait* in the scale.

I also agree that scales having to do with external factors such as social adjustment or work efficiency probably have been grossly underused. The self-report issue is an interesting one. In fact, many of the judgments that a clinician makes on his rating are from the self-reports of the patient. Now the question is: Why isn't it then more efficient and reliable to use the self-report of the patient in the first place? If he says he is sad, why isn't it better for him to say that he is sad rather than for you to rate him sad? Obviously, the clinician must make some sort of transformation; otherwise, there is no additional value. That transformation is the question he places in some kind of context that gives it some weight. But, in fact, he is most often using data that is self-reported. I would like not to see a sort of antithesis but a combination. It is a regression issue in the sense that one should have self-report scales along with the observer scales, and then see what combination of these scales predicts best for the purpose at hand.

Finally, it seems to me that one can go too far in the direction of scaling in the sense that one spuriously assumes that somehow having a more refined judgment is both more reliable and valid. This sometimes is absolutely false. A good example is the study that Dr. Werry did in New Zealand on the activity level of hyperactive kids and the effects of haloperidol. He used a sort of classical time sampling observation scale with very refined categories. These are highly reliable and their face validity is very high. But it turns out that that system is absolutely unpredictive of treatment response, whereas a simpler adjective check list is. Why is that? I think the answer is that the human observer does, in fact, do a lot of on-line computing. For example, when you ask a teacher or a clinician, "Is this person sad or is he experiencing excitement?" You have in mind a standard of numerous patients that you have seen before against which you place this particular observation; this evaluation therefore might be much more meaningful than a more molecular judgment in which you are simply saying the patient weeps, the patient does this or that, which is very precise for the number of tears that flow, but quite uninformative without relating the behavior to a larger context. I have always thought that psychiatry should use a sort of middle level of observation, neither very molecular judgments nor very global judgments, but something in between.

DR. GALLANT: As Dr. Weissman will emphasize in her paper, uniform selection criteria are lacking in depressive studies and a number of other psychopharmacologic areas of investigation. Dr. Hamilton states this problem in clear terms, and it is quite apparent that future collaborative studies must utilize a uniform approach in the criteria of patient selection. Otherwise, no additional valid information will result from future psychopharmacologic studies which attempt to delineate drug differences in regard to therapeutic efficacy and target symptom response.

Concerning the search for improved measures of depression, it is my strong feeling that specific factors evaluating *formal thought disorder* as well as *ideational* and emotional *content* have to be incorporated into most of these psychologic scales if we are to accomplish the goal of delineating drug differences in the depressive syndrome (or in any other psychiatric disease or syndrome). Ianzito's data on the prognostic and diagnostic value of *formal thought disorder* in speech and thought pattern disturbances in contrast to *ideational content,* which is more responsive to specific questions, emphasizes the importance of distinguishing these two areas of thought disorder (Ianzito et al., 1974). The results of the study by Ianzito and his associates showed that the presence of formal thought disorder was associated with a more serious prognosis for depressive illness and more likely to indicate the diagnosis of schizophrenia.

DR. HAMILTON: A number of points have been raised in the discussion. First of all, concerning the question of the correlations, they do indeed depend upon the variance. If you take a narrow range of severity, the correlation will decrease. But I am querying Dr. Conners' statement that the clinican bases his opinion on the patient's statements. I am sorry but this is quite untrue. If I ask a patient, "Have you ever thought of doing away with yourself?" and he states at me for a second with a sort of panic-striken expression on his face, turns red or pale and swallows hard, and then he says, "No," I put him down as being suicidal. In other words, it is not the patients' statements but the totality of their behavior, and one of the important things about training in psychiatry is precisely that it teaches the psychiatrist to learn to observe the patient's behavior and to interpret it appropriately. In turn, too great refinement of the scales may sometimes be misleading, but again and again we have reports by investigators who complain that there are difficulties in getting adequate information concerning differences which they are convinced are present but which the scales they use or the methods of judgment they use have not been able to delineate. The most obvious one is the use of so-called global judgments. I am referring not only to global judgments about mood but also to the totality of symptoms. There is no question that this is the great advantage of the use of scales rather than global judgments because they give information about the details of the symptoms and the patient's condition. It is noticeable to me, for example, when using scales, that the depressive symptoms tend to diminish before anxieties decrease. Many patients who never lose all of their symptoms do not come down to a low score on the rating scale because they still retain many of their anxieties, even though they have lost most of their depressive symptoms. This is then one of the reasons for using itemized scales. Clinical judgments are a very obscure way of recording information about the patients.

I want to emphasize that the self-rating scales and the observation scales have very different functions. They really are recording only a moderate amount of common variance. The self-rating scale records what the patient feels within and this can be very important. For example, the manic patients may be full of jokes and activity to the observer, but if you ask them how they feel, they may say that inwardly they feel very depressed and hopeless. Thus there may be significant differences between the external and internal manifestations of emotional and mental illness.

Self-rating scales, used alone, can produce misleading results. We recognize that the patient should be sufficiently literate to be able to read in order to answer the questions, but we do not take enough cognizance of the differences in interpretation of words we use. I know from my own experience that it is useless to ask a patient if he or she is depressed. Patients use the word depression to mean anything but depression. They use it to mean anxiety, preoccupation, loss of interest, aggression, all sorts of things, but not to mean what we mean by depression. I suspect that, in the United States, social and racial differences as related to the different cultural patterns may result in a use of the same words with somewhat different meanings. This is the point of the observer's scale, the business of the clinician to penetrate to the meaning of what the patient is saying and to see the underlying illness.

DR. RASKIN: I would just like to make one minor point. It has to do with the correlation between the self-report and the psychiatry report or the observer report. In one of our studies, we had the patient complete a mood scale, and then we had the nurse complete the mood scale for the patient based on his behavior and those correlations were very high. On the other hand, if you correlated the patient's mood scale with the psychiatrist symptom rating scale, correlations weren't very high, which is somewhat like correlating apples and oranges. In other words, the mood or affective component of depression generally is not well represented on symptom rating scales, so you are getting two different aspects of behavior. This goes back to my experience when I was working with Dr. Lorr in outpatient psychotherapy trials. In these trials, the mood scales completed by the patients tended to be relatively sensitive to treatment effects. However, you also have to be selective in your choice of a mood scale. For example, the Clyde Mood Scale, developed for use with schizophrenics, may not work too well with depressed patients because it does not contain many of the items that sample a depressed patient's behavior.

DR. HAMILTON: I think that is a very good point. One should recognize that the scale is designed for a particular purpose, and to use a scale outside its purpose puts one on very unsure grounds. It is perfectly possible to take an anxiety scale designed for neurotic anxiety reactions, apply it to depressed or schizophrenic patients with anxiety, and arrive at a false conclusion. One cannot transfer scale results or make cross-comparisons in this manner.

REFERENCES

Beck, P., Gram, L. F., Dein, E., Jacobsen, O., Vitger, J., and Bolwig, T. G. (1974, in press). Quantitative ratings of depressive states. Correlation between clinical assessment, self-rating scale (Beck) and objective rating scale (Hamilton). *Psychol. Med.*

Bojanosky, J., and Chloupkova, K. (1966). Bewertungsskala der depressionzustande. *Psychiat. Neurol. Bael.* 151:54–61.

Brown, G. L., and Zung, W. W. K. (1972). Depression scales: self or physician rating? A validation of certain clinically observable phenomena. *Compr. Psychiat.* 13:361–67.

Coppen, A., Noguera, R., Bailey, J., Burns, B. H., Swane, M. S., Hare, E. H., Gardner, R., and Magge, R. (1971). Prophylactic lithium in affective disorders. *Lancet* II:276.

Downing, R. W., and Rickels, K. (1972). Some properties of the Popoff index. *Clin. Med.* 79:11–18.

Garside, R. F., Kay, D. W. K., Roy, J. R., and Beamish, P. (1970). M. P. I. scores and depression. *Brit. J. Psychiat.* 116:429–32.

Guttman, L. (1944). The quantification of a class of attributes. In S. A. Stouffer, ed., *The Prediction of Personal Adjustment.* New York: Social Science Research Council.

Ianzito, B. M., Cadoret, R. J., and Pugh, D. P. (1974). Thought disorder in depression. *Am. J. Psychiat.* 131:703–07.

Kerekjarto, M. von, and Lienert, G. A. (1970). Depressionsakalin als forschungsmittal inder psychopathologie. *Pharmakopsychiat. Neuro-Psychopharmakol.* 3:1–21.

Lubin, B. (1965). Adjective check lists for measurement of depression. *Arch. Gen. Psychiat.* 12:57–62.

Metcalfe, M., and Goldman, E. (1965). Validation of an inventory for measuring depression. *Brit. J. Psychiat.* 111:240–42.

Paykel, E. S., Weissman, M., Prusoff, B. A., and Tonks, C. M. (1971). Dimensions of social adjustment in depressed women. *J. Nerv. Ment. Dis.* 152:158–72.

Pinard, G., and Tetreault, L. (1974). Concerning semantic problems in psychological evaluation. In P. Pichot, ed., *Psychological Measurements in Psychopharmacology.* Basel: Karger.

Raskin, A., Schulterbrandt, J. G., et al. (1967). Factors of psychopathology in interview, ward behavior and self-report ratings of hospitalized depressives. *J. Consult. Psychol.* 31:270–78.

————, Schulterbrandt, J. G., et al. (1969). Replication of factors of psychopathology in interview, ward behavior and self-report ratings of hospitalized depressives. *J. Nerv. Ment. Dis.* 148:87–98.

————, Schulterbrandt, J. G., et al. (1970). Differential response to chlorpromazine, imipramine and placebo: a study of subgroups of hospitalized depressed patients. *Arch. Gen. Psychiat.* 23:164–73.

Schulterbrandt, J. G., Raskin, A., et al. (1974). Further replication of factors of psychopathology in the interview, ward behavior and self-report ratings of hospitalized depressed patients. *Psychol. Rep.* 34:23–32.

Schwab, J. J., Bialow, M. R., and Holger, C. G. (1967). A comparison of 2 rating scales for depression. *J. Clin. Psychol.* 23:94–96.

Snaith, R. P., Ahmed, S. N., Mehta, S., and Hamilton, M. (1971). The assessment of the severity of primary depressive illness. *Psychol. Med.* 1:143–49.

Tan, B. K. (1969). Ein voorlopig onderzoek naar de praktische brulkberheid van drie vertaalde depressieschalen. *Bull. Coord. Comm. Biochem. Onderzooch* 3:49–57.

Wechsler, H., Grosser, G. H., and Busfield, B. L., Jr. (1963). The depression rating scale. *Arch. Gen. Psychiat.* 9:334–43.

Zealley, A. K., and Aitken, R. C. B. (1969). Measurement of mood. *Proc. RSM* 6-2:993–96.

Zung, W. W. K. (1972). The depression status inventory: an adjunct to the self-rating depression scale. *J. Clin. Psychol.* 28:539–43.

CHAPTER VII

Classification and Treatment of Childhood Depression and Depressive Equivalents

C. K. Conners

A recent comprehensive review by Nissen (1971) points out that the literature on childhood depression shows at least five different ways of viewing depressive symptoms: depressive moods are unknown in children; all types of childhood depression are "masked"; the symptoms do not differ from those in adults; the symptoms have a distinct psychopathological expression in children; and the symptoms consist of specific psychosomatic or hypochondriacal expression. Depressive *moods* as a reaction to loss or stress are in fact quite common in children although perhaps not always evident due to the child's more limited vocabulary and cognitive system.

Many observers, especially psychoanalytically oriented ones, have described a depressive state occurring before five years of age, some as early as the first year of life. Mahler (1961) maintained that depression in adults is regularly preceded by depression in early infancy, a concept consistent with the view first proposed by Abraham (1953) of a primary parathymia or "Ur-depression," and later developed by Melanie Klein (1960) as the concept of a "depressive disposition" in infants. Spitz's (1946) work on "anaclitic depression" described a typical course of infant depression as progressing from a stage of protest, to withdrawal, to apathy. His observations on deprived children suffering from "hospitalism" included the fact that the children had a characteristic forlorn and woebegone facies, disturbances of appetitive and sleep functions, disruption of motility patterns, and developmental arrest. (The term "anaclitic" was used by Freud in his classic formulation of

Mourning and Melancholia [Freud, 1957] to refer to the child's love for his parents which is based upon the biologic and instinctual dependence of the child upon the parent.)

Freud's position has, of course, served as the basis of most subsequent thinking by psychoanalytic theorists. This position holds that adult depressions are usually triggered by a loss which elicits memories of events associated with the loss of love of some important individual in childhood. Having introjected the love object, the child's anger against that object is turned against the self. As Ostow (1970) says, ". . . it is important to keep in mind that the essence of the psychology of depression lies in the struggle between the patient and the one he loves." In these formulations, the early infant or childhood dependency forms the basis upon which subsequent experiences of bereavement or loss evoke a depressive reaction. This theory has promoted a good deal of research on the role of early bereavement as a cause of subsequent depression in adults, a subject we will review presently.

Controversy over the existence of a depressive syndrome in middle childhood (the "latency" period) is much more marked. Some authors, such as Rie (1966), maintain that classical depressive disorders cannot occur in children because of their inadequate superego formation and lack of an adequate concept of future time which would allow them to develop a sense of hopelessness, which he sees as the primary cause of the typical despair of the depressed state. There is also controversy regarding the existence of manic-depressive disorders in childhood.

Because the child is in a continual process of development, most authors stress the fact that the expression of depressive tendencies in children will be conditioned by the particular stage of development and show itself in diverse manifestations, either for defensive reasons or because the repertoire of cognitive and affective behaviors is limited (Rie, 1966; Toolan, 1962; Malmquist, 1971). This raises the problem of "depressive equivalents" or "masked depression," especially among adolescents. Under this concept, sadness, inhibition, guilt and a sense of impending doom are absent or rarely noted; instead, a single dominant symptom or group of symptoms, most frequently phobic-obsessive, neurasthenic, or conduct disorders, will be found. This approach requires that some decision rules must be formulated in order to ascertain that the "equivalents" are in some way related to the primary depression. As one author suggests, the diagnosis of depressive equivalents in childhood or adolescence is made when it is possible to observe in the same patient the coexistence of true psychopathological substrates of depression and clinical aspects which are dependent on these substrates but not characteristic of depression, as, for example, when it is observed over time that an adolescent acts out when not depressed, and does not act out when depressed (Mastropaolo, 1972).

The problem with the various formulations referred to thus far is that they explain either too little or too much. At the one end of the spectrum, there is little doubt that severe reactions to loss occur in children and infants and that sad affect can be inferred from overt behavior, especially in infants as described by Spitz. This approach, however, fails to explain how these early states become transmuted into the typical forms of depression in later life, require often untestable assumptions, and are so qualitatively different from (though overlapping with) adult depressions, that their explanatory value is quite weak. On the other hand, if most or all of the symptoms and signs are qualitatively different "equivalents" from those found in adults, the concept of depression can be used to explain virtually all psychopathological expressions in childhood and adolescence.

It is possible, however, that adult concepts of depression can serve a useful heuristic function in pointing to certain clinical manifestations, precipitating factors, and biological variations that might otherwise fail to be interrelated. Ideally, one would like to emerge with a well-defined list of signs and symptoms, the causes for those symptoms, and the ability to predict the course and outcome, including the role of different treatments for the different types of disorder. As we shall see, although there is some merit to the concept of a depressive illness that begins in early childhood, adequate data still remain to be collected on a number of important issues.

BEREAVEMENT AND REACTIVE DEPRESSION IN CHILDREN

If it were possible to identify some common antecedent of a depressed state—assuming that the latter could be defined by some set of objective criteria—an important step would be taken toward an explanation of the disorder. One might at least be able to identify a "reactive" depression in contrast to other, possibly biologically conditioned forms of the disorder by establishing that a patient had a significant loss or bereavement at some stage of development. Even though the form of expression of the disorder might vary considerably, a highly correlated antecedent of depression in adults could lead to a clear picture of the origin of the depressive process and to the interrelating of diverse clinical phenomena in children.

Felix Brown (1972) has proposed that bereavement and loss are the most common cause of depression, with the incidence of bereavement before age fifteen increased among adult depressives to about double that of controls. He studied 331 depressed patients compared with 296 controls from general practice and found that the death of fathers was more common and just as significant as that of mothers in the history of depressed patients. Dennehy (1966) found an excess of male depressives who had lost mothers and of female depressives who had lost their fathers. Ripley and Dorpat (Ripley et al., 1965) found a high rate of bereavement among adult suicides, and Greer (1966), among attempted suicides. Hill and Price (1967), comparing depressed and nondepressed inpatients, found a raised incidence of loss of fathers occurring between the ages of ten to fourteen in female patients. Beck (Beck et al., 1963) used Beck's Depression Index and showed that 27 percent of those high on the index had a loss before the age of sixteen compared with 12 percent for controls. The figures for clinical ratings of severely depressed patients were 36.4 percent vs. 15.2 percent for controls.

Arthur and Kemme (1964) conducted an intensive case study of the families of eighty-three disturbed children who had experienced the death of a parent; they found a high incidence of both intellectual and emotional problems directly or indirectly related to the loss, with extremely variable forms of expression of the anxiety and depression. Caplan and Douglas (1969) compared a group of seventy-one depressed children who demonstrated a "persistent and severe sad mood" with a control group of "mixed neurotics." "For almost every type of separation studied, that is, separation due to death, divorce, desertion, illness or foster home placement, the percentage of depressive subjects was higher than that of the mixed neurotic control group."

Thus it would appear that childhood bereavement has a significant likelihood of eventuating in either childhood or adult forms of depression. However, these results are at variance with those of Pitts (Pitts et al., 1965) and Gregory (1966), who found no raised incidence of childhood bereavement in depressive or other patients. Similarly, Lokare (1972) compared the scores of 567 normal controls and 170 clinic children on two scales of a modified Maudsley Personality Inventory and found that "children with depression show no greater liability than a group of control patients to parental deprivation or object loss." Nevertheless, even "partial maternal deprivation" has been shown to be more likely in the histories of children diagnosed as depressed (Remschmidt et al., 1972), and careful studies of suicides and suicide attempts in adolescents (Otto, 1972) show a raised incidence of object loss, especially in early childhood.

These conflicting results might be accounted for by a number of obvious factors such as differences in diagnostic criteria, but another explanation is suggested by the report of d'Elia and Perris (1972), who found that it is among unipolar depressives that one finds an increased incidence of bereavement. Most of the studies did not differentiate between unipolar and bipolar depression, either in the adults or the children studied, nor did they classify the cases according to the presence of a history of depression in the parents; therefore, conflicting results might be due to the operation of a biological variable leading to samples of different composition in different studies. They report that the mean value from eight papers on childhood bereavement was 26 percent among patients and 17 percent for controls, but the figure is significantly lower among bipolar depressives. Also, the age of onset of depressive illness is nearly ten years lower if the depression is unipolar and home conditions are poor, suggesting that these depressions reflect early reactions to environmental stress. This finding is entirely consonant with the theories of object loss and early bereavement proposed by many authors among the psychoanalytic school, as long as one separates unipolar and bipolar variants.

CLASSIFICATION, SIGNS AND SYMPTOMS

Cytryn and McKnew (1972) describe a classification scheme that grew out of a research project at D. C. Children's Hospital. They state:

> We think in terms of depressive illness rather than of depressive affect when the depression is of long duration (of at least several months) and is associated with severe impairment of the child's scholastic and social adjustment and with disturbances of the vegetative functions, especially those of food intake and sleep. [p. 152]

Restricting themselves to neurotic depressive reactions of mid-childhood, they find three categories. Masked depression, which is the most frequent, refers to children whose personalities and families display severe psychopathology and whose typical clinical features include hyperactivity, aggressive behavior, psychosomatic illness, hypochondriasis and delinquency. "In such cases the underlying depression is largely inferred from periodic displays of a purely depressive picture and from depressive themes on projective tests such as the Rorschach, Thematic Apperception Test (TAT), figure drawings and fantasy material." The second category, a more purely depressive syndrome, includes symptoms of persistent sad affect, social withdrawal, hopelessness, helplessness, psychomotor retardation, anxiety, school and social failure, sleep and feeding disturbances, and suicidal ideation or attempts. This group is further divided into an acute and chronic variety, depending upon the presence of a clearly identifiable object loss in the former case, and multiple losses and considerable psychopathology in the family, especially a history of depression in the latter.

This schema has the virtue of specifying the symptoms, premorbid history, precipitating factors, and duration of illness for the proposed forms of the illness. Unfortunately, no data are presented to clarify the frequency with which the diagnoses are made, the reliability of the judgments, or, most importantly, the differential course and treatment response of the three types. However, the effort is rare in attempting a straightforward definition along classical descriptive lines and could serve as the basis for screening, epidemiologic, genetic and treatment studies. It is interesting to note that the authors comment on the uncanny degree to which chronically depressed children mimic their parents' illness in age of onset, a phenomenon noted by others (Campbell, 1952). Although such phenomena are usually interpreted as imitative reactions along the lines suggested by Anna Freud (1965) in which the child "produced the mother's mood in themselves," one might conceive of such reactions as stage-specific genetically determined responses which emerge as the child undergoes some maturational or developmental shift.

Nissen (1971) studied 105 children admitted as inpatients to a hospital ward with moderate to severe grades of depressive states and mood swings. Although the English summary of his monograph does not indicate how depression was originally defined, the five most common symptoms found in children so diagnosed were difficulty in establishing contact, anxiety, inhibition, "outsider" and "uncertainty." These psychic symptoms were contrasted with psychosomatic ones: aggressiveness, enuresis, disturbed sleeping-waking rhythm, mutism and nail-biting. This sample excludes short-term depressive reactions, neglect-based depressions, and depressions secondary to other diagnoses. Nissen found that boys tended to show symptoms of difficulty in establishing contact with others, which combined with learning inhibitions and irritability lead to difficulties in school and aggressiveness, while girls tended toward brooding, quiet and inhibited behavior.

By a procedure not clear from the summary, various syndromes were defined and contrasted with respect to presenting symptoms, but "it did not prove possible to distinguish sets of depressive symptoms specific to certain syndromes which would have enabled a differential typology to be worked out." Approximately 17 percent of his sample parents had a clearly defined affective illness. Another interesting finding, albeit of unknown reliability, was the fact that only 55 percent of the children had normal EEG's. Follow-up of the cases failed to confirm the original diagnosis of suspected bipolar manic-depressive illness, though a number of children had become schizophrenic (N=9). Perhaps the most important finding in Nissen's study was the fact that symptoms of brooding, dysphoria, daydreaming, inhibition of learning, suicide attempts, "vital sadness," restlessness and mutism were prognostically highly unfavorable. "Mood swings" seemed to be a sure sign of impending schizophrenia rather than depressive disorder of adult life. Finally, "the diagnostic and nosological syndromes do not supply useful prognostic criteria for the subsequent development or course of the illness."

Poznanski and Zrull (1970) used as a primary criterion for selection of cases the child's appearance in the interview (sad, unhappy, depressed reaction) or a description by the child of similar affective states within himself. In addition, symptoms of self-criticism, feelings of inadequacy, difficulty sleeping, excessive concerns about death were required as criteria for selection. From a pool of ninety-eight records, only fourteen were selected for intensive study on the basis of having complete information. In these children, five symptoms were found that had been included in a set of nine symptoms used in a study from the Hampstead Clinic. These five symptoms were: child looked sad, unhappy, depressed; withdrawal; child expressed feelings of being unloved or rejected; insomnia; autoerotic activities. Negative self-image was the most frequent symptom seen. A mournful crying and withdrawal in some form ran through the case histories consistently. The authors comment that the depressed behavior was not reactive to an immediate loss but was more comparable to characterological depressions in adults in whom depression episodically occurs as a character defense. From a diagnostic point of view, the fact that some difficulty in the handling of aggression was the most frequent presenting complaint (twelve of fourteen) suggests that aggressive conduct disturbance may frequently be the result of a more complex depressive syndrome.

Another observation of interest from this study was the frequency of enuresis. Several observers have noted the high prevalence of primary enuresis among depressed children. In a family study, Mendelwicz and Klotz (1974) report that primary enuresis was the most frequently reported childhood disturbance among the offspring of their patients and occurred only in sons of bipolar probands. But among the 204 affectively ill probands, only one (a bipolar) reported enuresis in his childhood. Sacks (1974) observed that many of his patients with primary enuresis have parents with endogenous depressions and suggested that disturbance of sleep processes may be common to both disorders, a possible reason why imipramine may be useful in both disorders.

Frommer (1968) conducted a study of 190 depressed children contrasted with 74 neurotic children. She notes that "illness in childhood presents most commonly as a non-specific somatic malaise, often with abdominal pain as the reason for referral." Frommer is not clear as to the original criteria for making the diagnosis, but she compares the depressed children with neurotic children on the following symptoms, all of which are highly statistically significant in terms of greater frequency among depressives: irritability, weepiness, complaint of depression, tension and explosiveness, moodiness, difficulty getting off to sleep, and abdominal pain. The sample is undoubtedly biased toward somatic symptoms because of the nature of the general medical service for which this clinic serves a consultation function.

On the basis of response to treatment and general pattern of illness, Frommer divided the depressives into a phobic and nonphobic group, and the latter group was divided according to whether or not there was a past history of enuresis/encopresis. Thus she compares enuretic-depressives, depressives, phobic-depressives, and neurotics. The enuretic-depressives seem quite similar to the children described by Poznanski and Zrull (1970), and corresponds to Cytryn and McKnew's chronic depressive group. The description of these children suggests that they might well be diagnosed as cases of maturational lag or minimal brain dysfunction: "Over half gave a clinical impression of being immature for their age, or else showed evidence of immaturity in their tackling of the psychometric tests; nearly a third displayed antisocial behavior . . . ." Interestingly, almost half of this group also showed sleep difficulties, although this is also true of the other two depressive groups in contrast with neurotics. This group also showed the best response to amitriptyline.

The "uncomplicated depressive" group showed irritability, weepiness, and explosive and miserable behavior without adequate external cause. They had a high incidence of sleep disturbances, but of the form similar to adult depressives who wake unusually early or in the middle of the night. They tended to complain spontaneously of feeling depressed and had the most suicidal ideas. Unlike the enuretic-depressives, this group appeared warm and friendly, and in some respects conformed to the description given by Campbell (1952) of the cyclothymic children seen in his practice.

In a more recent survey of 200 children under five years of age referred to a psychiatric clinic, Frommer (Frommer et al., 1972) compared depressed, anxious and aggressive children and found that the group of depressed children showed the highest incidence of sleep disturbance, abdominal pain, enuresis and anorexia. Unfortunately, no information is given as to the criteria for defining depression itself. This depression group (N = 122) was the only group in which having a mentally ill mother was significantly more frequent, being found in 46 percent of the cases. Seventy-three percent showed disrupted sleep patterns and 65 percent had enuresis (after age three).

In the only study surveyed which used clearly defined operational criteria, Weinberg and associates (1973) used a set of criteria developed by Ling (Ling et al., 1970) for the detection of depression in children presenting with migraine. Those criteria are:

A. The presence of both symptoms I and II:
    I. Dysphoric mood
    II. Self-deprecatory ideation
B. Two or more of the following eight symptoms:
    III. Aggressive behavior (agitation)
    IV. Sleep disturbance
    V. A change in school performance
    VI. Diminished socialization
    VII. Change in attitude toward school
    VIII. Somatic complaints
    IX. Loss of usual energy
    X. Loss of usual energy
    X. Unusual change in appetite and/or weight
C. These symptoms had to represent a change in the child's usual behavior.
D. These symptoms had to be present for a period of more than one month.

The most significant finding for background characteristics of the depressed group of children (N = 45) was a positive family history for affective disorders: the depressed group showed 89 percent with a positive history compared with 30.7 percent of the nondepressed group. Binge drinking and alcoholism were significantly greater in families of depressed children. Twenty-seven of forty-two depressed children's mothers met the criteria for adult affective illness, and twelve were actively depressed. The depressed children also showed a high incidence of hyperactivity, school phobia, enuresis, temper tantrums and destructiveness. The differentiation of these complaints from those found in hyperkinetic children or other neurotic disturbances was possible because the symptoms tended to appear only when the children were depressed.

Bauersfeld (1972) found that approximately 13.7 percent of children referred to a child psychiatric clinic for learning and behavioral disturbances presented with depressive mood or other depressive conditions. Many of the children reported a wide variety of subjective somatic symptoms as well as neurotic complaints and antisocial behavior. It was noted that in most cases the development of chronic depression had passed unnoticed by the parents and teachers.

In another large series of over 10,000 children seen at a Turkish clinic (Cebiroglu et al., 1972), the incidence of depressive diagnosis for children was approximately 0.8 percent, with the bulk of these considered reactive depressions (82%). Like many authors, Cebiroglu and associates commented on the fact that the depression is usually hidden behind psychosomatic complaints, anxiety and hyperactivity.

MANIC-DEPRESSIVE PSYCHOSIS IN CHILDREN

In reviewing the literature on manic-depressive psychosis in children, Campbell (1952) notes that Kraepelin observed rare cases with onset before age ten, as did Bleuler. Kanner (1946) felt that the number of cases before age fifteen was negligible, but Kasanin reported ten cases, and several of the older generation of psychiatrists reported such cases in early or mid-childhood. Campbell described eighteen cases: one aged six; one, seven; one, ten; one, twelve; four, thirteen; five, fourteen; three, fifteen; two, sixteen. All of these cases were said to possess in their prepsychotic phase a cycloid type of personality, including an outgoing, likable disposition. They had a high drive to succeed, and there was nothing schizoid, introverted or eccentric about them; however, they seemed to feel they were ill with some force that interfered with their normal wishes and desires. Few precipitating factors could be found, and their lives at home were, in general, unremarkable. They had little insight and were not introspective or self-reflective. The presenting complaint in most cases was a change in mood. Campbell, unlike Frommer, observes that these patients seldom go to a physician because of somatic complaints.

A strong familial tendency was noted, with earlier onset in those with a stronger family history of affective disturbance, but early onset seemed not to predispose to more severe attacks or poorer prognosis. "Their psychiatric illnesses almost consistently developed 'out of the blue,' and there was a striking absence of introverted or schizoid features in the patients themselves . . . ." It is interesting to note that the four cases under age thirteen were all depressed types, without a previous manic episode. Campbell seems to have placed great emphasis on the family history in making his diagnosis, with fourteen of the eighteen cases having a diagnosis of manic-depressive illness among his patients, but on ten-year follow-up none of these diagnoses was supported. Cebiroglu (Cebiroglu et al., 1972) found only two cases of manic-depressive psychosis among the 10,661 examined over a ten-year period, but his description of these cases conforms to

Campbell's in that a cyclothymic personality, family history of psychosis, and intermittent attacks were present. His cases were aged twelve and sixteen. Frommer (1968) identified nineteen cases of children with cyclothymic personalities whom she describes as follows:

> They are children who display depressive features with extreme forms of temper outbursts alternating with brief states of reasonableness, or else a condition of continuous unconstructive mechanical activity quite out of contact and keeping with the normal requirements of their surroundings. They also frequently suffer from sleep disturbances. [p. 127]

The main difference between her findings and Campbell's was a much lower incidence of affective disorder in the parents (33%); family histories were also less positive for the disorder.

Eggers (1972) described cyclothymic episodes at the beginning and during the course of schizophrenic psychoses in fifty-three prepubertal children. It is not clear whether the primary disorder was schizophrenia or affective disturbance.

In summary, it is unclear to what extent true biphasic mood disturbances in the presence of psychotic disturbance of thinking processes actually occur in children before puberty. Some authors feel that it is much more common than recognized, but the clinical syndrome is much less convincing in their descriptions than the family history and cyclothymic personality trend. It seems reasonable to suppose that some characteristic personality features might be apparent in children whose parents or immediate family have manic-depressive illnesses, but the evidence makes it seem likely that the full-blown disease state is rarely observed before age thirteen. Some of the presumed cases are likely to include organic brain syndromes with a waxing and waning effect; hyperkinetic children often give the appearance of cyclic patterns because of a tendency to react poorly in some circumstances and not others. It may well be true that some forms of hyperactivity in children, some impulse-ridden adolescent mood changes, and some manic-depressive illness in adults are variations of the same disease caused by an underlying genetically determined chemical imbalance (Hava, 1973). Annell (1969) points out that the depressive manifestations of bipolar manic-depressive illness may only be apparent in children and is likely to be confused with the unipolar illness. Here the differentiation must be made between precipitating factors, family history and course of the illness rather than the clinical picture itself.

TREATMENT OF DEPRESSION IN CHILDREN

There is no question that the advent of antidepressant drugs has stimulated an interest in the concept of depressive states and depressive equivalents in children (Annell, 1972). With so much uncertainty regarding classification and diagnosis, it is hardly surprising that relatively little solid information is available on the treatment of depression in children.

Weinberg and associates (1973) recommended treatment with amitriptyline or imipramine to thirty-four depressed children, of whom nineteen accepted. These groups were reviewed three to seven months later and also were compared with a group of twenty-six nondepressed children. Results were that "Eighteen of the 19 in the depressed-treated group demonstrated definite improvements; 12 children had improved to the point where the family considered them recovered. None of this group had worsened. In contrast, only 6 of the 15 depressed nontreated children and 11 of the 26 nondepressed ones showed any improvement." There are a number of flaws in the study, including lack of double-blind nonobjective criteria of improvement, and lack of specification of dosage or side effects. However, there was a careful selection of patients, and this type of study deserves careful replication.

Frommer (1968) reported extensive use of amitriptyline, imipramine, phenelzine and isocarboxazid in her sample of depressed patients. In general, she found the enuretic-depressives to be less responsive to treatment (41% recovered, 35% moderately improved) than depressives (74% recovered, 6% moderately improved). Amitriptyline was used as the drug of first choice for the enuretic-depressives, unless there was a clear-cut precipitating factor, in which case phenelzine (an MAO inhibitor) was used. Phenelzine was the drug of first choice for the uncomplicated depressives, and these were treated with the addition of imipramine if there was a failure to improve. She considers imipramine the drug of first choice for children with an endogenous depression. Phobic-depressives were treated first with phenelzine, which was combined with a tranquilizer if a great amount of anxiety was present. Chlordiazepoxide was used sometimes from the beginning, and sometimes the MAO drug was combined with isocarboxazid.

In a double-blind crossover study, Frommer (1967) compared phenelzine and chlordiazepoxide with phenobarbitone and placebo. Although the drug that was given first showed the greatest effect, she felt that the results demonstrated the superiority of the combination of the MAOI drug and the minor tranquilizer over the sedative. The study is unfortunately flawed in several respects but is one of few that undertake systematic drug comparison in carefully diagnosed depressed children. Success in noncontrolled trials with MAOI drugs in combination with minor tranquilizers has also been reported by others (Abdou, 1967). Although certainly suggestive, Frommer's work with phenelzine needs more careful study. In her crossover trial, there was no difference between the first combination of phenelzine and chlordiazepoxide (treatment A) and the second combination of phenobarbitone and placebo (treatment B) during the first two weeks: eleven of fifteen improved vs. eleven of seventeen. In the second two weeks, the results were fourteen of seventeen vs. five of fifteen. But as Graham (1967) points out, "These results appear to be just as consistent with the hypothesis that children with neurotic illnesses tend to benefit from being taken off phenobarbitone as with the suggestion that they derive any advantage from phenelzine and chlordiazepoxide."

Recent work by Gittelman-Klein (Gittelman-Klein and Klein, 1971) provides evidence that imipramine is beneficial in the treatment of intractable school phobia. Gittelman-Klein's work was initiated on the assumption that school phobia is often based upon an underlying depressive reaction, a position consistent with previous work which frequently mentions school phobia as a depressive equivalent or manifestation. Rapoport (Rapoport et al., 1974) has also recently done careful double-blind work with imipramine showing some advantage over placebo among hyperkinetic children. But the effects are not especially striking, and one wonders whether a separation of patients with "depressive disposition," history of affective disturbance, or family history for affective illness might show more clear-cut differences. There seems little doubt that a distinction between a depression-based hyperkinesis and one based on organic or maturational brain dysfunction could be an important basis of clinical subgrouping.

Ludiomil (BA 34276) is an antidepressant which is said to be unlike imipramine in that it exerts a marked sedative and antiaggressive action with no amphetamine-potentiating effect. It has apparently been used with great success in Europe (Kuhn-Gebhardt, 1972) in the treatment of depressive states in children and adolescents, although information on controlled trials is not available.

LITHIUM IN CHILDREN

Frommer (1968) tried lithium in the treatment of an eight-year-old boy who had been in an apparent hypomanic state for years and found that within two weeks there was a dramatic alteration in mood toward stability and calm. Dosage ranged from 50 mg/day to 250 mg/day. Other children with similar phasic patterns of hypomania and depression were treated with success, although some became worse and had to be treated with antidepressants.

In another case report (Dyson and Barcai, 1970), two "manic-depressive' children of lithium-responding parents were first treated unsuccessfully with amphetamine, and then given up to 1500 mg/day of lithium carbonate. They showed marked decrease of symptoms, which returned when the medication was discontinued. Several phobias in one patient were relieved during the treatment, suggesting that these symptoms were somehow related to the depression.

Annell (1969) treated eight children (with severe symptoms appearing before the age of ten) with lithium when the children were between the ages of eight and fifteen. The case reports are extremely interesting in that they point to very diverse early clinical manifestations that would usually be considered to reflect some obscure organic or schizophrenic type of illness of great severity. The dramatic improvement described lends credence to the supposition that the various manifestations of illness reflect a primary or endogenous disturbance for which lithium is a specific remedy. For instance, a nine-year-old girl showed a dramatic personality change from a sweet, likable disposition to a stubborn, disorderly child who disrupted her school class with obscene verbalizations, and had a sudden onset of poor sleep complicated with intense night terrors and sleepwalking. When she was treated with lithium at age sixteen, the longstanding pathological pattern was reversed, and the child remained essentially normal for several years at follow-up. Another child described by Annell was a seven-year-old boy who showed an apparent catatonic-like stupor with periodic remissions. He became completely well when treated with lithium at age eighteen. A third child, who had been considered an imbecile (with an IQ of 58 at the age of eight), appeared to be schizophrenic at the age of fifteen). Because of her rapid mood shifts, she was treated with lithium and showed remarkable improvement.

None of the eight children described showed the typical manic state found in adults, but several showed deep depression, and most showed a rather sudden change to a depressive state or alternated between depression and hyperactivity.* Most also had vegetative disorders and physical complaints, and all had a sleep disorder. Three had encopresis. Although sufficient evidence is lacking from controlled studies using objective criteria of diagnosis and double-blind controlled drug trials, the case reports surely suggest that a form of endogenous mood disorder may occur more frequently than supposed and may often be confused with other diagnoses. It should be noted that in most studies of these severe forms of disturbance, the children will have been hospitalized; also, as pointed out by experienced clinicians (Frommer, 1968; Cytryn and McKnew, 1972), depressed children often show marked improvement when placed in a hospital setting away from their disturbed environment.

CONCLUSIONS AND RECOMMENDATIONS FOR FUTURE RESEARCH

The literature on childhood depression reviewed in this paper would appear to suggest that depression as a persistent sad affect may occur quite early in children, either as a reaction to loss or as a somewhat spontaneous change in personality suggestive of cyclothymic patterns. In general, however, most of the work indicates that disturbances of affect in children are likely to be accompanied by, or displaced by, other behavior such as aggression, psychosomatic complaints, and disturbances of vegetative patterns, especially sleep and bladder control. Several authors have made a reasonable argument for the fact that typical adult depressive symptoms of self-accusation, despair and hopelessness may not be apparent until adolescence, although low self-esteem as a personality trait is not

---

*It is interesting to note that this picture of a rapidly alternating state of excitement and depression has been noted among women suffering from postpartum depressive psychosis (Herzog and Detre, 1974). One cannot but wonder whether some common endocrine imbalance underlies both the cyclothymic picture in childhood and that in postpartum states. The fact that true mania is rare before puberty suggests that the sex hormones may be involved in both cases.

uncommon in children and may be accompanied by verbal signs that the child feels stupid, inept, etc.

Although there is no clear agreement on a typology, and indeed significant differences among the classification systems exist, I believe that in view of the complexity of environmental, developmental and genetic variables interacting with each other, this is not surprising. What is needed is some method of ordering the existing data into a meaningful form.

The following facts warrant explanation by any theory of affective disorder among children:

1. The *length of the premorbid history* appears to be correlated with the form in which symptoms appear: in general, those children with acute onset are described as having cyclothymic personality patterns prior to their disturbance, while those with a long premorbid history tend to be described as introverted, irritable, aggressive and often antisocial in adolescence.

2. There is a significant association between *early object loss* and bereavement on the one hand, and subsequent depressive illness on the other, but this association is low in terms of absolute frequency.

3. Some studies show a high incidence of *positive family history* for affective illness in children with depression, while others do not.

4. There is a high incidence of *primary nocturnal enuresis* among depressed children.

5. There is a high incidence of *disturbed sleep patterns,* with some studies describing difficulties falling asleep, others describing early-morning waking.

6. There is disagreement as to the role of *somatic complaints* as a manifestation of depression, especially those related to autonomic function.

7. The incidence of *EEG abnormalities* is quite high in the few studies that have mentioned the problem.

8. If *alternating states of manic excitement and depression* are found at all in children below age thirteen or fourteen, the cycles are much more rapid and shorter in duration than found in manic-depressive disease of adulthood; it is much more common for only the depressive state to be clearly manifest over any length of time prior to puberty.

On the basis of developmental theory and observations, the following premises would seem to be valid:

A. Primary love, support, mother-contact and affectional-dependent relations between the child and mother are essential for maintaining moderate variations in infant arousal levels and smooth rhythmicity in basic appetitive and autonomic response systems.

B. The degree of lability of the autonomic system as well as the balance between the sympathetic-parasympathetic axis is normally distributed in the population.

C. Sudden infant arousal, followed by crying and other forms of "protest," is a natural consequence of separation from mother and other primary support objects in the child's environment, having biological survival value as a signal to the mother as to the child's whereabouts and state of need. The affective state accompanying such changes may be presumed to be "anxious" or fearful.

D. Prolonged separation, bereavement or deprivation of primary support persons in the child's environment lead to a shift from active protest to apathy and withdrawal, a shift also having survival value for conserving the child's energy supply.* This shift probably involves a shift from sympathetic to parasympathetic reactions and a shift from endocrine reactions preparing for emergency to those preparing for conservation. The affective state accompanying such changes may be presumed to be "depressed" or sad in nature.

E. Subsequent development will depend upon learning and the extent to which environmental cues trigger previously acquired response patterns. (According to McClelland, a motive is the redintegration by a cue of a change in affect.)

On the basis of these assumptions, many of the observations regarding depression in children can be explained as an interactive effect between the baseline state of autonomic balance (the integration and regulation of which will develop with age) and the timing and amount of "object loss." Those children with severely deprived early environments and multiple object losses will tend early to develop a range of parasympathetically related somatic symptoms (colic, headache, abdominal pain) and will have difficulty establishing bladder and/or bowel control. Later object loss will have in general a less profound impact, and if it occurs will tend to be less associated with parasympathetically controlled bodily functions. Whether or not such loss eventuates in depressive symptomatology at all will depend upon the level of autonomic integration and stability, as well as the portion of the normal curve within which the particular child falls with respect to autonomic balance. The loss of a parent may have less profound impact, for example, (a) if adequate primary support is forthcoming from others, (b) the child is autonomically stable; and (c) neural integration and maturation are according to the normal timetable. Children with EEG slowing and other irregularities indicative of delayed or impaired CNS function can be expected to be less capable of homeostatically regulating autonomic response following trauma.

Chronic, sustained loss can be expected to leave the child more likely to attach cues to the apathetic and withdrawn affective states, while frequent minor or less traumatic events will more often leave the child susceptible to learned reactions involving more "anxious" states. Rapid alternation between overarousal and underarousal may represent a strongly genetically determined trait of the nervous system and is suggestive of a system undergoing positive feedback augmentation or resonance, rather than the usual negative feedback homeostatic

---

*I am indebted to Dr. Don Klein for suggesting the adaptive value of Bowlby's and Spitz's stages of reaction to maternal deprivation.

control conditions. It is possible that some type of disruption due to the onset of sexual maturation leads to this state since it so rarely appears full-blown before puberty.

Aggressive symptomatology is prominent in the clinical descriptions offered by most authors. However, there is undoubtedly a difference between aggressive behavior due to frequent trauma in early childhood and "acting out" behavior which serves a function of self-stimulation or arousal-seeking. Hyperactivity as a depressive equivalent may exist as a form of self-stimulation, just as amphetamine abuse, stealing cars or gang-fighting might serve the same function.

Severe object loss may, as we have argued above, lead to an ultimately apathetic state, depending on post-traumatic support; a similar state, however, could be the result of an extreme variation on the normal curve of arousal (naturally low arousal presumably being genetically determined) so that such children, although predisposed to low arousal, would not necessarily have histories of object loss or bereavement.

In any case, regardless of the precise mechanism involved, it seems reasonable to make the following distinctions in further research with depressive states of childhood and adolescence: acute vs. chronic, phobic-anxous vs. nonphobic, early vs. late onset, positive vs. negative family history, and if positive whether there is bipolar or unipolar affective illness. These variables would seem to be natural markers for establishing clinical subtypes and might well account for much of the apparent disagreement in the literature regarding depressive states in children. Whether any such subtypes are uniquely responsive to tricyclic antidepressants, MAOI drugs, lithium, or other therapies has not been satisfactorily demonstrated, and it is precisely the failure to control the aforementioned variables that may cloud the picture of treatment specificity and response.

With the exception of the anxious-nonanxious distinction, these variables are related to etiology and background characteristics rather than the phenomenology of depression. This seems almost inevitable since the particular signs and symptoms of the disorder will vary with age (somatic early, nonsomatic later, for instance), cognitive level (self-reference and superego functions develop later), basic personality, culturally permitted expressions (e.g., boys don't cry), and undoubtedly many other developmentally determined factors. But the relevance of these factors has repeatedly been shown in adult studies of depression and virtually ignored in the childhood studies until quite recently.

COMMENTARIES

DR. WERRY: A point much belabored by child psychiatrists is that children are not simply miniature adults. As is clear in Dr. Conners' review, nowhere is this more apparent than in the nosology of depression and in the psychopharmacology of antidepressant drugs in children. The adolescent, on the other hand, while admittedly standing in the no man's land between childhood and adulthood, is much more akin nosologically and therapeutically to the adult than to the child, though the proverbial (and probably exaggerated) morose turmoil of adolescence carries its own peculiarity. I propose therefore to center most of the discussion on childhood defined as the period from birth to the onset of puberty, or from ages (approximately) zero to twelve years inclusive. I should like to examine briefly the two most important issues made by Dr. Conners, and in so doing, emphasize their distinctiveness from each other as he perhaps failed to do. These two issues are (1) the nosology and symptomatology of depressive states and equivalents, and (2) the psychopharmacology of the antidepressant drugs in children.

Depressive States

The most competent review of these (until Dr. Conners' paper) is that by Graham (1974), which in its careful scientific scrutiny stands in sharp contrast to other efforts such as that by Malmquist (1971) and most of the papers in Annell's book (1972) consisting largely of anecdotal, private clinical material, generalizations and reassertion of others' assertions. On the basis of scientifically acceptable epidemiological, symptomatological, etiological, family, suicide (Shaffer, 1974) and follow-up data, Graham concludes: (1) manic-depressive or true depressive disorders, as they are understood in adult psychiatry, are rare in children, (2) transitory dysphoric (note the use of the generic term) states in the presence of stress and in association with most childhood psychiatric disorders are common (these dysphoric states are too situation specific, too short-lived, too nondiscriminatory, and too varied in etiology, in family history and background, in prognosis and response to treatment, to form a nosologically distinct or clinically useful category called "depression"), and (3) the term depressive equivalents or masked depression as presently used is too vague, too inferential, and too polyglot to be credible or heuristically useful. Similar critiques have been well made by Gittelman-Klein and Klein (1973).

Child psychiatry has been and is bedeviled by a "pre-Kraepelinian" nosological anarchy based on a number of the following: (1) conceptual confusion among etiology, symptomatology, developmental processes and intellectual level (hopefully soon to be ameliorated somewhat by the ICD9), (2) undeserved prognostic optimism and pious hopes about treatment efficacy, (3) animosity to parents, and (4) empirical data of limited universality obtained by methods of uncertain but probably dubious reliability. Nosology cannot afford to be further wracked by a new Pandora's box called "depressive equivalents," most of which, e.g., enuresis, stomach aches, sleep disturbances and underachievement, are common to almost all psychiatric conditions of children. Diagnostic methods and a nosology which, according to NIMH statistics (Rosen et al., 1964), assign 40 percent of children to adjustment reactions and a further 30 percent to "undiagnosed" give little cause for comfort. Do we really wish to see a substitution of "depression" for "adjustment reaction" caused by the very ubiquitousness of these dysphoric symptoms or so-called depressive equivalents? Child psychiatry would do well to give more attention to the reliability and validity of its data-gathering process before espousing a new nosology. For example, a recent paper (Weinberg et al., 1973), laudable for its effort to define necessary and sufficient criteria (albeit too broadly to be really useful), failed on this very point, while most proselytizers of childhood depression cited by Dr. Conners simply ignore all methodological issues.

Psychopharmacology of Antidepressant Drugs in Children

Both the monoamine oxidase inhibitors and the tricyclics have been shown in reasonably well-controlled studies (Gittelman-Klein and Klein, 1973; Frommer, 1968; Waizer et al., 1974; Rapoport et al., 1974; Werry et al., 1975) to ameliorate certain behavioral symptoms such as school phobia, enuresis, hyperactivity, aggressivity, and attention disorders, and to produce clinical global improvement. As Graham (1974) points out, to deduce from this that such symptoms are therefore depressive equivalents ignores the fact that tricyclics have other actions besides antidepressant ones. For example, recent work by Dr. David Shaffer at the Institute of Psychiatry in London suggests that the efficacy of imipramine in enuresis *may* be due to its local anesthetic action. Further, stimulant drugs are known to be effective in hyperactive-aggressive states in children, and current thinking, as referred to by Dr. Conners, favors a neurophysiologic arousal disorder rather than a mood disorder as the etiological base. The use of lithium in hyperactive states in children (Annell, 1972) is unconvincing and uncontrolled, and the diagnoses, as inferred from illustrative case histories, dubious. In the light of the etiological theories of hyperkinesis and the effects of stimulants in such children, it is probably more parsimonious to assume that both MAO inhibitors and tricyclics probably have stimulant rather than true antidepressant properties in children. Indeed, we ourselves (Werry et al., 1975) have evidence to suggest that the effects of imipramine in children may well be indistinguishable symptomatologically, physically and cognitively from methylphenidate. (Perhaps, as suggested by Dr. Mendels in this symposium, we should drop the term antidepressant as prejudicial and procrustean and, as with the phenothiazines or benzodiazepines, substitute chemical terms like tricyclics.)

Rather than infer nosology from drug action, the more heuristic approach to pediatric pharmacotherapy is likely to ask: (1) what objectively defined and reliably measured psychopathological symptoms and physical and neurophysiological functions are affected by which drugs, and (2) which variables predict drug responsiveness. (Some of these have been listed by Dr. Conners.) If a nosology is to be derived from drug action, it should be a new one, atomistic, and related to cellular or neurophysiological systems as proposed by Wender (1973), rather than a rehash of molar ones that have already failed.

Finally, I should like to discuss a third area (additional to nosology and psychopharmacology) elaborated by Dr. Conners, namely, etiology. If—using objective methods of measurement and a set of exclusive and inclusive diagnostic criteria—dysphoric states called childhood depression having useful clinical, therapeutic and prognostic value should emerge (of which I am doubtful), then Dr. Conners' genetic-developmental-psychophysiological-learning theory of etiologies becomes of interest. His theory has many of the hallmarks of earlier ones, most relatively unfruitful scientifically, such as: (1) the psychoanalytic notion of "fixations," (2) Wenger's (1941) concept of autonomic imbalance, and (3) Engel's (1962) update of Cannon's orthosympathetic and parasympathetic systems; it does relate well, however, to the animal models and methods described by Dr. McKinney, and it would be educative if Dr. Conners would now deduce some specific hypotheses and indicate how they might be tested.

DR. GALLANT: Dr. Werry, could you add some observations resulting from your research with dose-response correlation in drug therapy in children?

DR. WERRY: One of the problems of pediatric psychopharmacology is the large differences in the doses of psychotropic drugs which are used in children in Europe and the United States. My colleague, Dr. Sprague, and I have done some studies in which we have used dosage as a variable. One of the interesting things which has come out of these studies is that, for example, with methylphenidate one can get a significant therapeutic effect at a level which is approximately one quarter that recommended in pharmacological texts. In a recent study of haloperidol, which I have just completed, I took as my low dose half the lowest dose that I could find in the literature and took as my high dose the lowest dose I could find in the literature. Thus I was able to show that haloperidol probably improves cognitive functioning in children in the low dose and depresses it in the high dose. In short, I think that doses of psychotropic drugs in the United States tend to be too high, which is a matter of concern to people who have an interest in the future of pediatric psychopharmacology. If we aren't very careful about trying to evaluate dosage as a variable, we are liable to impede the advance of pediatric psychopharmacology. Society is "hung up" enough on giving drugs to adults, but when it comes to giving them to children there are even more reservations, so I think we have to be extra careful. However, I can see that there could be some children (e.g., poor gastrointestinal absorbers) who need high doses, and there could be some conditions, such as school phobia (Gittelman-Klein and Klein, 1971), in which high doses may be indicated.

DR. KLEIN: I would like to reemphasize the problem of differential diagnosis of depression in childhood. Insufficient attention has been devoted to depressive criteria in children. The whole issue of masked depression is a "bag of worms" and I heartily agree with Dr. Werry's opinion.

The papers in the child psychiatry literature remind me of an old line I read somewhere, I think it was a British review, which said that everything in this book is either obvious or dubious. The fact that conditions approximating adult depression (especially conditions in which there is a marked loss of interest, marked loss of ability to enjoy one's self, to experience pleasure) are infrequent, if not almost absent, in the child psychiatric population contrasts with the data on the ubiquity of protest and despair in animal models and humans.

There does seem to be fair evidence that there is a high degree of stereotypy of this particular reaction to separation. Dr. McKinney feels that perhaps more recent evidence indicates that the degree of stereotypy has been exaggerated. It is easy to relate the protest-separation anxiety phase to the separation anxiety reaction you see in children labeled school phobic. This, of course, is a misnomer, as these children are not afraid of school. They have acute or chronic homesickness and want to be with their mothers. The fact that these conditions do respond very well to antidepressants might lead one to think that if you have a disorder of the protest phase, you can have an equivalent disorder of the despair phase that would similarly respond to antidepressants. This basic reaction may be what depression is in adults, but in that case why don't we find it in children? Children despair easily enough, so why don't disorders of the despair phase occur in children? I simply don't have any answer to that. Dr. Conners feels that such conditions do occur. Documentation would be valuable.

It is conceivable, as Dr. Conners mentioned in his paper, that the relative lack of clear-cut depression in children may have to do with maturation, the endocrines, or with the development of sex hormones that interact with the normal psychophysiology of the despair phase and thus fail to lay the groundwork for the depressive syndromes in children. Of course, that is entirely speculative. There has been recent work indicating that there are age-related enzyme changes, like levels of MAO, that may have some important modulating effect upon the despair phase. I believe there is some data on MAO blood levels in children by Rapoport and Murphy. It might be extremely interesting to look at that particular aspect of psychophysiology in children.

In his paper Dr. Conners says that it was our belief that school phobias were related to adult depression that led us to use antidepressants in school phobias. Actually, that is not correct. The relationship, in our opinion, was between adult agoraphobic and school phobics because half of the adult agoraphobics had a history of early separation anxiety. What is interesting is that adult agoraphobics are not, in my opinion, depressed. They don't have a loss of pleasure and interest; they frequently are very active when they are not in a panic; they have no vegetative signs; they don't have much sleep disturbance; their sex lives are satisfactory, etc.

In our evaluation of school phobics, we were looking for two things, depression and enuresis, but we found neither. The children were not enuretic, and although a number of them expressed feelings of futility and demoralization that they couldn't go to school, these complaints were only expressed by a quarter of them and they weren't depressed. So, despite the effects of imipramine in this population, I think that it would probably be wrong to refer to them as a type of depression or as a masked depression. One more qualification along these lines is that many agoraphobes, who are called masked depression, receive ECT which may make them worse.

DR. GITTELMAN-KLEIN: I think that both Dr. Werry and Dr. Klein have covered the theoretical problems involved in diagnosis of childhood depression; in addition, what is necessary is an attempt to distinguish between unhappy, miserable children and depressed children. There has been no effort made to define the clinical differences between depressed adults who have vegetative signs and phobic or emotionally upset children in whom the vegetative signs are virtually absent. Obviously, the depressive equivalents are creating more problems than they are solving, and I think that in children we need to turn our attention to very clear criteria for distinguishing reactive states, either realistic or unrealistic reactions to loss or disappointment, from endogenous depressive disorders if they exist at all. We cannot use the adult depressive criteria in children since these are lacking in the young population.

I am a little concerned about some of the data presented by Dr. Conners in terms of the incidence of family history of depression among "depressed children" vs. controls where the controls had a 30 percent prevalence of depression in the parents. Assuming that these were prepubertal children, most of these parents were probably in their thirties. Thirty percent prevalence of depression in people in their thirties in a control group is extraordinary.

DR. CONNERS: They were not a control group. They were clinic patients who were visiting the clinic for problems other than depression.

DR. GITTELMAN-KLEIN: Diagnostically they are a comparison group, and a prevalence of 30 percent of depression in these relatively young adults is extraordinarily high; it would be high even in older patients.

We have done a study of the presence of depression in parents of school phobic children and compared it to that of the parents of hyperactive children. We found no significant difference. About 8 percent of the parents of both the phobic and hyperactive children had a history of depression. I thought it was very high, but it was nowhere near what has been reported in the paper presented. I am therefore puzzled by studies which report such a very high level of depression in the families of children treated for a variety of psychiatric disorders.

DR. CONNERS: I would like to make a couple of very brief comments. First of all, I would disagree with Dr. Gittelman-Klein that these persistent dysphoric moods with vegetative and motor signs do not occur in children. Both the case material and my own experience show that they do occur. Now, it is true that it is not exactly the same as in adults, and we do have to pay more attention to precisely these kinds of things in making the definition. The main point that I wanted to make in the paper is that I think it is heuristically valuable to take the concepts of adult depression and see what they lead to in children. When a very aggressive adolescent or young person comes in, it may be helpful to consider that there is a bereavement present, and it might be better to think about treating his sadness than to worry about reducing his aggression.

Concerning a couple of the points that Dr. Klein and Dr. Werry made, I didn't want to get into the position of having to defend the literature. I am well aware of the inadequacy, but I am very impressed with the fact that the family history and the cycloid nature of some of these disorders has been, in fact, minimized and obscured. I don't want to open a Pandora's box. On the other hand, I think it would be silly to ignore what looked to me like interesting ways of broadening our understanding of childhood psychopathology. Dr. Klein, you did tell me in a personal communication that you were studying school phobics because they might be depressed.

DR. GALLANT: I would like to ask either Dr. Conners or Dr. Werry about the findings by Steinberg and his associates, who recorded a higher psychopharmacological response rate in those hyperkinetic children who had either one hard neurologic sign or two soft neurologic signs. If my memory serves me correctly, amphetamines were superior to chlorpromazine but produced more side effects in this particular group of children.

DR. CONNERS: There is other good evidence for that statement. The best paper is by Millichap (1973), in which he had a very nice correlation between the number of soft signs and degree of response to methylphenidate. I think there is something to that, but it is obvious there are a lot of children without soft signs who also respond, so it clearly is not a one-to-one issue.

REFERENCES

Abdou, F. A. (1967). Psychotropic drug therapy in children and adolescents. *Va. Med. Monthly* 94:464–67.

Abraham, K. (1953). A short study of the development of the libido. In *Selected Papers on Psychoanalysis.* New York: Basic Books.

Annell, A.-L. (1969). Manic depressive illness in children and effect of treatment with lithium carbonate. *Acta Paedopsychiat.* 36:292–301.

———— (1972). Ed., *Depressive States in Childhood and Adolescence.* Stockholm: Almqvist & Wiksell.

Arthur, B., and Kemme, M. L. (1964). Bereavement in childhood. *J. Child. Psychol.* 5:37–49.

Bauersfeld, K. H. (1972). Diagnose und behandlung depressiver krankheitzustande in einer schulpsychiatrischen beratungsstelle (diagnosis and treatment of depressive conditions at a school psychiatric center). In A.-L. Annell, ed., *Depressive States in Childhood and Adolescence.* Stockholm: Almqvist & Wiksell.

Beck, A. T., Sethi, B. B., and Tuthill, R. W. (1963). Childhood bereavement and adult depression. *Arch. Neurol. Psychiat.* 9:295–99.

Brown, F. (1972). Depression and childhood bereavement. In A.-L. Annell, ed., *Depressive States in Childhood and Adolescence.* Stockholm: Almqvist & Wiksell.

Campbell, J. D. (1952). Manic-depressive psychosis in children: report of 18 cases. *J. Nerv. Ment. Dis.* 116:424–39.

Caplan, M. G., and Douglas, V. I. (1969). Incidence of parental loss in children with depressed mood. *J. Child. Psychol. Psychiat.* 10:225–32.

Cebiroglu, R., Sumer, E., and Polvan, O. (1972). Etiology and pathogenesis of depression in Turkish children. In A.-L. Annell, ed., *Depressive States in Childhood and Adolescence.* Stockholm: Almqvist & Wiksell.

Cytryn, L., and McKnew, D. H., Jr. (1972). Proposed classification of childhood depression. *Am. J. Psychiat.* 129:149–55.

d'Elia, G., and Perris, C. (1972). Childhood environment and bipolar and unipolar recurrent depressive psychosis. In A.-L. Annell, ed., *Depressive States in Childhood and Adolescence.* Stockholm: Almqvist & Wiksell.

Dennehy, C. (1966). Childhood bereavement and psychiatric illness. *Br. J. Psychiat.* 112:1049–69.

Dyson, W. L., and Barcai, A. (1970). Treatment of children of lithium-responding parents. *Curr. Ther. Res.* 12:286–90.

Eggers, C. (1972). Cyclothyme phasen im beginn und im verlauf schizophrener psychosen des kindesalters (cyclothmic episodes at the beginning and during the course of schizophrenic psychosis in childhood). In A.-L. Annell, ed., *Depressive States in Childhood and Adolescence.* Stockholm: Almqvist & Wiksell.

Engel, G. (1962). *Psychological Development in Health and Disease.* Philadelphia: Saunders.

Freud, A. (1965). *Normality and Pathology in Childhood.* New York: Intl. Univ. Press.

Freud, S. (1957). *Mourning and Melancholia,* Standard Edition. J. Strachey, ed. London: Hogarth Press.

Frommer, E. (1967). Treatment of childhood depression with antidepressant drugs. *Br. Med. J.* 5542.729–32.

——— (1968). Depressive illness in childhood. *Br. J. Psychiat.* 2:117–36.

———, Mendelson, W. B., and Reid, M. A. (1972). Differential diagnosis of psychiatric disturbances in preschool children. *Br. J. Psychiat.* 121:71–74.

Gittelman-Klein, R., and Klein, D. F. (1971). Controlled imipramine treatment of school phobia. *Arch. Gen. Psychiat.* 25:204–07.

——— and Klein, D. (1973). School phobia: diagnostic considerations in the light of imipramine effects. *J. Nerv. Ment. Dis.* 156:199–215.

Graham, P. (1967). Childhood depression (a letter). *Br. Med. J.* 5551:576.

——— (1974). Depression in pre-pubertal children. *Develop. Med. & Child Neurol.* 16:340–49.

Greer, S. (1966). Parental loss and attempted suicide. *Br. J. Psychiat.* 112:465–70.

Gregory, J. W. (1966). Retrospective data concerning childhood loss of a parent. II. Category of parental loss by decade of birth, diagnosis and MMPI. *Arch. Gen. Psychiat.* 15:362–67.

Hava, F. A. (1973). Lithium, the hyperactive child and manic-depressive illness. *J. Ark. Med. Soc.* 69:299–300.

Herzog, A., and Detre, T. (1974, in press). Post-partum psychoses: a follow-up study. *Dis. Nerv. Syst.*

Hill, O. W., and Price, J. S. (1967). Childhood bereavement and adult depression. *Br. J. Psychiat.* 113:743–51.

Kanner, L. (1946). *Child Psychiatry.* Springfield, Ill.: C. C. Thomas & Co.

Klein, M. (1960). A contribution to the psychogenesis of manic-depressive states. *Intl. J. Psychoanal.* 16:145–74.

Kuhn-Gebhardt, P., (1972). Results obtained with a new antidepressant in children. In P. Kielholz, ed., *Depressive Illness: Diagnosis, Assessment, and Treatment*. Baltimore: Williams & Wilkins.

Ling, W., Oftedal, G., and Weinberg, W. (1970). Depressive illness in childhood presenting as severe headache. *Am. J. Dis. Child.* 120:122–24.

Lokare, V. G. (1972). Neuroticism, extraversion and the incidence of depressive illness in children. In A.-L. Annell, ed., *Depressive States in Childhood and Adolescence*. Stockholm: Almqvist & Wiksell.

Mahler, M. S. (1961). On sadness and grief in infancy and childhood: loss and restoration of the symbiotic love-object. *Psychoanal. Study Child.* 16:332–51.

Malmquist, C. P. (1971). Depressions in childhood and adolescence. *N. Eng. J. Med.* 284:887–93.

Mastropaolo, C. (1972). Depressions and adolescence. In A.-L. Annell, ed., *Depressive States in Childhood and Adolescence*. Stockholm: Almqvist & Wiksell.

Mendelwicz, J., and Klotz, J. (1974). Primary enuresis and affective illness (a letter). *Lancet* I (7860):733.

Millichap, J. G. (1973). Drugs in management of minimal brain dysfunction. In F. F. de la Cruz, B. H. Fox and R. H. Roberts, eds., *Minimal Brain Dysfunction. Ann. N. Y. Acad. Sci.* 205:321–34.

Nissen, G. (1971). *Depressive Syndrome in Kindes- und Jugendalter*. Berlin: Springer-Verlag.

Ostow, M. (1970). *The Psychology of Melancholy*. New York: Harper & Row, p. 13.

Otto, U. (1972). Suicidal attempts in childhood and adolescents—today and after ten years, a follow-up study. In A.-L. Annell, ed., *Depressive States in Childhood and Adolescence*. Stockholm: Almqvist & Wiksell.

Pitts, F., Winokur, G., et al. (1965). Adult psychiatric illness assessed for childhood parental loss. *Am. J. Psychiat.* Suppl. 112:12.

Poznanski, E., and Zrull, J. P. (1970). Childhood depression: clinical characteristics of overtly depressed children. *Arch. Gen. Psychiat.* 23:8–15.

Rapoport, J. L., Quinn, P. O., Bradbard, G., Riddle, K., and Brooks, E. (1974). A double-blind comparison of imipramine and methylphenidate treatments of hyperactive boys. *Arch. Gen. Psychiat.* 30:789–93.

Remschmidt, P., Strunk, P., Methner, C., and Tegeler, E. (1972). Kinder endogendepressiver eltern—verhaltensstorungen und personlichkeitsstruktur (children of depressive parents). In A.-L. Annell. ed., *Depressive States in Childhood and Adolescence*. Stockholm: Almqvist & Wiksell.

Rie, H. E. (1966). Depression in childhood: a survey of some pertinent contributions. *J. Am. Acad. Child Psychiat.* 5:653–85.

Ripley, H. S., Dorpat, L. D., and Jackson, J. K. (1965). Broken homes and attempted and completed suicide. *Arch. Gen. Psychiat.* 12:213–16.

Rosen, B. M., Bahn, A. K., and Cramer, M. (1964). Demographic and diagnostic characteristics of psychiatric outpatient clinics in the United States, 1961. *Am. J. Orthopsychiat.* 34:455–68.

Sacks, P. V. (1974). Childhood enuresis/adult depression (a letter). *Lancet* I(7856):508.

Shaffer, D. (1974). Suicide in childhood and early adolescence. *J. Child Psychol. Psychiat.* 15:275–97.

Spitz, R. A. (1946). Anaclitic depression: an inquiry into the genesis of psychiatric conditions in early childhood. *Psychoanal. Study Child.* 2:313–42.

Toolan, J. M. (1962). Depression in children and adolescents. *Am. J. Orthopsychiat.* 32:404–14.

Waizer, J., Hoffman, S., Polizos, P., and Engelhardt, D. (1974). Outpatient treatment of hyperactive school children with imipramine. *Am. J. Psychiat.* 131:587–91.

Weinberg, W., Rutman, J., Sullivan, L., Penick, E., and Dietz, S. (1973). Depression in children referred to an educational diagnostic center. Diagnosis and treatment—preliminary report. *J. Pediat.* 83:1065–72.

Wender, P. (1973). Some speculations concerning a possible biochemical basis of minimal brain dysfunction. *Ann. N. Y. Acad. Sci.* 205:18–28.

Wenger, M. (1941). The measurement of individual differences in autonomic balance. *Psychosom. Med.* 3:427–34.

Werry, J., Dowrick, P., Lampen, E., and Vamos, M. (1975, in press). Imipramine in enuresis-psychological and physiological effects. *J. Child Psychol. Psychiat.*

CHAPTER VIII

Diagnosis of Depression in Geriatric Patients and Treatment Modalities Appropriate for the Population

F. Post

For the purposes of this article, the word "geriatric" will refer to patients over the age of sixty, simply because the experiences reported here were gathered in a unit within a postgraduate psychiatric teaching hospital to which, for the sake of administrative convenience, patients above sixty tended to be admitted regardless of their diagnosis. Most people now think that old age and geriatrics start only after the age of seventy or seventy-five; when one is trying to explore problems related to depression, however, restricting oneself to the discussion of "really old" patients would remove from consideration the bulk of depressions recurring into, or first arising during late life. This point is demonstrated by Fig. 1, which is taken from an earlier article (Post, 1968a) and shows that only a small proportion of depressive illnesses first come to notice after the age of seventy.

The numbers represented in Fig. 1 refer to the early 1950's, when there were few facilities for treating any but mild depressions outside the hospital. First admission rates, as shown in the bottom row of histograms, are likely to be a fair reflection of the true incidence rates of severe depressions at different ages. While first attacks of depression requiring admission occur most commonly between the ages of 50 and 60, the incidence rate is seen to decline only slightly during the subsequent decade. The family doctor tended to see a much wider spectrum of depressive illnesses than the mental hospital psychiatrist of those years, and it is

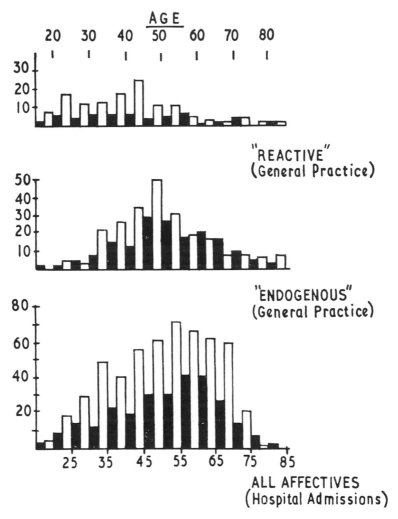

FIG. 1.   Age incidence of first depressive illnesses observed in general practice and through admission to three London mental hospitals (males, black; females, white) From *Recent Developments in Affective Disorders,* 1968

interesting that the numbers representing cases in a general (partly rural, partly urban) practice indicated that the less severe depressions tended to come to notice for the first time during the forties rather than the fifties.

Fig. 1 also illustrates the preponderance of women, especially among the more severe depressives, requiring inpatient treatment. The figure does not show that recurrence rates rise with age, and for this reason at any one time a considerable proportion of depressives receiving treatment in any setting belong to the higher age groups. The increased rate of suicide and attempted suicide in the elderly is so well-known that it does not require documentation here. However, we should perhaps touch briefly on the question of why depressions tend to become more frequent and more severe with rising age, at least until a time of life has been reached where gross anatomical brain changes become increasingly common. These matters have been fully discussed elsewhere (Post, 1968a, 1975; Cawley et al., 1973). In summary, common-sense assumptions have failed to explain the greater proneness of aging persons toward depressions severe enough to require treatment.

Bereavement and threatened bereavement, physical illness, and in general all losses of sources of self-esteem have become established as precipitating factors of depression at all ages, and obviously are especially common occurrences or threats after the middle of life has been reached. If they were the main reason why depressions became more common after that time, precipitating factors (especially those of bereavement and physical illness) should be discovered more frequently in late-onset than in early-onset depressions. Such has, on the whole, not been found to be the case. Again it might be thought one was dealing, in the case of late-onset depressives, with people badly equipped to stand the deprivations that late life brings with it. However, attempts to confirm that weaknesses of premorbid personality structure (as exemplified by the characteristics of the pre-involutional psychosis personality) were unduly frequent in late-onset depressives have failed. On the contrary, these patients seemed to have had more stable personalities than persons afflicted before the middle of life with recurring affective illnesses. In addition, a number of investigations have shown that the importance of hereditary factors decreases with age at first attack, and there is no evidence to suggest that late-onset depressions form a specific genetic group. The increase in depression in the elderly must therefore be considered either as a reaction or a fully blown illness related to the aging process itself. Central nervous system aging may diminish the efficiency of cerebral arousal systems, and thus facilitate the occurrence of depression following reactively produced emotional turmoil, or in a more general way (increase of monoamine oxidase concentration has been reported in blood platelets with rising age) biological age changes may make persons prone to depression.

Having sketched in this theoretical background, the remainder of this chapter will deal with practical matters. It is hoped, however, to show that clinical routine can remain linked with attempts at more systematic inquiries. First of all, diagnostic problems will be dealt with, the delineation of depression from other psychoses, those of schizophrenic type and those arising in relation to organic brain syndromes. The differentiation between milder depression and neurosis will be discussed. The meaningfulness of any distinction in this age group between psychotic and neurotic depression will be questioned, especially in relation to therapeutic response and prognosis. Finally, modern methods of treatment will be dealt with against the background of the recent past.

DIAGNOSIS OF DEPRESSION IN THE ELDERLY

A large proportion of the depressed elderly never reach the psychiatrist because the recognition of mild or masked depressions can present considerable difficulties. Presentation of the subject is facilitated by dealing first with patients who are obviously mentally ill. The possibility that the patient is suffering from an acute or chronic brain syndrome, from a manic state, or from a schizophrenic type of psychosis will no doubt be considered, but the mode of onset, the absence of cognitive impairment and disorientation, of schizophrenic features, of elation and its related thought content, will negate these possibilities. The diagnosis of a typical depressive illness will, in the great majority of elderly patients, be obvious on account of slowing or agitation affecting general psychomotor activity, facial expression and speech; on account of marked changes in sleep, appetite and weight; on account of clearly communicated mood of sadness usually mixed with anxiety; and finally on account of the classical thought content along the lines of self-belittlement, self-reproach, guilt, hypochondriacal beliefs of varying fixity, strength and bizarreness, and of hopelessness and fears and/or wishes of death. When the symptoms are less clear-cut, diagnostic difficulties will arise mainly in relation to two disorders: late schizophrenia and one of the brain syndromes common in late life.

Differentiation from Late Schizophrenia

This is desirable because abnormal thought content and experiencing due to a schizophrenic disturbance are specifically responsive to treatment with major tranquilizers (Post, 1966), which often make depression worse. The importance of schizophrenic states arising only late in life has come to be recognized in recent years (Post, 1966); on account of their limited nature and good preservation of many personality functions, David Kay and Martin Roth (1961) have suggested the label "late paraphrenia." Only a proportion of these patients exhibit symptoms which most psychiatrists would regard as undoubtedly schizophrenic rather than schizophreniform, and at least half suffer at some time or other from anxious-depressive mood changes. Otherwise, the symptomatology is paranoid: persecutory beliefs based largely on auditory hallucinations and on other experiences of a schizophrenic kind. Difficulties arise, as may be imagined, when there is well-marked depression as well as paranoid content of thought and experiencing. A diagnosis of depression can be made with confidence when there are only a few paranoid symptoms which can be clearly derived from self-depreciation and guilt: ideas of reference in the street—people talking about the patient, e.g., indicating that he is smelly, police patrol cars following him, etc. When the paranoid symptomatology is more florid, it may not be wise to make a definite diagnosis, but simply to decide if the patient should in the first instance be treated as a schizophrenic or as a melancholic. One would start with major tranquilizer treatment when the patient, though apparently quite depressed, hears voices discussing him in the third person, possibly commenting on his activities, or when the patient spontaneously and clearly describes experiences of passivity or influence. Even in the presence of some of these features, one might opt for antidepressant measures where these and similar experiences seem to derive from the patient's feeling of guilt and self-depreciation. Unfortunately, in the writer's experience, one will often make the wrong first choice, and the true nature of the disorder will only emerge at a later date.

It is worth stressing that real difficulties of this kind are met only very rarely. In a series of admissions of patients over sixty to the writer's facility over a five-year period, problems of differentiation between paraphrenia and depression were encountered in only 6 percent of cases and were speedily resolved in all but 4 percent. The question of whether or not there existed a schizoaffective reaction type was inconclusively examined (Post, 1971). What emerged clearly, however, was that these patients (exhibiting either concurrently or in rapid succession both affective and schizophrenic phenomena) had an unduly high loading with hereditary factors of various sorts and tended to have been badly adjusted persons. In spite of modern forms of treatment, their outlook turned out to be worse than that of elderly depressives or of pure paraphrenics. Finally (and this leads us into the next section), an unduly high proportion of schizoaffectives were found to be suffering from underlying acute or chronic brain syndromes.

Differentiation from "Dementia"

The large majority of general physicians and psychiatrists used to regard the appearance of depressive symptoms in late life, especially when there had not been any previous attacks of depression, as the beginning of senile mental changes. However, even in earlier times, some senile depressives survived their illness and made good and lasting recoveries. The introduction of modern forms of treatment has led to a much more widespread realization that depressive symptoms are only rarely a feature of one of the persistent organic brain syndromes of old age, and that elderly depressives as a group were no more at risk of developing deteriorative cerebral conditions than nonpsychiatric subjects of the same age. A full discussion will be found elsewhere (Post, 1968b), but the main results of the number of follow-up studies carried out in an English mental hospital (Kay et al., 1955), from a Swedish institution (Kay, 1962) and at the writer's own unit (Post, 1962, 1972) can be quickly summarized. Estimates of the frequency with which depressive and psycho-organic symptoms and signs coexist in elderly patients obviously vary relative to the criteria used for reporting patients (in spite of some brain changes) as depressives, and accordingly differ between 7 and 19 percent. The decision as to whether or not patients developed, during the follow-up period, definite evidence of a disabling brain syndrome is easier to make, but reports vary with method of observation and length of follow-up. The findings of different

Table I
Fresh incidence of arteriosclerotic and senile dementia in four
samples of elderly depressives followed up for varying periods

	N	Years observed (or death)	Percentages developing brain syndromes	Method of follow-up
Kay, 1955	189	0.75–3.25	2.5	case notes
Kay, 1962	97	16–25	18.5	case notes
Post, 1962	81	8	25.0	personal
Post, 1972	92	3	6.5	personal

investigators are summarized in Table I. In all studies, there was a much more frequent occurrence of brain syndromes associated with focal, presumably vascular, brain damage, than with global changes of a senile Alzheimer type. Evidence suggesting that the subsequent incidence of cerebrovascular and senile brain syndromes in these samples of elderly depressives occurs at the same rate as that "expected" over similar periods in mentally normal elderly populations with similar age distributions is rather circumstantial, but well-founded (Post, 1962).

It may thus be regarded as established that in the great majority of elderly patients depression is a self-limiting disorder, which only rarely coexists with or leads into an organic brain syndrome. In the United Kingdom, the differential diagnosis between depression and dementia seems to be made correctly in the great majority of instances. In order to test the stability of psychiatric diagnoses, Kendell (1974) drew a sample of 2,000 patients first admitted to a psychiatric bed of the National Health Service in 1964 and readmitted on at least one further occasion before the end of 1969. He found that in only 8 of 98 patients had the original diagnosis of dementia been changed to depression, and that only 23 out of 870 cases of depression had their diagnosis changed subsequently to one of dementia. The change from dementia to depression was made significantly more frequently than the other way around; in other words, there still is a slight tendency to mistake depression for a mental illness related to a brain syndrome. However, this is probably no longer due to lack of sophistication on the part of psychiatrists, but reflects the fact that certain depressive states mimic closely clinical pictures associated with organic cerebral failure. Madden and his colleagues (Hemsi et al., 1968) were perhaps the first to draw attention formally to the phenomenon of depressive pseudodementia, which had, however, been commented on by earlier writers. The practical and theoretical aspects of the condition have been fully discussed elsewhere (Post, 1975). Memory complaints may be severe, and there may be marked disabilities in performing simple household tasks. The patient may make ridiculous mistakes in orientation, e.g., maintaining the season is winter though evidence to the contrary is pointed out to him through the window. In other words, some patients with depressive pseudodementia may approach features seen in a Ganser state. However, it can be shown readily that cognitive failure in elderly depressives is not due to unwillingness to cooperate or to hysterical mechanisms, as patients failing on some clinical and laboratory tests of mental ability do well on other tests in the same session. Moreover, subclinical lowering of some cognitive functions has been found to be measurably present in a majority of elderly depressives, especially those of a predominantly psychotic type. In one series, some 16 percent of patients whose follow-up confirmed the diagnosis of depression scored in the same range as dementing patients on a learning test and a speed test. In another series (Post, 1975; Hemsi et al., 1968), it was demonstrated that the learning ability and psychomotor speed of depressives could be increased by successful treatment to a significant degree, confirming the reversibility of these changes. There was a similar lowering of barbiturate sleep thresholds in some depressives down into the range of dements, and a subsequent increase of values in depressives successfully treated. The suggestion that pseudodementia is related to a temporary and reversible lowering of some aspects of cerebral arousal continues to be investigated, but from a practical point of view the often subclinical yet sometimes clinically striking reduction of memory, learning, orientation and speed in elderly depressives is of little significance.

The rapid onset of a severe depressive, manic, or mixed manic-depressive state is at all ages associated with considerable changes in the level of awareness, subsequent amnesia of part of the illness, and often disorientation and perseveration. Usually, these patients are clinically and psychologically untestable. Many patients are understandably misdiagnosed as suffering from acute brain syndromes. But this is not a serious error, as it will lead to a particularly thorough physical work-up. By the time its largely negative results have come through, the clinical picture is likely to have crystallized into one of mania or melancholia. A combination of depressive symptoms and cognitive deficits in a less severe and more slowly developing illness should no longer lead to therapeutic inactivity. Even in a setting of ongoing cerebral deterioration, the treatment of depressive phenomena is usually successful. The prognosis is obviously that of the brain syndrome, but in the meantime antidepressant measures can be of greatest benefit Antidepressant drugs are especially prone to trigger off delirious reactions in elderly patients with brain damage and should be increased in dosage only slowly. The intensity of the treatment and the decision whether or not to turn, as a last resort, to electroconvulsive therapy will depend on the degree of probability with which a given patient can be allocated to a predominantly brain-damaged or cerebrally intact depressive group. Neurological deficits are reliable indicators of structural brain changes only when they are clear-cut, severe and systematic (Prakash and Stern, 1973). When discussing pseudodementia, we noted that the evaluation of depressives on psychological tests was likely to suggest the presence of cognitive defects similar to those found in dementing patients in a considerable proportion of cases. Severely bewildered, agitated or retarded patients usually prove altogether untestable. Simple clinical assessment, taking particular note of the points in Table II, is likely to be more useful. However, it may take many months to discover if some patients presenting with depressive symptoms are also suffering from cognitive impairment and, even more important, if this impairment is progressive at a significant rate. Decisions on therapy should, in the meantime, be arrived at independently of questions of prognosis.

Differentiation from Neurosis

Elderly neurotics are an elusive group of people. They are only rarely referred to psychiatrists by their family doctors, though many may continue attending their psychiatrists since an earlier age. The low referral rate of elderly neurotics for psychiatric treatment may be due to the fact that there is a shift toward physical complaints with age in the form of neurotic symptomatology: hysterical anxious and phobic symptoms tend to be replaced by somatic ones, either unpleasant physical sensations or hypochondriacal fears, nondelusional in type (McDonald, 1967). When elderly patients with various fears and complaints suggesting a neurotic disorder, often after rather too strenuous attempts at excluding physical disease, are finally referred to the psychiatric clinic, a high proportion show mild depressive symptoms. In fact, an entirely *de novo* appearance of neurotic symptoms after the age of sixty (albeit usually in persons with some neurotic personality traits) is almost always associated with some degree of depression (McDonald, 1973).

For the above reasons, the present writer sees too few elderly patients with predominantly neurotic disturbances to conduct properly controlled investigations. For what they are worth, a few impressions may be recorded. Episodic or continuous tension and anxiety are the most frequent complaints. Fears of physical disease or excessive preoccupations with existing physical handicaps, especially referring to eyesight and hearing, including the presence of tinnitus, occur on this background. In addition to anxiety, diminution of interests, changes in sleep and appetite patterns, and fleeting ideas of hopelessness will indicate that there is some depression as well. The association of phobic and obsessional symptoms with mild depression is almost equally strong in the elderly as some somatic preoccupations. In treating patients with neurotic symptoms, the question first to be answered will not be "Is this patient depressed rather than neurotic?" Instead, attempts will be made to gauge the extent to which the patient's depressive symptoms and neurotic problems each contribute to his disability. In practice it usually pays off to treat depression first, as in a large majority of patients their neurotic difficulties will cease to be a problem once their affective state has

Table II
Some features useful in the differentiation of "organic" from
"functional" depressives

	Likelihood of progressive cerebral failure being present	
	Small	Large
Memory and cognitive impairment reported as having been noted before depression	−	+
Memory and cognitive defects only noted since onset of depressive symptoms	+	−
Denial of knowledge of items of orientation and memory questionnaires	+	−
Evasive, near-miss confabulatory or perseverative replies	−	+
Dysphasias, dysgnosias and dyspraxias	−	+
Previous, personal or family history of affective disorders	Irrelevant as cerebral disorders frequently remobilize affective disorders in predisposed persons	

become normalized. In other patients, psychotherapeutic guidance beyond that employed to ensure successful antidepressant drug therapy will be required, and much of it may have to be directed to members of the patient's family, especially perhaps the single daughters with whom elderly neurotic women tend so frequently to live. Phobic symptoms, especially fears of going out or staying indoors alone, respond surprisingly well to various forms of behavior therapy, usually again in association with the use of thymoleptic preparations. Hysterical symptoms, as against histrionic types of behavior, hardly ever occur in elderly persons of our culture. The only behavior disorder sometimes first arising in late life is alcoholism. Here again, depression is usually a triggering mechanism, and its treatment together with psychotherapeutically orientated supervision makes the management of elderly alcoholics far more feasible than might be expected.

Table III
Grouping of patients according to some saliant features of mental state

Clinical picture	N
A. Severe depression with delusions and/or guilt	27
B. Severe depression without delusions or guilt	7
C. Mild depression with delusions and/or guilt	14
D. Depressive delusions or guilt without overt depression	8
E. Mild depression without either delusions or guilt	16
F. Neither overt depression nor depressive thought content	20

THE TYPOLOGY OF LATE-LIFE DEPRESSIONS

Once depression has been recognized as the main or an important source of a psychological disturbance, its treatment would be greatly facilitated if different types of depression of the elderly, each responding specifically to a different kind of therapy, could be distinguished. It would also be useful if typing a patient's depression led to a valid assessment of prognosis. It has to be said straightaway that the present writer's efforts in this direction have been unsuccessful and that he is not aware of any typology of depression in the elderly which has been shown to make a significant contribution to their management. On the whole, unipolar or bipolar depressions recurring before the age of forty were distinguished by better and more lasting recoveries than depressions starting in later life, i.e., the so-called involutional and senile depressions. Depressives over seventy did less well than those between the ages of sixty and seventy, probably largely because they also suffered from more physical diseases. Extroverts did better than introverts. Though just about statistically significant, these various differences would be of little use in deciding on the treatment and prognosis of individual patients (Post,

1962). In a more recent study (Post, 1972), an attempt was made to test the usefulness of classifying elderly depressives in terms of their presenting symptomatology.

In this last series there were ninety-two depressives over the age of sixty. They were all under the writer's care as inpatients and at the time of their discharge were deemed to be free of any cerebral disorder. They were personally followed by the investigator over the subsequent three years. There were numerous contacts with the patients' relatives and friends. Extracting and categorizing all the accumulated data from the case notes presented a considerable task, and for this reason independent ratings by a second investigator could not be arranged.

In terms of general severity of the illness, patients could be distributed over six categories as set out in Table III. The only comment required concerns the twenty patients in Group F. It might be thought that they were not suffering from depressive illnesses at all. In actual fact, they had been found in need of inpatient treatment on account of restlessness, poor sleep, loss of interest, somatic complaints—all failing to respond to outpatient therapy and becoming unfit for family care. Possibly the term of masked depression might be applicable, and this group is probably largely identical with patients discussed in the foregoing section: elderly neurotics with affective features.

Numbers in the six groups were too small for further analysis, and three groups were formed as follows.

AB patients: clearly communicated and *severe depression.* Most AB patients also exhibited typical melancholic thought content; in a few this was not obtainable. Patients in group AB could be called descriptively "Severely Psychotic Depressives."

CD patients: similar melancholic thought content—delusional or almost delusional ideas of guilt, poverty, self-belittlement, physical illness or change. In some there was a well communicated depressive mood, but not as severe as in AB patients; in others no depressive symptoms were obvious. This group will be referred to as "Intermediate Psychotic Depressives."

EF patients: mild or no overt depression. They had no delusional or "near-delusional" beliefs. They suffered reduction of interest and drives, tended to be restless, and were concerned with somatic sensations of an unpleasant kind, often leading to hypochondriacal, nondelusional fears. These patients were labeled "Neurotic Depressives."

As might be expected, members of these three clinical subgroups differed from one another on a number of characteristics. Considering, first of all, certain symptoms, only one Severely Psychotic Depressive exhibited complaining, whining and histrionically exaggerating behavior, but this was a striking feature in nearly half of the Neurotic Depressives. To a large extent, anxiety replaced depression in the Neurotic Depressives and was a marked feature in 75 percent. Conspicuous anxiety was noted in the Severely Psychotic group to a significantly smaller extent, but even so in nearly half of them. This confirms that anxiety and

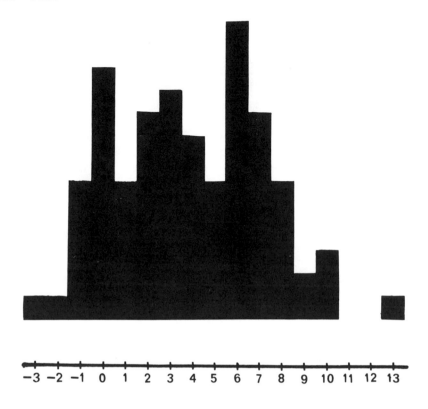

NEWCASTLE DIAGNOSTIC INDEX SCORE

FIG. 2.   Distribution of patients in terms of their Newcastle diagnosis scores

its psychomotor equivalent of agitation are common in elderly depressives as a group.

Turning to the background on which the depressions occurred, there was a tendency for the Severely Psychotic Depressives to have had slightly less evidence for previous maladjustment than patients belonging to the other two groups. Well over half of this series of elderly depressives—in fact, 50 percent of the Severe Psychotics and 75 percent of the Neurotic Depressives—had experienced longstanding interpersonal difficulties; similar but smaller differences were registered in the area of sexual and emotional maladjustments. They were, however, statistically significant only for past obsessive-phobic traits, which usually also colored the current illness; these were recorded in 24 percent of Severe Psychotics and in 44 percent of Neurotic Depressives. Surprisingly, a family history of affective illnesses in first-degree relatives was only insignificantly most frequent in Severe Psychotic Depressives, in 44 percent as against 31 percent of the

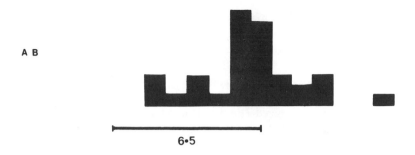

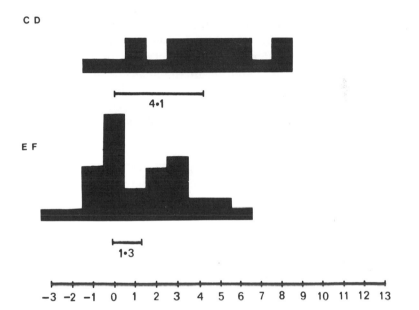

NEWCASTLE DIAGNOSTIC INDEX SCORE

FIG. 3.   Distributions of Newcastle diagnosis scores of three groups of patients

Neurotic Depressives. There were no differences among the three groups in frequency of reported loss of parents in childhood, in other childhood deprivation, in age at first depression, or whether or not there had been previous attacks.

Carney, Roth and Garside (1965) of Newcastle have worked out a method of rating depressives in terms of symptomatology and of various background factors, which allows them to classify depressives as either endogenous-psychotic or as reactive-neurotic with very little overlap. Patients are scored on a number of items. Features commonly thought to occur in neurotic depressives (anxiety, hysterical features, blaming others rather than oneself) carry negative points, and features of endogenous depression (early waking, self-blame, guilt feeling, and retardation) are given positive point values. Thus neurotic patients aggregate at the lower end of the Newcastle scale, and endogenous psychotic depressives at the higher end. It will be seen in Fig. 2 that rating our series of elderly depressives by the Newcastle measure produced a distribution which looked trimodal, though the writer has been advised that this trimodality might easily have occurred by chance.

When breaking down this population into Severe Psychotic Depressives (AB), Intermediate Psychotic Depressives (CD), and Neurotic Depressives (EF) (Fig. 3), it becomes obvious that the Psychotics are grouped near the upper end and the neurotics near the lower end of the scale. However, it is also clear that there is a degree of overlap between the groups, which makes it unlikely that their members belong to basically different populations. In keeping with this failure in a series of elderly depressives to allocate any but a few clearly to either a reactive or an endogenous group, it was found that precipitating factors could, with good reason, be suspected of having been present in all three types of depression with equally high frequencies. Among the various traumatic experiences which have been invoked as precipitating factors in depression, loss of a significant person is the most firmly established one. It was very striking to find that bereavement or threatened bereavement appeared to be related to the current depression in 29 percent of Neurotic Depressives, in 39 percent of Intermediate Psychotic, and in 41 percent of Severely Psychotic Depressives. In other words, the most potent reactive factors were found most frequently in patients with hereditary loading, scoring toward the "endogenous" end of the Newcastle scale.

The suggestion arose that all late-life depressions (serious enough to lead to hospital admissions) resulted from an interplay between inherited or acquired constitutional factors on one side, and the impact of life events on the other. Both types of factors were found with quite similar frequency in all types of elderly depressives. It was further suggested that the clinical picture, whether psychotic or neurotic, depended very much on personality structure. By totaling scores on personality items indicating abnormality, deviation scores were obtained for each patient (on the basis of their case notes). To a highly significant degree, Neurotic Depressives scored highest, and Severe Psychotic Depressives lowest (with Intermediate Psychotics occupying an intermediate position) for personality deviation noted during adult life. Obviously, this preliminary finding requires confirmation using properly controlled and validated measures. Also, it may be that patients with bipolar affective illnesses occupy a special position. There were, among ninety-two depressives, only seventeen with mostly dubious evidence for the presence of manic symptoms at one time or other, but interestingly all except three were members of the two psychotic groups.

It is tentatively concluded that depressive states in late life differ from patient to patient, in that there is an interplay of specific and highly personal factors in each individual. The evidence is, on the whole, against the existence of groups of persons suffering from this or that type of depressive "illness."

In a far more sophisticated fashion, a theoretical paper by Blumenthal (1971) states a similar view. Starting from the observation that depressions vary in terms of their etiology, symptomatology and response to different kinds of treatment, the simplest causal chain would be that etiology 1 is followed by depressive symptom pattern 1 which responds to therapy 1, that etiology 2 precedes symptom pattern 2 responding to therapy 2, etc. Blumenthal demonstrates that this model is implicit in a great deal of present-day investigations of the psychobiology of depression, and she thinks that this may be the reason why little progress has been made toward a real understanding of the disorder. She shows that there is, in fact, a far greater heterogencity in the etiology, symptomatology and treatment of depression. Future research should have to take account of this complicated situation through simultaneous studies of a number of variables, employing modern techniques of statistical analysis. Depressive states are best visualized as common final paths reached through an overlapping variety of etiological processes and responding, for this reason, far from specifically to different kinds of treatment. The matter is further complicated by etiological factors working together or in a chain sequence, e.g., starting from psychic event, via hormone imbalance, electrolyte disturbance, and transmitter imbalance, leading to depression. Moreover, this sequence of events could be set off at any point, and Blumenthal speculated that treatment would be effective only if applied at the right point. For instance, she considers that no amount of treatment directed at transmitter imbalance would be effective in a depressive whose illness was related to some continuing psychic stress, since strain would repeatedly renew the imbalance.

As a clinican and especially as a geriatric psychiatrist, one would suggest that the theoretician was wrong in making this and similar submissions. The whole point of treatment of depression in elderly persons is that good or reasonable results can be obtained by therapies affecting transmitter imbalance or electrolyte disturbance in spite of irremovable psychic stresses arising from the patient's life situation. Also, removal of depression not infrequently leads, even in the elderly, toward active steps on the patient's behalf of changing the life situation or of experiencing it no longer as a great stress. What is true, however, and borne out by experience, is that there is no specific relationship between pattern of depressive symptomatology and type of therapy. A high proportion of patients in our series were admitted because treatment with thymoleptic preparations by their family doctors or in the outpatient department had failed. It is not surprising, therefore, that electroshock therapy was the first choice of treatment following admission in 59 percent of Severely Psychotic Depressives. This form of treatment is supposed to produce only inferior results in neurotic depressives. All the same,

24 percent of Neurotic Depressives were initially treated with a course of ECT. Many patients required both types of therapy, ECT and drugs (mostly in this series amitriptyline or imipramine) in succession rather than concurrently. The treatment which immediately preceded the patient's discharge was, on the whole, thought to have been the most effective one. The practical irrelevance of any subclassification of elderly depressives is confirmed by the fact that ECT rather than drug therapy rendered patients fit for discharge only slightly more often in the case of Severe Psychotic Depressives (53%) than Neurotic Depressives (41%). Also, prognosis is said to be much worse in relatively mild and neurotic depressions and better in acutely severe psychotic illnesses. No difference was found to exist among our three clinical groups in outcome over the course of three years, assessed either in terms of further symptomatology or in a more global fashion.

TREATMENT AND MANAGEMENT

In the light of these experiences, the writer has evolved a treatment policy which is no longer much influenced by the clinical picture presented by the patient. The one exception must be stressed: electroconvulsive therapy is more likely than drug therapy to terminate quickly potentially dangerous psychotic states. Tricyclic and other psychopharmacological preparations used in large doses are prone to cause side effects leading to cardiac complications or falls, and may thus entail more risks to the patient than ECT. On the other hand, the choice of treatment must also be influenced by the fears and wishes of patients and their relatives; indications for giving ECT to depressives against their wishes are only very rarely present.

Apart from relatively infrequent emergency situations, therapeutic action is taken on the assumption that each patient suffers from a state of psychopathological and psychophysiological deviation which is called depression, but whose nature is, as yet, only imperfectly understood. This deviation will right itself in time, though this is not always the case in the elderly, in whom depression not infrequently becomes chronic. A number of remedies have been shown to abolish the psychopathological state or to remove some of its most disabling aspects in ways which are as yet ill understood. As emotional turmoil and anxiety are so frequently precipitating causes of depression, their continuation (especially in persons with longstanding emotional and neurotic difficulties) is likely to militate against remission of depression and may lead to early recurrence. In addition to determined somatic treatment of the depressive state, the "neurotic" aspects of the patient's condition should therefore receive attention through social, psychodynamically orientated, or behavior therapy. Often these environmental and personality problems prove irremovable, but it is almost always possible to reduce the degree of depression to a bearable level by adequate doses of tricyclic drugs, repeat sets of ECT, the use of monoamine oxidase inhibitors, and, very occasionally, the use of these preparations in combination with tricyclics. It has been some years since recommendations of psychosurgery had to be made in depressed patients over the age of sixty.

The writer has, in the past, attempted to evaluate the results of the treatment of elderly depressives under his care (Post, 1962), and he has recently carried out a similar study (Post, 1972). Table IV compares the earlier with the recent series of patients. The only significant difference concerns treatment for the current depression before admission. Nowadays, the great majority of depressives are admitted to the hospital only when ambulant treatments have failed. In other words, in the later series the more readily treatable and less persistently ill patients were, for the most part, excluded. On account of changes in admission policy, more members of the later series were socially disadvantaged and possibly more vulnerable to precipitating trauma.

Table V compares the treatments used during the index illness between the 1950 and the 1966 series. Around 1950, a high proportion of patients received no specific treatment, the only one available at the time being electroshock therapy. In spite of the introduction of tricyclic antidepressants, a total of 45.7 percent received ECT around 1966. "Other treatments" in 1950 signifies one patient receiving a modified leukotomy, and, in 1966, one operation as well as the use of MAOI drugs or lithium. Like other geriatric conditions, depression in the elderly often does not remit completely or lastingly. Outcome will be considered presently, but Table VI indicates that only one quarter of the earlier series of patients received further active treatment (other than hospitalization) and that this consisted of ECT in half. By contrast, only 8.7 percent received no further treatment following discharge around 1966, though in an additional 16.3 percent drugs were eventually and lastingly stopped. The remainder continued to receive antidepressant drugs continuously or intermittently, and a slightly higher proportion of these subjects received additional ECT as compared to those patients discharged around 1950.

It is at first sight disquieting that in spite of this tremendous increase of therapeutic activity, the sample of patients treated recently did no better longterm than the 1950 sample. As shown in Table VII, outcome in terms of further symptomatology following discharge from the hospital differed little between the 1950 and 1966 series. Recently, intermediate rather than strikingly good or bad results were recorded more frequently, but not to a statistically significant extent. Outcome was also expressed in terms of classes, taking account not only of further symptomatology but also of social adjustment in various areas and of needs of readmission. Again intermediate outcome was insignificantly more frequent after discharge around 1966. Though during their index illness in or around 1966, only 41 percent of the patients remained in hospital for more than three months, as against 78 percent in 1951, somewhat more patients of the later sample (42% as against 33%) had to be readmitted during a shorter observation period.

Rather disquieting was the discovery that during the three years after 1966,

Table IV
Some differences between two series of depressives over 60

	Elderly depressives admitted to same hospital	
	1950	1966
Number of patients	81	92
Received treatment for current attack of depression before admission	14.8%	60.9%
Low socioeconomic class	13.0%	25.0%
Precipitating factors regarded as present	58.0%	78.0%

Table V
Therapies employed during index illness in the case of patients
admitted around 1950 and 1966, respectively

Therapies employed	Percentage of patients	
	1950 (N = 81)	1966 (N = 92)
Supportive, occupational and social therapies, alone	46.9	2.1
Additionally, with electro-convulsive therapy	51.9	17.4
Additionally with tricyclic drugs	–	31.5
Electroshock and tricyclic drugs, both successively used	–	28.3
Combination of these with other antidepressant therapies	1.2	20.7

Table VI
Therapies employed after discharge from hospital around
1950 and 1966, respectively

Treatments applied during follow-up period	Percentages of patients	
	1950 (N = 81 over six years)	1966 (N = 92 over three years)
None for affective disorder	74.1	8.7
Tricyclics, eventually stopped	–	16.3
Tricyclics, intermittently or continuously	–	43.5
Electroconvulsive therapy	12.3	19.6*
Other (usually additional) therapies	13.6	11.9

*All but two of these patients also received antidepressants.

seven patients made suicidal attempts, three of them successfully. During a six-year follow-up of the earlier series, only one patient killed himself and three made attempts. However, taking account of the fact that the more recently treated sample of depressives probably contained a higher proportion of persistently ill patients than the earlier sample, some slight progress in treatment can be claimed. More recently, maintenance therapy with lithium salts has been introduced not only for patients showing tendencies towards bipolar illnesses, but also for those with more than one recent recurrence of depression. On a preliminary impression, this new approach will mark an important advance in the treatment of geriatric depression.

SUMMARY

Depression which has proved disabling in elderly persons is likely to continue as a source of trouble even when the original response to treatment has been good. A comparison of long-term results achieved before and after the introduction of thymoleptic drugs is reported.

Most severe depressions occur for the first time in life between the ages of fifty and sixty. Regardless of age of onset, depressive illnesses tend to recur increasingly frequently with rising age, and for this reason depression is probably the most common disorder leading to admission to psychiatric facilities between the ages of sixty and seventy-five. In this age group, chronic brain syndrome

Table VII
Comparison of long-term symptomatology in two samples
of elderly depressives

Long-term outcome	Percentage of patients	
	1950 (over 6 years)	1966 (over 3 years)
Lasting recovery	30.8	26.1
Further attacks with good recoveries	28.4	37.0
Some degree of depressive invalidism usually with further attacks	23.4	25.0
Continuously ill	17.4	11.9

patients begin to take the place of depressives. Possible mechanisms operating during later life in favoring the occurrence of depression have been discussed briefly.

The diagnosis of depression in the elderly is, as a rule, easy and straightforward. The presence of paranoid symptoms may make differentiation from late schizophrenic (paraphrenic) illnesses difficult. Perplexity, confusion and slowing may suggest the presence of an acute or chronic brain syndrome. The recognition of depression is highly important in terms of immediate treatment, but also of long-term prognosis, because the presence of cognitive defects in a depressive setting (depressive pseudodementia) usually presents no barrier to successful treatment. In mild depressions, differentiation from neurotic disorders is rarely of practical importance, as both conditions frequently coexist, with depression usually the more easily reversible condition.

The treatment of depression in the elderly would be greatly facilitated if different types of the disorder, each responding specifically to a different kind of therapy, could be distinguished. Failure in achieving a subdivision of late-life depressions has led to the suggestion that methods of management should be determined individually, according to the way in which depressive changes and personality structure interact in each patient.

COMMENTARIES

DR. VARGA: One of the real problems in psychiatry is that a close relationship between etiology and symptoms is rare, even in such obvious conditions as traumatic psychoses. It is difficult to say that the post-traumatic psychosis has one single cause—the *preceding trauma*—since even in the same person the same cause can lead at different times to various pictures. Just as in involutional depression in the same person, the clinical picture may switch from AB type (severe psychotic depression) to CD (intermediate) or to EF (neurotic form), or vice versa. In addition, we may see, during the depressive phase, manifestations of reversible dementia (cognitive impairment) with difficulty in remembering and learning, as well as in orientation.

The functional psychoses have a resemblance in their course to the Jacksonian principle. That is, the primary disturbances may lead to positive or negative secondary symptoms which then may manifest in tertiary disturbances. In a depressive episode, the primary anxiety and guilt may lead to paranoid delusions, which then may swing to manic-like agitation. Besides this stratification, we are reminded by every patient whom we treat that psychiatric illnesses are interrelated with three levels of existence: biological, psychological and social. These three-axis coordinates move on a time scale from the past memories to the future plans.

Depression may exhibit different manifestations in different ages in the same patient. It is true, however, that we do not know much more today than we did in the past about involutional and senile depressions, but we do know more about gerontology.

The old person is similar to his own younger version except that he is his own caricature. A man, known throughout his life as frugal, will become stingy when he becomes senile. Normal egotism becomes selfishness. Collectors become hoarders. The personality features go to extremes, and these character changes usually are not parallel with the decline of intellectual capacity; however, insight is missing. Many authors believe affective disorders in senescence are not one subgroup of affective disorders since withdrawal, morosity, reduced appetite, hopelessness, inertia, sleep changes, apathy and past-oriented rather than future-oriented views are as much symptoms of the normal aging as the symptomatology of depression.

DR. GALLANT: As Dr. Post has mentioned, monoamine oxidase activity apparently increases with age in association with a possible decrease in the incidence of mania and an increase in depression. Dr. Mendels, would you care to comment on these biochemical and clinical observations?

DR. MENDELS: There is indeed evidence along the lines Dr. Post indicated. However, there are a couple of reports that some depressed patients have low platelet MAO irrespective of their age. The evidence is that this occurs primarily, but not exclusively, in patients with bipolar illness or with a family history of bipolar illness. Dr. Post's closing remark about the recent indications of the effectiveness of lithium in this group of people raises a question about the association between levels of MAO and lithium responsiveness. We do have some data suggesting that there is a good correlation between those patients with low MAO levels in their platelets and lithium responsiveness. However, one cannot necessarily extrapolate from platelet to brain MAO. Nevertheless, given the fact that MAO is under genetic control, there is the possibility that MAO platelet levels may serve as a marker for the predisposition to depression or drug responsiveness to antidepressant therapy.

DR. PERRIS: Affective disorders in the elderly have not received enough attention in the past. As Dr. Post pointed out, the picture has been made even more difficult by the peculiar symptomatologic pattern that affective disorders may show in senile patients. Figures from several epidemiological studies of patients, age sixty or more, admitted to psychiatric hospitals have given quite consistent results and point to the fact that affective disorders are responsible for about one-half of the admissions, whereas the incidence of organic syndromes is not higher than about 25 percent. It has also been realized that only a minor part of the affective disorders of the elderly is due to manic-depressive psychosis or other recurrent depressive disorders, whereas the biggest group is represented by depressive breakdowns first occurring in the elderly. Awareness of the occurrence of such disorders has permitted the implementation of active therapeutic measures and consequently the discharge of a great number of patients, who under other circumstances would probably have become chronic cases. The therapeutic strategies outlined by Dr. Post are well-grounded, and I am pleased to find them to be quite consistent with our own therapeutic policy in such cases. Considering the possibility of an increased risk for the elderly of unwanted toxic reactions with current antidepressants, we do not hesitate to give unilateral (nondominant) ECT to old patients if their condition is severe enough to warrant an intensive treatment of this kind. Taking into account that existential problems very often play a prominent role in the etiopathogenesis of depressive reactions in the aged, we suggest that adequate supportive psychotherapeutic measures should be considered in each case.

A few other issues should be briefly commented upon. Concerning clear-cut instances of schizoaffective disorders not secondary to organic damage, the risk of first onset in the age group here considered is almost nil. In a recent monograph devoted to these disorders (Perris, 1974), I pointed out that the number of nonorganic recurrent schizoaffective disorders occurring for the first time after the age of fifty is hardly greater than a handful.

An increased content of MAO in platelets with increasing age, according to Dr. Post, might shed some light on the increased rate of depressive disorder in the elderly. Very recent brain investigations by Dr. Gottfries (Gottfries et al., 1974) in our department have confirmed the relationship between age and the MAO content in the brain. However, these results also show that there is a lower MAO content in the brains of individuals who committed suicide than in a control series. Even if not all cases of suicide can be attributed to a depressive illness, these apparent conflicting findings must be taken into account.

Concerning the arousal disorder in elderly depressed patients, we have collected evidence from three independent series (d'Elia and Perris, 1974; Perris, 1974) which supports the hypothesis that the dominant brain hemisphere may be more involved than the nondominant one in depressive processes. Thus it could be assumed that such an involvement is even more pronounced in the elderly and may account, to a large extent, for the transient intellectural impairment of the pseudo-dementia depressive type seen in older patients.

DR. MENDELS: The point that concerns me about Dr. Perris' data is his reference to what he calls "precipitating factors" and their relationship to the onset of depression. This term was also mentioned quite often in Dr. Klein's presentation. I don't mean to suggest that environmental factors in life do not play an important role in the onset of depression. The part that bothers me is how do you know, or how does the patient know? It seems to me that part of the nature of man is to have a ready explanation for things. We feel much better when we believe that we know why something happens, even if we're deceiving ourselves.

Depression is often of an insidious onset, and as a result of the increasing impairment associated with depression people start to have troubles in life. Thus many so-called precipitating factors may in fact be symptoms or consequences of the depression. I am not suggesting that life events of one kind or another are not important, but I think we should be much more precise in our use of the term "precipitating factors."

DR. WEISSMAN: Prospective studies can solve the problems in life-events research, described by Dr. Mendels, but there are many difficulties in following a group of people through stress to see how many get the disease and how many don't. Therefore, we are going to continue to rely on these retrospective studies. In association with this problem, I would like to comment on the interesting data Dr. Post presented on social maladjustment. Over half his patients had interpersonal maladjustments. Here, too, it is important to define what one means by interpersonal maladjustment and to look at the relationship between the maladjustment and the current symptom state. Did the maladjustment occur before, during or after the illness—or was it chronic? We have found that if you ask people about their maladjustments at the height of illness and compare them to normal samples, the depressives report considerable maladjustment whether they are psychotic or neurotically depressed. In these studies, maladjustment was defined as interpersonal functioning in current social situation. However, if you look at depressives after recovery when the consequences of having an illness have had a chance to resolve, the incidence of maladjustment is really not much different from normals. Now, if you obtain retrospective information about premorbid maladjustment, you find the problems of reliability and reporting that Dr. Mendels discussed, and we can't put much weight on such data. I think that many of the severe personality problems and maladjustment attributed to depressives are based on their reported life situations at the height of their illness. Long-term follow-up studies of depressives through symptom-free periods may resolve some of the problems of reporting found in retrospective studies. They may also help us to discriminate maladjustments due to a symptom state from maladjustments that are enduring and perhaps predisposed to further episodes.

DR. HAMILTON: The problem of reactive and endogenous depression is one which is so difficult that the French have completely rejected such classification of depressions on the grounds that it involves an etiological hypothesis for which there is no evidence, as has just been pointed out by Dr. Weissman. When one talks to patients about their stresses and difficulties, one has to take into account the fact that their guilt, self-accusation and self-denigration make them exaggerate the difficult problems they have had in the past and blame themselves for the sort of thing they believe they have done to bring about their illness. Even more important, whether or not one can see these relationships depends on one's judgment and common sense. Given enough enthusiasm and lack of judgment, one can always find some psychological precipitant to explain an attack of illness.

Once an illness starts, the pattern of its manifestation is almost certainly independent of what started it off. The particular features are determined very much by the characteristics of the individual. To consider, therefore, that the dichotomy between endogenous and reactive bears some relationship to the dichotomy between retarded and anxious or between "psychotic" and "neurotic" is one which is extremely questionable and, in my opinion, quite invalid. I would like to reemphasize Dr. Post's point that the "psychotic" vs. "neurotic" dichotomy is a complete waste of time, illogical, and clinically senseless. All of these terms would be better abandoned. We should talk about severe and mild depressions and about patterns of symptoms such as a retarded, anxious or hypochondriacal pattern, and clearly use terms which have a specific meaning in relation to what the patient is suffering from and how his illness came about.

DR. PERRIS: As stated in my presentation, we use four independent factors for describing the patient. The first one is concerned with the most prominent symptomatology, and by prominent I mean symptoms which are relevant for the patient. The second factor refers to the degree of severity when we use the terms psychotic or nonpsychotic without using neurotic and its implications. In our usage, the term psychotic is acceptable as it means severe, and the term nonpsychotic means not severe. The third factor is the course of the disorder which can help to differentiate bipolar from unipolar, etc. The fourth factor is etiology, where different factors can be combined if they are important.

DR. SCHOU: In reference to Dr. Post's comments about drug therapy, it should be remembered that the elderly are more sensitive to side effects of lithium therapy and require lower dosages for a therapeutic response.

DR. POST: Dr. Varga used the term "reversible dementia"—a term I don't like very much; I don't like the term "dementia" at all. Intellectual and cognitive impairment are more acceptable and are cerebral physiologic problems. Cognitive impairment occurs in depressives and in other conditions. Dr. Varga mentions the changes in character and personality in depressive types. The interesting thing is that these symptoms were described in a group of volunteers at Duke. The incidence of depressive symptomatology was 25 percent, and it was more prevalent among the poorer and more elderly. However, these people had not sought help, and one should not confuse a miserable, unhappy existence with a specific depressive illness.

I don't like to say anything about "schizoaffective," as it is a very complicated problem, but I would like to confirm that in an investigation of elderly patients diagnosed as schizoaffective there was a very high proportion of cerebral organic disorders but it was not as high as Dr. Perris found.

Next, I would like to refer to Dr. Schou's comments. I was delighted to hear Dr. Schou say that older people are particularly sensitive to lithium, and if I understood him rightly the effective level is somewhat lower than in younger people.

That leaves just the two very important and critical points made by Dr. Mendels and Dr. Weissman. Now, the question of precipitating factors is a subject to which one can devote a whole day. There are two ways of approaching it. First of all, in my paper, I cautiously said that precipitating factors are strongly suspected. A man of seventy would have been at risk to develop a depressive illness for the last forty years. If then he actually develops his first depression at the age of seventy two months after his wife's death, I would have thought the probability of there being a causal relationship to be quite high. Also, regarding retrospective falsification, and I think that is a term that Dr. Hamilton has used, there are certain precise things that happen to people, such as bereavement, physical illness, loss of job, moving away of children, etc. These are very clear events, and one again and again finds this close connection. The other point is experimental, and there are very respectable methods in which one can show that some schizophrenic relapses are connected to life situations; there are respectable data to support the idea that there is a connection between life stress and depressive reactions which are not retrospective falsifications (Birley and Brown, 1970). Aubrey Lewis reported such findings in 1936. Then, there is Dr. Weissman's point that people may give false accounts of themselves on self-report scales.

DR. GALLANT: Before leaving the subject of the diagnosis and treatment of depression in geriatric patients, I want to reemphasize that there is a need for additional caution in utilizing drug therapy in this population. In one review of 265 patients admitted to a medical geriatric unit (Learoyd, 1972), approximately 20 percent of the new psychiatric geriatric admissions were precipitated by adverse reactions to psychotropic drugs. Impaired drug metabolism and decreased renal function as well as the appearance of organic disease processes may account for the increase in drug-induced deaths in the elderly (Bottinger et al., 1974). For example, the mean plasma half-life of antipyrine is 45 percent greater in geriatric patients than in young control groups (Eisdorfer and Fann, 1973). Thus it may be wiser to spread the dosage to a t.i.d. regimen in geriatric patients because one large nighttime dose of medication such as amitriptyline may cause a higher incidence of cardiovascular side effects or atropine-like mental symptoms of confusion in these patients, who are more susceptible to these side effects. At the same time, it should be pointed out that socioeconomic and general medical help may be of more importance for many of the isolated, deprived and depressed elderly citizens than a specific type of somatic therapy.

I would like to end this discussion by stating that Dr. Post's paper will be an important teaching manuscript for physicians in training and for those individuals concerned with clinical research in the geriatric population. Less than twenty years ago, an NIMH-sponsored conference on research in gerontology, producing thirty-two papers and involving forty-one participants, made no mention of chemotherapeutic treatment modalities (Anderson, 1956). It appears that this problem of depression in the elderly has received more extensive and adequate evaluation and treatment in Britain than in this country.

REFERENCES

Anderson, J. E. (1956). *Psychological Aspects of Aging: Proceedings of a Conference on Planning Research*. Wisconsin: George Banta Co.
Birley, J. L. T., and Brown, G. W. (1970). Crises and life changes preceding the onset or relapse of acute schizophrenia: clinical aspects. *Br. J. Psychiat*. 116:327–33.
Blumenthal, M. D. (1971). Heterogeneity and research on depressive disorders. *Arch. Gen. Psychiat*. 24:524–31.
Bottinger, L. E., Norlander, M., Strandberg, I., and Westerholm, B. (1974). Deaths from drugs: an analysis of drug induced deaths reported to the Swedish adverse drug reaction committee during a five year period, 1966–1970. *J. Clin. Pharm*. 14:401–07.
Carney, M. W. P., Roth, M., and Garside, R. F. (1965). The diagnosis of depressive syndromes and the prediction of ECT response. *Br. J. Psychiat*. 111:659–74.
Cawley, R. H., Post, F., and Whitehead, A. (1973). Barbiturate tolerance and psychological functioning in elderly depressed patients. *Psychol. Med*. 3:39–52.
d'Elia, G., and Perris, C. (1974). Cerebral functional dominance and memory functions. *Acta Psychiat. Scand*. Suppl. 255.
Eisdorfer, C., and Fann, W. E. (1973). *Psychopharmacology and Aging*. New York: Plenum Press.
Gottfries, C. G., Oreland, L., Wiberg, A., and Winblad, B. (1974). Monoamine oxidase in human brain: a comparison between a control material and a material of suicides. 1st World Congress of Biological Psychiatry, Buenos Aires.

Hemsi, L. K., Whitehead, A., and Post, F. (1968). Cognitive functioning and cerebral arousal in elderly depressives and dements. *J. Psychosomat. Res.* 12:145–56.

Kay, D. W. K. (1962). Outcome and cause of death in mental disorders of old age: a long-term follow-up of organic and functional psychoses. *Acta Psychiat. Scand.* 38:249–315.

——— and Roth, M. (1961). Environmental and hereditary factors in the schizophrenias of old age ("late paraphrenia") and their bearing on the general problem of causation in schizophrenia. *J. Ment. Sci.* 107:686–91.

———, Roth, M., and Hopkins, B. (1955). Affective disorders arising in the senium: (1) their association with organic cerebral deterioration. *J. Ment. Sci.* 101:302–18.

Kendell, R. E. (1974). The stability of psychiatric diagnosis. *Br. J. Psychiat.* 124:352–56.

Learoyd, B. M. (1972). Psychotropic drugs and the elderly patient. *Med. J. Aust.* 1:1131–33.

Lewis, A. (1936). Melancholia: prognostic study and case material. *J. Ment. Sci.* 82:488–558.

McDonald, C. (1967). The pattern of neurotic illness in the elderly. *Aust. N.Z. J. Psychiat.* 1:203–10.

——— (1973). An age-specific analysis of the neuroses. *Br. J. Psychiat.* 122:477–80.

Perris, C. (1974). A study of cycloid psychoses. *Acta Psychiat, Scand.* Suppl. 253.

——— and d'Elia, G. (1974). Electroencephalographic hemispheric differences and affective disorders. 1st World Congress of Biological Psychiatry, Buenos Aires.

Post, F. (1962). *The Significance of Affective Symptoms in Old Age.* London: Oxford University Press.

——— (1966). *Persistent Persecutory States of the Elderly.* Oxford: Pergamon Press.

——— (1968a). The factor of aging in affective illness. In A. Coppen and A. Walk, eds., *Recent Developments in Affective Disorders. Br. J. Psychiat.* Spec. Pub. No. 2:105–16.

——— (1968b). The development and progress of senile dementia in relationship to the functional psychiatric disorders of later life. In C. Muller and L. Ciompi, eds., *Senile Dementia.* Bern: Hans Huber, pp. 85–100.

——— (1971). Schizoaffective symptomatology in late life. *Br. J. Psychiat.* 118:437–45.

——— (1972). The management and nature of depressive illnesses in late life. *Br. J. Psychiat.* 121:393–404.

——— (1975) in press). Dementia, depression, and pseudo-dementia. *Psychiat. Sem.*

Prakash, C., and Stern, G. (1973). Neurological signs in the elderly. *Age & Aging* 2:24–27.

CHAPTER IX

Some Problems in Clinical Trials of New Antidepressant Agents

A. Issues in the Evaluation of New Drugs: A Double-Blind Trial of Maprotiline (Ludiomil) and Amitriptyline (Elavil) in Outpatient Depressives

M. M. Weissman

Maprotiline (BA 34,276) is a new antidepressant, pharmacologically related to the conventional tricyclic drugs but chemically different from them by the presence of a bridge across the central ring, thus forming a tetracyclic ring system (Amin et al., 1973). In a four-week double-blind clinical trial with outpatient depressives, maprotiline was compared to amitriptyline hydrochloride in order to determine if it had clinical advantages over the usual tricyclics and to see if a different clinical profile could be detected (Kielholz, 1972; Lauritsen and Madsen, 1974).

This paper will illustrate several issues in the evaluation of new drugs, derived from the clinical trial. The results of the double-blind comparison of maprotiline and amitriptyline will be presented and will demonstrate the difficulty in showing a different clinical profile between antidepressants despite different chemical structures. The results of this trial illustrate the need for consideration of outcome criteria in drug comparisons where differences are apt to be subtle, and for closer attention to the statistical analysis of such trials, particularly the criteria for inclusion of patients in the analysis.

METHOD

Patient Selection for the Trial

Included were male and female outpatient depressives, between the ages of twenty-one and sixty-five, who exhibited a primary depressive disorder. The depression was characterized by a predominant affect of sadness accompanied by disturbances of sleep, appetite, sex and drive in patients who reached a score of at least 7 on the Raskin 3-Area Scale (range 3–15), which measures verbal report, behavior and secondary symptoms of depression (Raskin et al., 1967).

Patients were excluded if they had a predominant affect of anxiety; a primary diagnosis of schizophrenia, including schizoaffective type, depressed; or a past history or evidence of schizophrenia. Also excluded were patients with a history of drug abuse or alcoholism; patients who had had ECT within the last six months or who had shown no response to an adequate dose of tricyclic antidepressants in the past three months; patients who were pregnant; and patients who had a history or evidence of serious medical illness, known drug allergies or hypersensitivity reactions.

Sample Size

A sufficient number of patients entered the study so that sixty patients (thirty in each treatment group) completed four weeks of treatment.

Design

The study was double-blind, randomized and parallel-design, and lasted four weeks. Patients were seen twice during the first week and weekly thereafter.

Medication and Doses

Each tablet contained either 37.5 mg of maprotiline or 25 mg of amitriptyline. The dose for the first three days was fixed at three tablets per day and for the next four days at four tablets per day, given in divided doses. The balance of the study after week 1 was conducted in a flexible dose format between four and eight tablets per day. The investigator was instructed to build up to the optimum dose as rapidly as possible and maintain it for at least one week. The maximum dose could not exceed 300 mg of maprotiline or 200 mg of amitriptyline per day (eight tablets). Patients were given a minimum of two extra days' medication beyond the next visit. No other psychotropic medications were allowed, with the exception of hypnotics for sleep where indicated. Patients were instructed to return all unused medication at each visit. Pill-taking was monitored by direct questioning and by pill count.

Assessments

Basic sociodemographic, historical and diagnostic information was collected. The main outcome was manifest psychopathology, assessed by psychiatric interview. This assessment was made weekly by the treating psychiatrist on the Hamilton Rating Scale (Hamilton, 1960) and the Raskin Depression Scale (Raskin et al., 1967), and by a global assessment of illness. All treatment emergent signs and symptoms and vital signs were recorded weekly, and laboratory evaluations and electrocardiograms were obtained at the pretreatment and termination visits.

Data Analysis

The data were anlyzed independently by CIBA-Geigy and by the Yale investigators. Statistical analysis undertaken by the Yale group included chi square for categorical variables and analysis of covariance for rating data with the pretreatment scores as the covariate. Homogeneity of covariance was first tested. Early terminators were handled by the end-point analysis in which termination ratings, or ratings of the last visit in which patients were on adequate medication, were substituted in the final analysis. Results presented are for the period after one week of treatment and at the end of the trial.

RESULTS

Attrition and Completion

As shown in Table I, attrition and completion were comparable in the two treatment groups. Eighty-four patients entered the study. Of the eighty-four, sixty patients (71%) completed four weeks of treatment (thirty patients in each treatment group) and twenty-four patients (thirteen on maprotiline and eleven on amitriptyline) terminated early, usually due to noncooperation.

Table II gives a more detailed description of the early terminators, including their medication group, time and reason for termination. As can be seen, most of the termination was early, usually in the first week. There were no differences between treatment groups in time of termination, age or sex of terminators. All early terminators were diagnosed as depressive neurosis, as were most patients.

Criteria for Withdrawal of Patients from the Statistical Analysis

Prior to the analysis, the Yale group established criteria for the exclusion of patients from the final statistical analysis. Early termination was not a criterion for exclusion. For early terminators, the final rating scored at the time the patient was taking an adequate dose of medication was used in the statistical analysis. The criteria for exclusion from the analysis were as follows:

Table I
Termination status and reason for termination in two drug groups

Termination status	Drug groups		Totals	
	Maprotiline N	Amitriptyline N	N	%
Reasons for early termination				
Noncooperation	8	5		
Clinical worsening	1	2		
Clinical improvement	0	2		
Side effects	4	2		
Subtotal for those terminating before four weeks	13	11	24	29
Completed four weeks	30	30	60	71
Total	43	41	84	100

    1. Inadequate dose of medication, which was defined as an average of 75 percent or less of the minimum daily dose allowed. Therefore, an average of less than 3 pills a day over the entire study and less than 2.7 pills per day for the first week was considered inadequate.
    2. Use of psychotropic medication other than hypnotics during the study.
    3. Concurrent illness.
By these criteria, seventeen out of eighty-four patients (20%) were eliminated from the analysis (eight on maprotiline and nine on amitriptyline) (Table III).
    Four of the sixty patients (7%) who completed the study were eliminated from the analysis because of the use of other medications or other illness (two were on thyroid extract, one was taking Percadon, and one was diagnosed as hyperthyroid). These patients were divided evenly between drug groups. Thirteen patients, all noncompleters, were withdrawn from the analysis due to inadequate doses of medication. The final end-point analysis included sixty-seven patients (thirty-five on maprotiline and thirty-two on amitriptyline).

Table II
Medication group, termination time, reason for termination
for patients who did not complete the 4-week trial (N = 24)

Drug	Termina-tion week	Reason
	3	Noncooperation, stopped taking pills
	1	Noncooperation, wanted other treatment
	1	Noncooperation, did not take pills
	1	Noncooperation, did not return
	1	Noncooperation, did not take pills
	2	Noncooperation, did not return
Maprotiline	2	Noncooperation, stopped taking pills
	1	Noncooperation
	2	Clinical worsening, anxious and somatic complaints
	2	Side effects, skin rash
	1	Side effects, seizure
	1	Side effects, worsening of urinary problem since intake
	2	Side effects, toxic psychosis
	1	Noncooperation, missed appointments
	1	Noncooperation, did not return
	1	Noncooperation, refused to return
	1	Noncooperation, stopped taking pills
	1	Noncooperation, did not take pills
Amitriptyline	1	Clinical worsening, suicidal
	2	Clinical worsening, hospitalized
	1	Clinical improvement after four pills
	3	Clinical improvement, refused to take pills
	1	Side effects, dazed, depersonalized
	2	Side effects, constipation and no response to treatment

Characteristics of the Patients

The sixty-seven patients who were included in the statistical analysis were between the ages of nineteen and sixty-three (average age, thirty-six); mostly female (89%); white (85%); commonly from the middle and lower middle class (Social Class 3 and 4) according to the Hollingshead index; currently married

Table III
Status of patients included and excluded from the end-point sample

	Maprotiline	Amitriptyline	Total
Status of patients included in end-point analysis			
Completed study	28	28	56
Did not complete study	7	4	11
Total	35	32	67
Status of patients excluded from end-point analysis			
Completed study	2	2	4
Did not complete study	6	7	13
Total	8	9	17
Total sample entered study	43	41	84

(61%); and Catholic (58%). The most common diagnosis (89%) was depressive neurosis. Six percent of the patients were diagnosed as psychotic depression and 5 percent as manic-depressives. Sixty-three percent had experienced at least one previous depressive episode. The majority (67%) had experienced depressive symptoms for at least eight weeks before coming for treatment, but only 16 percent had received an antidepressant in the past six months. The average Hamilton Total Score at entrance into the study was 19.9 (S.D.=8.03). No significant differences were found between treatment groups, or between completers and early terminators on any of these variables. In summary, typical patients were women, moderately depressed, ambulatory, nonpsychotic and nonbipolar, and for the most part had had a previous depressive episode; these patients were typical of our clinic population.

Clinical Status After One Week

Table IV compares the clinical status of the patients by drug group at the end of one week of treatment, using the Hamilton factor scores derived from the Early Clinical Drug Evaluation Unit (Guy and Bonato, 1970), the Hamilton Total Score, the Raskin Depression Scale, and the global illness rating. These analyses

Table IV

Comparison of maprotiline and amitriptyline by analysis of covariance on symptom status after one week of treatment

| Symptom ratings | Adjusted means[1][2] | | F-Test |
	Maprotiline N = 32	Amitriptyline N = 30	
Hamilton factor scores			
Sleep disturbance	1.40	0.88	1.72
Somatization	2.66	2.79	0.07
Anxiety depression	4.29	3.82	0.52
Apathy	1.87	2.03	0.30
Hamilton total score	11.47	10.99	0.10
Raskin total score	6.81	6.33	1.15
Overall degree of illness	3.51	3.16	2.92

[1]Means are adjusted for the initial level of the items.

[2]Five patients were eliminated from the end-point sample of 67 for this analysis because of inadequate dosage in the first week.

were also done using alternate Hamilton factor scores (anxiety/agitation; retarded/endogenous; delusional guilt; general factor) (Hordern et al., 1965). Results were similar and will not be presented here. Five patients were eliminated from the one-week analyses due to inadequate doses of medication during that first week. As can be seen, there are no significant differences between groups after one week of treatment.

Clinical Status at the Termination of the Study

Table V presents similar analyses at the termination of the study and shows that results are essentially the same as for one week. There are no significant differences in symptoms between groups. Both treatment groups improved.

Table VI shows the patients' and the physician's opinion of therapeutic effect and, again, shows no differences between drugs. However, both the patients and the physician reported moderate to marked improvement in the majority of cases.

Table V
Comparison of maprotiline and amitriptyline by analysis of covariance on symptom status at the termination of the study

| Symptom ratings | Adjusted means[1] | | F-Test |
	Maprotiline N = 35	Amitriptyline N = 32	
Hamilton factor scores			
Sleep disturbance	0.72	0.07	0.0
Somatization	1.90	1.89	0.0
Anxiety depression	3.05	3.12	0.01
Apathy	0.69	0.99	1.71
Hamilton total score	7.46	7.70	0.02
Raskin total score	5.37	5.26	0.05
Overall degree of illness	2.64	2.55	0.08

[1]Means are adjusted for the initial level of the item.

Clinical Course

Fig. 1 presents these results graphically and shows the patients' clinical status by drug groups, using the Hamilton Total Score at the initial visit, after one week of treatment, and at the termination of the study. As can be seen, both groups improved and most of the improvement occurred during the first week. The change in clinical status between entrance, week 1 and termination was highly significant in both groups.

The mean onset of a therapeutic effect was noted to be similar in both groups: 5.7 days (S.D.=5.2) for maprotiline and 5.4 days (S.D.=5.1) for amitriptyline.

Dose

The flexible dose range after one week of treatment was 4 to 8 tablets per day, which was 150 to 300 mg for maprotiline and 100 to 200 mg for amitriptyline. The optimum dose for a therapeutic effect was judged by the investigator to be 5.2 tablets per day (194.3 mg) maprotiline and 5.3 tablets per day (131.5 mg) amitriptyline. Although the number of pills taken was similar in both drug groups, maprotiline had an optimum therapeutic dose in the higher range. The average

Table VI
Patients' and physician's opinion of therapeutic effect at the termination of the study (N = 67)*

Therapeutic effect	Patients' opinion		Physician's opinion	
	Maprotiline N	Amitriptyline N	Maprotiline N	Amitriptyline N
Marked improvement	10	7	11	9
Moderate improvement	16	17	16	16
Minimal improvement	3	5	2	3
No change	3	1	3	3
Worse	3	0	3	0

*Data were missing for patients' opinion on two patients and for physician's opinion on one patient in the amitriptyline groups.

Chi Square between drug groups for patients' or physician's opinions were not significant.

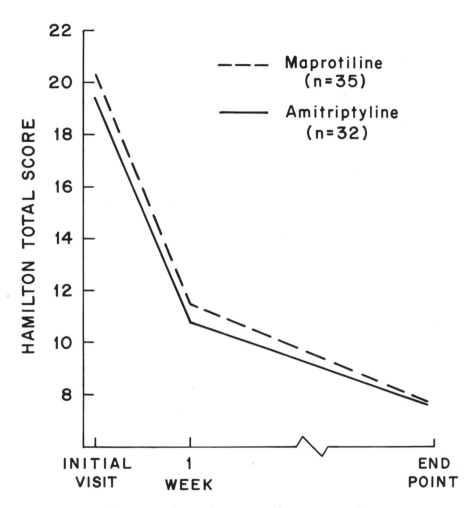

FIG. 1.   Hamilton total score in two drug groups over time

dose over four weeks was 4.3 tablets (161 mg) maprotiline and 4.2 tablets (105 mg) amitriptyline.

Side Effects

Treatment emergent signs and symptoms were recorded pretreatment and at weekly intervals. Table VII notes the number and percent of patients in each drug group who had a particular side effect at any time during the course of treatment that had been either absent or less severe during pretreatment. Side effects are ranked by frequency of their appearance in the maprotiline group. None of the side effect differences between drugs was significant, with the exception of headaches. This is within chance expectation. The rank order correlations of the individual side effects in the drug groups were tested by the Spearman's Rho. Results were highly significant (Rho = .92.) As can be seen, most patients in both drug groups reported an increase of dry mouth, drowsiness, increased appetite with a craving for sweets, feelings of dizziness, and constipation. This is similar to side effects commonly reported with antidepressants and to results published by DiMascio, Klerman, and Prusoff (1975) from the New Haven-Boston collaborative trial of maintenance amitriptyline. One patient taking maprotiline had a seizure two weeks after a dose of 150 mg daily had been attained. The patient recovered fully and was found subsequently to have had a history of episodes of loss of consciousness.

Side effects, in general, were usually considered insignificant and rarely interfered with treatment. Table VIII shows the investigator's opinion of the side effects. As can be seen, every patient reported at least one side effect which either first appeared or became worse during the study. Of those patients included in the end-point analysis, only four on maprotiline and one on amitriptyline required termination of the trial due to side effects.

Increase in Appetite

Since an increase in appetite, weight gain and craving for sweets, especially in obese patients, had been observed by Paykel in the New Haven–Boston eight-month maintenance trial of amitriptyline, attention was given to appetite changes in the current trial (Paykel et al., 1973). No differences in appetite were observed between drugs. Appetite was rated pretreatment and at termination on a 13-point scale: 1 = maximum increase; 7 = normal; 13= maximum decrease from normal appetite. Appetite changes in the two drug groups were compared by analysis of covariance, covarying for pretreatment appetite and weight. No significant differences in appetite were noted and the patients' appetite was rated as about normal in both groups at the termination of the study. This requires further study with patients on maintenance therapy before definite conclusions can be reached.

Table VII
Treatment emergent signs and symptoms by drug group[1][2]

Treatment emergent signs and symptoms	Maprotiline (N = 35)		Amitriptyline (N = 32)	
	N	%	N	%
Dry mouth	30	85.7	25	78.1
Drowsiness	22	62.9	24	75.0
Complaint of increased appetite	19	54.3	23	71.9
Feelings of dizziness, faintness or weakness	18	51.4	21	65.6
Craving for sweets	18	51.4	20	62.5
Craving for chocolates	16	45.7	19	59.4
Constipation	15	42.9	19	59.4
Blurred vision	15	42.9	15	46.9
Tachycardia	14	40.0	14	43.8
Feelings of jitteriness	12	34.3	8	25.0
Nasal congestion	10	28.6	10	31.3
Nausea	10	28.6	10	31.3
Difficulty with urination	8	22.9	8	25.0
Excessive sweating	8	22.9	8	25.0
Feeling of numbness or tingling	8	22.9	7	21.9
Headaches	8	22.9	1	31.1
Complaints of palpitations	7	20.0	6	18.8
Visible tremor at interview	5	14.3	5	15.6
Diarrhea	5	14.3	4	12.5
Insomnia	5	14.3	2	6.3
Hypotension	4	11.4	8	25.0
Vomiting	4	11.4	2	6.3
Complaint	2	5.7	4	12.5
Dystonic symptoms	2	5.7	3	9.4
Increased salivation	2	5.7	3	9.4
Skin rashes	2	5.7	1	3.1
Akathisia	1	2.9	4	12.5
Excitement	1	2.9	3	9.4
Convulsion	1	2.9	0	0
Toxic confusional state	1	2.9	0	0
Hypomania	0	0	2	6.3
Report of syncope	0	0	0	0
Rigidity	0	0	0	0

Laboratory Values, Vital Signs, ECG

Laboratory values, blood pressure, pulse and ECG were examined in detail over the study. No trend of abnormalities was noted in either treatment. Sporadic abnormal laboratory values did occur and were judged to be of no clinical importance.

DISCUSSION

These results clearly demonstrate the difficulty in showing a different clinical profile in antidepressants that are pharmacologically similar but have dissimilar chemical structures. The results should be reviewed in conjunction with other double-blind clinical trials of maprotiline. As can be seen in Table IX, over 900 patients spanning many countries have been studied (Amin et al., 1973; Lauritsen and Madsen, 1974; Welner, 1972; De S. Pinto et al., 1972; Roy et al., 1973; Guz, 1972). Results have been remarkably similar between countries and with the Yale data presented today. Before accepting the hypothesis that there is no clinical difference between the drugs, the possibility of a Type II error due to the choice of outcome criteria should be considered. Moreover, these studies raised questions about the criteria for patient inclusion in the statistical analysis, an issue which deserves attention when findings are examined across studies.

Issues of Assessments

All of the double-blind studies, including the one presented here, used as the main outcome criteria manifest psychopathology assessed by the treating psychiatrist during an interview. All used as the instrument for assessment the Hamilton Rating Scale for Depression. This scale has the most international acceptance, and therefore was useful in multinational studies where data were pooled. However, the absence of additional types of outcome criteria and different assessment techniques, when the differences anticipated were expected to be subtle, may have been an error.

A recent article by Katz and Itil (1974) is relevant to this issue. Katz and Itil have stressed that the capacity to measure behavior and symptomatology through

---

[1]TESS observed during therapy which were either absent or less severe pretreatment are recorded.

[2]The differences between drug groups for each TESS were tested by Fisher's exact test. There were no significant differences except for headaches ($p < .05$). The rank order correlation of TESS between drug groups was tested by Spearman's Rho .92 $p < .001$.

Table VIII
Physician's opinion of treatment emergent signs or
symptoms at the termination of the study

| | Maprotiline | | Amitriptyline | |
	N	%	N	%
Side effects absent	0	0	0	0
No significant interference	28	81	26	81
Significant interference	3	9	5	16
Therapeutic effects nullified	4	11	1	3
	35	100	32	100

expert clinician observers has reached a plateau. This pateau is evident in the capacity to assess the less severely disturbed nonschizophrenic patients, especially when applied to finding subtle differences between drugs with similar modes of action but different chemical structures. In these drugs general effects may be common, but slightly different and clinically important patterns of actions may exist. As an alternative technique, they propose the use of video-taped segments of brief structured interviews with the patient before and after treatment, which can be rated randomly by several judges, independent of the treatment. As a test to see if this method was more effective than standard psychiatric interview ratings in detecting changes, Katz and Itil used the two methods (video tape and interview) to compare two treatments in which differences were likely to be subtle and not very large. They compared two similar drugs, thiothixene and thioridazine, administered double-blind for chronic brain syndrome, to see if different profiles of actions could be detected. Results from the psychiatric interview revealed no differences, whereas results of the video tape interview, during which independent and "blind" raters could observe patient behavior, showed that the drugs did have different profiles of action consistent with their differences in chemical structure, although one drug was not "better" than the other.

Other less experimental rating techniques that might have been added to the traditional psychiatric assessment of symptoms are patient self-reports of symptoms or assessments of social adjustment judged by clinical interview, by the patient through self-report or by "significant others." Shapiro and Post (1974), Carroll (Carroll et al., 1973), Prusoff (Prusoff et al., 1972) and others (Arfwids-

Table IX

Double-blind controlled clinical trials of maprotiline

Place	Comparison drug(s)	Sample	Length of trial	Reference
Denmark, Finland Netherlands, Sweden (8 centers)	Amitriptyline	Hospitalized patients (N = 211)	28 days	Lauritsen, 1974 Welner, 1972
Austria, Brazil, France, Germany, Spain, Switzerland, Italy	Imipramine or Amitriptyline	Any patient depressed enough to need an antidepressant (N = 639)*	28 days	De S. Pinto, 1972
Canada	Amitriptyline	Hospitalized patients (N = 20)	8 weeks	Amin, 1973
Canada	Imipramine	Hospitalized patients (N = 46)	28 days	Roy, 1973

*Eight hundred fifty patients will be included in the final analysis.

son et al., 1974; Williams et al., 1972; Zung, 1973) have shown that the concordance between clinicians' and patients' ratings is sufficiently modest to merit the use of both. The New Haven–Boston collaborative maintenance trial of amitriptyline found many of the differences between amitriptyline, placebo and no pill in patients who did not have a major clinical relapse but who experienced mild return of symptoms on self-report assessments. These findings suggest that the patient rather than the clinician may be a better detector of mild differences in affect and motor activity.

Lastly, consideration should be given to the use of social adjustment as an outcome measure. Here changes in motor activity or affect that are particularly sensitive to the social situation or measures of milder psychopathology may be detected. The social adjustment measure is not a substitute for symptom measures. We have found an absence of correlation between symptom and social adjustment ratings at the height of a depressive illness and low correlations in recovered patients (Weissman and Paykel, 1974). We have also found little agreement in symptom and social adjustment ratings that conceptually overlap. For example, we found that the symptom rating of "work and interest" did not correlate with specific assessments of work performance derived from ratings of attendance, interest, feeling of adequacy, and actual performance. We found that patient hostility, as rated in the psychiatric interview, was discrepant with the degree of hostility expressed by patients in the social situation with intimate relations (Weissman et al., 1971). An adequate gauge of the patient's hostility required specific questioning about the patient's relationships with a variety of persons. Such inquiries are characteristic of social adjustment scales. These assessments are usually made by trained raters during an interview but can be made by patient self-report. Moreover, it might also be useful to obtain the view of others close to the patient; for this, social adjustment scales completed by "significant others," such as the widely used Katz Adjustment Scale, are available (Katz and Lyerly, 1963).

There are many such examples. While manifest psychopathology as rated by a psychiatrist should remain the standard measure of outcome included in all clinical trials, multiple outcome assessments and new methods for enhancing the sensitivity of observations should be considered.

Patient Selection for the Statistical Analysis

The statistical analyses of these data were conducted independently by CIBA-Geigy and by our research group. The results of both analyses were nearly identical. However, somewhat different decisions were made about the inclusion of patients for the statistical analysis. As we compared the analysis of data between the different studies, we became aware of the lack of standard criteria for patient inclusion in the analysis. As in our previous trials, the Yale group did not exclude early terminators from the statistical analysis. For the early terminators we used the patient's termination rating in the final end-point analysis. Patients were excluded from the analysis if they took an inadequate dose of medication (defined as 75 percent or less of the minimum prescribed dose over the study period), used other medications or had a concurrent medical condition. By these criteria seventeen out of eighty-four (20%) were excluded from the analysis, and the final analysis included sixty-seven patients (fifty-six completers and eleven early terminators).

The CIBA-Geigy analysis eliminated all early terminators and also eliminated patients who took other drugs, had a concurrent medical condition or took inadequate medication which was defined more strictly as 80 percent of prescribed dosage for the entire study. In addition, they eliminated patients who had unacceptable severity of mental illness, exceeded the specified dosage at week 1, had less than four or greater than ten days between visits after the first week, or had less than twenty-one or greater than thirty-five days between visits 1 and 6 (the termination of the trail). By these criteria forty-one patients out of eighty-four (49%) were excluded from the analysis, and their final analysis included forty-three patients as contrasted with our sixty-seven.

There are merits and drawbacks of both exclusion criteria and there is an absence of guidelines. A literature exists on selection criteria of patients for clinical trials (Klerman, 1971; Wittenborn, 1971) and on the value of end point vs. survivor analysis, but no mention could be found of other criteria for inclusion in the statistical analysis. Insufficient attention has been given to criteria regarding pill-taking, attendance, etc., which occurs during the course of a clinical trial and which could disqualify for inclusion in the statistical analysis. Although in these independent analyses alternate methods yielded similar results, investigators should be alert to the possibility that different inclusion criteria can alter results. The absence of uniform analytic criteria can hinder comparison of data between studies.

CONCLUSION

A double-blind clinical trial of maprotiline, a tetracyclic, and amitriptyline, a conventional tricyclic, found no difference in onset of action, efficacy, or side effects between drugs. Maprotiline was as effective as amitriptyline, produced an effect in less than one week, and was tolerated well in a group of ambulatory neurotic-depressives. However, no different clinical profile could be found. These results are similar to double-blind trials of maprotiline and other tricyclics conducted in several countries, including over 900 depressed patients and using similar outcome measures.

Further attention should be given to the outcome criteria of such trials, and multiple outcomes should be considered including patient self-report of symptoms, social adjustment measures by clinician, patient or relative, or video-taped interviews. Conventional techniques may not be sensitive to the subtle differences anticipated in clinical profiles and may lead to a Type II error. In addition, attention should be given to the criteria for inclusion of patients in the statistical analysis. Clinical efficacy is usually established by the compilation of data from a number of trials. The use of different inclusion criteria in the statistical analysis can potentially alter results and prevent comparisons between studies.

ACKNOWLEDGMENTS

This study was supported by a grant from CIBA-Geigy. Appreciation is expressed to Eugene S. Paykel, M.D., for initiating the study; the late Mason de la Vergne, M.D., and Julian Lieb, M.B., for psychiatric care and assessments of patients; Brigitte Prusoff, M.P.H., for statistical consultation, and Janis Tanner, for data analysis; Sallye Bothwell, M.A. Ed., for study coordination; and Gerald L. Klerman, M.D., for manuscript review and comment.

B. Double-Blind Evaluations in Psychopharmacology
J. L. Claghorn

The past twenty years of psychopharmacology may be divided roughly into two decades for purposes of evaluating trends in experimental methodology. To a large degree, the first decade was one of fascination with the highly dramatic and exciting properties of phenothiazine compounds. The absence of effective therapies had resulted in massive numbers of untreated, seemingly hopeless cases of mentally ill patients in hospitals throughout the world; the effectiveness of major tranquilizing drugs, disputed for a short period early on, was so obvious that even the most pessimistic and doubtful professionals realized these patients could be treated with success. The primary task of the researcher was to examine in a free form and creative way all the varying applications to which these drugs could be put. State legislatures had to be convinced that the new compounds merited substantial investments of taxpayer funds, and hospital procedures required change to meet the needs of patients receiving the new and effective treatments. As an increasing number of agents with relatively similar properties came to the marketplace, there developed a skepticism about the excessive enthusiasm of preliminary reports on these new drugs. The investigator's sensibilities were already somewhat blunted by the existence of growing numbers of effective drugs; thus psychopharmacology entered its second and contemporary period.

The evolvement of the second decade pointed up the need for more precision in drug appraisal; biostatistics became more important than it had been in the early years. This new emphasis on experimental design and statistical method directed attention away from the individual investigator's clinical opinions and toward more objective methods of evaluation. This change represents a two-edged sword: while the obvious biased influence of placebo drug action, inadequacies of sampling procedures, and the tendency to exaggerate the importance of rather trivial differences can be controlled by biostatistical methods, undoubtedly there has been a loss of important analogue data that best come from the human computer in the form of "clinical impressions."

Although clinical impressions are subject to many forms of distortion, they have the clear purpose of raising questions in the hypothesis-generating stage of experimental development. Too often an investigator's concern about "soft data" which does not lend itself readily to objective quantification has caused more relevant but less measurable traditional clinical assessments to be ignored. For example, when the psychotic patient reduces the importance of his delusional system and begins to see his home, family and occupational attainments as his greatest interest, he may concomitantly experience a decrement in performance on flicker fusion tests and tasks involving accurate size assessment. The goals of patient, doctor and family, however, are that the patient be a tolerably well-adjusted, functioning member of society; in this instance, the physiologic measures may be seen as accurate but irrelevant. Fortunately, a series of well-standardized and widely accepted scales for rating clinically relevant treatment attributes does exist. The Brief Psychiatric Rating Scale (Overall and Gorham, 1962) and the Hamilton Anxiety and Depression Scales (Hamilton, 1959, 1960) are outstanding examples of instruments which effectively measure difference when utilized by experienced raters.

Methods of experiment design in current psychopharmacological research have been fashioned in the interest of attaining complete objectivity; unfortunately, the "tight" appearance of a design may be fallacious, masking variables which may bias the outcome of a study. The "crossover" trial is a notable example. The persistence of this notion as a viable technique for controlling psychotropic drug evaluations overlooks the fundamental requirement that all patients be symptomatically at the same clinical state when they are exposed to each treatment condition. In our subject samples, continuous clinical changes over time occur for drug and placebo patients, with substantial "carry-over" effects from one treatment condition to the next. Patients treated with clinically active drugs tend to respond favorably to subsequent placebo treatment, while those treated initially with placebo who fail to get a clinical response have a poor response to active drug when it is administered at a later time; factors of patient expectation play a large part in achieving therapeutic results. "Washout" periods are often interpolated between crossover episodes. However, as a practical matter, the periods of time allowed are usually insufficiently long for complete metabolic removal of the drug previously tested, and behavioral response to such washout periods unfavorably affects the patient's return to initial clinical state. The crossover design would appear limited to a population of essentially healthy people who have a predictably recurrent symptom.

The double-blind experimental procedure is now accepted with an almost religious fervor in psychopharmacological studies. Obviously, the hazard of both investigator and patient seeing the "blind" exists, especially when there are characteristic physiological effects produced by the experimental drug which are not seen in the other treatment conditions. In most three-way comparison trials, both experimental drugs will produce qualitatively similar side effects, and, as any investigator who has worked extensively with placebo will confirm, a large number of placebo subjects will complain of drowsiness, nausea, dizziness and a variety of additional side effects. It can be asserted safely that the double-blind procedure, while far from foolproof, does represent a highly valuable experimental design, when a sufficient number of open studies have clearly indicated effective dosage ranges and have suitably defined target symptoms. Unfortunately, double-blind techniques are sometimes invoked too early in the course of a drug's overall evaluation, clouding the interpretation of the final data. In such situations, questions may arise concerning the adequate dosing and proper assessment procedures. It is perhaps a hazard of our trend toward increasing obsessionalism in psychotropic drug research that this kind of premature control is becoming more commonplace.

Points to be stressed regarding double-blind research are the needs for placebo washout and placebo control. Because of the powerful influence exerted by the patient's first contact with the treating physician and the initially distressing events surrounding entrance into a drug trial, the period of placebo observation during which the subject is only conditionally accepted can be most helpful. One week of placebo from the time of initial evaluation, discussion of the study, and necessary consent, to the period of baseline evaluation is adequate to separate those individuals who experience emotional relief from having found a therapist from those whose symptoms are sufficiently well established to persist. The investigator's ability to establish a proper baseline severity rating for each symptom requires more than one observation and removal of the uneasiness which typically accompanies a patient's first visit.

Often in clinical research an unfortunate assumption is made when two reputedly active compounds are compared to one another: a lack of difference between them is supposedly indicative of activity in the unknown compound. This assumption is frequently far from true, through every clinical investigator, for practical reasons, falls regularly into the trap. While the evaluation of acutely psychotic individuals is not conducive to the mistake, the recent emphasis on the less readily evaluated syndromes of anxiety and depression makes its occurrence more likely. In such situations, the independent evaluations of each experiment become imperative; it is essential that each drug trial be placebo-controlled so that the validity of the study may be confirmed. In a three-way comparison involving adequate dosages of a known active drug, unknown possibly active drug, and placebo, a failure to differentiate placebo from either or both of the other compounds indicates that either the assessment techniques or patient population used were inappropriate.

Subject selection and mode of assignment to treatment conditions strongly influence the outcome of a double-blind study. In an effort to avoid systematic differences between patients who are assigned to varying treatment conditions, a population with roughly similar degrees of disability, as measured by a criterion level measurement on an accepted rating scale, can be assigned to therapy regimens via a random numbers table. In any given investigation, the nature of the experimental sample may be uniform enough; difficulty arises, however, when one compares studies of varying investigators which have been carried out in a variety of settings. For example, Rickels has demonstrated several times the differences between patients evaluated by practitioners in their private offices and patients treated with similar medications in a clinic. There is indication from his studies that these dissimilarities are partially racial and relate in part to variations in investigator attitude, time spent with the subject, and the educational level and treatment expectations of the patient. Subject differences of this type and magnitude would be expected to exist in a public health clinic, a general hospital or a publically operated community mental health center (Rickels et al., 1969).

For many good and practical reasons, investigators often use what I shall call "professional" patients. Particularly very early clinical investigations and many later trials may involve patients who for a number of years have received their treatment on an experimental basis. They are well-accustomed to the process of clinical investigation and often feel a deep personal investment in the procedures. They are, however, metabolically and psychologically different from comparatively naïve patients who come for first-time therapy in a new setting, and enter a research trial. Hepatic microsomal enzyme induction produced by medication and the long persistence in the body of many psychotropic medications cause the professional patient to exhibit a particular set of metabolic influences not found in the population at large. Also, stability and chronicity of these patients' symptoms are more fixed, and they are less often labile in a treatment situation, causing the measured differences to be of a smaller magnitude. While professional patient populations offer the advantage of a small dropout rate, as compared to the approximately 30 percent dropout rate customarily experienced in outpatient studies of naïve individuals, they present the disadvantage of being, in many respects, unrepresentative of the population for whom the treatment is being proposed.

The rate of subject attrition experienced in double-blind research is an influence which may bias the outcome of a study of extended duration. For example, should the dropout rate among placebo patients be higher than the attrition for either treatment condition, it would be reasonable to assume that the placebo regimen was losing its most symptomatic individuals at a higher rate than the therapeutic groups. If data supported this contention, the placebo group would selectively appear healthier by contrast than either of the treated groups. As often happens, the difference between placebo and other treatment groups will emerge most clearly in the second and third weeks of therapy and will diminish thereafter, as the dropout rate of placebo patients begins to increase. Inherent in many such study designs is the freedom for the investigator to discontinue patients who are unimproved or worsened; ethically and morally this requirement is necessary, and if the investigator does not elect this option in an outpatient population the subject may do so for himself by not returning for subsequent treatment. An appropriate device for handling such data is the modification of a life table technique, computing the differential rates of dropout for each of the involved treatment conditions. By this means, the influence of placebo attrition can be objectively tested.

The study I would like to describe is not an ideal of its kind, but an example of practical application of the numerous compromises necessary to accomplish the reliable late-phase evaluation of a psychotropic drug. All patients were seen by the principal investigator at virtually all of their visits; the study took place over a protracted period of time, but the distribution of treatment conditions was uniform for the duration of the trial.

THE TRIAL

A Double-Blind Study of Maprotiline (Ludiomil) and Imipramine in Depressed Outpatients

The new antidepressant maprotiline (Ludiomil, BA 34,276) is a dibenzocyclooctadiene with a tetracyclic structural formula. While the compound emulates many of the pharmacological properties of imipramine, unlike its tricyclic counterpart maprotiline produced a marked histaminolytic action and a weaker sedative effect in animal studies (BA 34,276 Orientation Brochure, 1972).

Clinical research trials have indicated the potential therapeutic value of maprotiline. Efficacy studies have shown the agent to possess beneficial antidepressant properties in adults as well as children (Kielholz, 1972; Carney et al., 1972; Deniker et al., 1972). Although previous comparative investigations with imipramine and amitriptyline did not demonstrate any superiority of maprotiline, the new compound seemed to elicit a favorable therapeutic response in both unipolar and bipolar depressive cases (Pinard et al., 1972; Maprotiline, 1972; Amin et al., 1973). In general, investigators of maprotiline in both Europe and America have concurred that the drug is an asset to antidepressant treatment (Amin et al., 1973).

The current investigation compared the therapeutic efficacy, dosage levels, onset of action, and side effect profile of maprotiline (Ludiomil) vs. imipramine (Tofranil) vs. placebo in depressed adult outpatients.

Subject Sample

Subjects for this investigation were chosen from the outpatient clinic at the Texas Research Institute of Mental Sciences in Houston. Sixty-two adults, males and females, were assigned to the research project. At the conclusion of the trial, twenty-two individuals with erratic attendance and/or interrupted dosage schedules were excluded from the final analyses.

The forty patients used for analyses all manifested a primary depressive disorder, with symptomatology including a sad or gloomy affect as well as disturbances of sleep, food intake, sex and drive; severity of illness was rated in a majority of cases as moderate. A breakdown of demographic and medical variables is presented in Table I; appropriate statistical procedures determined that there were no significant differences among treatment groups and that these groups were comparable.

Design and Procedures

The study was parallel and double-blind in design, with a placebo control. Sixty-two depressed outpatients were randomly assigned to one of three treatment regimens, maprotiline, imipramine or placebo. A one-week placebo "washout" period took place prior to the initiation of drug therapy (designated as the "baseline" period); duration of the active treatment schedule was four weeks (visit 1 through visit 5).

Medication was supplied in identical appearing tablets: 50 mg maprotiline, 50 mg imipramine, and placebo. Placebo for use during the pretreatment washout was labeled as such and supplied in bulk; all medication for the study (maprotiline, imipramine, placebo) was packaged individually for each patient. A fixed dosage regimen of 1 tablet t.i.d. (50 mg maprotiline, 50 mg imipramine, or placebo) was maintained during the initial seven days of treatment. Subsequently, a flexible dosage was employed in which the investigator adjusted dose levels as necessary to achieve optimum therapeutic results; the maximum daily dose did not exceed 300 mg of either maprotiline or imipramine per day.

Laboratory evaluations were obtained on all subjects prior to visit 1 and at the conclusion of treatment. These determinants included hemoglobin, hematocrit, WBC, platelet counts, urinalysis, fasting blood sugar, BUN, alkaline phosphatase, SGOT, SGPT, and serum bilirubin. In addition, electrocardiograms were performed at baseline and termination; treatment emergent symptoms were recorded as necessary.

Mental status was assessed weekly, at visits 1 through 5, through use of the Hamilton Depression Scale (Hamilton, 1960). At the conclusion of treatment,

Table I
Demographic characteristics

Treatment group	Sex		Mean age	Mean no. weeks since onset of depression	Severity of illness	
	males	females			mild	moderate
Maprotiline (13 pts.)	8	5	29.6 yrs.	35.4 wks.	3	10
Imipramine (13 pts.)	5	8	37.9 yrs.	30.2 wks.	1	12
Placebo (14 pts.)	3	11	36.2 yrs.	22.0 wks.	0	14

both physician and patients were asked to comment globally on therapeutic response.

RESULTS

The primary instrument used to evaluate therapeutic efficacy was the Hamilton Depression Scale. Treatment differences were examined with regard to the following scores: Total Hamilton, Mean Hamilton Item, Factor 1—Anxiety/Agitation, Factor 2—Retarded Endogenous Depression, Factor 3—Delusion Guilt, and Factor 4—"General." Score changes for visits 1 through 5 were analyzed within each treatment group through use of the Student-Newman-Keuls Multiple Range Test.

Results for all three treatment regimens indicated a statistically significant (p ≤ .05) decrease from visit 1 in the Total Hamilton, Mean Hamilton Item, and Retarded Endogenous Depression scores at 7, 14, 21 and 28 days after treatment. Maprotiline and placebo treatment produced a significant decrease from visit 1 in the Anxiety/Agitation and Delusional Guilt factor scores after 7, 14, 21 and 28 days of treatment; in these same two factor scores, imipramine treatment showed a significant decrease after 14, 21 and 28 days of treatment. Maprotiline and imipramine were also associated with significant decreases from visit 1 in the "General" factor scores after 21 and 28 days of therapy; placebo treatment produced no significant decreases in this factor score.

The differences among treatment means at each post-treatment visit were also analyzed via the Student-Newman-Keuls Multiple Range Test. Results indicated that the pretreatment scores for the Total Hamilton, Mean Hamilton Item, and each of the four factors were homogeneous among the treatment groups. Analyses of the post treatment visit scores revealed that maprotiline was associated with the lower mean scores among the treatment groups for the Total Hamilton, Mean Hamilton Item, and each factor. The only exception was Delusional Guilt after 21 days of treatment, where imipramine treatment produced the lower mean score. Detailed results regarding these differences among the means are presented in Table II.

These results indicate that the greatest separation among the treatment groups occurred after twenty-one days of treatment (visit 4). At this time the mean differences between maprotiline scores and placebo scores were significant (p ≤ .05) in favor of maprotiline for the Total Hamilton, Mean Hamilton Item, and each of the four factors. At visit 4, the mean differences between imipramine and placebo scores were significant in favor of imipramine for the Delusional Guilt factor; in addition, after twenty-one days of treatment the mean differences between imipramine and placebo scores for the Total Hamilton and "General" factor were significant in favor of imipramine at the 10 percent level of probability.

The possibility that patient attrition could significantly bias the outcome of

Table II

Treatment comparisons: Hamilton score differences between treatment groups (mean ± S.E.)

	Total Hamilton	Mean Hamilton Item	Anxiety agitation	Retarded endogenous depression	Delusional guilt	"General"
Maprotiline vs. placebo						
Visit 2	7.0 ± 2.5*	0.32 ± 0.12*	0.43 ± 0.19**	0.43 ± 0.16*	0.26 ± 0.16	0.47 ± 0.20**
Visit 3	8.7 ± 2.7**	0.43 ± 0.13*	0.51 ± 0.18*	0.44 ± 0.17**	0.14 ± 0.12	0.44 ± 0.21
Visit 4	11.4 ± 3.3*	0.56 ± 0.16*	0.64 ± 0.22*	0.57 ± 0.19*	0.36 ± 0.17*	0.64 ± 0.23*
Visit 5	6.5 ± 2.9**	0.29 ± 0.15	0.28 ± 0.20	0.38 ± 0.18**	0.15 ± 0.13	0.38 ± 0.22
Maprotiline vs. imipramine						
Visit 2	5.1 ± 2.3**	0.23 ± 0.11**	0.36 ± 0.17**	0.26 ± 0.13	0.21 ± 0.17	0.25 ± 0.20
Visit 3	4.2 ± 2.3	0.20 ± 0.11	0.23 ± 0.18	0.26 ± 0.17	0.05 ± 0.12	0.31 ± 0.21
Visit 4	5.8 ± 2.3**	0.30 ± 0.12**	0.33 ± 0.14	0.32 ± 0.13**	-0.02 ± 0.09	0.26 ± 0.15
Visit 5	3.2 ± 2.5	0.14 ± 0.13	0.23 ± 0.18	0.17 ± 0.15	0.08 ± 0.15	0.31 ± 0.17
Imipramine vs. placebo						
Visit 2	1.9 ± 3.0	0.09 ± 0.15	0.07 ± 0.22	0.17 ± 0.19	0.05 ± 0.20	0.22 ± 0.23
Visit 3	4.5 ± 3.2	0.23 ± 0.16**	0.28 ± 0.21	0.18 ± 0.21	0.09 ± 0.16	0.13 ± 0.22
Visit 4	5.6 ± 3.8**	0.26 ± 0.19	0.31 ± 0.23	0.25 ± 0.22	0.38 ± 0.16*	0.38 ± 0.23**
Visit 5	3.3 ± 3.6	0.15 ± 0.18	0.05 ± 0.26	0.21 ± 0.21	0.07 ± 0.17	0.07 ± 0.26

* $p \leq .05$

**significant at the 10 percent probability level, $.05 < p \leq .1$

data exists in all clinical drug trials. To account for this variable, survival patterns (using a follow-up table) were calculated for all research participants within their respective treatment groups. Results revealed the following: a 69.7 percent probability that fourteen of the initial twenty maprotiline subjects would complete the study, 71.8 percent for eighteen of the twenty-two original imipramine participants, and 73.2 percent for sixteen of the twenty placebo patients; comparisons among treatment groups produced no statistical significance. The dynamics of these calculations are presented as Appendix A.

At the conclusion of treatment (visit 5), both physician and patient assessed overall therapeutic effects; again, the Student-Newman-Keuls test was used to compare the weighted means associated with the treatment global. Results indicated that both maprotiline and imipramine regimens induced a higher mean improvement rating than placebo for both physician's and patients' evaluations; these differences were significant ($p \leq .05$). No statistically significant difference occurred between the mean improvement scores of maprotiline and imipramine. Table III summarizes these findings.

Review of the data regarding onset of treatment effects (determined from therapist's impressions) shows an average of 3.8 ± 1.8 days (Mean±Standard Error) for the maprotiline group, 8.1 ± 2.3 days for the imipramine, and 8.2 ± 1.8 for the placebo; statistical analysis revealed no significance among the regimens, although maprotiline did appear to induce the most rapid therapeutic action.

Optimum therapeutic dosage, as expressed by the physician, was also reviewed for each treatment group. Median optimum dose for both maprotiline and imipramine was approximately 200 mg/day. In the placebo group, nine out of fourteen patients achieved optimum results while on the maximum dosage allowed by the protocol (6 tablet/day); in addition, four placebo subjects experienced no therapeutic effect as rated by the physician.

The most commonly reported side effects for all three groups were somnolence, dry mouth and gastric disturbances. Of the patients included in the analyses, nine on maprotiline, nine on imipramine and five on placebo claimed one or more of these symptoms; of those not included, three on maprotiline and five on imipramine experienced one or more side effects. Treatment emergent symptoms were not, in any case, severe enough to warrant discontinuance from the trial. Laboratory evaluations, ECG and vital sign data showed no important fluctuations at the study's end.

CONCLUSION

Treatment comparison data obtained through the Hamilton Depression Scale and clinical global impressions demonstrated no statistically significant difference between the two therapeutic agents; the investigation, however, showed a significant difference between placebo and both active drugs. While scrutiny of the

Table III
Global impressions treatment comparisons

Patient opinion			
Treatment comparison	Mean difference	S.E.	Probability level
Maprotiline vs. placebo	1.29	0.42	p ≤ .05
Maprotiline vs. imipramine	0.25	0.32	p < .1
Imipramine vs. placebo	1.04	0.46	p ≤ .05

Physician opinion			
Treatment comparison	Mean difference	S.E.	Probability level
Maprotiline vs. placebo	1.36	0.43	p ≤ .05
Maprotiline vs. imipramine	0.31	0.37	p < .1
Imipramine vs. placebo	1.05	0.46	p ≤ .05

data reveals a trend toward ranking of the medications (maprotiline −1, imipramine −2, placebo −3), it must be concluded that maprotiline and imipramine exhibit similar treatment properties.

COMMENTARIES

DR. HEIM: As one of the discussants, I have been requested to comment on issues of evaluation of new drugs. The NIMH-FDA Academic Community Cooperation (NIMH-FDA, 1971) recently produced a clear, definite guide listing and defining on twenty pages the following issues concerned in new psychiatric drug evaluation: phases, methodology, monitoring, ethics, data collection and recording, and data presentation and interpretation.

Rather than repeating their clear statements, I would prefer to concentrate on an issue too seldom taken into consideration: that of so-called nonspecific factors. As Hamilton (1973) once put it: "Nonspecific factors are important for small treatments and small illnesses." I feel tempted to generalize this truism: nonspecific factors modify the results of every study and may sometimes even be the best treatment.

I would like to mention a few of these factors, especially those concerning the *doctor-patient relationship*. One necessity for the conduct of a study is to recruit suitable subjects. This poses the problem of motivating the *patient*. Many researchers are aware of the possibility of "volunteer-error," well-known in laboratory studies. It may be that one of the best ways to motivate a patient is to convince him that it is he who is evaluating the drug, that he is not just a test subject, an anthropomorphic guinea pig. To do so we have to be very careful about the kind of question asked, as was recently shown in a study by Smith and associates (1974). When the question format separated three different questions, they were able to show significant treatment differences but failed to do so when the question was asked in such a way that it combined the three. Like the form of the question, the so-called "response option" can be important; continuously distributed variables are, in general, more sensitive than dichotomous criteria.

Of even greater concern is the extent of the patient's cooperation in taking or not taking drugs. Many patients fail to follow orders in one way or another: as Joyce (1966) puts it, in "not doing what they are told or doing what they are not told." One of his own studies in which two classes of patients could be separated, according to whether or not they returned an acceptable number of unused pills and satisfied urine controls for a marker substance, illustrates this point. The patients defined in this way as "cooperators" showed significant differences in treatment efficacy and toxicity, whereas the "noncooperators" showed a significant difference in subjective symptoms—quite probably the experience that had caused some of them at least to become noncooperative. The "cooperators" were rewarded by the disappearance of symptomatic differences (Joyce, 1962). Few studies allow for rigorous control of patient compliance, so Type II errors may occur in many studies for this reason.

It would be of interest to know more about the psychological characteristics of the "cooperator" and to compare these with the well-known "placebo reactor," whose idiosyncrasies have been described (Honigfeld, 1964). One might suppose that lack of cooperation would be part of the patient's response to the research setting. But patients may more often see themselves as being "treated" rather than "researched," and this may provide a highly favorable setting for drug action (Fisher et al., 1964). How patients really feel about being subjected to research methods and treatments has rarely been a research topic itself. An ingenious experiment by Park and associates (1966) surprisingly showed that about 80 percent of their patients had no notion whatsoever that research goals were involved. In the present climate of opinion about informed consent, the proportion would presumably be substantially less. Dare one suggest that it would be interesting to discover if this assumption is correct?

Indeed, to protect the patient's welfare against any hazards of research, the National Institutes of Mental Health recommended "that investigators carefully consider the risks involved, inform patients of the nature of procedures and obtain their permission to use the data obtained" (NIMH-FDA, 1971). This point leads to consideration of nonspecific factors influenced by the *experimenter or doctor* involved. The influence of the personality of the leading experimenter is usually underestimated. This may result in failure of the whole experiment. His qualities should include being energetic, reliable, persistent and capable of motivating his collaborators.

The impact of the doctor's beliefs and enthusiasms has been proved in many experiments and is just one feature of a more general law, as Rosenthal (1964) has pointed out in his classic papers on the influence of the experimenter's expectations. But just how important enthusiasm can be, especially for new treatments, is revealed by the history of medicine. A saying of the great Canadian nineteenth-century physician, William Osler, took this into consideration: "Use new drugs quickly while they still have the power to heal." All of us are familiar with this kind of "placebo-dependency" in ourselves as well as in our patients.

The influence of the treating doctor's expectation is presumably more subtle than that of his enthusiasm but is nonetheless important, as, for example, a study by Uhlenhuth (Uhlenhuth et al., 1959) showed: Dr. A expected no differences in treatment outcome and found none, whereas Dr. B fulfilled his own prophecy that there would be treatment differences. It is crucial to mention that this happened in spite of a careful double-blind design, indicating that doctors' and patients' perceptual thresholds for differences in effectiveness were changed and/or the patient's actual response was affected by his doctor's expectation. Similar results have been reported in other studies.

These and other possible sources of bias call for *adequate control.* "The description of a trial as 'controlled' is often meant by its designers to indicate that it was held under single-, double-, or multiple-blind (blindfold) conditions: that is, with patients, doctors, or other parties clinically involved ignorant of the treatment received by each individual" (Joyce, 1966). Although double-blind design has become commonly accepted only since the mid-Fifties, Rivers had in fact already used it in 1908 in evaluating the effects of alcohol on fatigue (Joyce, 1962). Of the many thousands of studies relevant to this point, let me just mention one by Loranger and collaborators (1961). A simple placebo was presented to staff and patients, either as a new tranquilizer or as a new energizer. In a first study conducted under open conditions, about 80 percent of the patients seemed to benefit; in a second study, using a double-blind design, the same placebo "drug" was of help to only a few patients.

Critics of the traditional blindfold design suggest that not only the type of treatment but also the dosage levels should be kept blind, especially in a trial permitting variable dose. Open or blind conditions affect, besides treatment outcome variables, the evaluation of side effects and the number of dropouts (Heim et al., 1972). On the other hand, such sophisticated trials have been criticized as elaborate rituals for self-deception—not without justification, as some of the evidence given above seems to prove. Other critics assume that a Type II error has occurred when strict double-blind conditions apparently prevent the expected differences of effect on pain between salicylamide, aspirin and placebo from appearing. However, the error may be logical rather than statistical, as illustrated in a study conducted by Battermann and Grossman (1955).

A last and serious criticism arises from the fact that the typical controlled clinical trial is concerned with differential improvement rates between groups of patients, whereas the traditional doctor, even if he is research-minded, still cares primarily for the individual patient. There is no doubt of the need for new techniques and methods that allow the patient to go on living in his usual setting, without being bothered too much by the research design. Some "n = 1" designs have already been published (Liberman et al., 1973), and more are no doubt to be expected.

ACKNOWLEDGMENT: I would like to thank Dr. C. R. B. Joyce for his valuable advice.

DR. DELINI-STULA: I am concerned about Dr. Weissman's statement that maprotiline possesses classical antidepressive pharmacologic properties.

The first impression was that maprotiline, pharmacologically, was a classical antidepressant and very comparable to imipramine. However, additional pharmacologic studies have shown that maprotiline has a very different pharmacological profile compared to imipramine and amitriptyline. A unique distinction is that maprotiline influences noradrenaline metabolism, but serotonin metabolism is not influenced at all by this drug. We know that all of the presently available antidepressants affect serotonin as well as noradrenaline metabolism. In the studies we have done, in animals and human beings, maprotiline failed to influence serotonin metabolism. We also evaluated the effect of maprotiline on concentrations of free plasma tryptophane. We know that free tryptophane concentrations will influence the brain metabolism of serotonin. However, in this study in human subjects, maprotiline, unlike clomipramine and other tricyclic agents, failed to change the concentration of free tryptophane. These biochemical findings are of importance since some investigators hypothesize that serotonin as well as noradrenaline is involved in the pathogenesis of the affective disorders.

There are additional pharmacological differences between maprotiline and the tricyclic agents. In contrast to imipramine, maprotiline does have sedative and antiaggressive properties but does not potentiate amphetamines. Maprotiline can also be distinguished from amitriptyline by the fact that it has only weak anticholinergic and adrenolytic properties. So it is no problem for us to distinguish maprotiline from the classical antidepressant agents.

DR. PERRIS: In my position, I have been called many times to check the literature presented by the pharmaceutical industry when they apply for registration of new drugs in Sweden. In this way, I became interested in methodology, and my remarks will be directed to the comments made by Dr. Weissman and Dr. Heim:

namely, the quite frequent occurrence of a Type II error in evaluating differences between two drugs.

The possible occurrence of a Type II error is a very important issue, which should always be taken into account in comparative drug trials. In this regard, one of the most common sources of this kind of error is a low inter-rater reliability of the rating instrument used to assess possible changes in psychopathology. The fact that a rating scale has good reliability in the hands of the constructor is not sufficient for assuming that the same high-reliability coefficients apply in the case of other investigations carried out by different (and not "co-trained") investigators in other settings and with different patient populations. Before starting a trial, it is necessary that all the doctors participating in the ratings "co-train" in order to achieve a satisfactory degree of agreement.

Another problem to be taken into account regards the assessment of possible side effects. Many of the new antidepressants have been introduced with the claim that they induce less pronounced side effects than other drugs already on the market. Although we have reached some degree of sophistication concerning the rating of therapeutic effects, the ratings of side effects are still made in a very crude way. Our suggestion is that objective measures should be used, especially for the assessment of anticholinergic side effects. In our experience (Jacobsson et al., 1973, 1974), the use of objective measures might demonstrate differences between drugs when subjective judgments fail to give correct formation.

DR. HAMILTON: Concerning the question raised by Dr. Perris regarding the inter-rater reliability of the Hamilton Scale, it varies between 0.88 and a scarcely believable 0.98.

DR. PERRIS: I agree, but what I wanted to say is that the inter-rater reliability should be checked every time a new rater is involved in the use of the scale because the reliability depends to a great extent on how familiar one is with the scale.

DR. GALLANT: In addition to the issues raised by Dr. Heim, one of the main problems in patient selection in many studies is that the exclusion criteria for administrative withdrawals and treatment dropouts, as contrasted to treatment failures, are not adequately defined *prior* to the trial. Adherence to the definitions by the investigator would at least minimize the problems of patient inclusion criteria and result in a more reliable study. Additional valuable information could be obtained if the clinical measurements utilized for the evaluation of results were also used for the follow-up comparison evaluations of the administrative dropouts as compared to treatment failures. When feasible, this procedure should be routinely incorporated into a controlled outpatient study.

In relation to the specific study results by Dr. Weissman and her associates, they noted that both of the active drug groups displayed much of their improvement during the first week of treatment. At Tulane, in the double-blind studies of nonpsychotic patients with symptomatology of depression and/or anxiety, we have utilized a placebo washout for all drug groups during the first week of the study after the baseline measurements are completed and prior to beginning the double-blind trial. It has been our experience that the clinical measurements show an approximate improvement of 50 percent or more in the global ratings and total morbidity scores of the psychologic scales as well as in most of the individual factors. It is my impression that this clinical observation may partially explain the apparent rapid onset of action of both drugs in this study conducted by Dr. Weissman.

Concerning the comments by Dr. Delini-Stula, the structural, animal profile, and biochemical differences of the tricyclic agents do suggest that some clinical psychopharmacologic differences should exist in human subjects. As noted by Dr. Delini-Stula, maprotiline differs from imipramine in that it does not potentiate amphetamines while it displays antiaggressive actions and more hypnotic qualities; yet, like imipramine, it does inhibit uptake of norepinephrine. In addition, modifications *within* the tetracyclic group result in distinct differences in the animal profiles of behavior and biochemical changes (Bein, 1972). Maprotiline lacks the muscle relaxing and tranquilizing action of benzoctamine (Tacitin), an antianxiety agent, which is another tetracyclic compound. These two tetracyclic agents also differ in their effects upon brain NE and DA. Another type of tetracyclic structure is dibenzopyrazinoazepin, which has the generic name mianserin. This compound apparently possesses antidepressant properties similar to those displayed by maprotiline (Itil et al., 1972) (Fig. 2).

Dr. Wilhelm has written about the stereochemical structural and activity differences of the tricyclic and tetracyclic compounds. He has compared the flexible tricyclic antidepressant structures with the tetracyclic dibenzobicyclooctadiene agents which have a rigid structure and can be defined sterically. It is interesting to note that a short methylaminomethyl substituent at the bridge head (benzoctamine) displays anxiolytic effects, but the addition of two carbon atoms to this side chain results in maprotiline, an agent with antidepressant properties. Dr. Wilhelm has suggested that the basic psychotropic activity of the polycyclic compounds is dictated by the arrangement of the primary skeleton with the specific nature of activity depending on the angle of flexure of the polycyclic framework (Wilhelm, 1972). I would like to ask Dr. Wilhelm if mianserin, another tetracyclic antidepressant agent, has the same type of stereochemical rigidity as maprotiline.

DR. WILHELM: I would say that mianserin is more rigid. It is not completely rigid, but the energy barrier required to change the constellation for mianserin is higher than it is for maprotiline. However, with the tetracyclics it is almost impossible to change the constellation. One practically has to destory the molecule.

DR. KLEIN: This whole stereochemical concept is interesting, but I am not sure how much can be generalized from stereochemical theory. I remember du Pont

TETRACYCLIC COMPOUNDS

MIANSERIN

1,2,3,4,10,14b-hexahydro-2-methyl-dibenzo (c,f)-
pyrazino (1,2-a) azepin monohydrochloride

MAPROTILINE

CH_2-CH_2-CH_2·NH -CH_3 ·HCl

1-(3-methylaminopropyl)-dibenzo-/b,e/-bicyclo-/2,2,2/-octadiene
hydrochloride

BENZOCTAMINE

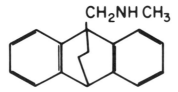

CH_2NHCH_3

1-methylaminomethyl-dibenzo (b,e) bi-
cyclo (2,2,2) octadiene hydrochloride

had a compound that was completely rigid and it did mimic the NE structure; however, the compound did not display antidepressant activity.

DR. WERRY: There is one statement in Dr. Claghorn's presentation that I really must challenge: that the crossover trial has demonstrated its limited scope of accuracy. The crossover design, like any other particular kind of experimental design, has its strengths and its weaknesses, and perhaps I should list the weaknesses first. With the crossover design, one might have problems with "hangover" of effect and, of course, of illness; also, it is logistically more cumbersome. I suppose the fatal error in the crossover design in depression studies is the assumption that the therapeutic effect is reversible. If the depression is alleviated during the first phase of a study, then the patient may not deteriorate after the crossover to placebo. Now, the crossover design of antidepressant studies in children is really quite different and there are strengths in the use of the crossover design. The first one is that it controls for individual subject error and also for the observer's error. Secondly, it enables one to get by with a smaller sample. So the only fatal flaw in the design that I can see is really the question of whether or not the effect must be reversible.

DR. HAMILTON: Additional problems need to be considered, such as dropouts. Dr. Weissman quite correctly compared the dropouts with those who stayed in. Because dropouts are a very serious problem, one which can taint the results of any trial, the protocol should include plans to deal with them.

Another problem is the great improvement in the first week. I am convinced that most of this is nonspecific, and I would suggest that it would be better to make the baseline assessment at the end of the first, or even the second week. Trials of treatments of depressions lasting four weeks are far too short. I have worked for many years with imipramine and phenelzine and have found that those patients who have shown improvement at the end of two months show a further improvement by the end of four months. This does not suggest the appearance of spontaneous recovery.

Video tape interview is a good idea but it is obviously a research technique not yet applicable to ordinary clinical trials.

Dr. Weissman has mentioned the criteria for inclusion in a trial and in the analysis. It is fundamental that these criteria be clearly defined at the beginning of a trial.

REFERENCES

Amin, M., Braham, E., Bronheim, L. A., Klingner, A., Ban, T. A., and Lehmann, H. E. (1973). A double-blind, comparative clinical trial with Ludiomil (BA 34,276) and amitriptyline in newly admitted depressed patients. Curr. Ther. Res. 15:10:691–99.

Arfwidsson, L., d'Elia, G., Laurell, B., Ottosson, J. O., Perris, C., and Persson, G. (1974). Can self-rating replace doctor's rating in evaluating antidepressive treatment? *Acta Psychiat. Scand.* 50:16–22.

BA 34,276 Orientation Brochure (1972). Summit, N.J.: CIBA-Geigy Laboratories.

Battermann, R. C., and Grossman, A. J. (1955). Effectiveness of salicylamide as an analgesic and antirheumatic agent. *JAMA* 159:1619–22.

Bein, H. J. (1972). The activity of two structurally analogous psychoactive compounds. In P. Kielholz, ed., *Depressive Illness*. Berne: Hans Huber.

Carney, M. W. P., et al. (1972). Pilot trial of BA 34,276. *Psychopharmacol.* (Berl.) 23:96–98.

Carroll, B. J., Fielding, J. M., and Blashki, T. G. (1973). Depression rating scales. *Arch. Gen. Psychiat.* 28:361–66.

Deniker, P., et al. (1972). Clinical and electroencephalographic study of methylaminopropyldibenzo-bicyclo-octadiene (BA 34,276) in depressive states. *Psychopharmacol.* (Berl.) 26:Suppl. 57.

De S. Pinto, O., Afeiche, S. P., Bartholini, E., and Loustalot, P. (1972). International experience with Ludiomil. In P. Kielholz, ed., *Depressive Illness*. Vienna: Hans Huber, pp. 253–66.

DiMascio, A., Klerman, G. L., and Prusoff, B. A. (1975). Relative safety of amitriptyline in maintenance treatment of depression. *J. Nerv. Ment. Dis.* 160:34–41.

Fisher, S., et al. (1964). Drug-set interaction: effect of expectations on drug response in outpatients. In P. B. Bradley, F. Flügel and P. Hoch, eds., *Neuro-Psychopharmacology*, Vol. 3. Amsterdam: Elsevier, pp. 149–56.

Guy, W., and Bonato, R. (1970). *ECDEU Assessment Battery*, 2nd rev. Chevy Chase, Md.: U.S. DHEW, PHS, HSMA, NIMH.

Guz, I. (1972). A controlled, double-blind, between-person trial comparing BA 34,276 and imipramine in depressive states. In P. Kielholz, ed., *Depressive Illness*. Vienna: Hans Huber, pp. 234–44.

Hamilton, M. (1959). The assessment of anxiety states by rating. *Br. J. Med. Psychol.* 32:50.

────── (1960). A rating scale for depression. *J. Neurol. Neurosurg. Psychiat.* 23:56–62.

────── (1973). Personal communication.

Heim, E., Joyce, C.R.B., and Martin, K. H. (1972). A comparison of open and blind dosage in an antidepressant trial. In P. Kielholz, ed., *Depressive Illness, Diagnosis, Assessment, Treatment*. Intl. Symp., St. Moritz. Berne: Huber.

Honigfeld, G. (1964). Nonspecific factors in treatment. I. Review of placebo reactions and placebo reactors. *Dis. Nerv. Sys.* XXV:145–56.

Hordern, A., Burt, C. G., and Halt, N. F. (1965). Factor and discriminant function analyses. In A. Hordern, ed., *Depressive States: A Pharmaco-Therapeutic Study*. Springfield, Ill.: Charles C. Thomas, pp. 97–108.

Itil, T. M., Polvan, N., and Hsu, W. (1972). Clinical and EEG effects of GB-94, a tetracyclic antidepressant-EEG model in discovery of a new psychotropic drug. *Curr. Ther. Res.* 14:395–413.

Jacobsson, L., Glitterstam, K., and Palm, U. (1974, in press). Objective assessment of anticholinergic side effects of tricyclic antidepressants. *Acta Psych. Scand.* Suppl. 255.

────── , Lundin, G., Palm, U., and Perris, C. (1973, in press). Some methodological aspects of trials of new antidepressants. 3rd Yugoslav. Psychopharmacol. Congr., Opatija.

Joyce, C. R. B. (1962). Patient cooperation and the sensitivity of clinical trials. *J. Chron. Dis.* 15:1025–36.

────── (1966). Psychopharmacology—dimensions and perspectives: psychological factors in the controlled evaluation of therapy. In M. Balint, ed., *Mind and Medicine Monographs*. Tavistock, J. B. Lippincott, pp. 214–42.

Katz, M. M., and Itil, T. M. (1974). Video methodology for research in psychopathology and pharmacology. *Arch. Gen. Psychiat.* 31:204–10.

────── and Lyerly, S. B. (1963). Methods for measuring adjustment and social behavior in the community: I. Rationale, description, discriminative validity and scale development. *Psychol. Rep.* 13:503–35.

Kielholz, P. (1972). Ed., *Depressive Illness: Diagnosis, Assessment, Treatment*. Bern, Switz.: Hans Huber.

Klerman, G. (1971). Methodology for drug evaluation in affective disorders—depression. In J. Levine, B. Schiele and L. Bouthelet, eds., *Principles and Problems in Establishing the Efficacy of Psychotropic Agents*. Public Health Services Publ. No. 2138, pp. 91–136.

Lauritsen, B. J., and Madsen, H. (1974). A multinational, double-blind trial with a new antidepressant maprotiline (Ludiomil) and amitriptyline. *Acta Psychiat. Scand.* 50:192–201.

Liberman, R. P., Davis, J., Moon, W., and Moore, J. (1973). Research design for analyzing drug environment—behavior interactions. *J. Nerv. Ment. Dis.* 156:432–39.

Loranger, A. W. (1961). The placebo effect in psychiatric drug research. *JAMA* 176:920–25.

Maprotiline: New drug shows promise in depressed patients (1972). *JAMA* 220:661–62.

NIMH-FDA: Antipsychotic, antidepressant, antianxiety guide-lines (1971).

Overall, J. E., and Gorham, D. R. (1962). The brief psychiatric rating scale. *Psychol. Rep.* 10:799.

Park, L. C., et al. (1966). The subjective experience of the research patient: an investigation of psychiatric outpatients' reactions to the research treatment situation. *J. Nerv. Ment. Dis.* 143:199–206.

Paykel, E. S., Mueller, P. S., de la Vergne, P. M. (1973). Amitriptyline, weight gain and carbohydrate craving: a side effect. *Br. J. Psychiat.* 123:501–07.

Pinard, G., et al. (1972). Comparative evaluation of Ludiomil. *Psychopharmacol.* (Berl.) 26:Suppl. 57.

Prusoff, B. A., Klerman, G. L., and Paykel, E. S. (1972). Concordance between clinical assessments and patients' self report in depression. *Arch. Gen. Psychiat.* 26:546–52.

Raskin, A., Schulterbrandt, J., Reatig, N., and Rice, C. E. (1967). Factors of psychopathology in interview, ward behavior, and self-report ratings of hospitalized depressives. *J. Consult. Psychol.* 31:270–78.

Rickels, K., et al. (1969). Doxepin and diazepam in general practice and hospital clinic neurotic patients: a collaborative controlled study. *Psychopharmacol.* (Berl.) 15:265.

Rosenthal, R. (1964). Experimenter outcome-orientation and the results of the psychological experiment. *Psychol. Bull.* 61:405–12.

Roy, J. Y., Pinard, G., Hillel, J., Gagnon, M. A., and Tetreault, L. (1973). Evaluation comparative de la dibencycladine (Ludiomil) et de l'imipramine chez le déprimé psychotique. *Intl. J. Clin. Pharmacol.* 7:1:54–51.

Shapiro, M. B., and Post, F. (1974). Comparison of self-ratings of psychiatric patients with ratings made by a psychiatrist. *Br. J. Psychiat.* 125:36–41.

Smith, G. M., et al. (1974). Use of subjective responses to evaluate efficacy of mild analgetic-sedative combinations. *Clin. Pharmacol. Ther.* 15:118–29.

Uhlenhuth, E. H., et al. (1959). The symptomatic relief of anxiety with meprobamate, phenobarbital and placebo. *Am. J. Psych.* 115:905–10.

Weissman, M. M., and Paykel, E. S. (1974). *The Depressed Woman: A Study of Social Relationships*. Chicago: University of Chicago Press.

———, Klerman, G. L., and Paykel, E. S. (1971). Clinical evaluation of hostility in depression. *Am. J. Psychiat.* 128:41–46.

Welner, J. (1972). A multinational, multi-centre, double-blind trial of a new antidepressant (BA 34,276). In P. Kielholz, ed., *Depressive Illness*. Vienna: Hans Huber, pp. 209–19.

Wilhelm, M. (1972). The chemistry of polycyclic psychoactive drugs—serendipity or systematic investigation. In P. Kielholz, ed., *Depressive Illness*. Berne: Hans Huber.

Williams, J. G., Barlow, D. H., and Agras, W. S. (1972). Behavioral measurement of severe depression. *Arch. Gen. Psychiat.* 27:330–33.

Wittenborn, J. R. (1971). The design of clinical trials. In J. Levine, B. Schiele and L. Bouthelet, eds., *Principles and Problems in Establishing the Efficacy of Psychotropic Agents*. Public Health Services Publ. No. 2138, pp. 222–59.

Zung, W. W. K. (1973). From art to science. *Arch. Gen. Psychiat.* 29:328–37.

Appendix A
Statistical determination of survival patterns

Column X is a partition of the complete time period (4 weeks) allotted to the study. Each successive interval represents the weekly visit of the subjects.

Column Ox represents the number of subjects participating in the study at the beginning of the corresponding intervals.

Column nDx represents the number of patients who had withdrawn from the study.

Column nQx is the estimate of the probability of dropping out during the interval.

Column nPx is the probability of surviving the interval, or the survival rate of the subjects.

Column Px represents the cumulative proportion surviving the interval or the cumulative survival rate.

The Standard Error of the last interval cumulative rate was calculated to determine the extent to which the computed rate may have been influenced by sampling variations.

A z-score was derived to determine if there was a significant difference between the survival rates for the groups.

	X	Ox	nDx	nQx	nPx	Px
	1	20	0	0.00	1.00	100.0
	2	20	3	0.15	0.85	100.0
Maprotiline	3	17	3	0.18	0.82	85.0
	4	14				69.7
				S.E. = 9.76		

	X	Ox	nDx	nQx	nPx	Px
	1	22	2	0.09	0.91	100.0
	2	19	3	0.16	0.84	91.0
Imipramine	3	18	1	0.06	0.94	76.4
	4	18				71.8
				S.E. = 7.18		

	X	Ox	nDx	nQx	nPx	Px
	1	20	1	0.05	0.95	100.0
	2	17	3	0.18	0.82	95.0
Placebo	3	16	1	0.06	0.94	77.9
	4	16				73.2

$$S.E. = 7.32$$

Maprotiline vs. imipramine
    f = 0.055   no significance

Maprotiline vs. placebo
    f = 0.067   no significance

Imipramine vs. placebo
    f = 0.126   no significance

CHAPTER X

Adverse Reactions of Thymoleptics

D. H. Mielke

Adverse drug reactions are divided into side effects (expected, undesirable pharmacologic actions) and toxic reactions (unexpected, direct cellular damage or allergic reaction). The spectrum ranges from mildly bothersome drug reactions to those endangering the health or life of the patient. The ready availability of colorful, aesthetically pleasing medications, often in large quantities, has resulted in accidental or deliberate poisoning in adults and children. As always, the risks involving the use of any pharmacologic agent must be carefully weighed against its benefits, particularly in treating the less seriously ill.

Along with other psychopharmacologic agents, the use of antidepressants has increased. Their place in the therapeutic armamentarium has been established over the last twenty years, and their use is likely to increase further. The thymoleptics are generally divided into lithium, the monoamine oxidase (MAO) inhibitors (subdivided into the hydrazine and nonhydrazine groups) and the non-MAO inhibitors. The non-MAO inhibitors include the tricyclic and tetracyclic antidepressants and will be considered first. The undesired drug reactions will be divided into side effects, toxic reactions, and poisoning.

In considering the adverse clinical reactions to psychoactive agents, two points should be kept in mind. First, side effects of the active agent must be dissociated from negative placebo reactions. Drowsiness and gastrointestinal complaints are among the most common reactions to administration of placebo. In addition, palpitations, weakness and dizziness have been reported along with diffuse itchy erythema and maculopapular rashes, abdominal pain, urticaria and edema of the legs (Shapiro, 1964). Rickels states that private psychiatric patients report the lowest incidence of negative placebo effects, and general practice patients, the highest incidence (Rickels, 1968). Secondly, there have been numerous reports in the medical and psychiatric literature of poor response or mood alterations in undesired directions as a result of psychoactive agents. It would appear that the lack of response, clinical deterioration, or other complaint attributed to drug treatment may be due to administration of the compound to inappropriately selected patients. The need for careful diagnosis and thoughtful prescribing cannot be overemphasized.

THE TRICYCLIC ANTIDEPRESSANTS

The most widely used drugs are imipramine (Tofranil and Presamine), desipramine (Norpramine, Pertofrane), amitriptyline (Elavil), protriptyline (Vivactyl), nortriptyline (Aventyl and doxepin (Adapine, Sinequan). Each is a 6-7-6 tricyclic compound.

Side Effects

Recent reviews have shown a significant percentage of side effects associated with tricyclic use. The incidence ranges from 15 to 30 percent, with larger samples producing more stable estimates (Sigg, 1968; Boston, 1972). Less than 5 percent are considered major reactions (Boston, 1972).

The most frequent side effects are atropine-like in character and include dry mouth and skin, tremor, blurred vision and impaired accommodation, constipation, dizziness, palpitations and tachycardia, mydriasis, and urinary retention. Anorexia, insomnia and excessive perspiration have also been reported. Although individual susceptibility to side effects at any age varies markedly, the elderly seem particularly susceptible to atonic bladder and adynamic ileus. These agents must be used with caution in glaucoma and benign prostatic hypertrophy.

Administration of high dosages of tricyclics has been associated with difficulty in thinking and concentration (Goodman, 1970). Orthostatic hypotension, muscle tremors, fatigue, nightmares, and edema are occasionally reported with tricyclic use. Skin reactions include photosensitivity similar to that produced by phenothiazines (Goodman and Gilman, 1970); rash and pruritus may also occur (Litvak and Kaelbling, 1972). Headache and epigastric distress are fairly common. Gastrointestinal complaints include nausea, vomiting, diarrhea, anorexia, stomatitis and peculiar taste sensations. Some members of the tricyclic group such as amitriptyline produce sedation; others such as imipramine have been reported to produce hypomanic or manic excitement (Goodman and Gilman, 1970). In general, adaption to most of the side effects occurs following continued administration; in some cases, a reduction in dosage is helpful.

Toxic Reactions

The electrocardiographic changes related to the use of the tricyclic antidepressants have received much attention. The tricyclic antidepressants tend to exhibit a quinidine-like effect in that they prolong A-V conduction which may progress to first degree A-V block. The drugs reach high concentrations in the heart and thus can produce direct toxic effects upon the conduction system (Copeland, 1972).

The most common ECG changes are broadened QRS complex, depressed S-T segment, and flat or inverted T waves. Bundle branch block to complete heart block can occur with or without exercise. Further changes frequently reported include A-V and I-V block, bradycardia or tachycardia, ventricular extrasystoles, and atrial and ventricular arrhythmias. Occasionally, bizarre QRS complexes are mentioned.

ECG abnormalities are generally accepted as derived from two drug actions. First, in low doses anticholinergic blockade of vagal endings can occur (Cairncross and Gershon, 1962). Second, at high doses a direct toxic effect occurs on the myocardium itself (Copeland, 1972; Cooperative Study, 1973; Nemec, 1973). Another hypothesis for alteration of cardiac function by tricyclic agents was proposed by Auclair, who suggested a severe imbalance between the intracellular and extracellular potassium ratio (Auclair et al., 1969). However, this hypothesis has not been proved (Kristiansen, 1961). Copeland has suggested that the cardiac effects are caused by tricyclic potentiation of circulating catecholamines or alteration of the balanced sympathetic-parasympathetic control of the heart (Copeland, 1972).

The tricyclics may produce potentiation of or hypersensitivity to circulating catecholamines, and the physician should be cautious when he administers local anesthetic preparations containing adrenalin or noradrenalin to patients receiving tricyclics (Copeland, 1972). Recently Kaufmann (1974) reported a hypertensive episode following four doses of imipramine in a patient with surgically proved pheochromocytoma. The patient experienced increased blood pressure and seizures. This case reflects an exaggerated response to released catecholamines from the pheochromocytoma. Freeman's hypothesized mechanism, especially operative in poisoning, is one of flooding the system with catecholamines or their breakdown products (Freeman and Loughhead, 1973).

Investigations into tricyclic use in patients with heart disease have produced contradictory findings. Moir and his group (1972) have reported 13 sudden, unexplained deaths in 119 patients with the diagnosis of heart disease after they were given amitriptyline, while only three deaths occurred in a comparison group. Four out of 87 cardiac patients on imipramine died unexpectedly. He concluded that amitriptyline has cardiotoxic effects in therapeutic dosages in the presence of preexisting heart disease. However, Moir later followed up 91 percent of the original 119 amitriptyline patients; at a five-month to five-year follow-up period, the only difference between the amitriptyline patients and the comparison group was the association of amitriptyline with sudden, unexpected death in patients over the age of seventy years (Moir et al., 1973). The Boston Collaborative Drug Survey Program (1972) found no evidence of cardiotoxic effects; the mortality rate was similar in the amitriptyline and control groups. Each of the 80 patients involved had a previous diagnosis of cardiovascular disease, a diagnosis possibly very different from the more specific "heart disease"noted in other studies. We find ourselves comparing studies from different countries and patients with different diagnoses (cardiovascular vs. heart disease). Recently, Moir (1973) found the ultimate prognosis in terms of mortality rate to be similar in an amitriptyline and control group but suggested that amitriptyline hastened by a number of months or years an inevitable sudden death.

Also lending weight to the notion that the drug has definite myocardial and conduction tissue effects is the finding that congestive heart failure may be produced or aggravated by the tricyclic antidepressants (Raisfeld, 1972). Thus the use of tricyclic antidepressants is particularly contraindicated in the post-myocardial infarction period (Luke, 1971). In summary, there is strong evidence that the tricyclic antidepressants, perhaps some more than others, can be cardiotoxic in therapeutic dosages. In treating the elderly, particularly those with heart disease, the risk involved compared to possible usefulness must be carefully considered. The increased incidence of side effects and toxicity associated with the use of the tricyclic antidepressants in the elderly has prompted Prange (1972) to recommend divided doses rather than the once daily (Klein and Davis, 1969) bedtime dose frequently recommended.

The tricyclic antidepressants do not display the classical extrapyramidal phenomena seen with phenothiazines, nor do they potentiate narcotics and anesthetic agents as the parent compounds do (Gallant, 1963). A fine, persistent non-parkinsonian tremor may occur in the elderly on high dosage (Goodman and Gilman, 1970). An allergic type of cholestatic jaundice, identical to that seen with the phenothiazines, tends to clear when the drug is discontinued (Short, 1968). This hypersensitivity reaction is very uncommon compared to the mild transient elevations of SGPT which return to normal levels without discontinuance of the drug. Fatalities which were possibly a result of liver damage in association with the use of one or more tricyclic antidepressants have occurred (Powell, 1968).

Agranulocytosis, an uncommon toxic effect, is due to a hypersensitivity reaction to the tricyclic compounds (Goodman and Gilman, 1970). Blood abnormalities including eosinophilia, purpura thrombocytopenia, or granulocytopenia are also uncommon. Rachmilewitz studied two patients with thrombocytopenia and found evidence for serum antibodies against desipramine (Rachmilewitz et al., 1968). Other manifestations of allergic reactions in patients who were administered these medications include: rash, urticaria, generalized edema, and edema of the face and tongue.

The rare syndrome of nephrogenic diabetes insipidus associated with tricyclic antidepressant therapy was first reported by Schwartz (Schwartz et al., 1957). This syndrome is characterized by hyponatremia and serum hypotonicity with relative urine hypertonicity in the presence of normal adrenal, renal, cardiac and hepatic function. The repetitive association of the presence of the antidepressant and the syndrome is well established, as is the unresponsiveness to vasopressin (Luzecky et al., 1974).

Inordinate weight gain, sometimes associated with a craving for carbo-hydrates, has been noted with the use of amitriptyline in maintenance dosages (Arenillas, 1964; Gander, 1965). Occasionally a patient will refuse medication in order to avoid this unwanted weight gain. In a placebo-controlled study with amitriptyline, it was shown that weight increased with the active drug and de-creased when the drug was discontinued (Paykel et al., 1973). This weight gain is dose related with the mechanism being unknown, but changes in carbohydrate metabolism may be involved (Gander, 1965).

The controversy over the effects of tricyclic antidepressants on glucose metabolism remains unresolved. Observing five mildly diabetic patients, Kaplan noted that imipramine produced a diminution in glycosuria which again increased when the drug was discontinued (Kaplan et al., 1960).

Neurotoxic reactions are rare but do occur with imipramine and amitrip-tyline. Cerebellar dysfunction may occur with these agents and is generally as-cribed to the drug's central anticholinergic properties; it is dose-related (Duvoisin, 1968). Signs of neurotoxicity may include ataxia, nystagmus, dysarthria, slurred speech, tremor, agitation, chorea, hyperpyrexia, myoclonia, hyperreflexia, pares-thesias of the extremities, hallucinations, and a depressed level of consciousness.

A related atropine-like delirium has been attributed to the use of drugs with anticholinergic properties. This is most often seen when two or more such agents are given concomitantly (Cole, 1972). Raising the dosage slowly and avoding polypharmacy will help prevent this problem. Klein (1965) reported 12 of 209 patients on high dosages of imipramine had isolated visual hallucinations, but these reactions disappeared with a reduction in dosage.

Interference with the pituitary-gonadal axis by the tricyclic antidepressants can produce symptoms which are distressing to the patient but are generally harmless (Hanse, 1923; Ripley and Papanicolao, 1942). Menstrual irregularities, breast enlargement and galactorrhea have been reported (Klein et al., 1964; Klein, 1964). Testicular swelling, impotence and gynecomastia in males have been as-sociated with tricyclic agents (Koang, 1957; Molina et al., 1957). Libido can be enhanced or diminished in the course of therapy.

The possible teratogenicity of imipramine and related drugs has resulted in numerous letters, editorials and articles in the medical literature. McBride began the flurry by reporting the possible association of imipramine treatment with congenital limb deformities (McBride, 1972). Subsequent studies have not borne out the relationship, even when the drug was given in early pregnancy (Crombie et al., 1972; Wheatley, 1972). Animal studies have noted congenital abnormalities in various species. Recently, the chicken embryo was used and toxic teratogenic effects were noted (Gilani, 1974). The use of drugs in pregnancy demands a large measure of caution although those risking their use can take some comfort in the 1973 report of the Australian Drug Evaluation Committee (Tricyclic, 1973). This report states: "Avalilable information does not support the contention that tricyc-lic antidepressants are a cause of limb reduction deformities."

Should the tricyclic antidepressants be abruptly withdrawn, an akathisia-like

Table I
Drug interactions and the tricyclic antidepressants

Drug	Resultant Effects
Minor tranquilizers	Side effects additive
Nitroglycerine	Sudden fail in blood pressure is exaggerated
Guanethidine and related adrenergic blocking agents (Mitchell et al., 1967; Prange, 1973; Fann et al., 1971)	1) Patient needs more guanethidine 2) Increased guanethidine suddenly excessive if tricyclic is stopped
MAO inhibitors	Hyperpyrexia and convulsions
Barbiturates	Antidepressant plasma levels are reduced
Methylphenidate (Fann, 1973; Wharton et al., 1971)	1) Increased antidepressant blood levels 2) Paradoxical sedation
Acidifiers (NH_4Cl)	Antagonizes antidepressants
Alkalinizer	Potentiates antidepressants
Reserpine	Inhibits reserpine
Phenothiazines (Alexander and Nino, 1969)	Atropine-like side effects are additive; phenothiazine blood level increased

syndrome may develop. Sathananthan reported three patients who experienced withdrawal symptoms after administration of imipramine for three to four weeks with doses between 300 mg and 450 mg per day (Sathananthan and Gershon, 1973b). This syndrome was characterized by acute anxiety and restlessness; readministering imipramine caused the symptoms to abate. The authors suggested a sudden functional depletion of dopamine at the receptor, similar to that seen in parkinsonian akathisia. Other withdrawal reactions have included malaise, muscular aches, coryza, nausea, vomiting, dizziness and anxiety (Kramer et al., 1961; Mann and MacPherson, 1959; Anderson and Kristiansen, 1959). These reactions are seen equally in males and females, responders and nonresponders, and in unipolar and bipolar illnesses; they always disappear when the drug is reinstituted.

Desipramine and imipramine, administered throughout pregnancy, produced tachycardia, tachypnea, sweating, cyanosis, irritability and wakefulness in the neonate during the first week (Webster, 1973; Eggermont, 1973).

Drug Combinations and Interactions

The combined use of the tricyclic antidepressants with selected drugs produces a spectrum of reactions, as summarized in Table I. It should be noted that the MAO inhibitor interaction is controversial and not well documented. The interested reader is directed to the original references for more detailed information about each type of interaction.

Tricyclic Antidepressant Poisoning

Since the severity of intoxication depends partly upon individual tolerance (Goel and Shanks, 1974a), the treating physician must assess the clinical picture, not simply the blood levels or the dose ingested. Blood and urine levels only serve to verify the diagnosis.

Tricyclic antidepressants are absorbed quickly and mainly bind to plasma proteins. There is rapid tissue accumulation so that serum concentrations are never very high (Rasmussen, 1965). With overdosage, the onset of symptoms can be sudden, almost apoplectic at times. Life-threatening cerebral excitation, respiratory depression, and myocardial toxicity occur in the first twenty-four hours. Consciousness is invariably depressed to some degree during the first day.

With mild overdosage, symptoms develop in one to four hours, and one observes a reduced level of consciousness, dizziness or ataxia, disturbed posture, restlessness, flushing of the face (Goel and Shanks, 1974a), and occasionally thirst (Steel et al., 1967). Tachycardia without ECG abnormalities is usual, as is some degree of mydriasis (Goel and Shanks, 1974a; Steel et al., 1967). Even in mild cases, extreme agitation may be seen to alternate with periods of drowsiness. Some patients may hallucinate with mild or moderate intoxication.

With moderately toxic dosages, ataxia, dysarthria, nystagmus, hyperreflexia, and a Babinski response occur. Convulsions and systemic hypertension may or may not appear (Goel and Shanks, 1974a).

With full-blown intoxication or poisoning, the clinical picture develops rapidly, beginning with irritability, agitation and delirium. These give way to increased deep tendon reflexes, convulsions, respiratory depression, and coma. Hyperpyrexia to 108 degrees and higher has been recorded (Sedal et al., 1972;

Gallant, 1966). Also appearing in the first four hours is a profound hypotension with tachycardia or bradycardia and respiratory depression. Anticholinergic effects and cardiac complications will demand attention relatively soon after the overdose.

ECG changes progress quickly from sinus tachycardia to a wide variety of abnormalities reflecting the myocardial and conducting tissue response to the drug's anticholinergic effects, direct toxic effect, and increased levels of catecholamines (Sedal et al., 1972). Most authors reporting fatal cases describe conduction defects including RBBB or complete heart block (Sedal et al., 1972), which is often difficult to treat; if the patient survives the first twenty-four hours, recovery is likely. Typically, a patient presents in a deep state of unconsciousness with cyanosis, muscle twitching, and frequent grand mal convulsions, the blood pressure being unrecordable.

The importance of metabolic acidosis has become increasingly recognized by those faced with tricyclic overdosage (Kanarek et al., 1973; Gerst et al., 1966; Farquharson, 1972; Brown et al., 1973). Our knowledge of this metabolic influence on the cardiovascular system stems largely from animal work, which formed a basis for clinical success in treating tricyclic overdosage. Some patients develop metabolic acidosis which is often accompanied by considerable reduction in potassium, both of which predispose to major arrhythmias (Farquharson, 1972). In his work with puppies, Brown has shown that arrhythmias caused by amitriptyline disappeared when acidosis was corrected (Brown et al., 1973). Plasma protein-binding capacity of amitriptyline increases as the pH rises, thus reducing the unbound fraction. Considering these mechanisms, Brown postulates that the antiarrhythmic action of sodium bicarbonate (in tricyclic antidepressant poisoning) results from an increase in the pH. Metabolic acidosis probably depresses myocardial contractility in man. The blood gases, pH and potassium must be monitored over time.

Treatment of Poisoning with the Tricyclic Antidepressants

Treatment is symptomatic, as no antidote exists. Vomiting should be induced, if possible, otherwise, lavage is recommended. Resuscitative measures, including defibrillation, may be required.

Metaraminol and norepinephrine have no place in the treatment of hypotension secondary to tricyclic overdosage (Steel et al., 1967; Kanarek et al., 1973; Locket, 1973). Metaraminol may produce forward cardiac failure (Rasmussen, 1965). Steel points out the added cardiac work load inflicted by vasopressor agents (Steel et al., 1967). In addition, there is evidence that the tricyclic antidepressants have already elevated the plasma concentration of catecholamines (Sedal et al., 1972). Recently glucagon was shown to be of value as a cardiotonic agent and particularly useful in the management of refractory cardiac failure (Brogan et al.,

1969). Oxygen and diuretics are usually the treatments of first choice for ventricular failure.

Central stimulation is the mechanism behind convulsions which may usher in stupor and coma (Trubohovich, 1973). Seizures cause an increased work load on the heart (Steel et al., 1967); therefore, it is imperative that they be controlled. Most authorities agree that diazepam is of great value if not the drug of choice for counteracting the drug-induced seizures (Young and Galloway, 1971; Gallant, 1966; Locket, 1973; Treitman, 1972; National Clearinghouse, 1973). Usually 5 to 10 mg (or 0.2 mg/Kg) is slowly given intravenously for adults and correspondingly less in children. Young and Galloway (1971) have outlined the use of paraldehyde as an anticonvulsant in children, and the relative lack of respiratory depression is noteworthy, but local irritation can be a problem when paraldehyde is used via the intramuscular route. Diphenylhydantoin alone or in combination with diazepam is sometimes recommended. Succinylcholine is used only with mechanical ventilation and as a last resort to control seizures.

The drug of choice is not yet established for rhythm disturbances resulting from conduction defects. Arrhythmias are prominent and life-threatening. The physician must support rate and stroke volume for the first twenty-four hours. Diphenylhydantoin is a less effective antiarrhythmic agent than quinidine, procainamide, or lidocaine (AMA, 1973). It has been useful for supraventricular premature beats, ventricular premature contractions, ventricular tachycardia, and atrial tachycardia with or without A-V block. One hundred mg is given intravenously every ten minutes until the desired effects occur, the total dose not exceeding 10 mg per Kg body weight. Parenteral diphenylhydantoin in the first twenty-four hours may prevent the convulsions and cardiac arrhythmias mentioned above (Cardiovascular complications, 1971; Locket, 1973; Goel and Shanks, 1974b). In the presence of partial heart block, diphenylhydantoin or lidocaine is least likely to increase the block.

Lidocaine hydrochloride (lignocaine, Xylocaine) is being used increasingly in the treatment of ventricular premature beats and tachycardia. It has a less depressing effect on cardiac conduction and less negative inotropic action than quinidine and procainamide (AMA, 1973), thus producing less hypotension and less depression of contractility (Young and Galloway, 1971). A continuous intravenous infusion of 5 percent dextrose in water is used. The initial adult dose is 25 to 50 mg i.v. (not to exceed 100 mg), followed by 1 to 4 mg/minute (Steel et al., 1967). The dosage in children is 1 mg/Kg as a bolus to be repeated from time to time should the arrhythmia reappear (Young and Galloway, 1971). The drug is generally withdrawn over a period of forty-eight to seventy-two hours. There is some evidence that lidocaine may have anticonvulsant properties (Taverner and Bain, 1958); nevertheless, its antiarrhythmic action is similar to that of Dilantin. Lidocaine reduces automaticity, shortens the effective refractory period, and raises the fibrillation threshold. It acts by increasing the stimulatory threshold of the ventricules during diastole (Young and Galloway, 1971). The lidocaine-adrenalin combination must be avoided.

Procainamide (Pronestyl) prevents ventricular premature contractions and ventricular tachycardia (Bellet, 1972). It increases the effective refractory period and reduces cardiac automaticity. Like lidocaine, it is less effective with the supraventricular tachycardias. No more than 100 to 200 mg should be given every five minutes until reaching 1000 mg or abolition of the arrhythmias. Subsequently, 1 to 3 mg may be administered i.v. to maintain rhythm.

Neostigmine (Prostigmin) and physostigmine indirectly produce a cholinergic effect by inhibiting acetylcholinesterase, which results in an accumulation of acetylcholine at the site of cholinergic transmission. This stimulates muscarinic receptor sites of effector cells of smooth muscle and various organ systems. Physostigmine can act centrally as well and rapidly improve coma, depressed respirations and abnormal motor movements. Neostigmine in the dose of 1 mg has been of value in treating supraventricular tachycardias (Young and Galloway, 1971; Bellet, 1972). It may be given intramuscularly or intravenously. Kanarek found that arrhythmias and bizarre ECG changes respond dramatically to parenteral neostigmine (Goel and Shanks, 1974a). However, its beneficial effects are transient, and it can produce severe cholinergic manifestations.

Rasmussen first reported the use of intravenous pyridostigmine (Mestinon) at the rate of 1 mg every four hours. Subsequently, others have used this medication to counteract the atropine-like cardiovascular effects of the tricyclic antidepressants (Cardiovascular complications, 1971; Steel et al., 1967; Kanarek, et al., 1973; Ruddy, et al., 1972). The use of anticholinergic drugs is logical and seems most effective in treating the supraventricular arrhythmias.

Propanolol has been used for virtually every type of tachycardia. It decreases the rate of ectopic atrial or ventricular foci and may abolish them, and it slows the conduction through the A-V node (Bellet, 1972). Although propanolol sometimes prevents recurrent supraventricular tachycardia, it is not considered the drug of choice. Roberts described a poisoning from the combination of amitriptyline and phenothiazine which he treated with 1 mg of atropine to prevent bradycardia, prior to the administration of 1 mg of propanolol (Roberts et al., 1973). (One to 2 mg is commonly used in children.) Ramsey (1967) has noted that the use of 15 mg may have contributed to depression of myocardial contractility. Freeman used 18 mg and thought it contributed to the patient's hypotension (Freeman et al., 1969). Doses approaching 15 mg are usually counterproductive and cannot be recommended.

Practolol is a relatively cardioselective beta-adrenergic blocker effective in the treatment of supraventricular tachycardia. It has no local anesthetic properties but does demonstrate intrinsic sympathomimetic activity. This drug is preferable for use in cases which are complicated by asthma and bronchitis (Bellet, 1972; Meyler and Herxheimer, 1972). It is known to depress the myocardium in dosages between 15 and 25 mg (Sowton et al., 1968). It is probably less likely to precipitate heart failure than propanolol (Meyler and Herxheimer, 1972). Brown administered practolol for imipramine toxicity when 1 mg of neostigmine proved ineffective (Brown, et al., 1972). He gave 1 mg, then 2 mg, and finally 3 mg intravenously, producing a slowing of the rate and a narrowing of the QRS complex with each dosage. The blood pressure rose and respirations improved. Brown then gave 1 mg per minute by i.v. drip over the next thirty-six hours. The possibility of inadequate dosage can make it difficult to evaluate the drug effect.

It must be remembered that in the presence of A-V block with ventricular extrasystoles, the use of cardiac glycosides is contraindicated. The use of potassium chloride, which was first reported by Penney (1968), has fallen into disuse because its therapeutic and hypothetical value has remained unproved.

Some cardiologists prefer electrically induced cardioversion and/or cardiac pacemakers for some arrhythmias and complete or partial heart block, with drugs being used as an adjunct to maintain normal rhythm. Although most of the severe symptomatology will abate in the first twenty-four hours, occasionally a death will occur as late as seventy-two hours after the overdosage (Sedal et al., 1972; Locket, 1973). The value of gastric aspiration, lavage and catharsis is questionable (Goel and Shanks, 1974a; Young and Galloway, 1971; Kanarek et al., 1973; Trubohovich, 1973; Locket, 1973; Sesso et al., 1973).

Metabolic acidosis is usually treated with sodium bicarbonate administered intravenously. Brown and his group (1973) have described the use of sodium bicarbonate in children and the dramatic results achieved in the presence of episodic bradycardia, supraventricular tachycardia, and wide QRS complexes. This group has discontined the use of other cardioactive drugs and now use sodium bicarbonate alone to treat cardiac complications of tricyclic antidepressant overdosage.

Blood clearing methods such as forced diuresis or dialysis are of questionable value (Cardiovascular complications, 1971; Rasmussen, 1965; Steel et al., 1967; Young and Galloway, 1971; Kanarek et al., 1973; Crammer and Davies, 1972). They must never be the first measure instituted, although some reports have indicated the usefulness of such techniques. Asbach reported two cases of severe imipramine poisoning in children (Asbach and Schuler, 1974). They were placed in a renal unit for hemodialysis, and the authors were encouraged by the return of consciousness in four to five hours. They were prompted to investigate this modality based on their *in vitro* studies and previous case reports. They concluded that the duration of coma was favorably shortened and that the amount of drug recovered in the dialysate was not as small as previously thought. In general, the normal metabolism and excretion can be relied on to remove the drug (Crammer and Davies, 1972). Dialysis should be used only in conjunction with vital symptomatic treatment; the value of this technique is yet to be proved.

The use of activated charcoal has been suggested by Crammer (Crammer and Davies, 1972). This treatment approach is based on the fact that the tricyclic antidepressants undergo enterohepatic circulation with large amounts being secreted into the bile and passed on to the intestine, only to be reabsorbed later. The benfit of activated charcoal therapy is an open question at this time (Activated charcoal, 1972).

After the patient recovers from the acute intoxication phase, mental disturbances such as an organic brain syndrome with or without psychosis may appear (Sedal et al., 1972; Locket, 1973); these symptoms may be a result of the central stimulatory effects of the drug.

In summary, the treatment of poisoning with the tricyclic antidepressants requires prompt transfer to an intensive care unit. The onset of life-threatening symptoms is extremely rapid and requires that resuscitative measures be close at hand. Fatalities usually occur in the first twenty-four hours and relate to direct effects on the cardiovascular system, central nervous system, and respiratory system. The patient should receive bed rest and careful monitoring for at least seventy-two hours after the ingestion of toxic amounts of the tricyclic antidepressants.

THE MONOAMINE OXIDASE INHIBITORS

Psychiatrists in the United States have relegated these agents to a lesser role in the treatment of depression. Because of lesser efficacy and greater toxicity than the tricyclic antidepressants, they are often used when less hazardous drugs or electroconvulsive therapy have failed. Adverse reactions cover a wide spectrum from mildly bothersome side effects to severe and dramatic life-threatening reactions.

Side Effects

The monoamine oxidase (MAO) inhibitors produce anticholinergic effects similar to those observed with tricyclic antidepressant agents (Gallant, 1963). Dry mouth and skin, hyperhydrosis, constipation, blurred vision, impaired accommodation, and orthostatic hypotension are frequent. The elderly have a proclivity to develop atonic bladder and bowel. Symptoms attributed in part to the atropine-like activity of these compounds are tachycardia, anorexia and insomnia.

Orthostatic hypotension is generally seen with the administration of high doses and characteristically develops during the first week of treatment. It occurs with all MAO inhibitors available in the U.S.A. This symptom may be treated with recumbancy, reduction in dosage, or termination of drug treatment. Although the underlying mechanism is generally accepted as a depression of the sympathetic action through peripheral ganglionic blocking, the exact site of action remains controversial. Besides the MAOI activity shared by each member of the group, phenelzine and particularly tranylcypromine have an amphetamine-like pharmacologic action (Hendley and Snyder, 1968). The increase in available amines may result in CNS stimulation to the point of insomnia, restlessness, hypertension, headache and palpitations.

In rats, the MAO inhibitor alters glycolysis, which is reflected by an increase in pyruvate and lactic acid levels and lowered glucose levels (Gey and Pletscher, 1961). Hypoglycemic action has also been reported in man (Weiss et al., 1959; Leak and Dormandy, 1961). Cooper suggests caution when administering these agents to depressed diabetics who may also be receiving insulin (Cooper and Ashcraft, 1966). The hydrazine MAO inhibitor potentiates and prolongs the insulin-induced reduction in blood glucose (Cooper and Ashcraft, 1966).

Other side effects associated with the administration of this group of drugs include abnormal cardiac rate and rhythm, confusion, peripheral edema, muscle fasciculations, nervousness, asthenia, rashes, and weight changes. Less frequent complaints are black tongue, dysuria, euphoria, changes in libido, photosensitivity, and inhibition of ejaculation. Spermatogensis was investigated in a depressed male on phenelzine and found to be increased (Blair et al., 1962).

This group of agents also displays "anti-anginal effects." The drugs block the response of the cardiovascular system to exercise, thus producing a delay or disappearance of the onset of angina (Goldberg et al., 1962). Caution should be used since anginal pain can serve as a warning to the patient with a compromised cardiac reserve.

Leukopenia has been reported but is rarely of consequence. Muscle twitches, muscle pain, and muscle weakness are associated with use of the hydrazine subdivision of the MAO inhibitors, but are usually insignificant.

Toxic Reactions of Hydrazine MAO Inhibitors

The hydrazine group includes phenelzine (Nardil), nialamide (Niamid) and isocarboxazid (Marplan). They have been associated with hepatocellular damage (Gallant, 1963; Remmen et al., 1962, Scherbel, 1960), which represents a drug-induced hypersensitivity (Goodman and Gilman, 1970). Elevated transaminases may be the first sign of hepatotoxicity (Pader, 1960), although this finding may be transient, and the laboratory values can return to normal with continued drug treatment. Due to the low incidence of hepatocellular degeneration, the use of these agents is considered a justifiable risk in cases of severe depression not responding to the usual techniques.

Very rarely, a peripheral neuropathy may develop; this toxic effect is apparently related to pyridoxine deficiency. The peripheral neuropathy may be ushered in with neuralgia and paresthesias, and its development demands that the drug be stopped immediately and pyridoxine replacement instituted (Gallant, 1963). Invariably, peripheral neuropathy appears at doses well above those required for antidepressant activity.

Blood dyscrasias are uncommon but have occurred. In the U.S.A., cardiac toxicity and arrhythmias have received scant attention, possibly reflecting the group's relatively minor role in the treatment of depression in this country. In general, the arrhythmias have been observed as an exaggerated response to an increase of sympathomimetic amines associated with MAO inhibition.

Toxic Reactions of Non-hydrazine MAO Inhibitors

The two medications in this classification are tranylcypromine (Parnate) and pargyline (Eutonyl).

Psychomotor overstimulation has been observed following tranylcypromine administration and may not respond to a reduction in dosage (Gallant, 1963). Brandt and Hoffbauer (1964) reported a case of hepatotoxicity, secondary to tranylcypromine administration. Upon recovery, the patient was given a challenging dose of tranylcypromine, which produced a recurrence of her symptoms (along with abnormal laboratory values) from which she again recovered after cessation of medication.

There is evidence that the greatest number of side effects will occur with the positive isomer of tranylcypromine, while the negative isomer may be the more therapeutically effective (Escobar et al., 1974). Should future investigators support this finding, the presently available racemic mixture may be replaced by the appropriate isomer.

Hypertensive Crises

The most dramatic adverse effect is the clinical entity called paradoxical hypertension which is associated with the concomitant use of an MAO inhibitor with food substances high in tyramine content or with certain sympathomimetic agents. The patient experiences headaches, palpitations, nausea, vomiting, flushing of the face, photophobia, arrhythmias, and sometimes pulmonary edema, hyperpyrexia (Goldberg, 1964) and even cerebral hemorrhage and death. One generally accepted explanation for these reactions is based on the rapid absorption of tyramine or other pressor agent into the general circulation instead of being destroyed by the inhibited MAO in the bowel or elsewhere (Pettinger et al., 1968). The net result is the same as if norepinephrine were injected from an exogenous source. Any other substance capable of releasing stored epinephrine will produce a similar picture (amphetamines, ephedrine, etc.). Also, the administration of an MAO inhibitor results in the release of an increased amount of effective norepinephrine (Pettinger et al., 1968). In addition, the enzyme inhibition may produce a supersensitivity to circulating catecholamines (Pettinger et al., 1968). Recent work suggests that the inhibition of hepatic microsomal oxidative enzymes may be involved (Renton and Eade, 1972). Tyramine is probably the substrate for this enzyme as well as for MAO.

The incidence of cerebral vascular accidents cannot be determined with accuracy. An estimated 3.5 million people have received tranylcypromine. Goodman and Gilman (1970) report fifty CVA's of which fifteen died. They believe that pathology which is not drug-related played a role in these deaths. Another study reported thirteen cases of subarachnoid hemorrhage occurring in a fifteen-month period involving 833 psychiatric patients on MAO inhibitors. There were no

Table II
The following substances in combination with an MAO inhibitor may be associated with hypertensive crisis in some patients

Foods with Significant Amounts of Tyramine

Cheese	Red wines
Pickled herring	Chicken livers
Canned figs	Broad beans
Chocolate	(fava beans)
Yeasts	Beer
Game	Meat extracts
	Yogurt

Other Vasopressor Agents

Amphetamines	Dopamine
Adrenalin	Certain cold remedies
Noradrenalin	Nasal decongestants
	(containing vasocon-
	strictors)
Dopa	Anorexiants

fatalities, but several patients had residual effects (de Villiers, 1966). The importance of close dietary restrictions cannot be overemphasized. Raskin reported a nine-hospital depression study consisting of 110 patients, following appropriate dietary restrictions, in whom no hypertensive crises occurred (Raskin, 1972); 2.7 percent were terminated for other serious reactions which disappeared one week after terminating the drug.

Table II summarizes those substances currently known to be associated with hypertensive crises in some patients receiving MAO inhibitors. Not every patient taking a MAOI and ingesting one of the substances listed in Table II will experience the severe reaction. It can be anticipated that these reactions will be more frequent in general medical practice than in carefully supervised hospital trials.

Interaction of the MAO Inhibitors and Other Drugs

Some of the better-known interactions are summarized in Table III. Those which are not self-explanatory will be commented on briefly.

L-DOPA is capable of producing a hypertensive crisis due to its release of stored catecholamines in association with an MAO inhibitor. The narcotics, par-

Table III
The combination of an MAO inhibitor with each drug
may produce the corresponding reaction

Patient on an MAO Inhibitor and Administered:	Possible Reaction
Insulin	Enhances hypoglycemic action
Other hypoglycemics	Enhance hypoglycemic action
L-DOPA, methyldopa	Hypertensive crises
Antiparkinson agents	Potentiation of these agents
Meperidine, morphine, dextromethorphan	Potentiate narcotic, cardiovascular shock, death
Thiazide diuretics	Potentiate hypotension
Another MAO inhibitor	Agitation, tremor, hyperthermia, opisthotonus, coma
Coffee	Rare hyperexcitability
Tricyclic antidepressants	Hypertension, convulsions, hyperpyrexia
Other CNS depressants: Anesthetics, general Barbiturates Codeine Alcohol Chloral hydrate Cocaine Minor tranquilizers	Potentiation of CNS depression, hypertension or hypotension, shock, coma, and sometimes death
Amphetamines	Hypertensive crises
Phenothiazines	May interfere with MAO inhibitors

ticularly meperidine and morphine, have been associated in some cases with cardiovascular collapse leading to death. The cause remains obscure. In addition to the reactions mentioned in Table III, meperidine in combination with an MAO inhibitor could depress respiration, elevate temperature and produce agitation (Goldberg, 1964).

The prescribing of an MAO inhibitor together with a tricyclic antidepressant may increase the toxicity of the latter (Goodman and Gilman, 1970). The combination potentiates the anticholinergic activity leading to a severe atropine-like reaction with tremors, fever, general clonic convulsions, delirium, and death.

The development of hypertensive crises may occur within minutes after introducing imipramine in the presence of MAO inhibition (Gong and Rogers, 1973). When rabbits pretreated with pargyline were injected with imipramine, marked hyperthermia developed; PCPA antagonized this side effect (Gong and Rogers, 1973). There is pronounced individual variation in sensitivity to the combination of an MAO inhibitor and a tricyclic antidepressant (Rom and Benner, 1972). Similarly, not all patients taking the other combinations develop the untoward reactions. However, because of the potential for serious effects, the concurrent use of more than one potent chemical agent should be reserved for those severely ill patients considered truly refractory to the use of a single medication.

MAO Inhibitor Poisoning

Acute overdosage may not produce clinical manifestations for twelve or more hours (Locket, 1973). Thus it is necessary to observe a patient with suspected overdosage for at least twenty-four hours. There is a gradual onset of headache, chest pain, and hyperactivity leading to confusion, delirium, hallucinations, and eventually coma (Locket, 1973). Nausea, vomiting, restlessness, mydriasis and photophobia are frequent. Hyperventilation, hypertension and tachycardia are usually present to some degree and may be marked. Attacks of paroxysmal hypertension are a classical and feared symptom which may lead to death from acute circulatory collapse, pulmonary edema or intracranial hemorrhage. Muscle spasms or twitching are common. Trismus, laryngeal stridor and hyperreflexia may be noted. As the clinical manifestations continue to develop, the initial hypertension is followed by a profound drop in blood pressure. Hyperpyrexia is always present by this time, if not earlier. CNS stimulation, convulsions, and increased neuromuscular activity are prominent as the clinical picture unfolds (Ciocatto et al., 1972).

Treatment of MAO Inhibitor Poisoning

Since there may be a long latent period before the appearance of toxicity, the inducement of vomiting may be safe and result in the recovery of the ingested drug. The management of respiratory distress is similar to that employed in severe overdosage with potentially depressing substances.

The elevated blood pressure which appears early may respond to the short-acting alpha-adrenergic blocker, phentolamine. However, this drug does not block the cardiac stimulatory properties of the sympathomimetic amines; therefore, tachycardia and arrhythmias are not necessarily reversed. Phentolamine is generally given slowly 5 mg at a time by the i.v. route. An alternate is pentolinium given 3 mg subcutaneously.

For convulsions, one may administer diazepam or paraldehyde. With the use of mechanical ventilation, barbiturates or even 10 to 15 mg of succinylcholine may be administered since respiratory depression would not be of concern.

Hyperpyrexia is a constant symptom in severe poisoning and is life-threatening. External cooling techniques can control this dangerous reaction. Chlorpromazine, 25 mg administered intramuscularly immediately and repeated in one hour, can be helpful (Robertson, 1972), but not always (Locket, 1973). Its sedative and hypotensive properties can be an added benefit (Ciocatto et al., 1972), but its use in the presence of hypotension requires extreme caution. As a last resort to control temperature, a continuous i.v. infusion of succinylcholine together with mechanical cooling has been advocated (Ciocatto et al., 1972).

Electrolytes, acid-base balance, hydration, electrocardiographic changes, pulse, and blood pressure require continuous monitoring. (See above for discussion of cardiac arrhythmias.) Only small amounts of these agents are excreted in the urine; acidification will slightly increase excretion. The maximum amount of ingested drug excreted via the urine is less than 8 percent (Locket, 1973).

When muscle spasms do occur, they may last for several hours (Robertson, 1972). The patient should be carefully followed for approximately ten days. As an additional precaution, liver function studies during the recovery period should be repeated monthly for six months.

THE ADVERSE REACTIONS ASSOCIATED WITH LITHIUM THERAPY

The symptoms of lithium poisoning generally appear with blood levels of 2.0 to 2.5 meq/l. Although an occasional patient may be seen with levels of 2 to 3 meq/l without intoxication, others may be extremely uncomfortable in the therapeutic dose range of less than 1.5 meq/l. A concentration of 2.0 meq/l is now considered undesirable, and a level of 1.5 meq/l is now the maximum recommended for the manic state (Simpson, 1974).

Side Effects

It is usual for side effects to appear in the first days of treatment and then fade by the second week as the patient adapts to the presence of the chemical.

Such transient symptoms include nausea, vomiting, abdominal pain, thirst, polyuria, dazed feelings, muscle weakness, fine tremor of the hands, sluggishness, slight fatigue, and sleepiness. Loose or thin stools may be prominent at the beginning. These side effects can occur at blood levels less than 1.0 meq/l; Schou (1968) has suggested their possible correlation with the steepness of rise rather than the peak of the lithium level. Spreading the dosage can curtail these side effects (Simpson, 1974). Caution must be exercised in treating the manic-depressive female who is pregnant; renal lithium clearance rises in pregnancy, only to fall in the postpartum period, a time of increased hazard with regard to toxicity (Schou et al., 1973a).

The use of lithium at therapeutic levels may be associated with persistent side effects. These reactions include a feeling of thirst and polyuria, and a fine tremor of the hands; the latter does not respond to anti-parkinsonian agents. It is characterized by spontaneous variations. Most patients will adapt and learn to accept the slight inconvenience. Should lowering the lithium dosage be ineffective in curtailing the tremor, one may consider propanolol (Kirk et al., 1972, 1973). The usual dosage is 30 to 80 mg per day, but it must not be given to a patient with asthma, bronchitis or hayfever (Kirk et al., 1973). The combination of lithium and a tricyclic antidepressant can produce a tremor which does not respond to propanolol (Kirk et al., 1972). Schou considers both the polyuria and the tremor harmless.

Toxic Reactions

Electrocardiographic changes may occur during lithium therapy. The more serious ECG changes seem to be markedly idiosyncratic. Depression of T waves was frequent in Demers' six patients but was not serum level related (Demers and Heninger, 1971). These nonspecific changes were consistent with those noted by others and are generally considered benign and reversible. However, one case of reversible premature ventricular contractions was associated with lithium therapy (Tangedahl and Gau, 1972). Tseng (1971) reported a patient who developed an arrhythmia and bundle branch block while on lithium, the latter persisting after lithium was discontinued. Resumption of lithium therapy resulted in death. Post-mortem examination demonstrated interstitial myocarditis.

The net effect of lithium treatment is intracellular accumulation of lithium with equal displacement of sodium and potassium (Keynes and Swan, 1959). Since renal mechanisms excrete extracellular potassium, the resulting hypokalemia prolongs repolarization and facilitates the occurrence of ectopic beats and various arrhythmias.

The development of a diffuse nontoxic goiter while undergoing lithium therapy is not a rarity. It usually appears during the first two years of lithium administration (Schou et al., 1968a; Candy, 1972), and it is seen much more frequently in females than males (Lloyd et al., 1973); ages twenty to sixty are most affected (Schou et al., 1968a). These thyroid enlargements are usually small to moderate, although one patient did require partial thyroidectomy for trachial compression (Schou et al., 1968a). Those who become clinically hypothyroid respond to thyroid administration, which occasionally reduces gland size as well.

Schou, reporting on a group of 330 patients on lithium, estimated the likelihood of goiter formation in patients taking lithium for one year as 4 percent, while the expected rate in the general population is 1 percent (Schou et al., 1968a). Although others have reported a higher incidence of lithium-induced goiter (Fieve and Platman, 1969), it should be emphasized that the majority remain euthyroid.

Laboratory values demonstrate an actual reduction in protein-bound iodine, reflecting an actual decrease in the level of circulating thyroid hormone (Candy, 1972; Whybrow, 1972). In addition, both T_3 resin uptake and 24-hour I^{131} uptake are frequently diminished. TSH is transiently elevated (Bennie and Lazarus, 1972) in about one-third of those patients on lithium (Singer and Rotenberg, 1973).

The available data imply that an underlying thyroid defect may be a prerequisite. Should thyroid reserves be low for any reason (genetic, chronic thyroid disease, antithyroid factors, etc.), goiter develops. Schou states that the condition is neither a frequent complication nor a serious one (Schou et al., 1968a). To date, this diffuse, nontender thyroid enlargement has been readily reversible, and no malignancies have evolved. Since lithium and iodine may act synergistically to produce hypothyroidism (the reason for this occurrence remains unclear [Whybrow, 1972; Shopsin et al., 1973]), the combination should be avoided.

An acquired, reversible nephrogenic diabetes insipidus has been observed at therapeutic dosages (Lithium, 1972) and occurs in possibly one-third of the patients on lithium (Singer and Rotenberg, 1973). Angrist reported two cases of polyuria and polydipsia and suggested a mechanism based on a temporary hypokalemic nephropathy (Angrist et al., 1970). The most discussed mechanism for this drug-induced phenomena centers around the physiologic activity of c-AMP (adenosinemonophosphate) (see Fig. 1). At what point or points lithium interferes with the series of events in Fig. 1 is not yet clear.

Increased human red blood cell fragility in media containing lithium has been observed by those handling blood samples. In those patients on lithium, blood levels of magnesium are often found to be slightly elevated. The significance, if any, is not known.

Lithium dermatitis is the cutaneous response to the presence of this element and is observed from time to time. Callaway reported on five patients, four of whom had pruritic maculopapular eruptions (Callaway et al., 1968). Also, two of these patients had cutaneous ulcers of the lower extremity. One patient had cutaneous ulcers without a rash. The symptoms responded to the use of steroid cream and a reduction in dosage. Kusumi (1971) described two cases with pruritic acneform papules which finally coalesced before subsiding. The eruption cleared in one patient although lithium treatment was continued, and the other cleared

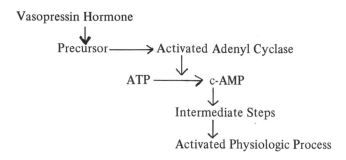

Fig. 1
Probable series of events occurring in the renal cell
membrane as summarized by Singer (Singer and Rotenberg, 1973).

when lithium was discontinued and did not return when lithium was reintroduced. Both skin reactions began in the first week of therapy. Acneform eruptions may be confined to the face and shoulders (Ruiz-Maldonado et al., 1973). Stopping lithium may allow subsidence of the dermatitis; however, readministering the lithium may cause return of the lesions (Ruiz-Maldonado et al., 1973). Posey (1972) wrote of a papular and pruritic dermatitis confined to the elbows. Kurtin (1973) found seventeen cases of folliculitis associated with lithium use. Hyperkeratotic, erythematous, follicular papules were described as occurring in the first year of therapy; most of these remitted with discontinuance of lithium, although some partly remitted with continued treatment. The general consensus of these authors is that the skin reactions are not harmful. They appear to be toxic reactions rather than allergic reactions (Kurtin, 1973).

Hematologic changes such as leukocytosis have been reported in patients on lithium (O'Connell, 1970). Shopsin reported a reversible leukocytosis in general psychiatric patients with different diagnoses, all treated with lithium (Shopsin et al., 1971). He observed a trend toward neutrophilia and lymphotcytopenia, which is drug related but not dose or blood level related. These are innocuous and reversible reactions. One account of fatal aplastic anemia in a fifty-year-old female manic-depressive patient on lithium is difficult to explain or relate to drug therapy (Hussain et al., 1973).

An unusual case was Duffield's (1973) patient who was taking lithium (for recurrent depression) and experienced an unpleasant taste and smell with butter, celery, and other selected foods. This peculiar reaction disappeared when lithium was discontinued.

The development of a mild confusional state in the presence of recommended levels of lithium has been reported by several investigators. Mayfield and Brown described a confusional state occurring in their patients (diagnosed as schizoaffective) receiving subtoxic doses of lithium. Shopsin describes signs of "neurotoxicity" as manifested by confusion, memory loss, disorientation, grimacing and dyskinesias in eight patients (Shopsin et al., 1970). Lithium levels ranged from 0.2 to 1.8 meq/1. Interesting and noteworthy was the finding that this group of symptoms was most common in those patients diagnosed as schizophrenic, thus suggesting the possibility that the mental deterioration may have been due to the use of a drug that was not efficacious for schizophrenia and not due to the activity of lithium. In addition, the relatively vague diagnostic criteria used in these studies further obscured the reported observations.

It has long been known that the presence of lithium in the media of eggs of certain lower organisms and mammals can produce developmental anomalies (Herbst, 1893; Schou et al., 1973b). Some studies have failed to show interference with morphogenesis (Schou et al., 1973b). Schou cites a retrospective study of 118 children whose mothers had taken lithium in the first trimester of pregnancy. The total number of malformed children was nine. The cardiovascular system was involved in six of the nine cases, and two children had Down's syndrome. Schou and his associates (1973b) have concluded that the risk of teratogenicity was not statistically significant and was lower than expected from animal studies. Some investigators are not satisfied with this conclusion and are still collecting data about lithium babies.

Abnormal findings may occur in neonates born to mothers taking lithium. Usually seen is the triad of flaccidity, cyanosis, and heart murmur (Wilbanks et al., 1970; Tunnessen and Hertz, 1972). In one child, the blood level was 2.4 meq/1 (Wilbanks et al., 1970). Tunnessen described a newborn as floppy but responsive to stimuli, as having a grade 3 over 5 systolic murmur, a temperature of 34.9°C., and associated cyanosis (Tunnessen and Hertz, 1972). Amdisen (1969) observed a female child born to a mother who had received lithium throughout pregnancy. The infant was born with generalized edema and a large goiter but recovered without treatment.

Any unnecessary ingestion of drugs is undesirable and sometimes potentially dangerous. The nursing infant will ingest lithium in the milk and achieve serum concentrations one-third to one-half the concentration of the mother's serum level (Schou and Amdisen, 1973). Although arguments can be presented for and against permitting a lithium-treated woman to breast-feed her child, Schou and Amdisen think that bottle feeding is advisable.

Lithium Poisoning

Intoxication with lithium generally occurs in one of three ways: cumulative overdosage occurring in a patient on a lithium regime, diminished excretion in a patient on optimal subtoxic dosage, and in acute self-administered overdosage (Saran and Gaind, 1973). In each occurrence there is more drug administered than can be eliminated by the kidneys. Most manifestations of intoxication relate to depression of the central nervous system (Schou et al., 1968b), and signs of CNS intoxication usually begin in the range of 2.0 to 2.5 meq/1. The accumulation of lithium over a period of days raises the blood and tissue levels with a progressive increase in sluggishness, a languid feeling, drowsiness, coarse tremor, muscle twitches, dysarthria, loss of appetite, vomiting and diarrhea. Thirst and polydipsia do not occur (Schou et al., 1968b). Not all of the symptoms are present in any one case. Hypertonic muscles, body rigidity, or hyperactive deep tendon reflexes along with impairment of consciousness may progress to convulsions, coma and possibly death. Muscle tremors are to be expected (Schou et al., 1968b), and fasciculations are often seen. Other clinical characteristics of lithium intoxication are attacks of hyperextension of the arms and legs, sometimes combined with gasping, grunting, and wide opening of the eyes, lasting a few seconds to half of a minute. These may appear spontaneously or as a result of stimulation. Convulsions are not uncommon. The clinical picture may simulate cerebral hemorrhage with transitory neurological asymmetries, conjugal lateral deviation of the eyes, lateral rotation of the head, one-sided extensor plantar reflex, as well as occasional stiff neck or transient vertical nystagmus. The course tremor mentioned above is usually prominent.

The electrocardiographic changes seen with lithium overdose do not play the primary or life-threatening role found with tricyclic antidepressant overdosage. The T waves are sometimes flat or inverted in leads I or II. The blood pressure tends to be stable throughout the course of lithium poisoning (Schou et al., 1968b), but vasopressors are occasionally indicated.

The electroencephalogram recorded during lithium poisoning shows a decrease in alpha activity and an increase in theta and delta activity, with the latter at times paroxysmal and maximal frontally (Schou et al., 1968b). Periods of beta activity with or without the appearance of sharp waves have been observed. The changes are reversible (Schou et al., 1968b).

Schou noted that most of his patients sooner or later developed pyrexia, generally related to the semicomatose state (Schou et al., 1968b).

Plasma sodium and potassium are usually unchanged. There is evidence from human and animal work of sodium wasting in lithium intoxication (Baer et al., 1973). A negative sodium balance coinciding with the onset of lithium intoxication has been observed in manic-depressive patients. A pathological cycle of renal sodium wasting associated with increased retention of the lithium has been described. The net result is greater lithium toxicity associated with the sodium loss.

A moderate increase in BUN and creatine without uremia is very common and probably relates to decreased renal output. A transient proteinuria is frequent.

The Treatment of Lithium Poisoning

The treatment plan is very similar to that used with barbiturate overdosage (Simpson, 1974). Lacking a specific antidote, the physician endeavors to remove lithium, apply supportive measures, and prevent complications.

Adequate renal function is critical in the detoxification of these patients. Oliguria, low salt diet, and renal or cardiac disease are some of the factors associated with diminished lithium excretion (Saran and Gaind, 1973). Hydration is important. The merits of the administration of sodium chloride or potassium chloride or both as a treatment measure is currently the subject of debate.

Hemodialysis readily decreases blood levels of lithium and has been used with much success. The blood levels drop with active dialysis, then rise as the tissue reserves release lithium into the blood (Saran and Gaind, 1973; Hawkins and Dorken, 1969). Although blood levels are reduced, consciousness may not return for several days (Amdisen and Skjoldborg, 1969). Indications for dialysis are reduced urinary output coupled with high lithium levels and a serious static or worsening condition (Simpson, 1974). Dialysis may have to be continued for a time or reinstituted if the blood levels once again rise due to tissue release of lithium.

Several measures aimed at increasing the lithium excretion over the normal rate may be used if urinary output is adequate. Osmotic diuresis (urea) is established as a method to speed renal elimination of lithium from the blood (Saran and Gaind, 1973; Thomsen and Schou, 1968). Aminophylline can double the twenty-four-hour excretion of lithium (Simpson, 1974) by increasing renal blood flow and by possible direct action on the tubular transport system. It is given intravenously in amounts of 500 mg t.i.d. or q.i.d. The third procedure helpful in lowering blood levels of lithium is the use of lactate or sodium bicarbonate. These agents enhance excretion by the probable mechanism of obligatory excretion of cation with un-reabsorbed bicarbonate (Thomsen and Schou, 1968), resulting in a reduced lithium reabsorption in the proximal tubule. An osmotic diuretic, aminophylline, and an alkalinizer of the urine can be utilized alone or in combination. Another drug known to increase lithium excretion is the carbonic anhydrase inhibitor, acetazolamide (Thomsen and Schou, 1968). The mechanism of action is the same as for sodium bicarbonate and is based on sodium thiosulfate studies which elucidated the concept of obligatory cation excretion.

Correcting fluid and electrolyte balance may be necessary. This procedure and proper hydration are usually sufficient to maintain blood pressure, to maintain circulation to the vital organs, and to regulate renal function. Electrolytes should be monitored daily until the patient is no longer stuporous, and the blood level is less than 2.0 meq/l.

Permanent neurological sequelae after lithium poisoning have been reported. Von Hartitzsch reported three cases of poisoning, two of which were exposed to high blood levels for a "prolonged" period of time before recovery (Von Hartitzsch et al., 1972). Both had permanent changes in the basal ganglia and cerebellar connections. One had ataxia and choreiform movements of the upper body at six-month follow-up, and the other had ataxia and choreoathetoid movements at one-year follow-up. Why the vast majority recover without permanent sequelae is not yet understood. There is generally no difference in blood levels between those with and without permanent sequelae.

Post-mortem examination following fatal lithium poisoning has revealed only nonspecific findings (Chapman and Lewis, 1972).

SUMMARY

Although the thymoleptic drugs are generally safe, dangerous reactions and poisonings do occur. The clinical management of the adverse reactions and poisonings is outlined for the prescribing physician and his colleague in the emergency room. It is anticipated that adverse reactions and poisoning will continue to be a problem as greater amounts of these drugs are dispensed annually. The side effects are mostly inconvenient, and proper supervision of the patient will reduce the risk of toxic reactions or poisoning to the point of being negligible when weighed against the distress of the severely ill patient. In this context, a preventive approach is important since these drugs should be used only when specifically indicated. With thoughtful patient selection and a familiarity with the compound prescribed, gratifying results can be achieved.

COMMENTARIES

DR. HAMILTON: In addition to the problems reviewed by Dr. Mielke in his wide-ranging paper, there is that of idiosyncratic reactions which I think are much more important than is realized. Many so-called side effects are probably of this nature. Human metabolism is extraordinarily varied, and some people cannot eat even ordinary food. I suspect that even the hypertensive crisis with the MAOI agents is primarily an idiosyncratic reaction.

Concerning the treatment of side effects, I am firmly of the opinion that any which appear with large doses should be treated primarily by reduction of the dose to see how much we can diminish the side effects and yet retain the therapeutic effect we want. This is not a fashionable attitude. The common practice is to add a second toxic substance to mask the side effects of the first. For idiosyncracy there is only one solution, and that is to stop the drug. This incidentally is one of the advantages, insufficiently understood, of having available a variety of drugs and particularly of chemical structures, for treatment of any one disorder, because the patient who shows an idiosyncracy to one may not do so to another.

DR. SIMPSON: Dr. Hamilton, concerning the combination of monoamine oxidase inhibitors and tricyclics, an area in which Dr. Mielke has taken the North American line, I wonder if you might give the London party line.

DR. HAMILTON: I am against polypharmacy on principle and have managed on the whole to avoid giving more than one drug. However, Dr. William Sargant and quite a number of others have been giving both these drugs for many years with no obvious increase in mortality rate of their psychiatric patients. I doubt that the interaction between these types of drugs is as serious as has been suggested. However, I suspect that the resultant therapeutic effect is also not quite as impressive as has been suggested.

DR. SCHOU: I find no reason to comment in any great detail on Dr. Mielke's excellent and comprehensive review. He ended with the question of lithium poisoning and its prevention. I would like to point out that it looks as if many, if not all, of the lithium poisonings we have seen during recent years have developed under one or the other of two sets of circumstances. We know from animal experiments (Thomsen and Schou, 1973) and we confirmed in humans (Petersen et al., 1974) that prolonged administration of thiazides and other salts-depleting diuretics leads to lowering of the lithium clearance. If under these circumstances the lithium dosage is not reduced appropriately, poisoning will develop. This has happened in a number of cases and is worth noting, especially since edema is occasionally seen as a side effect of lithium treatment and diuretic treatment therefore frequently prescribed. The other group of patients who developed lithium poisoning had had flu before the poisoning. It seems as if the kidney function, particularly the renal lithium clearance, may be temporarily lowered during influenza, and if the lithium dosage is not correspondingly reduced, we have the vicious cycle of lithium poisoning.

Lithium-induced hand tremor may often be effectively counteracted only by reducing dosage. I do not think it is a good idea to give continuous treatment with beta-blockers as a routine procedure to patients with lithium tremor. The internists are beginning to report side effects from such treatment. It is therefore preferable to give pindolol or other beta-blocking agents only when they are particularly required.

We have no specific treatment for the weight gain seen during lithium treatment, nor for the weight gain resulting from treatment with neuroleptics or tricyclic antidepressants. But we should warn our patients against quenching their thirst with fluids of high calorie content and in general to cut down on the intake of calories. However, since a reduced food intake usually also means a reduced intake of salt which may lead to lowering of the lithium clearance, the patients should be advised to take extra salt during the slimming regimen.

A slight reduction of dosage may often be sufficient to remove the lithium-induced polyuria and polydipsia, but not in all cases. We have tried using a vasopressin derivative, DDAVP, but the benefit was doubtful. Lithium-induced goiter and myxedema are no longer major problems, since they are effectively treated with thyroxine, but it is, of course, important not to mistake a lithium-induced myxedema for a depressive relapse.

DR. SIMPSON: I just wanted to emphasize the point about the diuretics. The problem really is that very many people have very many doctors, who give and take away medications, including diuretics, without discussing it.

I would also like to comment on your statement about the elderly people, which interests me because we have been using a prediction loading dose method for estimating optimal daily dosage of treatment. We have been treating a group of elderly patients with tardive dyskinesia, and three out of fourteen needed only 300 mg twice a day in our prediction in this elderly group, which is highly unusual. We only have about six out of one-hundred subjects who are getting less than 300 mg twice a day to maintain therapeutic levels.

Dr. Schou, would you comment about pindolol since it is not available in the U.S.

DR. SCHOU: Propanolol, practolol and pindolol all have beneficial effects on lithium-induced tremor. Pindolol has the advantage in that it is less apt to induce bronchial spasm.

DR. CLAGHORN: I would like to comment on the issue of sudden death. Admittedly there are describable changes on the electrocardiogram and in other cardiac functions in patients. However, the difficulties attendant on making the decision that sudden death is related to the use of drugs is complicated by the very low frequency with which sudden death occurs. Enormous sampling is required in order to establish incidence rates and control groups which are sometimes almost impossible to acquire. In 1946, the Armed Forces Institute of Pathology published studies on sudden death in young men who were in the service at the time, all of whom were under forty, ambulatory, and supposedly in good physical condition, yet died within twenty-four hours after the onset of some type of sudden illness. In a good many of the cases, it was determined that there was generalized atherosclerosis with cardiovascular disease or intracerebral hemorrhages and a variety of other readily diagnosable causes of illness. However, depending on how one reads the autopsy reports, numbers varying between 17 and 21 percent of these cases had no known cause of death. In a presumed healthy population, there is not an inconsiderable incidence rate of sudden death with unknown cause (it would be about one in 70,000 for the entire population of Armed Forces Institute of Pathology autopsies); it becomes even more difficult to interpret the etiology of the rare sudden deaths of patients who were on drugs at the time of death. In addition, the evidence is substantial that the incidence of cardiovascular, gastrointestinal and autonomic dysfunction is considerably higher in the psychiatric population than in the general population. In 1967, we attempted to determine the effects of chronic tranquilizer drug use on the death rates of our clinic population; we studied some 1,300 patients, and the only way we could establish any kind of control mechanism to age, sex and race was to correct the mortality rates against rates occurring in the country where these patients resided for those years. It is anything but a satisfactory comparison. However, to find 1,300 psychiatric patients who are not medicated is an obvious impossibility. Our computation of the incidence rates indicated that the death rates were not different from what would have been expected in the general population. So, while I have no answer to the question concerning the association of psychopharmacologic therapy with sudden death, I believe that statements about sudden death should always be highly qualified in view of the virtual impossibility of making a valid statement of the true incidence rates in any kind of comparable control group.

DR. KLEIN: I would like to ask two questions. The first one is for Dr. Schou. Is there any knowledge of the mechanisms of lithium-induced tremor? I was surprised to hear you say that practolol is a useful tremor blocking agent. Practolol doesn't cross the blood-brain barrier; therefore, if it is having an effect, it seems to be an entirely peripheral one. I really can't even conceptualize a peripheral mechanism that would reduce tremor.

DR. SCHOU: There is evidence to indicate the existence of beta-receptors in the muscles, and this may be where practolol exerts its anti-tremor action. Furthermore, even if practolol has difficulty crossing the blood-brain barrier, a little may, in fact, enter the brain.

DR. GALLANT: It is interesting to note that propanolol, with which I am more familiar, does cross the blood-brain barrier and is efficacious in the treatment of familial cerebellar tremor. Although there is no reasonable biochemical formulation for the etiology of familial cerebellar tremor, I could understand from a clinical point of view how propanolol could thus reduce the tremor seen with lithium administration.

DR. KLEIN: Concerning my other question, it seems that there is very little animal pharmacologic work reported on the interaction of the MAO inhibitors with the tricyclics and/or tyramine-containing foods. You would think that if there is any area in which animal models might prove illuminating, it would be in these particular areas. You would think that you could treat animals with MAO inhibitors and expose them to a wide variety of foods and see whether or not anything adverse occurs. I believe there is a lot of mythology floating around the MAO inhibitor–cheese reaction area. I just don't understand why there are not any extensive animal pharmacological studies in this area.

DR. SIMPSON: Dr. Klein, I have to say that the only reference that Dr. Mielke left out was by Blackwell, who first reported the MAOI-cheese reaction which was somewhat ignored at the time. I think it was Aubrey Lewis who suggested that Dr. Blackwell take some time off and go into the lab. He indeed went through all the cheeses and showed very clearly which cheeses were associated with the hypertensive crisis in cats, and later on he even discussed which parts of the specific cheese were involved. So there was a substantial amount of work performed on the problem at that time. However, I have not seen any further investigational work in animals in regard to problems of MAOI-tricyclic combinations.

DR. MENDELS: I would like to ask one question of Dr. Mielke. Considering the reports that you may enhance cardiotoxicity with tricyclics, is there any consensus that one tricyclic is safer than another for a patient with cardiovascular disease?

DR. MIELKE: In looking through the literature I didn't find a safer one; I only found that amitriptyline was mentioned more frequently in regard to cardiotoxicity, but it is also prescribed quite frequently.

DR. GALLANT: We are all aware that there are no controlled evaluations in this area, but the antidepressant drug that has been listed as being associated with most of the moderate to serious cardiac reactions is amitriptyline. It is undetermined at this time whether or not this reporting is due to the increased use of amitriptyline in certain patient populations and better reporting in certain areas where amitriptyline is used to a greater extent than other antidepressants.

DR. MENDELS: Some people believe, rightly or wrongly, that amitriptyline is more sedative than other tricyclics and that elderly people who are more agitated need a more sedative drug. Thus the apparent increased cardiotoxic incidence may be a reflection of clinical choice in this specific type of patient.

DR. GALLANT: Before we end this discussion, I would like to offer advice on two side effects or toxic problems observed with antidepressant agents. The anticholinergic effects in patients with glaucoma deserve additional attention. It should be noted that patients with open-angle glaucoma, which is the most common form of glaucoma, are relatively safe subjects for antidepressant and antipsychotic agents with anticholinergic activity. To avoid precipitating a first attack in acute-angle glaucoma, some type of screening for a narrow-angle anterior chamber (acute-angle) is necessary. Of course, pilocarpine eye drops should be used immediately if an attack does occur. With the exception of lithium, most antidepressant agents are capable of causing significant anticholinergic side effects. Therefore, ophthalmologic consultation should be sought before *long-term* therapy of antidepressant agents is initiated.

The second problem is concerned with overdosage. The emergency room physician should always remember the following symptom triad associated with suicide attempts with antidepressant agents: (1) atropine-like symptoms, (2) confusion and/or agitation, and (3) cardiac arrhythmias. For confirmation of the diagnosis of antidepressant overdosage, the physician can first use methacholine, 10 to 30 mg. If a flush does not appear, and there is no perspiration reaction, then physostigmine may be indicated for systemic treatment.

REFERENCES

Activated charcoal in tricyclic drug overdoses (two letters) (1972). *Br. Med. J.* 4(835):298.

Adams, P. H., Chalmers, T. M., and Davies, E. B. (1963). Tranylcypromine and acute intermittent porphyria (a letter). *Lancet* 2:692.

Agulnik, P. L., DiMascio, A., and Moore, P. (1972). Acute brain syndrome associated with lithium therapy. *Am. J. Psychiat.* 129(5):621–23.

Alexander, C. S., and Nino, A. (1969). Cardiovascular complications in young patients taking psychotropic drugs. *Am. Heart J.* 78:757–69.

AMA Drug Evaluations, 2nd edition. (1973). Acton, Mass.: AMA Dept. of Drugs, Publ. Sci. Group, Inc.

Amdisen, A. (1969). Lithium in psychiatry. *Acta Psychiat Scand.* Suppl. 207:55–58.

―――― and Skjoldborg, H. (1969). Hemodialysis for lithium poisoning. *Lancet* 2:213.

Anderson, H., and Kristiansen, E. S. (1959). Tofranil treatment of endogenous depression. *Acta Psychiat, Neurol. Scand.* 34:387–97.

Angrist, B. M., Gershon, S., and Levitan, S. J. (1970). Lithium-induced diabetes insipidus-like syndrome. *Comp. Psych.* 11:141–46.

Arenillas, L. (1964). Amitriptyline and weight gain. *Lancet* 1:432–33.

Arneson, G. A. (1964). Phenothiazine derivatives and glucose metabolism. *J. Neuropsychiat.* 5:181–85.

Asbach, H. W., and Schuler, H. W. (1974). Amitriptyline and imipramine poisoning in children. *Br. Med. J.* 2:386–87.

Auclair, M. C., Gulda, O., and Lechat, P. (1969). Étude du rôle du potassium dans l'action toxique cardiaque de l'imipramine. *Biologie Comptesendus* 5:1093.

Ayd, F. J. (1974). Ed., *International Drug Therapy Newsletter.*

Baer, L., Glassman, A. H., and Kassir, S. (1973). Negative sodium balance in lithium carbonate toxicity: evidence of mineralocorticoid blockade. *Arch. Gen. Psychiat.* 29(6):823–27.

Bain, D. J., and Turner, T. (1971). Imipramine poisoning (a letter). *Arch. Dis. Child.* 46(250):887.

Bellet, S. (1972). *Essentials of Cardiac Arrhythmias, Diagnosis and Management.* Philadelphia: W. B. Sanders Co. pp. 345–70.

Bennie, E. H., and Lazarus, J. H. (1972). Lithium-induced thyroid dysfunction. *Lancet* 2(766):44–45.

Bigger, J. T., Schmitt, D. H., and Kutt, H. (1968). Relationship between the plasma level of diphenylhydantoin sodium and its cardiac antiarrhythmic effects. *Circ. Res.* 38:363–74.

Blair, J. H., Simpson, G. M., and Kline, N. S. (1962). Monoamine oxidase inhibitors and sperm production (a letter). *JAMA* 181:172.

Boston Collaborative Drug Surveillance Program (1972). Adverse reactions to the tricyclic antidepressant drugs. *Lancet* 1(749):529–31.

Brackenridge, R. G. (1972). Cardiotoxicity of amitriptyline. *Lancet* 2(783):929–30.

Brandt, C., and Hoffbauer, F. W. (1964). Liver injury associated with tranylcypromine therapy. *JAMA* 188:752–53.

Brogan, E., Kozonis, M. C., and Overy, D. C. (1969). Glucagon therapy in heart failure. *Lancet* 1:482–84.

Brown, K. G., McMichen, H. U., and Briggs, D. S. (1972). Tachyarrhythmia in severe imipramine overdose controlled by practolol. *Arch. Dis. Child* 47(251):104–06.

Brown, T. C. K., Barker, G. A., Dunlop, M. E., and Loughnan, P. M. (1973). The use of sodium bicarbonate in the treatment of tricyclic antidepressant induced arrhythmias. *Anaesth. Intens. Care* 1:203–10.

Cairncross, K. D., and Gershon, S. (1962). A pharmacological basis for the cardiovascular complications of imipramine medication. *Med. J. Aust.* 2:372–75.

Callaway, C. L., Hendric, H. C., and Luby, E. D. (1968). Cutaneous conditions observed in patients during treatment with lithium. *Am. J. Psych.* 124:1124–25.

Candy, J. (1972). Severe hypothyroidism—an early complication of lithium therapy. *Br. Med. J.* 3(821):277.

Cardiovascular complications of tricyclic antidepressants (an editorial) (1971). *N.Z. Med. J.* 74(475):390–91.

Chapman, A. J., and Lewis, G. (1972). Iatrogenic lithium poisoning: a case report with necropsy findings. *J. Okla. State Med. Assn.* 65(12):491–94.

Ciocatto, E., Fagiano, G., and Bava, G. L. (1972). Clinical features and treatment of overdosage of monoamine oxidase inhibitors and their interaction with other psychotropic drugs. *Resuscitation* 1:69–72.

Cole, J. O. (1972). Atropine-like delirium and anticholinergic substances. *Am. J. Psychiat.* 128(7):898–99.

Cooper, A. J., and Ashcraft, G. (1966). Potentiation of insulin hypoglycemia by MAOI antidepressant drugs. *Lancet* 1:407–09.

———, Magnus, R. V., and Rose, M. J. (1964). Hypertensive syndrome with tranylcypromine medication. *Lancet* 1:527–29.

Cooperative Study (1973). Drug induced extrapyramidal symptoms. *JAMA* 224(6):889–91.

Copeland, P. S. (1972). Tricyclic antidepressives and cardiac death. *Drug & Ther. Bull.* No. 10:55–56.

Crammer, J., and Davies, B. (1972). Activated charcoal in tricyclic drug overdoses (a letter). *Br. Med. J.* 3(825):527.

Crombie, D. L., Pinsent, R. J., and Fleming, D. (1972). Imipramine in pregnancy (a letter). *Br. Med. J.* 1(802):745.

Davies, R. K., Tucker, G. J., Harrow, M., and Detre, T. P. (1971). Confusional episodes and antidepressant medication. *Am. J. Psychiat.* 128(1):95–99.

Demers, R. G., and Heninger, G. R. (1971). Electrocardiographic T-wave changes during lithium carbonate treatment. *JAMA* 218(3):381–86.

de Villiers, J. C. (1966). Intracranial haemorrhage in patients treated with monoamine-oxidase inhibitors. *Br. J. Psychiat.* 112:109–18.

Donsa, T., and Hechter, O. (1970). The effect of NaCl and LiCl on vasopressin sensitive adenyl cyclase. *Life Sci.* 9(1):765–69.

Duffield, J. D. (1973). Side effects of lithium carbonate (a letter). *Br. Med. J.* 1(851):491.

Duvoisin, R. C. (1968). Neurological reactions to psychotropic drugs. In *Psychopharmacology: A Review of Progress, 1957–1967.* PHS Publ. No. 1836, pp. 561–73.

Eggermont, E. (1973). Withdrawal symptoms in neonates associated with maternal imipramine therapy. *Lancet* 2(830):680.

Escobar, J. I., Schiele, B. C., and Zimmerman, R. (1974). The tranylcypromine isomers: a controlled clinic trial. *Am. J. Psychiat.* 133:1025.

Fann, W. E. (1973). Some clinically important interactions of psychotropic drugs. *So. Med. J.* 66(6):661–65.

———, Cavanaugh, J. H., Kaufmann, J. S., Griffith, J. D., et al. (1971). Doxepin: effect on biogenic amine transport in man. *Psychopharmacol.* 22:111–25.

Farquharson, S. (1972). Poisoning by tricyclic drugs (a letter). *Br. Med. J.* 1(796):378.

Forrest, J. N., Jr., Cohen, A. D., Torretti, J., Himmelhoch, J. M., and Epstein, P. H. (1974). On the mechanism of lithium-induced diabetes insipidus in man and the rat. *J. Clin. Inv.* 53(4):1115–23.

Fieve, R. R., and Platman, S. R. (1969). Follow-up studies of lithium and thyroid function in manic-depressive illness. *Am. J. Psych.* 125:1443–45.

Freeman, J. W., and Loughhead, M. G. (1973). Beta blockade in treatment of tricyclic antidepressant overdosage. *Med. J. Aust.* 1:1233–35.

———, Mundy, G. R., Beattie, R. R., and Ryan, C. (1969). Cardiac abnormalities in poisoning with tricyclic antidepressants. *Br. Med. J.* 2:610–11.

Gallant, D. M. (1963). Clinical management of side effects and toxicity in psychopharmacologic therapy. *Bull. Tulane Univ. Med. Faculty* 22(3):179–86.

——— (1966). A clinical investigator presents a brief survey of psychopharmacology for the practicing physician. Quebec Psychopharmacology Assn., Quebec, Canada.

Gander, D. R. (1965). Treatment of depressive illness with combined antidepressants. *Lancet* 2:107–09.

Gerst, P. H., Fleming, W. H., and Malm W. Jr. (1966). Increased susceptibility of the heart to ventricular fibrillation during metabolic acidosis. *Circ. Res.* 19:63–70.

Gey, K. F., and Pletscher, A. (1961). Increase of pyruvic lactic acid in rat blood by inhibition of monoamine oxidase. *Experimentia* 17:25–27.

Gilani, S. H. (1974). Imipramine and congenital abnormalities. *Path. Microbiol.* 40:37–42.

Goel, K. M., and Shanks, R. A. (1974a). Amitriptyline and imipramine poisoning in children. *Br. Med. J.* 1(902):261–63.

——— and Shanks, R. A. (1974b). Amitriptyline and imipramine poisoning in children. *Br. Med. J.* 1(907):575.

Goldberg, L. I. (1964). Monoamine oxidase inhibitors. *JAMA* 190:456–62.

———, Horwitz, D., and Sjoerdsma, A. (1962). Attenuation of cardiovascular responses to exercise as a possible basis for effectiveness of monoamine oxidase inhibitors in angina pectoris. *J. Pharm. Exp. Ther.* 137:39–46.

Gong, N. C., and Rogers, K. H. (1973). Mechanism of hyperthermia in the interaction between pethidine or imipramine and monoamine oxidase inhibitors. *Med. J. Malaysia* 27(4):280–83.

Goodman, L. S., and Gilman, A. (1970). *The Pharmacological Basis of Therapeutics,* 4th edition. Macmillan & Co., pp. 732–33, 181–92.

Greenblatt, D. J., Koch-Weser, J., and Shader, R. I. (1974). Multiple complications and death following protriptyline overdosage. *JAMA* 229:556–57.

Gwynne, J. F. (1971). Tricyclic antidepressants and heart disease. *N.Z. Med. J.* 74(475):414–15.

Hanse, A. (1923). Uber amenorrhoe bei geistes und nervenkrankheiten usw. *Arch. f. Psychiat.* 68:463.

Hawkins, J. B., and Dorken, P. R. (1969). Lithium. *Lancet* 1:839–41.

Hendley, E. D., and Snyder, S. H. (1968). Relationship between the action of monoamine oxidase inhibitors on the noradrenaline uptake system and their antidepressant efficacy. *Nature* 220:1330–31.

Herbst, C. (1893). Experimentelle untersicjimgem uber den einfluss der veranderten chemischen zusammensetzung des umgebenden mediums auf die entwicklung der tiere. I.Theil Versuche an Suigeleieren. *A. wiss. Zool.* 55:446.

Herrero, F. A. (1973). Lithium carbonate toxicity. *JAMA* 226(9):1109–10.

Hussain, M. Z., Khan, A. G., and Chaudhry, Z. A. (1973). Aplastic anemia associated with lithium therapy. *Can. Med. Assn. J.* 108(6):724–25.

Janowsky, D. S., David, J., el-Yousef, M. K., and Serkerke, H. J. (1972). Combined anticholinergic agents and atropine-like delirium. *Am. J. Psychiat.* 129(3):360–61.

Juul-Jensen, P., and Schou, M. (1973). Permanent brain damage after lithium intoxication (a letter). *Br. Med. J.* 4(893):673.

Kanarek, K. S., Thomson, P. D., and Levin, S. E. (1973). The management of imipramine (Tofranil) intoxication in children. *S. Afr. Med. J.* 47(19):835–38.

Kaplan, S. M., Mas, J. W., Pixley, J. M., and Ross, W. D. (1960). Use of imipramine in diabetes. *JAMA* 174:511–17.

Kaufmann, J. S. (1974). Pheochromocytoma and tricyclic antidepressants (a letter). *JAMA* 229:1282.

Keynes, R. D., and Swan, R. C. (1959). The permeability of frag muscle fibers to lithium ions. *J. Physio.* (London). 147:626–38.

Kirk, L., Baastrup, P. C., and Schou, M. (1972). Propanolol and lithium-induced tremor. *Lancet* 1(755):839.

———, Baastrup, P. C., and Schou, M. (1973). Propanolol treatment of lithium-induced tremor (a letter). *Lancet* 2(837):1086–87.

Klein, D. F. (1965). Visual hallucinations with imipramine. *Am. J. Psychiat.* 121:911–14.

———— and Davis, J. M. (1969). *Diagnosis and Drug Treatment of Psychiatric Disorders.* Baltimore: Williams & Wilkins Co.

Klein, J. J., Segal, R. L., and Warner, R. R. (1964). Galactorrhea due to imipramine. *N. Eng. J. Med.* 271:510–12.

Klein, M. (1964). Galactorrhea. *JAMA* 189:593.

Kline, N. S., Alexander, S. F., and Chamberlain, A. (1974). *Psychotropic Drugs: A Manual for Emergency Management of Overdosage.* Oradell, N. J.: Med. Economics Corp.

Koang, N. K. (1957). Endocrine function during treatment of pulmonary tuberculosis with INH. *Clin. Med. J.* 75:100.

Kramer, J. C., Klein, D. F., and Fink, M. (1961). Withdrawal symptoms following discontinuance of imipramine therapy. *Am. J. Psychiat.* 118:549–51.

Kristiansen, E. S. (1961). Cardiac complications during treatment with imipramine (Tofranil). *Acta Psychiat. Scand.* 36:427–42.

Kuenssberg, E. V., and Knox, J. D. (1972). Imipramine in pregnancy (a letter). *Br. Med. J.* 2(808):292.

Kurtin, S. B. (1973). Lithium carbonate dermatitis (a letter). *JAMA* 223(7):802.

Kusumi, Y. (1971). A cutaneous side effect of lithium: report of two cases. *Dis. Nerv. Syst.* 32:853–54.

Lavalle, B. (1965). *Toxicity and Adverse Reaction Studies with Neuroleptics and Antidepressants,* H. E. Lehmann and T. A. Ban, eds. Quebec Psychopharmacological Research Assn., pp. 129–30.

Leak, D., and Dormandy, T. L. (1961). Possible relations of hypoglycemia induced by monoamine oxidase inhibition and angina pectoris. *Proc. Soc. Exp. Biol. Med.* 108:597–600.

Levy, S. T., Forrest, J. N., Jr., and Heninger, G. (1973). Lithium-induced diabetes insipidus: manic symptoms, brain and electrolyte correlates, and chlorothiazide treatment. *Am. J. Psychiat.* 139(9):1014–18.

Lithium-induced diabetes insipidus (1972). *Br. Med. J.* 2(816):726.

Litvak, R., and Kaelbling, R. (1972). Dermatological side effects with psychotropics. *Dis. Nerv. Syst.* 33(5):309–11.

Lloyd, G. G., Rosser, R. M., and Cros, M. J. (1973). Effect of lithium on thyroid in man. *Lancet* 2(829)·619.

Locket, S. (1973). Clinical toxicology. VII. Poisoning by salicylates, paracetamol, tricyclic antidepressants and a miscellany of drugs. *Practitioner* 211(261):105–12.

Luby, E. D., Schwartz, D., and Rosenbaum, H. (1971). Lithium-carbonate-induced myxedema. *JAMA* 218(8):1298–299.

Luke, C. M. (1971). Tricyclic antidepressants and heart disease (a letter). *N.Z. Med. J.* 74(474):345.

Luzecky, M. H., Burman, K. D., and Schultz, E. R. (1974). The syndrome of inappropriate secretion of antidiuretic hormone associated with amitriptyline administration. *S. Med. J.* 67(4):495–97.

McBride, W. G. (1972). Limb deformities associated with iminodibenzyl hydrochloride. *Med. J. Aust.* 1:492.

Mahurkar, S. (1973). Imipramine associated with renal damage. *Lancet* 1(810):998.

Mann, A., and MacPherson, A. (1959). Clinical experience with imipramine (G-22355) in treatment of depression. *Can. Psychiat. Assn. J.* 4:38–47.

Marshall, A., and Moore, K. (1973). Pulmonary disease after amitriptyline overdosage. *Br. Med. J.* 1(855):716–17.

Meyler, L., and Herxheimer, A. (1972). Amsterdam: Excerpta Medica. p. 286.

Mitchell, J. A., Arias, L., and Oates, J. A. (1967). Antagonism of the antihypertensive action of guanethidine sulfate by desipramine hydrochloride. *JAMA* 202:973–76.

Moir, D. C. (1973). Tricyclic antidepressants and cardiac disease. *Am. Heart J.* 86:841–42.

————, Crooks, J., Sawyer, P., et al. (1972). Proceedings: cardiotoxicity of tricyclic antidepressants. *Br. J. Pharmacol.* 44(2):371–72.

————, Dingwall, F. I., and Weir, R. D. (1973). Medicines evaluation and monitoring group, a follow-up study of cardiac patients receiving amitriptyline. *Eur. J. Clin. Pharmacol.* 6(2):98–101.

Molina, C., Aberkane, B., and Conguy-Douard, T. A. (1957). Les gynecomastics chez les tuberculeux dulonaries, à propos de cinq observations. *Moroc. Med.* 36:635–36.

Morgan, M. H., and Read, A. E. (1972). Antidepressants and liver disease. *Gut* 13(9):697–701.

Morrow, A. W. (1972). Imipramine and congenital abnormalities. *N.Z. Med. J.* 75(479):228–29.

National Clearinghouse for Poison Control Centers (1973). *Diazepam as Therapy for Convulsive Seizures Precipitated by Chemical Intoxicants.*

Nemec, J. (1973). Cardiotoxic effects of tricyclic antipsychotics. *Toxicologie Exp.* 4–5:224–31.

O'Connell, R. A. (1970). Leukocytosis during lithium carbonate treatment. *Intl. J. Pharmacopsychiat.* 4:30.

Pader, E. (1960). Nardil. *Am. J. Psychiat.* 117:271–72.

Paykel, E. S., Mueller, P. S., and De la Vergne, P. M. (1973). Amitriptyline, weight gain and carbohydrate craving: a side effect. *Br. J. Psychiat.* 123(576):501–07.

Penn, A. S., Rowland, L. P., and Fraser, D. W. (1972). Drugs, coma and myoglobinuria. *Arch. Neurol.* 26:336–42.

Penney, R. (1968). Imipramine hydrochloride poisoning in childhood. *Am. J. Dis. Child.* 116:181–86.

Petersen, V., Hvidt, S., Thomsen, K., and Schou, M. (1974). The effect of prolonged thiazide treatment on the renal lithium clearance of humans. *Br. Med. J.* 3:143–45.

Pettinger, W. A., Mitchell, J. R., and Oates, J. A. (1968). Cardiovascular effects and toxicity of psychotropic agents in man. In *Psychopharmacology: A Review of Progress, 1957–1967.* PHS Publ. No. 1836, pp. 589–95.

Posey, R. E. (1972). Lithium carbonate dermatitis. *JAMA* 221(13):1517.

Powell, W. J. (1968). Lethal hepatic necrosis after treatment with imipramine and desipramine. *JAMA* 206:642–44.

Prange, A. J., Jr. (1972). *The Use of Antidepressant Drugs in the Elderly Patient.* Psychopharmacology and Aging Patient Symposium, Duke Univ., Durham, N.C.

――― (1973). The use of drugs in depression: theoretical and practical basis. *Psychiat. Ann.* 3:2–10.

Pritchard, M. J. (1972). Cardiotoxicity of amitriptyline. *Lancet* 2(780):760.

Rachelefsky, G. S., Flynt, J. W., Jr., Ebbin, A. J., Wilson, M. G., et al. (1972). Possible teratogenicity of tricyclic antidepressants. *Lancet* 1(755):838–39.

Rachmilewitz, E. A., Dawson, R. B., Jr., and Rachmilewitz, B. (1968). Serum antibodies against desipramine as a possible cause for thrombocytopenia. *Blood* 32:524–35.

Raisfeld, I. H. (1972). Cardiovascular complications of antidepressant therapy, interactions at the adrenergic neuron. *Am. Heart J.* 83(1):129–33.

Ramsey, I. D. (1967). Survival after imipramine poisoning. *Lancet* 2:1308–09.

Raskin, A. (1972). Adverse reactions to phenelzine: results of a nine-hospital depression study. *J. Clin. Pharmacol.* 12(1):22–25.

Rasmussen, J. (1965). Amitriptyline and imipramine poisoning. *Lancet* 2:850–51.

Remmen, E., Cohen, S., Ditman, K. S., and Frantz, J. R. (1962). Psychochemotherapy. Los Angeles: A Western Medical Publication.

Renton, K. W., and Eade, N. R. (1972). Microsomal enzymes and potentiation of tyramine pressor response. *Biochem. Pharmacol.* 21:1393–1402.

Rickels, K. (1968). Antineurotic agents: Specific and nonspecific effects. In *Psychopharmacology: A Review of Progress, 1957–1967.* PHS Publ. No. 1836, pp. 231–47.

Rifkin, A., Klein, D. F., and Quitkin, F. (1973). Organic brain syndrome during lithium carbonate treatment. *Compr. Psychiat.* 14(3):251–54.

Ripley, H. S., and Papanicolaou, G. N. (1942). The menstrual cycle with vaginal smear studies in schizophrenia, depression, and elation. *Am. J. Psychiat.* 98:567–75.

Roberts, R. J., Mueller, S., and Lauer, R. M. (1973). Propanolol in the treatment of cardiac arrhythmias associated with amitriptyline intoxication. *J. Pediat.* 82(1):65–67.

Robertson, J. C. (1972). Recovery after massive MAOI overdose complicated by malignant hyperpyrexia, treated with chlorpromazine. *Postgrad. Med. J.* 48(555):64–65.

Rom, W. N., and Benner, E. J. (1972). Toxicity by interaction of tricyclic antidepressant and monoamine oxidase inhibitor. *Cal. Med.* 117(6):65–66.

Rosen, D. H. (1973). Acute parotitis associated with depression and psychoactive drug therapy. *Compr. Psychiat.* 14(2):183–88.

Ruddy, J. M., Seymour, J. L., and Anderson, N. G. (1972). Management of tricyclic antidepressant ingestion in children with special reference to the use of glucagon. *Med. J. Aust.* 1(13):630–33.

Ruiz-Maldonado, R., Perez de Francisco, C., and Tamayo, L. (1973). Lithium dermatitis (a letter). *JAMA* 224(11):1534.

St. Jean, A., and Ban, T. A. (1965). *A Note on Amitriptyline, Haloperidol and Thioproperazine.* H. E. Lehmann and T. A. Ban, eds. Quebec: Psychopharmacologic Research Assn., p. 156.

Saran, B. M., and Gaind, R. (1973). Lithium. *Clin. Toxicol.* 6:257–69.

Sathananthan, G. L., and Gershon, S. (1973a). Renal damage due to imipramine. *Lancet* 1(807):833–34.

——— and Gershon, S. (1973b). Imipramine withdrawal: an akathisia-like syndrome. *Am. J. Psychiat.* 130:1286–87.

Scherbel, A. L. (1960). Clinical experience in treatment of over 2,000 cases with amine oxidase inhibitors. *Dis. Nerv. Syst.* 21:67–69.

Schou, M. (1963). Electrocardiographic changes during treatment with lithium and with drugs of the imipramine type. *Acta Psychiat. Scand.* 39(Suppl. 169):258–59.

——— (1968). Lithium in psychiatry. A review. In *Psychopharmacology: A Review of Progress, 1957–1967.* PHS Publ. No. 1836, pp. 711–18.

——— and Amdisen, A. (1973). Lithium and pregnancy. III. Lithium ingestion by children breast-fed by women on lithium treatment. *Br. Med. J.* 2(859):138.

———, Amdisen, A., Jensen, S. E., and Olsen T. (1968a). Occurrence of goiter during lithium treatment. *Br. Med. J.* 3:710–13.

———, Amdisen, A., and Steenstrup, O. R. (1973a). Lithium and pregnancy. II. Hazards to women given lithium during pregnancy and delivery. *Br. Med. J.* 2(859):137–38.

———, Amdisen, A., and Trop-Jensen, J. (1968b). Lithium poisoning. *Am. J. Psychiat.* 125:520–27.

———, Goldfield, M. D., Weinstein, M. R., and Villeneuve, A. (1937b). Lithium and pregnancy. I. Report from the register of lithium babies. *Br. Med. J.* 2(859):135–36.

Schwartz, W. B., Bennett, W., Curelop, S., and Bartter, F. C. (1957). A syndrome of renal sodium loss and hyponatremia probably resulting from inappropriate secretion of antidiuretic hormone. *Am. J. Med.* 23:529–42.

Scollins, M. J., Robinson, D. S., and Nies, A. (1972). Cardiotoxicity of amitriptyline. *Lancet* 2(788):1202.

Sedal, L., Korman, M. G., William, P. O., and Mushin, G. (1972). Overdosage of tricyclic antidepressants: a report of two deaths and a prospective study of 24 patients. *Med. J. Aust.* 2(2):74–79.

Segal, R. L., Rosenblatt, S., and Eliasoph, I. (1973). Endocrine exophthalmos during lithium therapy of manic-depressive disease. *N. Eng. J. Med.* 289(3):136–38.

Sesso, A. M., Snyder, R. C., and Schott, C. E. (1973). Propanolol in imipramine poisoning. *Am. J. Dis. Child.* 126(6):847–49.

Shapiro, R. K. (1964). Etiological factors in placebo effect. *JAMA* 187:136–38.

Shopsin, B., Friedmann, R., and Gershon, S. (1971). Lithium and leukocytosis. *Clin. Pharmacol. Ther.* 12(6):923–28.

———, Johnson, G., and Gershon, S. (1970). Neurotoxicity with lithium: differential drug responsiveness. *Intl. J. Pharmacopsychiat.* 5:170.

———, Shenkman, L., Blum, M., and Hollander, C. S. (1973). Iodine and lithium-induced hypothyroidism: documentation of synergism. *Am. J. Med.* 55(5):695–99.

Short, H. (1968). Cholestatic jaundice during imipramine treatment. *JAMA* 206:1791–92.

Sigg, E. G. (1968). Autonomic side effects induced by psychotherapeutic agents. In

Psychopharmacology: A Review of Progress, 1957–1967. PHS Publ. No. 1836, pp. 581–89.

———, Osborne, M., and Koral, B. (1963). Cardiovascular effects of imipramine. *J. Pharmacol. Exp. Ther.* 141:237–43.

Sim, M. (1972). Imipramine and pregnancy (a letter). *Br. Med. J.* 2(804):45.

Simpson, G. M. (1974). *Treatment of Lithium Toxicity.* Bergen Pines Medical Staff Report, Bergen Pines County Hosp., Paramus, N.J., p. 14.

——— and Cooper, T. B. (1969). Lithium and thyroid function (a letter). *Am. J. Psychiat.* 125:1132.

Singer, I., and Rotenberg, D. (1973). Mechanisms of lithium action. *N. Eng. J. Med.* 289:254–60.

———, Rotenberg, D., and Puschett, J. B. (1972). Lithium-induced nephrogenic diabetes insipidus: *in vivo* and *in vitro* studies. *J. Clin. Inv.* 51(5):1081–91.

Smith, E. E., Reece, C. A., and Kauffman, R. (1972). Ototoxic reaction associated with use of nortriptyline hydrochloride: case report. *J. Pediat.* 80(6):1046–48.

Sowton, E., Balcon, R., Cross, D., and Frich, H. (1968). Haemodynamic effects of ICI 50172 in patients with ischaemic heart disease. *Br. Med. J.* 1:215–16.

Spivak, J. L., and Conti, C. R. (1969). Post seizure myoglobinuria. *Johns Hopkins Med. J.* 124:18–24.

Standards in cardiacpulmonary resuscitation and emergency cardiac care (1974). *JAMA* 227:833–68.

Steel, C. M., O'Duffy, J., and Brown, S. S. (1967). Clinical effects and treatment of imipramine and amitriptyline poisoning in children. *Br. Med. J.* 3:663–67.

Tangedahl, T. N., and Gau, G. T. (1972). Myocardial irritability associated with lithium carbonate therapy. *N. Eng. J. Med.* 287(17):867–79.

Taverner, O., and Bain, W. A. (1958). Intravenous lignocaine as an anticonvulsant in status epilepticus and serial epilepsy. *Lancet* 2:1145–47.

Thomsen, K., and Schou, M. (1968). Renal lithium excretion in man. *Am. J. Physiol.* 215:823–27.

——— and Schou, M. (1973). The effect of prolonged administration of hydrochlorothiazide on the renal lithium clearance and urine flow of ordinary rats and rats with diabetes insipidus. *Pharmakopsychiat.* 6:264–69.

Treitman, P. (1972). Desipramine poisoning (a letter). *JAMA* 220(6):861.

Tricyclic antidepressant and limb reduction deformities. A further communication from the Australian Drug Evaluation Committee (1973). *Med. J. Aust.* 1(15):768–69.

Trubohovich, R. V. (1973). Tricyclic antidepressants: dangers with overdosage. *N.Z. Med. J.* 78:502–03.

Tseng, H. L. (1971). Interstitial myocarditis probably related to lithium carbonate intoxication. *Arch. Pathol.* 92(6):444–48.

Tuller, M. A., and Cohen, I. R. (1963). Tranylcypromine (a letter). *Lancet* 2:464.

Tunnessen, W. W., Jr., and Hertz, C. G. (1972). Toxic effects of lithium in newborn infants: a commentary. *J. Pediatr.* 81(4):804–07.

Van De Ree, J. K., Zimmerman, A. N. E., and Van Heijst, A. N. P. (1972). Intoxication with tricyclic antidepressants hemodynamic consequences. *Toxicologie Exp.* No. 5:302–05.

Von Hartitzsch, B., Hoenich, N. A., Leigh, R. H., Wilkinson, R., et al. (1972). Permanent neurological sequelae despite haemodialysis for lithium intoxication. *Br. Med. J.* 4(843):757–59.

Webster, P. A. (1973). Withdrawal symptoms in neonates associated with maternal antidepressant therapy. *Lancet* 2(824):318–19.

Weiss, J., Weiss, S., and Weiss, B. (1959). Effects of iproniazid and similar compounds on the gastrointestinal tract. *Ann. N.Y. Acad. Sci.* 80:854–59.

Wharton, R. N., Perel, J. M., Dayton, P. G., and Malitz, S. (1971). A potential clinical use for methylphenidate with tricyclic antidepressants. *Am. J. Psychiat.* 127:1619–25.

Wheatley, D. (1972). Drowsiness and antidepressant drugs in mild depressive illness. *Br. J. Psychiat.* 120(558):517–19.

Whybrow, P. C. (1972). Synergistic action between iodine and lithium (a letter). *JAMA* 221(5):506.

Wilbanks, G. D., Bressler, B., Peete, C. H. Jr., Cherny, W. B., et al. (1970). The toxic effects of lithium carbonate in mother and newborn infant. *JAMA* 213:865–67.

Young, J. A., and Galloway, W. H. (1971). Treatment of severe imipramine poisoning. *Arch. Dis. Child.* 46:353–55.

CHAPTER XI

Prophylactic and Maintenance Therapy in Recurrent Affective Disorders

M. Schou

A review of prophylactic and maintenace therapy in recurrent affective disorders should ideally include maintenance electric convulsive treatment and continuation treatment with monoamine oxidase inhibitors. We know little about the latter (Imlah et al., 1965), somewhat more about the former (Geoghegan, 1947; Geoghegan and Stevenson, 1949; Stevenson and Geoghegan, 1951; Karliner and Wehrheim, 1965; Barton et al., 1973). On this occasion I shall limit myself to a discussion of experiences with lithium and with tricyclic antidepressants.

As a preliminary note on terminology, it should be mentioned that Hartigan (1963) was the first to use the term "prophylaxis" in relation to the effect of long-term lithium treatment in depression because he found lithium ineffective in treating already existing depression and yet effective in preventing further depressive recurrences. Other terms have been suggested for the effect of long-term lithium administration in recurrent affective disorders: "normothymotic" or "mood-normalizing action" (Schou, 1963), "mood stabilization" (Baastrup et al., 1970), "compensatory action" (Freyhan, 1971), "regulatory action" (Glen and Reading, 1973), and—for tricyclic antidepressants—"continuation treatment" (Mindham et al., 1973). There is little reason to discuss their relative merits here. They all signify the ability of a treatment to attenuate or prevent further recurrences of the disease, and it is implicit in all of them that it is only the abnormal, not the normal, mood changes that are being stabilized, compensated for, regulated, etc.

The question of lithium prophylaxis has been the subject of so much debate that it hardly requires any extensive discussion. I need only remind you that the evidence is based on two types of prophylactic trials: the one-group, non-blind trials and the two-group, double-blind trials (Schou, 1973; Schou and Thomsen, 1975). The first kind of trial was based on two assumptions concerning the nature and course of recurrent endogenous affective disorders: (1) that observer bias and the effect of psychological factors would not be sufficiently strong to prevent further recurrences to any significant extent, and (2) that patients selected for having had frequent episodes during recent years would be at high risk of further recurrences during the following years. It was the validity of these assumptions that was at the center of the debate; both assumptions have now been substantiated experimentally (Schou et al., 1970). Since only the two-group, double-blind studies on lithium are comparable with the prophylactic studies on tricyclic antidepressants, only these will be reviewed here.

Table I outlines the design and special features of the double-blind lithium trials, presented chronologically. It will be noted that there were two types of design, the start design and the discontinuation design; that a frequency selection criterion was used in all but one of the studies; that the trial periods varied considerably in length; and that the serum lithium level was monitored in seven out of the eight studies. It should further be noted that the termination of one study (Baastrup et al., 1970) was determined according to a sequential analysis design. The remaining studies were terminated after a certain experimental period; it was not clear in all cases whether or not the length of the trial period had been decided prior to the trial, as ideally it should have been.

There are many ways in which the outcome of a prophylactic trial can be recorded; no single procedure can give a comprehensive picture of what happens to the patients and their disease when active prophylactic treatment is given. One may, for example, record the frequency of episodes, the intensity of episodes, the duration of episodes, the amount of additional drug or shock treatment required, the social adjustment and working ability of the patients during the trial period, etc. In Table II, I have chosen to record simply the total number of patients in the trial, the number of those who suffered one or more relapses during the trial period, and the number of those who did not relapse. This procedure obviously disregards valuable information; it was chosen because it is the only one that permitted comparison of the published studies. The figures in the table were derived in the following way: the total number of patients include those who entered the trial minus those who dropped out of it for reasons other than relapse, e.g., intercurrent disease, side effects, etc. The number of patients who relapsed during the trial includes those who dropped out because they relapsed as well as those who completed the trial in spite of one or more relapses.

Inspection of Table II leads to three conclusions concerning lithium prophylaxis. Firstly, lithium was superior to placebo in all eight studies. Secondly, this difference reached a high degree of statistical significance in most of the

Table I

Two-group double-blind trials with lithium: designs and features, from Schou and Thomsen

Author	Design	Selection criterion	Trial period (months)	Serum lithium (mmoles/liter)
Melia (1970)	Discontinuation	—	24	Not determined
Baastrup et al. (1970)	Discontinuation	≥ 2 ep./2 years	5	0.6–1.5
Coppen et al. (1971)	Start	≥ 3 ep./3 years	14	0.7–1.2
Hullin et al. (1972)	Discontinuation	≥ 5 ep./5 years	6	0.6–1.4
Cundall et al. (1972)	Discontinuation	≥ 2 ep./3 years	6	0.5–1.2
Stallone et al. (1973)	Mixed discontinuation and start	≥ 2 ep./2 years	24–28	0.8–1.3
Prien et al. (1973[b])	Discontinuation	—	24	0.5–1.4
Prien et al. (1973[a])	Discontinuation	≥ 2 ep./2 years and ≥ 3 ep./5 years	24	0.5–1.4

Table II

Two-group double-blind trials with lithium: patients having relapse and patients not having relapse during trial period. From Schou and Thomsen (Schou, in press)

Author	Diagnostic group	Medication	Total no. of patients[a]	No. of patients who during trial period relapsed[b]	– did not relapse	Significance[c]
Melia (1970)	Bipolar	Lithium	9	5	4	n.s.
	+ Unipolar	Placebo	9	7	2	
Baastrup et al. (1970)	Bipolar	Lithium	28	0	28	p < 0.001
		Placebo	22	12	10	
	Unipolar	Lithium	17	0	17	p = 0.001
		Placebo	17	9	8	
Coppen et al. (1971)	Bipolar	Lithium	16	3	13	p < 0.001
		Placebo	22	21	1	
	Unipolar	Lithium	11	2	9	p = 0.01
		Placebo	14	11	3	

Study	Type	Treatment				p
Hullin et al. (1972)	Bipolar + Unipolar	Lithium	18	1	17	$p = 0.05$
		Placebo	18	6	12	
Cundall et al. (1972)	Bipolar	Lithium	12	4	8	$p < 0.05$
		Placebo	12	10	2	
	Unipolar	Lithium	4	3	1	n.s.
		Placebo	4	2	2	
Stallone et al. (1973)	Bipolar	Lithium	19	5	14	$p < 0.005$
		Placebo	23	21	2	
Prien et al. (1973[b])	Bipolar	Lithium	85	36	49	$p < 0.005$
		Placebo	86	75	11	
Prien et al. (1973[a])	Bipolar	Lithium	14	5	9	$p < 0.05$
		Placebo	10	9	1	
	Unipolar	Lithium	23	13	10	$p < 0.05$
		Placebo	21	19	2	

[a]Excluding patients who dropped out of the study for reasons other than relapse.
[b]Including patients who dropped out of the study because they relapsed.
[c]One-tailed fourfold table test (Documenta Geigy, 1970) for $N \geq 60$; X^2 -test for $N > 60$.

studies. The studies in which the statistical significance did not reach, or just reached, the 5 percent level were those with small numbers of patients or short trial periods. (The study of Baastrup and associates [1970] reported the shortest of all trial periods, five months, but it was based on large patient groups and therefore yielded a high degree of statistical significance.) And thirdly, lithium exerted a clear-cut prophylactic action in the unipolar type of affective disorder as well as in the bipolar. This result needs to be emphasized because the claim has occasionally been made that lithium is prophylactically less active, or not active at all, in unipolar patients. That notion receives no support from the data presented here.

The percentages of patients who relapsed within the trial period varied considerably (Table III), because the trial periods varied in length. In the last column of Table III, the percentages have been extrapolated to a period of one year. The extrapolations were based on the assumption that the number of patients who had not yet fallen ill decreased exponentially over time; in other words, that a fairly constant proportion of the patients fall ill every month. This assumption is not unreasonable, and it is based on experimental evidence (Shou et al., 1970).

It will be noted than even when calculated in this way the percentages varied considerably: in the lithium groups, from 0 to 94 percent of the patients relapsed; in the placebo groups, from 54 to 97 percent of the patients relapsed. These figures show that the use of a frequency selection criterion is not sufficient to produce homogenous patient samples. The percentages are based on groups with different numbers of patients; in order to calculate a mean value, these numbers must be taken into consideration. The weighted means are 21 percent with relapse in the group of lithium treated patients and 71 percent with relapse in the group given placebo.

These figures require some comment. The figure of 71 percent with relapse within one year in the placebo patients reveals that we are dealing with patients who as a group have a serious prognosis with a high risk of further relapses if not given active prophylactic treatment. Administration of placebo did not prevent the dire outcome in these patients. The high percentage of patients who relapsed clearly substantiates the validity of the two assumptions on which the one-group, non-blind studies were based. More important, this figure may be useful for patient selection in future prophylactic studies, especially if, for ethical reasons, one should decide to abstain from including placebo treated groups.

The figure of 21 percent of the patients relapsing within one year in the lithium treated group might, at first sight, seem to serve as a quantitative measure of the prophylactic efficacy of lithium. The figure should, however, be assessed with some caution. Due to special features in the trial designs, the prophylactic power of lithium may be overestimated; due to other features, it may be underestimated.

The studies using a discontinuation design were based on patients who were already in lithium treatment and had been so for some time; these patient samples may well have an overrepresentation of lithium responders, which was unimportant as long as the trials merely tested the null hypothesis that lithium was no better than placebo. It does, however, limit the applicability of the data to the quantitative assessment of the effect of lithium in unselected patient groups. This limitation, of course, does not apply to the single study (Coppen et al., 1971) which used a start design. In this study, the percentages of patients suffering relapse during lithium treatment were actually lower than 21 percent; that figure may, after all, not overestimate the efficacy of lithium very much.

The 21 percent lithium relapse rate may underestimate the actual effect for the following reason: since more lithium-treated than placebo-treated patients completed the trials, the former were, as a group, exposed to longer trial periods and accordingly to a higher risk of suffering relapse. In the study of Melia (1970), for example, the lithium patients were in the trial for a mean of 433 days and the placebo patients for a mean of 224 days. In the study of Stallone and associates (1973), the corresponding periods were 672 and 250 days. The percentages of patients suffering relapse during treatment with lithium and during treatment with placebo should be seen in the light of this two to three times longer exposure period for the lithium patients. Another reason why 21 percent may be an underestimate is that the procedure used in Table II classified patients as treatment failures if they had had even a single relapse. The fact was therefore disregarded that many of them actually benefited very much from the lithium treatment in terms of lowered frequency of episodes, lessened intensity of episodes, improved social adjustment, and regained working ability, features which the relapse criterion ignored.

I have discussed these points in some detail because they are general to the problem of quantitative assessment of the prophylactic efficacy of a treatment and also because they illustrate the impossibility of expressing such efficacy with a single or a few measures. A considerable number of measures must be employed to obtain a full picture of prophylactic action.

We may now turn to the prophylactic trials with tricyclic antidepressants. These drugs have been used prophylactically for a long time. Many psychiatrists maintain their patients on tricyclic antidepressants after remission of the depressive episode, not only for three or six months but often for years. In some cases, the patients are treated with unaltered doses; in other cases, with reduced doses. Ayd (1974) recently deplored this procedure and called for what he termed "drug holidays" of some days or weeks in order to see if the patients still needed treatment and to reduce the cardiac risk of continued administration of tricyclic antidepressants. While sympathizing with the sentiments expressed by Ayd, I do not agree with his argument or advice. The question seems to me to be one not of shorter or longer drug holidays but one of finding out whether or not the tricyclic antidepressants do exert prophylactic action and, if so, to administer them continuously to patients with a high risk of depressive recurrences.

Clinical impressions, even those of experienced psychiatrists, have been controversial concerning the value of continued treatment with tricyclic antide-

Table III
Two-group double-blind trials with lithium: percentages of patients having relapsed within trial period and within one year

Author	Diagnostic group	Trial period (months)	Medication	Total no. of patients	% of patients relapsing within trial period	% of patients relapsing within one year (extrapolated)
Melia (1970)	Bipolar	24	Lithium	9	56	34
	+ Unipolar		Placebo	9	78	54
Baastrup et al. (1970	Bipolar	5	Lithium	28	0	0
			Placebo	22	55	80
	Unipolar	5	Lithium	17	0	0
			Placebo	17	53	78
Coppen et al. (1971)	Bipolar	14	Lithium	16	19	16
			Placebo	22	95	92
	Unipolar	14	Lithium	11	18	15
			Placebo	14	79	74

316

Study	Type	Duration	Treatment			
Hullin et al. (1972)	Bipolar + Unipolar	6	Lithium	18	6	12
		6	Placebo	18	33	56
Cundall et al. (1972)	Bipolar	6	Lithium	12	33	56
			Placebo	12	83	97
	Unipolar	6	Lithium	4	75	94
			Placebo	4	50	75
Stallone et al. (1973)	Bipolar	24–28	Lithium	19	26	14
			Placebo	23	91	70
Prien et al. (1973[b])	Bipolar	24	Lithium	85	42	23
			Placebo	86	87	64
Prien et al. (1973[a])	Bipolar	24	Lithium	14	36	20
			Placebo	10	90	68
	Unipolar	24	Lithium	23	57	34
			Placebo	21	90	68

pressants. Some psychiatrists claim that these agents are prophylactically effective, others that they are not. A number of more systematic studies have likewise failed to provide an unequivocal answer. Some studies (Agramonte, 1962; Oltman and Friedman, 1964; Hordern et al., 1964; Lindner, 1966) seemed to provide positive evidence for a prophylactic action while other studies (Grof and Vinar, 1966; Angst et al., 1969) failed signally to do so.

In the literature available to me, I have found six studies in which the results were presented in such a way that they could be entered in tables of the same type as Tables I–III. The studies with tricyclic antidepressants are listed in Tables IV–VI.

Table IV presents the trials in their chronological order. The prophylactic trials were all started after the depression had remitted as a result of active treatment with ECT or antidepressant drugs. Only one study (Prien et al., 1973a) lasted more than eight months, and only that study employed a specified frequency selection criterion.

The data shown in Table V indicate that the tricyclic antidepressant drugs exert a prophylactic action against depressive recurrences. In only one study (Mindham et al., 1973) was imipramine found to be no better than placebo. The study of Prien (Prien et al., 1973a) distinguished between bipolar and unipolar patients. In the unipolar patients, lithium and imipramine were both prophylactically effective and both significantly superior to placebo. In the bipolar patients, only lithium was significantly better than placebo. The patients treated with imipramine had as many recurrences as those given placebo; the recurrences were all manias.

Table VI shows the percentages of patients falling ill within the trial period and within one year, the latter extrapolated in the same manner as in Table III. It will be noted that in the imipramine group of Mindham (Mindham et al., 1973) the negative outcome was due, not to a high frequency of relapse among the imipramine treated patients, but to a low relapse frequency among the placebo treated patinets. This resolves the apparent discrepany between these results and the results obtained by Prien (Prien et al., 1973a).

As in the lithium trials, one finds a wide variation in relapse percentages. In the tricyclic antidepressant groups, 22 to 42 percent of the patients relapsed, whereas 36 to 91 percent of the patients relapsed in the placebo treated groups. Weighted means are 33 percent for the tricyclic antidepressant group and 67 percent for the group given placebo. (None of these percentages include bipolar patients.)

The prophylactic trials with tricyclic antidepressants require some comments. Changing patients from active medication to placebo might lead to diminution or disappearance of side effects, which could unmask the double-blind design. For this reason we excluded such patients from our discontinuation trial with lithium (Baastrup et al., 1970). That procedure does not seem to have been

Table IV
Prophylactic trials with tricyclic antidepressants: designs and features

Author	Design	Frequency selection criterion	Trial period (months)	Biochemical control
Seager and Bird (1962)	Initially together with ECT	None	6	None
Imlah et al. (1965)	Initially together with ECT	None	6	None
Kay et al. (1970)	Initially together with ECT	Non	7	None
Mindham et al. (1973)	Continuation of therapeutic use	None	6	None
Klerman et al. (1974)	Continuation of therapeutic use	None	8	None
Prien et al. (1973[a])	Continuation of therapeutic use	≥ 2 ep./2 years and ≥ 3 ep./5 years	24	Serum lithium 0.5–1.4 mmol/1 Imipramine:none

Table V

Outcome of prophylactic trials with tricyclic antidepressants: patients having relapsed and patients not having relapsed during trial period

Author	Diagnostic group	Medication	Daily dosage (mg)	Total no. of patients[a]	No. of patients who during trial period relapsed[b] – did not relapse		Significance[c]
					relapsed	did not relapse	
Seager and Bird	Depression treated with ECT	Imipramine	75–150	12	2	10	p<0.02
		Placebo		16	11	5	
Imlah et al. (1965)	Depression treated with ECT	Imipramine	75	25	5	20	p<0.02
		Placebo		41	21	20	
Kay et al. (1970)	Depression treated with ECT	Amitriptyline	50–150	34	8	26	p<0.05
		Diazepam		51	24	27	
Mindham et al. (1973)	Primary depression	Amitriptyline	75–150	34	8	26	p<0.001
		Placebo		27	18	9	
		Imipramine	75–150	16	3	13	n.s.
		Placebo		15	3	12	

Study	Diagnosis	Drug	Dose				Significance
Klerman et al. (1974)	Nonpsychotic depression	Amitriptyline	100–200	39	6	33	A vs P: p<0.05
		Placebo		33	14	19	A vs no pill: p<0.01
		No pill		34	13	21	P vs no pill: n.s.
Prien et al. (1973)[b]	Bipolar	Lithium	50–200	14	5	9	Li vs P: p<0.05
		Imipramine	50–200	10	8	2	I vs P: n.s.
		Placebo		10	9	1	Li vs I: p = 0.05
	Unipolar	Lithium	50–200	23	13	10	Li vs P: p<0.05
		Imipramine	50–200	18	8	11	I vs P: p<0.01
		Placebo		21	19	2	Li vs I: n.s.

[a]Excluding patients who dropped out of the study for reasons other than relapse.
[b]Including patients who dropped out of the study because they relapsed.
[c]One-tailed fourfold table test (Documenta Geigy, 1970) for $N \leq 60$; X^2-test for $N > 60$.

Table VI

Outcome of prophylactic trials with tricyclic antidepressants: percentages of patients having relapsed within trial period and within one year

Author	Diagnostic group	Trial period (months)	Medication	Total no. of patients	% of patients relapsing within trial period	% of patients relapsing within one year (extrapolated)
Seager and Bird (1962)	Depression treated with ECT	6	Imipramine	12	17	32
			Placebo	16	69	91
Imlah et al. (1965)	Depression treated with ECT	6	Imipramine	25	20	36
			Placebo	41	51	76
Kay et al. (1970)	Depression treated with ECT	7	Amitriptyline	34	24	39
			Diazepam	51	47	67
Mindham et al. (1973)	Primary depression	6	Amitriptyline	34	24	42
			Placebo	27	67	89
		6	Imipramine	16	19	35
			Placebo	15	20	36

Klerman et al. (1974)	Nonpsychotic depression	8	Amitriptyline	39	15	22
			Placebo	33	42	56
			No pill	34	38	52
Prien et al. (1973[a])	Bipolar	24	Lithium	14	36	20
			Imipramine	10	80	55
			Placebo	10	90	68
	Unipolar	24	Lithium	23	57	35
			Imipramine	19	42	25
			Placebo	21	90	69

followed in the studies under consideration. Dryness of the mouth, for example, was reported to decrease more frequently in the patients switched to placebo than in those continuing on tricyclic antidepressants (Mindham et al., 1973) and yet these patients were not excluded from the study. The possibility of "leakage" in the blindness of the trials may render them invalid in the eyes of some critics. I do not share this view. The prophylactic lithium trials have provided compelling evidence that even a strongly expectant attitude of patients and physicians does not suffice to prevent further recurrences of endogenous depression and mania. In my view, the trials with tricyclic antidepressants are not invalidated by not being entirely blind.

The short duration of the trial periods seems to me a more important matter. Five studies lasted only six to eight months; this is rather short for prophylactic trials. Some of the lithium trials were admittedly also of short duration, but the situation there was different. The lithium trials dealt with patients who were normothymic at the start of the trials and had been so for a long period. Such was not the case with the antidepressant drug trials. These patients had just emerged from a depressive episode; in fact, some of them had not even remitted completely. In the study of Mindham (Mindham et al., 1973), a number of patients rated themselves as "not completely well" when the trials started, and it is noteworthy that it was these patients who derived the most benefit from the continuation treatment. One cannot help feeling that in at least some of these cases the trials may have dealt with therapy and prevention of exacerbation of the *same* episode rather than with prophylaxis of *new* episodes. Mindham (Mindham et al., 1973) discusses that possibility.

This brings us to the important question of why the five trials with tricyclic drugs were not continued for a longer time. Were the trials terminated because too many patients dropped out? Were they terminated for ethical reasons? Or are the studies still in progress, so that we can eventually expect follow-up reports with longer observation periods? A fourth possibility is that the trials were terminated at the point when the required level of statistical significance had been achieved. Unless a sequential analysis design had been used, such a procedure might lead to false positive results and would be unacceptable. I do not, in fact, suspect the authors of having committed this error. I simply point out that in their published reports they fail to provide unequivocal assurance that they did not. The question may be clarified in the discussion.

The study of Prien (Prien et al., 1973a) differed in several respects from the five previous studies. It distinguished between bipolar and unipolar patients; the trial period of two years was established prior to initiation of the study; and it compared imipramine not only with placebo but also with lithium. As pointed out above, the trial showed agreement with the previous studies in regard to unipolar patients; with bipolar patients, imipramine was not found to be an effective prophylactic agent, at least not against manic recurrences.

The effect of long-term administration of tricyclic antidepressants may be summarized as follows: There is evidence, not yet conclusive but strongly suggestive, that these drugs exert a prophylactic action against depressive recurrences. The tricyclic antidepressants do not appear to prevent manic recurrences and may even provoke them.

On the basis of this evidence, lithium seems to be preferable to the tricyclic antidepressants for prophylactic purposes in recurrent affective disorders of the bipolar type. However, it should be kept in mind that only a single study (Prien et al., 1973a) has examined the prophylactic effect of tricyclic antidepressants in bipolar patients.

With unipolar patients, the prophylactic powers of lithium and tricyclic antidepressants have been compared directly in only that same study (Prien et al., 1973a). According to this study, lithium and imipramine are equally effective, but it is obviously not possible to draw any definitive conclusions from a single study. Further comparisons of lithium and tricyclic antidepressants are required.

It is important to emphasize that conclusions concerning the relative prophylactic efficacies of lithium and the tricyclic antidepressant drugs cannot be drawn from comparison of the studies that deal with lithium alone with those that deal with tricyclic antidepressants alone. These studies were designed merely to test whether or not lithium and the tricyclic antidepressants exerted any prophylactic action, i.e., an action better than placebo. Consequently, quantitative estimates of prophylactic efficacy cannot be assessed from these studies. For this purpose special trials must be designed in which the prophylactic efficacy of lithium is compared directly with one or more tricyclic antidepressants and the relative efficacies determined quantitatively through the use of a variety of measures as already described. Since determination of plasma concentrations of the tricyclic antidepressant drugs may be of use for monitoring treatment, this feature should ideally be included in the studies in order to give the tricyclic antidepressants a full and fair trial.

Finally, regardless of which prophylactic treatment measure or measures are or will become available, we shall need more information about the types of patients who can be expected to benefit from prophylactic treatment. In other words, we must know more about the factors which are associated with a high risk of recurrence in the near future. In their first study on lithium prophylaxis, Baastrup and Schou (1967) selected patients who had had two or more episodes during the two years preceding the trial with the assumption that such patients would be at high risk for further recurrences. This assumption proved correct. But presumably there are other "predictors"; one should focus attention on such items as: sex, age, age at first episode, number of previous episodes, polarity of episodes, intensity of episodes, duration of episodes, duration of intervals, etc. Some of these factors have been studied; others have not. Research in this field is essential for optimal handling of the recurrent affective disorders.

SUMMARY

Prophylactic studies raise important questions concerning concepts, definitions, spontaneous course of the disease, risk of recurrence, trial methodology, trial execution, and interpretation of data.

There is strong evidence for a prophylactic action of lithium in recurrent endogenous affective disorders, both of the bipolar and of the unipolar type. The data do not, however, provide reliable quantitative measures of the efficacy of the treatment.

Studies on the long-term administration of tricyclic antidepressant drugs have provided evidence which is strongly suggestive, although not yet conclusive, that these drugs exert a prophylactic action against recurrences of depression. They do not seem to prevent manic recurrences and may even provoke them.

The data available at present do not permit any definitive conclusions regarding the relative merits of lithium and the tricyclic antidepressants in prophylaxis of recurrent affective disorders of the unipolar type. For prophylaxis in the bipolar type, lithium seems clearly superior to the tricyclic antidepressant drugs.

COMMENTARIES

DR. GALLANT: Dr. Schou's presentation of his extensive work, as well as the reports of other investigators, is quite convincing in regard to the necessity for prolonged maintenance treatment of bipolar and unipolar illnesses. However, in maintenance therapy, it is essential to identify the "noncompliant patient" who, for socioeconomic reasons, may be more prevalent in the United States than in the majority of European countries (Gilliam and Barsky, 1974). One-third to one-half of the patients in the United States fail to comply with physicians' prescription orders. Predictors of noncompliance are: (1) a complex treatment regimen may confuse the patient (another reason to decrease polypharmacy); (2) poverty patients may have no source of free medication; (3) extremely high level of anxiety or depression tends to decrease the patient's memory of the physician's instructions; (4) patient denies the severity of illness, particularly after recovery from an acute episode; (5) patient shows ambivalence about prescription orders even before leaving the office; (6) negative physician-patient interaction; and (7) presence of family instability or a patient who is living alone. Approaches to decreasing the noncompliance rate, which are of major practical importance if one is to utilize maintenance therapy, are: (1) attempts must be made to mobilize family or socioeconomic resources to aid in the therapeutic regimen, particularly if the prescribed treatment is complex; (2) a specific educational approach to the patient must be made, stressing the importance of treatment measures and outlining the treatment regimen (individually or in groups); and (3) if personality attributes of the doctor-patient interaction conflict, the physician must be perceptive and initiate the accommodation before the patient leaves the office in order to decrease the noncompliance rate.

The extreme importance of maintenance therapy is emphasized by the increasing suicide rate in Western countries; steps must be taken to decrease this tragic condition. The suicide rate nearly doubled between 1960 and 1971 in Great Britain, Australia, Canada, Israel and the United States.

In addition to maintenance drug therapy, the use of socioeconomic and environmental variables should be more adequately studied in association with the use of these medications. Studies such as the collaborative project conducted at the Connecticut Mental Health Center and Boston State Hospital should be performed with patients presenting various syndromes of affective disorders. In depressive studies in nonpsychotic patients, Dr. Weissman and her group used a design with amitriptyline, placebo, and no drug in 150 females, with psychotherapy in 50 percent and without it in the other 50 percent, resulting in a total of six cells for comparison in the follow-up evaluations. At the eighth-month follow-up, the patients' self-assessment scale showed further symptomatic improvement and reduction of relapse rate in those patients who continued on active medication. In addition, as Dr. Weissman has stated, psychotherapy enhanced medication effects by promoting social adjustment and *tended* to reduce relapse or symptom return. The most appropriate environmental therapy as well as drug therapy should be selected for each patient; it should never be a case of using either one or the other.

There is no doubt about the efficacy of lithium in reducing the frequency and intensity of episodes in both bipolar and unipolar patients. Control trials now should be conducted in patients diagnosed in the United States as schizoaffective (in Sweden, as cycloid) in order to define further the efficacy of lithium for this serious disorder in which the suicide rate is the highest of all types of mental disorders. Electroshock therapy still plays an important role in the treatment of this particularly dangerous disease process. Definitive large scale evaluations of lithium, i.e., (1) lithium vs. (2) a combination of lithium plus a neuroleptic vs. (3) a neuroleptic alone, and other studies using tricyclic and tetracyclic antidepressant agents (in the place of lithium) with similar methodological approaches must be performed in this population since the response rate of the schizoaffective patients to the available standard forms of therapy is relatively low. It is hoped that these important studies will take place within the next two to three years. In the meantime, although I dislike the use of polypharmacy, I do tend to go along with Dr. Schou's suggestion that lithium plus a neuroleptic may be more efficacious in the schizoaffective patient than either drug alone.

DR. SIMPSON: I would like to ask Dr. Schou three questions. First, what is your feeling about the actual percentages of bipolar patients who relapse on supposedly adequate levels of lithium therapy? Second, for patients who relapse and have frequent depressive episodes on maintenance lithium and on maintenance tricyclics, do you have a plan for treating such cases? I am referring to the persistent recurring depressions. The third question concerns schizoaffective illness. I think that you have been to North America often enough to have some ideas about what we mean when we use the term schizoaffective illness. Since it seems to me to be mainly an affective disorder, I can't understand statements about lithium toxicity in patients who have been diagnosed as schizoaffective. Dr. Klein includes this category in his affective disorders, and many other investigators would as well.

DR. SCHOU: I will answer the questions out of order. The more often I come to this country, the less I know what schizoaffective illness is. We define these subjects quite simply as patients who have schizophrenic and manic-depressive symptoms at the same time or alternately. We have not seen the flare-up of schizophrenia or greater toxicity that the Gershon-Shopsin group reported when they gave lithium to schizoaffective patients.

DR. SIMPSON: And did you publish that?

DR. SCHOU: No, because we didn't do a systematic study of the phenomenon, we just never saw it. So we are handling schizoaffective patients, who are certainly a problem, by giving them lithium and long-term neuroleptics concomitantly. We have no systematic studies in this population, but we have had many good individual results and some very poor ones.

Your first question was how many refractory cases there are in the bipolar group and whether or not we published these data. That depends upon what you define as refractory. If you mean patients who never have a recurrence of a single symptom of disease, then I think that we would have to say that all cases are refractory. Even the patients who respond best occasionally have what I call "reminders," that is, a few days when they feel as if a depression or mania is coming on without this ever actually happening. Then we have a larger group who have relapses, but at much longer intervals and of much shorter duration, especially during the first half-year of the treatment. These patients are partial responders, and then we have some who do not respond at all. I would say that the last group is less than 10 percent of the entire population of bipolars.

Concerning the second question, I think that Dr. Weissman has good evidence that one should then try tricyclics, either alone or perhaps in combination with lithium.

DR. PERRIS: I want to add a few comments regarding the much discussed patients whom we don't call schizoaffective. Just to be sure that we understand each other, I should like to define this patient group. We prefer the term *cycloid* because it is more neutral than *schizoaffective*. These cycloid patients have recurrent affective symptoms, confusion, paranoia-like delusions and/or hallucinations, and motility disturbances. Complete remission of symptoms occurs between these severe episodic reactions.

We are studying a group of twenty-five cycloid patients who have been receiving prophylactic lithium therapy for a period of two to five years. In this study, there has been a reduction of the number of relapses, which is significant only in the group in which the conduction of treatment is defined as "regular." The term "regular" means that the blood levels of lithium are at least 0.8 meq/1. We have also reviewed the duration of time spent in hospitals, which was again significantly reduced only in the group in which the lithium levels were consistently 0.8 meq/1 or above. So lithium also has efficacy in this group of cycloid patients.

DR. MENDELS: The story of lithium's efficacy in bipolar, unipolar and schizoaffective illnesses obviously contradicts many of the current biochemical concepts of depression. I would like to hear Dr. Schou's opinions on the biochemical actions of lithium in affective illness.

DR. SCHOU: I am often asked about the biochemical mode of action of lithium, and it always embarrasses me because I do not know it. We do know a very large number of biological effects of lithium, but how are we to know which of them is relevant? It seems to me that we have to get away from the simple "up or down" hypotheses for mania and depression. We have to look for a mechanism by which lithium may stabilize something that is abnormally unstable, inhibition of a positive feedback or stimulation of a negative feedback in terms of brain metabolism. That is not so easy a model to construct. Last week I spent three days discussing the neurobiology of lithium with a group of basic scientists, endocrinologists and biochemists in Boston. The discussions of course did not lead to any comprehensive and immediately testable hypothesis about the mode of action of lithium, but among the things that emerged from the discussion, and which was new to me, is that lithium is not only closely related to sodium and magnesium but also, in a number of respects, to calcium. The proceedings of that meeting will be published in a year or so.

DR. KLEIN: I would like to make two points. First, I think Dr. Schou is right about the prophylactic effect of lithium in the unipolar patient. However, I think we should remember that the total number on which the conclusions have been based is really quite slim. The total number of patients treated with lithium in all of these controlled studies of unipolar patients adds up to about fifty-five, which is not an enormous sample size. As for the total number of patients treated with tricyclics, I think it is something like 190. Since there are more female than male unipolars, it is possible that the number of males treated prophylactically with lithium in all of these studies may be as low as twenty. In my opinion, you have a data base that could stand considerable expansion. I am sure that Dr. Schou would agree that further studies in this area would be to everybody's advantage, including the possibility of developing predictors.

DR. SCHOU: When you refer to a relatively small sample size, you disregard entirely the non-blind studies. We now have positive evidence that these were based on valid assumptions and that their results are therefore reliable. These studies comprise many hundred cases. But, obviously, further studies would provide additional evidence and might be of value for the discovery of "predictors."

DR. KLEIN: I think this point is important because there are many investigators in this country who are designing further prophylactic studies. One of the questions that arises is whether or not lithium efficacy has been established in the maintenance therapy of unipolar depression. If so, the goals of the proposed protocol would be to delineate the specific subgroups of patients who respond best to lithium. If the efficacy of lithium maintenance therapy of unipolar depression has not been established, then we still have to confirm efficacy of lithium in this illness.

I would like to make one point in regard to schizoaffective illness. We also use definitions for schizoaffective much like those that Dr. Perris used for cycloid psychosis. However, we have evaluated one aspect of the patient that was not included in the list, the premorbid personality. In our evaluation, the premorbid personalities of the schizoaffective patients were nonschizoid, but there was a small percentage of schizoid personalities. I think we had about 20 percent who could be considered schizoid. We did a three-year follow-up on these patients, and the patients who had good premorbid personalities looked just like our affective disorders in terms of what happened to them in the ensuing three years. However, the patients that had schizoid personalities before the onset of illness had not responded as well, moving along the same pathway as the schizophrenics. It was our conclusion that (within this heterogeneous group of schizoaffective patients) you can use the premorbid personality as a way of pinpointing who is going to be a lithium responder and who isn't. Now, in the Gershon-Shopsin study, which is the only one that reports lithium as being toxic in schizoaffective patients, they state quite specifically that the premorbid personality was schizoid in their patients.

DR. GALLANT: I think what has happened in this country is that we learned from other countries that the type of patient whom Vaillant described in 1964 is really not a "good prognosis" schizophrenic, but is what we now call schizoaffective or what Dr. Perris calls the cycloid patient; and the patient with this diagnosis never deteriorates. It is very easy to make the diagnosis of schizoaffective or cycloid when the patient is forty-two or forty-three because he really has not disintegrated over the years. The true homogenous schizophrenic deteriorates by the time he approaches the age of forty-two or forty-three. The problem in diagnosis always occurs when the patient is first hospitalized at twenty-two or twenty-three, and there is a lack of adequate biographical data and a lack of adequate family history. At the time of first hospitalization, misdiagnosis is not infrequent.

DR. PERRIS: I would just like to comment on the premorbid personality of the cycloid patient. I was not able to find any studies in the literature which evaluated the premorbid personality in a systematic way. In our study comprising sixty probands and their families, we have studied the personality traits during the symptom-free intervals with two different personality batteries, and we have not found any special personality characteristic in this group.

DR. RASKIN: Dr. Schou, Dr. Shopsin mentioned that raising the lithium dosage in those unipolar patients who had relapsed, instead of switching the patient to imipramine, was of benefit to them. Do you have any similar experiences?

DR. SCHOU: Bipolar and unipolar patients, in whom prophylaxis is not 100 percent successful, tend to alter their lithium levels during manic and depressive recurrence even while receiving the same dosage. This could have two explanations. One, it may reflect a change in the renal clearance. We checked this possibility and could find no difference between the renal clearance in the bipolar and unipolar patients who relapsed. Another explanation could be that the presence of a manic or depressive episode may alter the lithium-binding capacity of the polysaccharides in the connective tissue, which are large molecules with many negative charges. This binding capacity varies a great deal with the patient's endocrine condition, which can be affected by depression or mania.

DR. SIMPSON: Dr. Schou, I just wondered if Dr. Raskin was really asking if you have had any successful experiences with increasing the lithium rather than adding a tricyclic in those patients who relapsed.

DR. SCHOU: I think that we may tend to add an antidepressant, but we should first think of increasing the lithium dosage because the patient may relapse if he requires a higher blood level of lithium for therapeutic activity.

CONCLUDING REMARKS

DR. SIMPSON: I would like at this time on behalf of Dr. Gallant and myself to thank everyone present for his contribution to what was to me an outstanding and interesting meeting. The presentations were predictably of high caliber and the commentaries exceptionally stimulating. It appears to us that meetings such as this not only clarify, but also generate new problems, many of which are solvable. The disagreement is not a sign of confusion but of new hypotheses to be tested. This is particularly so in discussing the etiologies, diagnoses, and treatment modalities of affective disorders, which perhaps more than any other areas in psychiatry have advanced decisively in the past twenty and in particularly the last ten years. These rapid advances have emphasized national differences in diagnoses and treatment. The solution is obviously increased international collaboration. The last two days have seen precisely that and we are all the richer for it.

REFERENCES

Agramonte, E. G. (1962). El tratamiento preventivo de las depresiones con el Tofranil. *Rev. Cuba Med.* 1:110–12.

Angst, J., Dittrich, A., and Grof, P. (1969). The course of endogenous affective psychoses and its modification by prophylactic administration of imipramine and lithium. *Intl. Pharmacopsychiat.* 2:1–11.

Ayd, F. J. (1974). "Drug holidays" during maintenance tricyclic antidepressant drug therapy. *Intl. Drug. Ther. Newsletter* 9:17–20.

Baastrup, P. C., and Schou, M. (1967). Lithium as a prophylactic agent. Its effect against recurrent depressions and manic-depressive psychosis. *Arch. Gen. Psychiat.* 16:162–72.

————, Poulsen, J. C., Schou, M., et al. (1970). Prophylactic lithium: double-blind discontinuation in manic-depressive and recurrent-depressive disorders. *Lancet* II:326–30.

Barton, J. L., Mehta, S., and Snaith, R. P. (1973). The prophylactic value of extra ECT in depressive illness. *Acta Psychiat. Scand.* 49:386–92.

Coppen, A., Noguera, R., Bailey, J., et al. (1971). Prophylactic lithium in affective disorders. Controlled trial. *Lancet* II:275–79.

Cundall, R. L., Brooks, P. W., and Murray, L. G. (1972). A controlled evaluation of lithium prophylaxis in affective disorders. *Psychol. Med.* 2:308–11.

Documenta Geigy (1970). 7th ed. Basle: *Scientific Tables.*

Freyhan, F. A. (1971). Lithium treatment: prophylactic or compensatory? *Am. J. Psychiat.* 128:121–22.

Geoghegan, J. J. (1947). The "shock therapies" at the Ontario Hospital, London. *Can. Med. Assn. J.* 56:15–24.

———— and Stevenson, G. H. (1949). Prophylactic electroshock. *Am. J. Psychiat.* 105:494–96.

Gilliam, R. F., and Barsky, A. J. (1974). Diagnosis and management of patient noncompliance. *JAMA* 228:1563–67.

Glen, A. I. M., and Reading, H. W. (1973). Regulatory action of lithium in manic-depressive illness. *Lancet* II:1239–41.

Grof, P., and Vinar, O. (1966). Maintenance and prophylactic imipramine doses in recurrent depressions. *Activ. Nerv. Sup.* (Praha) 8:383–85.

Hartigan, G. P. (1963). The use of lithium salts in affective disorders. *Br. J. Psychiat.* 109:810–14.

Hordern, A., Burt, C. G., Gordon, W. F., and Holt, N. F. (1964). Amitriptyline in depressive states: six-month treatment results. *Br. J. Psychiat.* 110:641–47.

Hullin, R. P., McDonald, R., and Allsopp, M. N. E. (1972). Prophylactic lithium in recurrent affective disorders. *Lancet* I:1044–46.

Imlah, N. W., Ryan, E., and Harrington, J. A. (1965). The influence of antidepressant drugs on the response to electroconvulsive therapy and on subsequent relapse rates. In P. Bente and P. D. Bradley, eds., *Neuro-Psychopharmacology,* Vol 4. Amsterdam, London, New York: Elsevier, pp. 438–42.

Karliner, W., and Wehrheim, H. K. (1965). Maintenance convulsive treatments. *Am. J. Psychiat.* 121:1113–15.

Kay, D. W. K., Fahy, T., and Garside, R. F. (1970). A seven-month double-blind trial of amitriptyline and diazepam in ECT-treated depressed patients. *Br. J. Psychiat.* 117:667–71.

Klerman, G. L., DiMascio, A., Weissman, M., et al. (1974). Treatment of depression by drugs and psychotherapy. *Am. J. Psychiat.* 131:186–91.

Lindner, M. (1966). Vorbeugende langzeittherapie periodischer und rezidivierender depressionen. *Ärztl Prax* 18:279–81.

Melia, P. I. (1970). Prophylactic lithium: a double-blind trial in recurrent affective disorders. *Br. J. Psychiat.* 116:621–24.

Mindham, R. H. S., Howland, C., and Shepherd, M. (1973). An evaluation of continuation therapy with tricyclic antidepressants in depressive illness. *Psychol. Med.* 3:5–17.

Oltman, J. E., and Friedman, S. (1964). Relapses following treatment with antidepressant drugs. *Dis. Nerv. Syst.* 25:699–701.

Prien, R. F., Caffey, E. M., and Klett, J. (1973a). Prophylactic efficacy of lithium carbonate in manic-depressive illness. *Arch. Gen. Psychiat.* 28:337–41.

——, Klett, J., and Caffey, E. M. (1973b). Lithium carbonate and imipramine in prevention of affective episodes. *Arch. Gen. Psychiat.* 29:420–25.

Schou, M. (1963). Normothymotics, "mood-normalizers." Are lithium and the imipramine drugs specific for affective disorders? *Br. J. Psychiat.* 109:803–09.

—— (1973). Prophylactic lithium maintenance treatment in recurrent endogenous affective disorders. In S. Gershon and B. Shopsin, eds., *Lithium: Its Role in Psychiatric Research and Treatment.* New York and London: Plenum, pp. 269–94.

—— and Thomsen, K. (1975). Lithium in the prophylactic treatment of recurrent affective disorders. In F. N. Johnson, ed., *Lithium Research and Therapy.* London: Academic Press, pp. 63–84.

——, Thomsen, K., and Baastrup, P. C. (1970). Studies on the course of recurrent endogenous affective disorders. *Intl. Pharmacopsychiat.* 5:100–06.

Seager, C. P., and Bird, R. L. (1962). Imipramine with electrical treatment in depression—a controlled trial. *J. Ment. Sci.* 108:704–07.

Stallone, F., Shelley, E., Mendlewicz, J., and Fieve, R. R. (1973). The use of lithium in affective disorders. III: A double-blind study of prophylaxis in bipolar illness. *Am. J. Psychiat.* 130:1006–10.

Stevenson, G. H., and Geoghegan, J. J. (1951). Prophylactic electroshock. A five-year study. *Am. J. Psychiat.* 107:743–48.

Vaillant, G. E. (1964). Prospective predictors of schizophrenic remission. *Arch. Gen. Psychiat.* 11:509–18.

Index

Acetazolamide, 296

Acetylation and Monoamine Oxidase Inhibitor efficacy, 116,117

Acetycholine, 29, 42, 48-49, 52-53

Acetylcholinesterase inhibition, 49

Acute brain syndrome (*See* Organic brain syndrome)

Adaptine (*See* Doxepin)

Adenosine monophosphate (5' AMP), 45

Adenosine 3',5'-monophosphate (cyclic AMP), 35, 45-48, 292-293
    changes in affective illness, 46
    effect of norepinephrine on, 48
    effects of drugs on, 46-47
    excretion of, 46
    in receptor activity, 45
    production of, 45, 46

Adenosine triphosphatase (ATPase), 27, 28
    K-activated, 27-28
        activity in depression, 27
        in lithium treatment, 27
    Na-activated, 27-28

Adenosine triphosphate (ATP), 30, 45

Adenylate cyclase, 44-47, 62
    adrenergic receptor, 45
    effect of psychotropic drugs on, 46
    in the formation of cyclic AMP, 45
    in lithium side effects, 47
    in relation to receptor sensitivity, 44-45

Adoptee studies, 81

Adrenal cortical function, 23-24
    effect of anxiolytic drugs on, 23
    in depressed patients, 23-24

Adrenalin (*See also* Epinephrine), 29, 282, 287
    interaction with MAOI's, 287

Adrenergic receptors, 31, 45-48
    adenylate cyclase as, 45
    blocking agents of, 45
    cyclic AMP and, 45-46
    normetanephrine as an index of activity of, 31
    postsynaptic abnormalities in depression, 47

Adrenergic system, 61

Adrenocortical hormones, 23

Adrenocorticotrophic hormone (ACTH), 23-24

Affective disorders (*See also* entries for specific disorders), 19, 22-23,25, 29, 36, 41, 52-53, 62, 75-92, 94-95, 99-100, 127-128, 148, 226
    alcoholism and drug abuse, as equivalents, 148
    biogenic amine hypothesis, 29, 36, 41, 62
    DSM II definition, 127, 128
    epidemiology, 75-81, 99-100, 226
        disease expectancy, 78, 80
        frequency, 78
            factors affecting, 78, 81
        prevalence, 79, 80
    etiology, 19, 53, 96-98
    genetics, 79-92
        mode of transmission, 94-95
        morbidity risk in relatives, 84-86
        predisposition, 22, 79, 83, 91
    hypothalamic function, 23
    neuroendocrine function in, 22, 25
    spontaneous remission in, 52, 53

Affective psychoses, 86
  bipolar and monopolar, 86
    morbidity risk in relatives, 86
Aged persons, 205-229, 274-276, 284, 299
  alcoholism, 213
  dementia, 209-211
  depression
    age incidence, 205-207, 223
    classification, 214-220, 228
    cognitive functioning in, 210-212
    diagnosis of, 208
    differential diagnosis, 208-213, 224
      dementia, 209-211, 213
      late schizophrenia,
        208-209
      neurosis, 212-213, 224
    epidemiology, 226
    etiology, 207, 219
      precipitating factors, 207, 218,
        220, 227, 229
    genetics, 207
    neurotic, 212, 215-218, 220
    premorbid personality, 207, 218
    prognosis, 214, 221, 223-224
    pseudodementia, 210-211, 225-227,
      229
    psychotic, 214-220
    symptoms, 208, 210-216, 218, 225,
      227-229
    treatment, 213, 219-224, 226, 229, 230
      antidepressants, 209, 211,
        220-223, 226, 275, 276
        side effects, 274
        in cardiovascular disease,
          275-276
      behavior therapy, 213, 220
      ECT, 211, 219-223, 226
      lithium, 221, 223, 226, 227, 229,
        299
      MAO inhibitors, 220-221, 284
        side effects, 284
      psychotherapy, 213, 220, 226
      social therapy, 220
  organic brain syndromes, 209-210
Aging, 116
  MAO activity in, 116
Agitation, 128, 133, 137, 216
Agranulocytosis, 276
Akinesia, 128-129, 136, 140-143, 151
Alcoholism, 97-99, 102, 140, 148-149, 156, 213
  covert, 140

  in elderly, 213
  in relatives of unipolar depressives, 148
  symptomatic, 148-149
    tricyclics and lithium in, 149
Alpha-methyl-paratyrosine (AMPT), 24, 30, 42,
  55, 63
  amine depletor agent, 42
  in schizophrenia and affective disorders,
    42, 55
  biological induction, 9
Amine pump, 60, 61
Amino acids, 20, 53
Aminophylline, 296
Amitriptyline, 24, 32, 34, 36-37, 57, 60-61, 64,
  122, 140, 233-246, 249, 254, 263, 274-277,
  320-321, 324-325
  adverse reactions (See also tricyclic
    antidepressants)
    cardiotoxicity, 301
    in cardiac disease, 275-276
    neurotoxicity, 277
    sedation, 274
    weight gain, 276
  clinical trial vs. maprotiline, 234-246
  effect on biogenic amines, 37, 61
  in childhood depression, 187, 190-191
  in elderly depressives, 220, 230
  L-triiodothyronine, effect on, 24
  plasma levels, 110-111, 118
    and clinical response, 118
    enuresis, 118
    interindividual differences, 110
  urinary MHPG as a predictor of response
    to, 36
Amnesia, 131, 132, 151
  following ECT
Amphetamines, 149-151, 192, 202, 287-288
  interaction with MAOI's, 287-288
  with sedatives, 150-151
d-amphetamine, 37, 120, 135, 143, 151
Anancastic personality, 142, 150
Anaclitic depression, 11, 181
Anhedonia, 129-130
Animal behavior, abnormal, 1, 3-16
  biological induction methods, 1, 9-10
  brain functioning in, 5, 7, 13
  EEG studies in, 5
  rehabilitation in, 5, 10-11, 13-14, 16
  selective breeding in, 15
  social induction methods (See also
    Separation) 1, 4-9

learned helplessness, 4, 8, 9
mother-infant separation, 4
peer-separation, 4, 7, 8
social isolation rearing, 4
vertical chamber confinement, 4, 8
species differences, 3, 6, 12, 13
Anti-anginal effects of monoamine oxidase
inhibitors, 285
Antidepressants (*See also* Monoamine oxidase
inhibitors; Tetracyclic antidepressants;
Tricyclic antidepressants), 13, 31-35, 43-44,
52, 54-62, 89, 90, 102, 113, 119, 121, 190-
192, 196, 200, 211, 213, 220, 222, 223, 226,
230
biochemical classification of, 60, 61
correlation with stereochemical
parameters, 61-62
dosage adjustments in treatment failures,
113, 119, 121
delayed onset of response, 52, 54
effects on biogenic amines, 31-35, 54
in acute and chronic administration,
33-35, 52
effects on enzyme systems, 62
evaluation of (*See* Clinical trial
methodology)
genetic factors in response to, 13, 89, 90
in alcoholism and sociopathy, 102
in children, 190-192, 196, 200
in elderly depressives, 209, 211, 213, 220,
222-223, 226, 230
in school phobias, 200
monoamine precursors as, 43-44
stereochemical properties, 55-62
Antidiuretic hormone (ADH), 4
effect of lithium on, 4
Antiparkinson agents, 136
Antipsychotic agents, 128, 131-133, 135-137,
140-143
Akinetic reactions, 128, 136, 140, 143
differential indications, 133
in schizoaffective psychoses, 135-136
tardive dyskinesia risk, 133
Antipsychotic drug activity, 54
brain area deposition and, 54
cell membrane permeability and, 54
Antisocial personality, 129, 137
Anxiety, 23, 36, 208, 212, 215, 218, 220
in elderly, 208, 212, 215, 218, 220
Anxiolytics (*See also* entries for specific agents),
151, 278

interaction with tricyclic antidepressants,
278
Apathy, 129
Apomorphine, 25, 45
Assessment procedures (*See also* Rating scales)
159-161, 165-166, 172, 174, 178, 184, 235,
245, 251, 255, 257, 259, 264
Beck Depression Inventory, 159, 160, 184
Bojanovsky Scale, 161
Brief Psychiatric Rating Scale, 172
Clyde Mood Scale, 178
Guttman Scale, 165, 166, 172, 174
Hamburg Inventory, 159
Hamilton Depression Rating Scale,
159-161, 172, 235, 245, 251, 255, 257,
259, 264
Lubin Adjective Check List, 160
Minnesota Multiphasic Personality
Inventory, 160
Popoff Depression Inventory, 159, 161
Schutz's Scale, 161
Wakefield SADS, 159
Wechsler Scale, 161
Visual Analogue Scale, 159, 160
Zung Depression Status Inventory, 161
Zung SDS, 159-161
Atropine, 274, 277, 282
-like side effects with tricyclics, 274, 277
Autism, 11
Aventyl (*See* Nortriptyline)
Barbiturates, 278, 288
interaction with MAOI's, 288
interaction with tricyclics, 278
Beck Depression Inventory, 159-160, 184
Behavior therapy, 213, 220
in elderly, 213, 220
Benzoctamine (Tacitin), 265, 266
Benzodiazepines, 121, 139, 150
interaction with antidepressants, 121
Bereavement, 182-184, 194, 207, 218
and depression. 182
early
and depression, 183-184, 194
and suicide, 183-184
in elderly, 218
Bicyclic antidepressants, 56
Biogenic amines (*See also* entries for specific
amines), 22, 29-49
administration of precursors, 44
clinical studies of 35-41
cerebrospinal fluids, 37-40

post-mortem, 41
probenecid, 39-40
urinary, 35-37
depletion studies, 41-43
effect of antidepressant drugs on, 31-35
physiology and pharmacology of, 29-31
receptor deficit in affective disorders, 48
receptor sensitivity, 44-45
role in emotional behavior, 22, 29
Biogenic amine depletion, 1
Biogenic amine hypothesis of affective disorders,
29, 36, 41, 62
Bipolar affective illness (See also
Manic-depressive psychoses) 20, 36, 40, 52,
54, 86, 88-89, 91-94, 100, 102-103, 128, 131,
133, 142, 150, 184, 187, 214, 218, 223, 225,
228, 254, 310-328, 331
antidepressants in, 133, 254
prophylaxis, 318-322, 324-325
relapse rates, 318, 320-321, 324-325
enuresis in offspring, 187
in elderly, 218, 223, 225
lithium in, 223
prognosis of, 214
lithium in, 133
prophylaxis, 310-317, 322-323,
326-328, 331
relapse rates, 312-317
morbidity risk in relatives, 88, 89
sex distribution, 24, 89
twin studies, 91, 92
unipolar-bipolar dichotomy, 94, 100,
102-103, 128, 142, 150
Blood abnormalities, 276, 285, 293
secondary to
lithium, 293
MAOI's, 285
tricyclic antidepressants, 276
Blood groups, 93, 94
Blood levels of antidepressants (See Plasma
levels of antidepressants)
Bojanovsky Scale, 161
Brain, 130
pleasure center, 130
self stimulation, 130
Brief Psychiatric Rating Scale (BPRS), 172, 251
Butyrophenones, 33, 46
Calcitonin activity, 26
Calcium, 26, 50
Cannon, Walter, 29
Cardiotoxicity, 274-276, 279-283,
285, 289-290, 301
MAO inhibitors, 285, 289-290
tricyclic antidepressants, 274-276, 279-280,
301
treatment of acute, 280-283
Catecholamines, 25, 30-31, 36, 43-46, 52, 55,
275, 280
adenylate cyclase as receptor for, 45
changes secondary to membrane
permeability, 54
effect of psychotropic drugs on, 46
hypothesis of depression, 36, 51, 54
metabolism of, 31
potentiation by tricyclics, 275, 280
Catecholamine synthesizing enzymes, 7
increased levels in serotonin, 7
Catechol-3-0-methyl-transferase (COMT), 31,
50
erythrocyte levels in affective illness, 50
Cation transport, 27
Cell membrane, 27, 54
distribution and transport of cations across,
27
permeability, 54
Cerebral arousal, 211, 227
in elderly, 211, 227
Cerebral vascular accident, 286
Cerebrospinal fluid (CSF), 37-40, 46, 50-51
biogenic amines in, 37-40
cyclic AMP in, 46
probenecid studies, 39-40
tryptophan levels, 40-41
Character disorders, 129, 132, 137-138
depression in, 137
dysphoria in, 138
emotionally unstable, 129, 132, 138
histrionic, 129, 138
Children, 175, 181-202
depression, 181-199, 201
classification and diagnosis, 185-186,
188, 194-198, 201
depressive equivalents, 182-183, 192,
196-198, 201
differential diagnosis, 187-188, 190
EEG's in, 186, 194-195
family history, 188, 194, 201
in adolescents, 182
in infants, 181
in middle childhood, 182
masked, 181-182, 185, 197, 199
object loss, 194, 196

pharmacotherapy of, 190-193,
196-199
reactive depression, 183, 185
separation in, 184
suicide, 184
sympathetic-parasympathetic balance,
194-195
symptoms, 181, 185-189, 194, 196
and prognosis, 186
enuresis, 118, 186-188, 194, 197-198, 200
hyperactivity, 175, 188, 190, 192, 196, 198,
201
lithium, 192, 193
manic depressive psychosis, 182, 186, 189,
190, 197
minimal brain dysfunction, 187
school phobia, 14, 192, 198-202
Chlordiazepoxide, 135, 191
Chlorimipramine (See Chlomipramine)
Chlorpromazine, 5, 11, 14, 16, 122, 149, 202,
290
in isolation syndrome in animals, 5, 11, 14,
16
Cholinergic system, 49
in relation to
adrenergic balance, 49
mood, 49
Cholestatic jaundice, 276
Chromosome studies, 81, 92
Chronic brain syndrome (See Organic brain
syndrome)
Classification, 20-21, 127-129, 142, 145-148,
185 189
childhood depression, 185-189
late life depressions, 214-220, 228
endogenous vs. neurotic, 217, 218, 228
Newcastle Diagnostic Index, 216-218
multifactorial model, 145-146, 151
precipitants, 128
treatment-relevant, 129
treatment response, as criterion, 127-128,
142, 156
Clinical trial methodology, 115, 245-246,
248-249, 251-253, 260-267, 310, 314-315,
318, 322, 323
assessment and outcome issues, 245-246,
248-249, 264
video tape, 246
social adjustment, 248
designs, 251-252, 262-267
nonspecific factors, 260-262, 267

prophylactic trials, 310, 314-315, 318,
322-323
side effect evaluations, 264
statistical analysis
end point analysis, 249
subject inclusion criteria, 248-249,
264, 267
subject selection, 115, 249, 253
Clomipramine, 32, 37, 40, 59, 60, 121, 263
effect on biogenic amines, 60-61
Clyde Mood Scale, 178
Cognitive functioning in elderly depressives,
208, 210-212, 224-225, 229
Cognitive tests, 131-132
changes following ECT, 131, 132
Coma, 279, 295
in lithium overdosage, 295
in tricyclic antidepressant overdosage, 279
Confusion, 131, 149, 151, 285, 289, 293
following ECT, 131, 149, 151
in lithium overdosage, 293
in MAOI administration, 285, 289
Convulsions, 279-281, 289, 295
in lithium poisoning, 295
in tricyclic antidepressant poisoning,
279-280
treatment of, 281
in tricyclic-MAOI combinations, 289
Corpus striatum, 54
Cortical evoked potentials, 22
Corticotropin releasing factor, 23
C-21024, 61
Cushing's syndrome, 23
Cycloid psychoses (See also Schizoaffective
psychoses), 86-87, 93-94, 101, 144, 327-329
description of, 328-329
prophylactic lithium in, 327-329
Cyproheptadine, 25, 45
Death (See Suicide)
Death, sudden, 276, 299
Delirium, 279, 289
in MAOI hypertensive crises, 289
in tricyclic antidepressant poisoning, 279
Delusions, 120, 215
Dementia, 209-211, 213, 229
Demoralization, 128, 138, 139
Depression (See also Manic depressive psychosis;
Neurosis, depressive; Psychotic depressive
reaction; Bipolar psychosis, Unipolar
psychosis) 6, 20, 50-51, 53-54, 75-85, 96-100,
116-117, 127-138, 140, 142-143, 149,

150-152, 156-157, 161-162, 182-184, 217-218, 227-229

  age of onset, 85, 97-98

  assessment of, (*See also* Assessment procedures; Rating scales; Clinical trial methodology), 156-157, 161-162

  atypical, 116-117

  differential diagnosis, 127-129

  early experience, 6, 182-184

  endogenomorphic, 129-133

  endogenous, 80, 82-85, 128-130, 142, 149, 152, 157, 217-218, 228

  environmental factors in, 96-98

  epidemiology, 75-81, 99-100, 226

  hereditary factors (*See* Genetics)

  heterogeneity of, 20, 53-54

  in adolescence (*See* Children)

  in childhood (*See* Children)

  in elderly (*See* Aged Persons)

  in infants (*See* Children)

  in neuroses, 137

  in organic and toxic illness, 140

  in personality disorders, 137-138

  in schizophrenia, 136-137

  mania, biological similarities with, 50-51, 54

  neuroleptics and, 143

  precipitating factors in, 128-130, 227, 229

  primary vs. secondary, 128, 143, 150-151

  reactive depression, 128-129, 134-135, 143, 149

  retarded vs. agitated, 128

  sex ratio, 96-97

  symptoms of, 128-131, 134

  treatment of, (*See also* Antidepressants; Tricyclic Antidepressants; Monoamine oxidase inhibitors; Tetracyclic antidepressants; Electroconvulsive therapy; lithium), 52, 128, 131-133, 135-137, 139-141, 143-144, 148-149, 151, 156, 162, 172-175, 310-330

    criteria for selection, 156

    DSM II implications, 128

    electroconvulsive therapy, 131-133, 136, 143, 144, 149, 151

      vs. pharmacotherapy, 132-133

    evaluation of (*See also* Assessment procedures; Rating scales), 140-141, 162, 172-175

    genetic history, 148

    in children (*See* Children)

    in elderly (*See* Aged persons)

    interaction between biochemical and environmental treatments, 15

    maintenance therapy, 326, 327

    pharmacotherapy, 132-133, 135-137

      combinations, 133, 140, 148

      differential indications, 133

      dosage changes, 141

    predictors of noncompliance, 326

    prophylaxis

      lithium, 310-318, 322-323, 326-330

      tricyclic antidepressants, 315, 318-321, 323-325

Depressive equivalents (*See also* Masked depression), 97, 182-183, 197-198

  in children, 182-183, 197-198

Depressive neuroses (*See* Neuroses, depressive)

Depressive spectrum disease, 96-97, 102-103

Deprivation (*See also* Separation), 102, 181, 195

  experimental, 102

  in infants, 181, 195

Desmethylamitriptyline (*See* Nortriptyline; Protriptyline)

Desipramine (*See* Desmethylimipramine)

Desmethylimipramine, 31-32, 35, 37, 110, 119-121, 123, 274, 276, 279

  metabolism of, 120

  plasma levels, 110, 123

    and clinical response, 119, 121

Desmethyl doxepine, 115, 118

Dexamethasone, 23

Dextroamphetamine, 120

Diabetes, 285

  MAOI's in, 285

Diagnosis of depression, 127-130, 141-142, 147, 150, 156

  criteria, 127-128

  Diagnostic and Statistical Manual of Mental Disorders (DSM-II), 127-128, 141-142, 147

  differential, 127-129

  family history, 156

  precipitants, 128-130

  prognosis, 156

  statistical techniques for determining, 156

  treatment response, as criteria, 142, 150

Diagnostic and Statistical Manual of Mental Disorders (DSM-II), 127-128, 141-142, 147, 156
  deficiencies and drawbacks, 127, 141
  definitions, 127-128
  diagnoses in depression, 127-128
  proposed new categories, 129
  treatment response as criteria, 127-128
Diagnostic and Statistical Manual of Mental Disorders (DSM III), 149, 152
Dialysis, 283, 296
Diazepam, 281, 290, 320, 324
  MAOI induced convulsions, 290
  in tricyclic induced convulsions, 281
Dibenzepine, 61
Dibenzazepine derivatives, 32, 56, 61
Dibenzo-bicyclo-octadiene derivatives, 56, 59, 61
Dibenzocycloheptadiene derivative, 56
Dibenzocyclo-octadiene, 61
Dibenzopyrazinoazepin (See Mianserin)
Dibenzoxepine derivatives, 56, 61
L-Dihydroxyphenylalanine (See L-DOPA)
Diphenylhydantoin, 281
Disease expectancy, 76-78
  affective illness, 78
  definition, 77
Diuresis, 283
Diuretics, 281
DOPA, 55
L-DOPA (L-dihydroxyphenylalanine), 25, 30, 38, 44, 55, 287-288
  in depression, 44
  interaction with MAOI's, 287-288
Dopamine, 7, 9, 29-31, 36, 38, 40-45, 48, 287
  depletion by reserpine, 41
  enzymatic degradation of, 31
  interaction with MAOI's, 287
  levels in separation, 7
  receptors, 33, 45, 48
Dopamine-β-hydroxylase, 24, 42
Dopaminergic activity, 49-50
  pituitary growth hormone, 49-50
Doxepin, 32, 57, 274
Drug abuse, 129, 140, 148-149
  tricyclic antidepressants and lithium in, 149
Dysarthria, 277-279, 295
Dysphoria, 128-129, 134-141, 143, 148, 198
Dysphoric disorders, 129-141

classification of, 129
primary
  endogenomorphic depression, 129-136
    definition of, 130
    treatment, 130
  reactive or situational dysphorias, 134-135
    treatment, 134-135
  schizoaffective illness, 135-136
secondary
  to organic and toxic illness, 140-141
  to personality disorders and neuroses, 137-139
  to schizophrenia and schizoid states, 136-137
Dysphoric states in children, 197, 199
Early experience, role of in abnormal behavior, 4
Elavil (See Amitriptyline)
Elderly (See Aged persons)
Electrocardiograph, 274-275, 280, 282, 291, 295
  effect of lithium on, 291, 295
  effect of tricyclics on, 274-275
  in tricyclic poisoning, 280, 282
Electroconvulsive therapy, 111, 131-133, 136, 143-144, 148-149, 151, 309, 318-319, 327
  advantages and disadvantages, 131-133, 144
  cognitive changes following, 131-132, 143
  compared with pharmacotherapy, 132-133
  in elderly depressives, 211, 219-221, 226
  in schizoaffective illness, 136, 327
  in suicidal risk, 133
  maintenance, 132
  memory changes, 131-132, 143-144, 151
  muscle relaxants, 132, 149
  organic mental syndrome following, 131
  personality changes, 132
  unilateral, 132, 143
Electroencephalography, 5, 15-16, 22, 186, 194-195, 295
  depth electrodes, 15-16
    animals in isolation, 15
    in schizophrenia, 15-16
  in childhood depressives, 186, 194-195
  in lithium poisoning, 295
  sleep, 22
Electrolytes, 25, 26, 50
Electrolyte therapy, 296

for lithium toxicity, 296
Electromyography, 22
Electrophysiological measures, 22
    cortical evoked potential, 22, 51
Electroshock therapy (*See* Electroconvulsive therapy)
Emotionally unstable character disorder, 129, 132, 138
Endogenomorphic depression, 129-137, 142-143, 145, 148-152
    classification of, 129
    definition of, 130
Endogenous depression, 80, 82-85, 110, 116, 217-218, 228
    in elderly, 217-218, 228
    morbidity risk in relatives, 84-85
Enuresis, 118, 186-188, 194, 197-198, 200
    amitriptyline in, 118
    endogenous depression in parents, 187
    imipramine action, 198
    nortriptyline plasma levels, 118
Environmental stimulation, 13-14
    in treatment of depressed patients, 13-14
    in treatment of mania, 14
Epidemiology, 75-81, 99-101, 226
    diagnostic reliability, 77, 79, 101
    disorders of the aged, 226
    findings, 77-81
    methodological aspects, 76-78
    objective case criteria, 76
Epinephrine (*See also* Adrenalin), 29, 36
Erythrocytes, 21, 26-29
    cell membrane distribution and transport of Li, Na, K, 27
    lithium concentration in, 21
    magnesium concentration in, 26
    sodium concentration in, 26
Eutonyl (*See* Pargyline)
Family risk studies, 81-86, 88-89
    affective disorders, 84
    bipolar and monopolar psychoses, 86, 88-89
    early and late onset disorders, 85
    endogenous depression, 84
    investigations, 81-86, 88-89
    involutional melancholia, 85
    manic depressives, 82-84
Figure drawings, 185
FLA-63 (dopamine beta hydroxylase inhibitor), 24
Freud, Anna, 185

Freud, S., 135, 181-182
Fusaric acid, 42, 43
    in mania, 42-43
Galactorrhea, 277
Gamma-amino butyric acid (GABA), 22, 53
Ganser state, 211
Genetic control, 118, 120
    of absorption, diffusion and excretion of drugs, 120
    of monoamine oxidase activity, 118
    polygenetic factor in tricyclic metabolism, 118, 120
Genetics, 12-13, 22, 82-91, 96-98, 148, 207
    in animal models, 12-13
    of affective disorders, 22
    of depression, 82, 84-91, 207
        age of onset, 97-98
        in elderly, 207
        sex ratio, 96-97
    of drug response, 13
    of manic depressive psychosis, 82-85
    selection of treatment modality, 148
Genetic investigation, methods, 79, 81-94, 99, 101
    biological, 79, 81, 92-94
        association, 81, 93
        chromosome, 81, 92
        linkage, 81, 93-94
    clinical, 79, 81-92
        adoptee, 79, 81
        family, 81-86, 88-89
        twin, 81, 90-92, 101
    sources of error, 79, 82-84, 99, 101
Genetic predisposition to depression, 79, 83, 88, 91
    generic and specific predisposition, 88
Geriatric patients (*See* Aged persons)
Glaucoma, 274, 301
    and tricyclic antidepressants, 301
Glutamate, 22
Glycine, 22
Grief, pathological, 135
Growth Hormone, 25, 48-50
    effect of dopamine receptor-stimulating agent on, 48
    response to insulin-induced hypoglycemia, 25
Guttman Scale, 164-170, 172, 174
Haloperidol, 45, 175, 199
Hamburg Inventory, 159
Hamilton Depression Rating Scale, 159-161,

172, 235, 245, 251, 255, 257, 259, 264
Hepatotoxicity, 276, 285-286
   secondary to
      MAOI's, 285-286
      tricyclic antidepressants, 276
Heredity (*See* Genetics)
Hereditary factors (*See also* Genetics), 207, 209, 218
   in elderly depressives, 207, 209, 218
Histamine, 22
Histrionic character disorder, 129, 138
Homovanillic acid (*See*
   3-methoxy-4-hydroxyphenyl acetic acid)
Hospitalization, 133
   in suicidal risk, 133
Hydrazine, 54
Hydrogen ion activity, 28
6-Hydroxydopamine (6HDA), 9, 42
   monoamine depleting agent, 42
5-Hydroxyindoleacetic acid (5HIAA), 31, 34, 37-41, 43-44, 50
   antidepressant response and, 40
   cerebrospinal fluid levels in affective
      disorders, 50
   cerebrospinal fluid levels of, 38
5-Hydroxytryptamine (5-HT) (*See* Serotonin)
5-Hydroxytryptophan (5HTP), 30, 40, 44
Hyperkinetic children, 175, 188, 190, 192, 196, 198, 201-202
   depression in parents, 201
   psychopharmacology of, 202
   stimulants in, 198
Hypertension, 275, 284, 289-290
   secondary to
      MAOI's, 284
         poisoning, 289-290
      tricyclic antidepressants, 275
Hypertensive crises, 286-287, 290, 300-301
   secondary to
      MAOI's, 286-287, 300-301
         treatment, 290
Hypoglycemia, 25, 49
   insulin-induced, 25
Hypokalemia, 291
Hypokalemic nephropathy, 292
Hypomania, 274
Hypotension, 274, 280, 284
   secondary to,
      MAOI's, 284
      tricyclic antidepressants, 274, 280
Hypothalamus, 23, 54-55

Hypothyroidism, 129, 140
Imipramine, 12, 14-15, 24, 31-37, 42-44, 50, 52, 57, 59-63, 110-114, 119-121, 123, 137, 139, 187, 191-192, 198, 201, 220, 254-260, 263, 265-267, 274-275, 277-279, 283, 289, 318, 320-322, 324-325, 331
   adverse reactions (*See also,* Tricyclic
      antidepressants), 274-275, 277-279, 283
      hypertension, 275
      hypomanic or manic excitement, 274
      neurotoxicity, 277
      seizures, 275
   clinical trial vs. maprotiline, 254-260
   effect on biogenic amines, 37, 60-61●
   effect on glucose metabolism, 277
   in cardiac disease, 275
   in enuresis, 187, 198, 201
   in mania, 50
   in pregnancy, 279
   in school phobia, 192
   in separation, 14-15
   interactions with
      methylphenidate, 111-112, 120
      MAOI's, 289
   metabolism, 120
   plasma levels of, 110-114, 123
      and clinical response, 112-114, 119, 121
      dosage 112-114, 119, 121
      drug interactions, 111-112, 120-121
   prophylactic, 318, 320-322
   stereochemical characteristics, 59
   teratogenicity, 277
   L-triiodothyronine, effect on, 24
   urinary MHPG, as a predictor of response
      to, 36
   withdrawal, 278
Impotence, 277
Infants (*See* Childhood)
Insulin, 25
International Clissification of Disease, Injuries
   and Causes of Death, 9, 147, 152
Involutional melancholia, 82, 84-85, 96-97, 100, 207, 214, 225
   morbidity risk in relatives, 84-85
   premorbid personality, 207
Iprindole, 32, 35, 61
Isocarboxazid, 191, 285
Isolation, social (*See also* Separation) 1, 4, 5, 11, 15, 16
   as a model for psychosis, 11, 15, 16

in animals, 1, 4, 5
Klein, Melanie, 181
Kleist, 86
Kraepelin, E., 82
Lactate, 296
Leonhard, 86, 87
    classification of endogenous psychoses, 86,
        87
Leukocytosis, 293
Leukopenia, 285
Leukotomy, 221
Lidocaine, 281, 282
Limbic system, 48, 54
Linkage studies, 81, 93-94
Lithium, 21, 26-29, 33-34, 40, 46, 50, 52, 54,
    63, 102, 131, 138, 148-149, 192-193, 196,
    198, 221, 223, 225-226, 229, 290-299,
    310-318, 321-330
    biochemical mode of action, 329
    blood levels, 290
    distribution and transport, 27
    diuretic effect, 47
    diuretics and, 298
    in alcoholism and drug abuse, 149
    in bipolar disorders, 133, 310-317, 322-323,
        326-328, 331
    in children, 192-193, 196, 198
    in depression, 21, 132, 310-318, 322-323,
        326-331
    in elderly, 221, 223, 225, 226, 299
    in emotionally unstable character
        disorders, 132
    in neonates, 294
    in normals, 63
    in pregnancy, 291
    in schizoaffective psychoses, 136, 149,
        327-329
    in schizophrenia, 294
    in unipolar depressives, 310-317, 323, 326,
        329, 331
    poisoning, 294-295
        neurological sequelae, 296
        treatment, 295-297
    prophylaxis in affective disorders, 310-318,
        322-323, 326-329
        relapse rates, 312-317
        trial design, 310, 314-315, 323
    serotonin synthesis and, 33-34
    side effects, 290-291
        treatment, 291, 297-299
    sodium pump and, 28

substitution for sodium, 28
teratogenicity, 294
thyroid functioning and, 47, 291-292
toxic reactions, 291-294
Lubin Adjective Check List, 160
Ludiomil (See Maprotiline)
Lymphotcytopenia, 293
Magnesium, 26, 50
Major tranquilizers (See also Phenothiazines and
    entries for specific agents), 208
Mania, 22, 42, 50-51, 54
    AMPT in, 42
    biochemical similarities with depression,
        50-51, 54
Manic-depressive psychosis (See also Bipolar
    affective illness), 72, 82-86, 89, 93-94, 96-97,
    101-102, 148, 182, 186, 189-190, 192, 197,
    226, 312-317, 320-327
    genetic predisposition, 83
    in aged, 226
    in children, 182, 186, 189-190, 192, 197
        differential diagnosis, 190
        personality characteristics in, 189
    maintenance therapy, 326-327
    morbidity risk, in relatives, 82-85
    prophylactic lithium, 312-317, 322-323,
        326
    prophylactic tricyclic antidepressants,
        320-321, 324-325
Mania-depression relationship, 49-51, 54
    cholinergic-noradrenergic balance, 49
Maprotiline (BA34,276), 57, 59, 60-62,
    121-123, 192, 233-247, 249, 254-260, 263,
    265-266
    absorption kinetic, 122
    effect on biogenic amines, 61
    effect on norepinephrine and serotonin
        metabolism, 263
    in children, 192
    pharmacological properties, 263, 265-266
    pharmacokinetic model, 122
    plasma levels, 121-123
    stereochemical properties, 265
    summary of international double blind
        studies, 247, 254
    trials in outpatient depressives 263, 265-266
        vs. amitriptyline, 234-245
        vs. imipramine and placebo, 254, 260
Marplan (See isocarboxazid)
Masked depression (See also Depressive
    equivalents), 181-182, 185, 197, 199, 208, 215

adolescents, 182
children, 181, 185, 197, 199
elderly, 208, 215
Maudsley Personality Inventory, 184
in children, 184
Memory (*See also* Cognitive functioning),
131-132, 143-144, 151, 210
changes following ECT, 131-132, 143-144,
151, 210
Menstrual irregularities, 277
Meperidine, 288-289
Metabolic acidosis, 280, 283
Metanephrine, 36
Metaraminol, 280
3-Methoxy-4-hydroxyphenylacetic acid
(Homovanillic acid HVA), 31, 37-40, 43-44,
50
CSF levels of, 38
in affective illness, 50
3-Methoxy-4-hydroxyphenylglycol (MHPG), 31,
35-37, 39-40, 42
CSF, levels of, 39
urinary levels of, as a predictor of response
to imipramine and amitriptyline, 36
urinary studies of, 35-37
3-Methoxy-4-hydroxyvanillylmandelic acid
VMA), 31, 36
Methylphenidate, 49, 111-112, 120, 198-199,
202, 278
effect on tricyclic plasma levels, 111-112
interaction with tricyclic antidepressants,
278
Methysergide, 25, 45
Mianserin, 57, 60-61, 265-266
Minnesota Multiphasic Personality Inventory,
160
Minor tranquilizers (*See* Anxiolytics)
Models
animal, 1-5, 7, 10-11, 13-16, 199-200
acceptance by clinicians, 2, 11
criteria for evaluating, 3
of psychosis, 11, 15, 16
predictors of psychopharmacological
treatments, 5, 7, 10, 13, 14
relevance to human psychopathology,
2
value in psychiatry, 3-5
biochemical, 9
reserpine, 9
of depression, 22, 41, 53
psychobiological, 22

reserpine, 41
Monkeys, 2, 4, 6-9, 12-13, 42
bonnet, 6, 12-13
macaca speciosa, 42
pigtail, 6, 12
rhesus, 2, 4, 6-9
stumptail, 9
Monoamine oxidase activity, 25, 31, 50,
116-118, 200, 207, 225-226
age related changes, 116, 200
and lithium responsiveness, 226
blood levels in children, 200
catacholamines conversion, 31
in depressives, 116
in elderly, 116, 207, 225-226
in plasma, 116
in platelets, 116-117
inhibition of, 118
clinical response and, 117-118
levels in suicides, 226
sex differences in, 25
Monoamine oxidase inhibitors, 24, 31-33, 44,
56, 63, 116-118, 131-133, 135-136, 138-140,
143, 148, 191, 196, 198, 220-221, 273,
278-279, 284-290, 297, 298, 300-301, 309
acetylator status and response, 116
dietary restrictions, 287
differential indications, 133
drug interactions, 287-289, 300
tricyclic antidepressants, 140, 221,
278-279, 288-289, 297-298, 300-301
effect on biogenic amines, 31-32
hypertensive crises, 286-287, 297
in aged, 220
in atypical depression, 116-117
in children, 191, 196, 198
in endogenous depression, 116
in personality disorders, 138
maintenance therapy, 309
platelet MAO inhibition and clinical
response, 116-118
poisoning, 289
treatment, 289-290
potentiation by L-tryptophan, 44
REM sleep, 118
side effects, 284-285
treatment, 284, 297
toxic reactions, 285-286
Monoamines, 30-32, 34, 39, 41, 47, 49-50
depletion of, 30, 41-43
by AMPT, 42

by PCPA, 43
precursors of, 43-44
psychotropic drug effects on, 34
receptor abnormality in depression, 47
Monoamine systems, 49-50
effects of electrolytes on, 50
effects of steroid hormones on, 50
interactions between, 49
Mood disturbance, 127-129
dysphoria, 129
Morbidity rates of affective disorders, 75, 98-99
Morphine, 35, 288-289
interaction with MAOI's, 288-289
Mourning, 134, 135, 151
Nardil (See Phenelzine)
Neostigmine (Prostigmin), 282-283
Nephrogenic diabetes insipidus, 276, 292
secondary to
lithium, 292
tricyclic antidepressants, 276
Neural transmitters (See also entries for specific
transmitters), 29-30, 51-52
Neuroendocrine function, 22-25
growth hormone, 25
hypothalamic-pituitary-adrenal activity,
22-23
in affective disorders, 22
role of biogenic amines in, 22
sex hormones, 24
thyroid hormone, 23
Neuroendocrine studies (See also entries for
specific hormones), 22-25
Neuronal connections, simplistic, 53
model of, 53
Neuropathy, peripheral, 285
Neuroleptics, 34-35, 128, 136, 140, 143,
148-149, 151, 327-328
akinetic reactions, 128-136, 140, 143, 151
and lithium,
in schizoaffective disorders, 149,
327-328
changes in synaptic receptor activity,
34-35
long-acting agents
depressive reactions, 143, 151
Neuroses, 79-80, 86, 91, 96, 116, 128-129, 137,
212-213, 215-218, 220, 224
depressive
antidepressants in, 128
DSM II definition, 128
in elderly, 212, 215-218, 220

internal conflict, 128
MAOI's in, 116
morbidity risk in relatives, 86
precipitant, 128
prevalence estimates, 79-80
twin studies, 91
in elderly, 212-213, 215-218, 220, 224
obsessive compulsive, 129
treatment of depression in, 137
phobic, 12, 14, 191, 192, 198-202, 212-213
phobic anxious
treatment of depression in, 137
Neurotoxicity, 277, 279, 285, 289, 293-294
secondary to
lithium, 293-294
MAOI's, 285, 289
tricyclic antidepressants, 277, 279
Neutrophilia, 293
Nialamide, 285
Niamid (See Nialamide)
Noradrenalin, 275
interaction with tricyclic antidepressants,
275
Noradrenergic system, 10, 24, 49, 61
cholinergic balance, 49
in brain and social behavior, 10
in mania, 49
Norepinephrine, 7, 9, 24, 29-37, 40-45, 48-49,
52, 54-55, 60-63, 118, 263, 265, 280, 286-287
brain concentrations, 54
deficit in depression, 24
depletion agents, 42
effect of tricyclic antidepressants, 54-55, 60
effect on systolic blood pressures in
depressives, 48
enzymatic degradation of, 31
levels in separation, 9
MAOI's effect on, 286-287
metabolism, 263
plasma nortriptyline level and, 118
receptors, 45
synaptic transmission, 30
Normetanephrine, 31, 36
index of adrenergic receptor activity, 31
Norpramine (See Desmethylimipramine)
Nortriptyline, 32, 37, 40, 110-113, 118, 121, 274
plasma levels of, 110-112, 118
clinical response, 110-113
drug interactions, 111
in enuresis, 118
norepinephrine uptake, 118

side effects, 110
Obsessive-phobic traits, 216
in aged, 216
Organic brain syndrome, 129, 140, 209-211,
223-224, 229
in elderly
acute, 209, 211, 224
and depression, 209-211
chronic, 129, 140, 209-210, 223-224,
229
Organic mental syndrome, 131-132
following ECT, 131-132
Osmotic diuresis, 296

Parachlorophenylalanine (PCPA), 9, 30, 43,
63-64
depletion of serotonin by, 43
Paraldehyde, 281, 290
Paraphrenia, late, 208-209, 224
Parathymia, primary, 181
Pargyline, 286
side effects of, 286
Parkinson's disease, 44
Parnate (See Tranylcypromine)
Passive dependent personality, 129, 137
Pentolinium, 290
Personality, 142, 143, 145, 150, 189-190, 194,
207, 218
anancastic, 142, 150
cyclothymic
in children diagnosed as
manic-depressive, 189-190, 194
obsessive compulsive, 142, 150
premorbid
in elderly depressives, 207, 218
in involutional psychoses, 207
in unipolar depressives, 143, 145
Personality disorders, depression in,
129-137-139, 143
antisocial personality, 129, 137
emotionally unstable character disorder,
129, 138
histrionic character disorder, 129, 138
hysteroid dysphoria, 129, 138
description and treatment of, 138
inadequate and hypochondriacal, 138-139
Pertofrane (See Desmethylimipramine)
Pharmacotherapy, 11, 14, 16
combined with psychotherapy, 14, 16
Phenelzine, 31, 116-117, 139, 191, 267, 284-285
acetylation of, 116

inhibition of MAO activity and response,
117
side effects of, 284-285
2-Phenethylamine (PEA), 55
behavioral effects, 55
levels in depression, 55
Phenylethylamine hypothesis, 55
Phenobarbitone, 191
Phenothiazines, 33, 46-47, 133, 135-136, 138,
250, 276, 278
interaction with tricyclic antidepressants,
278
piperazine vs. aliphatic in retarded
schizoaffectives, 135-136
Phentolamine, 45, 290
Phobias, 12, 14, 191-192, 198-202, 212-213
agoraphobics, 200
in elderly, 212-213
school, 14, 191-192, 198-202
Phosphodiesterase, 45-47
inhibition by phenothiazines and tricyclic
antidepressants, 47
Physostigmine, 48-49, 282
in mania, 48-49
in schizophrenia, 49
Pindolol, 298-299
Pituitary, 23
Placebo, 135, 139, 252, 261-262, 265, 273
in clinical trials, 252, 265
in demoralization, 139
in reactive depression, 135
reactors, 261-262
side effect reactions, 273
Plasma binding, 113, 115, 118
Plasma levels of psychotropic drugs, 52
Plasma levels of tricyclic and tetracyclic
antidepressants, 109-123, 279
assay procedures, 114-115
drug interactions, 111-113, 115, 120-121
genetic factors, 118, 120
interindividual differences, 109-110, 118,
122
in tricyclic poisoning, 279
methodological issues, 110-111, 113-116,
123
plasma binding, 113, 115, 118
relationship to
clinical outcome, 110-114, 116-117,
119, 121
dosage, 112
side effects, 110

steady state
definition of, 109
sex differences, 110
time to reach, 109-110
therapeutic window, 119, 121
Plasma monoamine oxidase activity, 116
Platelet monoamine oxidase activity, 116-117
correlation with brain MAO activity, 116
genetic control of, 116
in depressives, 116
inhibition of, 117
"Pleasure center," 130
impairment in depression, 130
Polycyclic antidepressants, 56, 60
Polydipsia, 292, 298
Polyuria, 47, 291, 292, 298
with lithium, 47
Popoff Depression Inventory, 159, 161
Potassium, 27, 28
transport of, 27
Potassium chloride, 283
Practolol, 282, 299-300
Pregnancy, 279, 291
imipramine in, 279
lithium in, 291
Presamine (See Imipramine)
Probenecid, 34, 39-40, 44, 46
cyclic AMP concentrations (in CSF) in
affective illness, 46
in CSF studies of biogenic amines, 39-40
Procainomide, 281-282
Propranolol, 45, 122, 282-283, 291, 299-300
treatment of drug induced
arrhythmias, 283
bradycardia, 282
tachycardia, 282
tremor, 291, 299-300
Prostaglandin synthetase, 62
Protein binding (See Plasma binding)
Prothiaden, 61
Protriptyline, 32, 274
Pseudodementia in elderly depressives, 210-212,
224, 227
Psychological tests, 160, 184-185, 211-212
in children, 185
Figure drawings, 185
MPI, 184
Rorschach, 185
TAT, 185
in elderly, 211-212
MMPI, 160

Psychometric procedures (See Assessment
procedures; Rating scale methodology)
Psychomotor retardation, 119, 128, 137
Psychopathology
experimental (See also Animal behavior,
abnormal), 1, 2, 10
human, 2, 10
models of (See Models, animal)
Psychopharmacology, 162, 172-175
evaluation in, 162, 172-175
Psychosis, 128, 147
DSM-II use, 128, 147
Psychotherapy, 11, 14, 16, 139, 213, 220, 226,
327
combined with drug therapy, 14, 16, 213,
327
in elderly, 213, 220, 226
Psychotic depressive reaction, 96, 128, 147
DSM-II definition, 128
treatment implications, 128
Psychotropic agents (See also entries for specific
agents), 34-35, 52, 220, 230
adverse reactions in aged, 230
delayed onset of response, 52
Pyridostigmine (Mestinon), 282
Quinidine, 281
Quipazine, 45
Rapid eye movements (REM), 35, 118-119
effects of tricyclic antidepressants on, 35
MAOI response and, 118
Raskin Depression Scale, 234-235
Rating scales (See also Assessment procedures),
156-159, 161-162, 171-178, 228-229, 248, 264
global evaluations, 159, 161-162, 172,
174-175, 177
inter-rater reliability, 264
observer ratings, advantages and
disadvantages, 158, 176-177
concordance with self-scales, 177-178,
248
self-rating scales, 158, 174-175, 177,
228-229
sex differences in scores, 171-172
total pathology scores, 172-173
uses, 156-157, 172-174
in research, 157
patient selection criteria, 172-173, 176
Rating scale methodology, 157-163, 165-166,
172-175, 177
construction, 157
item weighting, 162-163, 165

problems, 172-174, 177
psychometrics, 162-163, 165-166
reliability, 158, 161, 175
    inter-rater, 161, 173-174
    test-retest, 161
scaling theory, 165, 174-175
sensitivity, 175
validity, 158-161, 175
    concurrent, 159-161
    construct, 159-160, 163
Reactive depression, 128-129, 134-135, 143, 149, 183, 185
    in children, 183, 185
Research, clinical (*See also* Clinical trial methodology), 172-173, 176
    patient selection criteria, 172-173, 176
    total rating scale scores, as entry criteria, 172-173
Research Diagnostic Criteria (RDC), 100
Reserpine, 9, 29, 30, 41, 63, 278
    induced depression in animals, 9
    interaction with tricyclic antidepressants, 278
    model of depression, 41
Rorschach, 185

Schedule for Affective Disorders and Schizophrenia (SADS), 100
Schizophrenia, 11, 15-16, 23, 38-40, 42, 85-87, 99, 101-102, 136-137, 162, 172, 186, 190, 208-209, 224, 229, 294, 330, 331
    alteration of transmitter amines in, 16
    AMPT in, 42
    antidepressants in, 136-137
    chronic defect state, 137
    depression in, 136-137
    good prognosis, 102
    in children, 186, 190
    late
        differentiation from depression, 208-209
    lithium in, 294
    non-systematic, 86-87
    systematic, 86-87
Schizoaffective psychosis (*See also* Cycloid psychosis), 36, 93, 101-102, 129, 135-136, 144, 147, 149, 209, 226, 229, 327-331
    diagnostic criteria, 101
    differential diagnosis, 330-331
    in aged, 209, 226, 229
    lithium in, 149, 328-329

combined with neuroleptics, 149, 327-328
premorbid personality, 330-331
suicide, 149
treatment, 135-136, 149, 327-329
twin studies, 101
urinary MHPG, 36
Schizoid states, 136-137
    depression in, 136-137
School phobia, 14, 191-192, 198-202
    treatment, 191-192, 200
    depression in parents, 201
Schutz's Scale, 174
Seizures (*See* Convulsions)
Separation (*See also* Deprivation), 4, 6-9, 11-12, 14-15, 184, 194-195, 200
    in animals, 4, 6-9, 11-12, 14-15
        biogenic amines in, 7, 9
        mother-infant, 4, 6, 7, 11, 14
            biphasic reaction, 6, 7
            sensory modalities in, 12, 15
            species differences, 6, 12
        peer, 4, 7-8, 11
            effect of age, 7
    in humans, 6
        in childhood depression, 184, 194-195, 200
Separation anxiety, 14, 200
    in agoraphobics, 200
Serotonin, 7, 25, 29-34, 37-39, 40-45, 49-53, 60-63, 263
    brain levels in suicides, 41
    effect of tricyclic antidepressants on, 31-34, 37, 40, 60
    growth hormone, 50
    metabolism of, 31
    norepinephrine balance, 49
    receptors, 45
Serum levels of antidepressants (*See* Plasma levels of tricyclic and tetracyclic antidepressants)
Sex differences, 25, 81, 89, 96-97, 110, 171-172, 206, 291
    activity of MAO, 25
    goiters secondary to lithium, 291
    incidence of depression, 206
        age, 97
        culture, 97
        diagnostic differences, 96
        race, 97
        social class, 96

treatment setting, 96
morbidity risk for depression, 96
morbidity risk of relatives of unipolar
depressives, 89
plasma levels, 110
Sex hormones, 24-25
Sexual disorders, 277, 285
Side effects (*See* Tricyclic antidepressants;
Monoamine oxidase inhibitors; Lithium; and
entries for specific agents)
Sinequan (*See* Doxepin)
Skin reactions, 274, 292-293
secondary to
lithium therapy, 292-293
tricyclic antidepressants, 274
Sleep, 51
Social incapacitation, 128
Social maladjustment, 216, 218, 227-228
in elderly depressives, 216, 218
Sociopathy, 97-98, 102
Sodium (Na), 26-28, 30, 50-51, 54
activity in
cerebral spinal fluid, 28
erythrocytes, 27
saliva, 27-28
erythrocyte levels of, 26
effect of lithium on, 29
in depression and mania, 51
relationship to clinical condition, 26, 29
transport of, 27
Sodium bicarbonate, 296
in lithium toxicity, 296
Sodium pump, 28
Spitz, R.A., 181, 183
Stereochemical classification of antidepressants,
56-62, 265, 267
parameters, 58
relationship to biochemical characteristics,
61
side chain constellations, 59
Stimulants (*See also* Amphetamine;
Methylphenidate), 138, 198
Subarachnoid hemorrhage, 286
Succinylcholine, 281, 290
Suicide, 96, 101, 131, 133, 143, 156, 183-184,
207, 223, 226, 327
adolescents early object loss, 184
attempters, 96, 207, 223
early bereavement in, 183
ECT in prevention, 131
in geriatric population, 223, 226
in schizoaffective psychoses, 143

risk
hospitalization, 133
indication for ECT, 133
with long term neuroleptic therapy,
143
Superego, 182
Tardive dyskinesia, 133
Temporal lobe epilepsy, 129, 140
Teratogenicity, 277, 294
lithium, 294
tricyclic antidepressants, 277
Testicular swelling, 277
Tests (*See* Assessment procedures)
Tetracyclic antidepressants (*See also*
Maprotiline; Mianserin), 54, 263, 265-266,
327
stereochemical structures, 265
Thematic Apperception Test (TAT), 185
in children, 185
Theories of depression, 29, 36, 38, 41, 44,
48-49, 54-55, 62, 182, 184
biogenic amine hypothesis, 29, 36, 41, 48,
62
catecholamine hypothesis, 36, 51, 54
cellular and intracellular membrane
concept, 54-55
cholinergic and adrenergic balance, 49
norepinephrine hypothesis, 44
"permissive" hypothesis, 38
phenylethylamine hypothesis, 55
psychoanalytic, 181-184
serotonin and norepinephrine balance, 49
Therapeutic window, 119, 121
Thiethylperazine, 54
Thioridazine, 122
Thymoleptics (*See also* Antidepressants;
Lithium), 213, 219, 223
Thyroid functioning and lithium, 291, 292
Thyroid hormone, 24, 47
in relation to
gland, 47
lithium, 47
Thyroid stimulating hormone (TSH), 24, 47
inhibition by lithium, 47
Thyrotropic releasing factor (TRH), 24, 55
therapeutic value in depression, 55
Tofranil (*See* Imipramine)
Toxicity, 274-297, 299-300
lithium
symptoms, 291-295
treatment, 295-297
MAOI's

symptoms, 285-289
treatment, 289-290
tricyclic antidepressants
symptoms, 274-280
treatment, 280-284
Tranylcypromine, 31-32, 43, 284, 286
side effects of, 284, 286
Tremor, 291, 295, 300
Tricyclic antidepressants (*See also* entries for
specific agents), 31-35, 37, 40, 46-47, 54,
56-64, 113, 118-121, 131-133, 135-139,
148-149, 198, 211, 219-223, 226, 230, 265,
274-284, 288-289, 297, 300-301, 315, 318-325
absorption, distribution and excretion, 120
biochemical classification of, 60-61
correlation with stereochemical
parameters, 61-62
biogenic amines and, 31-33, 37, 40
blood levels (*See* Plasma levels of tricyclic
and tetracyclic antidepressants)
differential indications, 133
dosage, 113, 119, 121
drug interactions, 120-121, 278-279,
288-289
MAOI's, 278-279, 288-289, 297-298,
300-301
genetic control of metabolism, 118, 120
glaucoma and, 301
in children, 198
in elderly, 220-223, 226, 230
adverse effects, 211, 219, 223
cardiac complications, 220, 230
confusion, 230
delirious reactions, 211
dosage, 230
in normals, 63-64
in personality disorders and neuroses, 137
in reactive depression, 135
in schizoaffective psychoses, 136
in schizophrenia, 136
pharmacologic effects of chronic
administration, 34-35
poisoning, 279-284, 301
treatment, 280-284
prophylactic therapy, 315, 318-321,
323-325
methodological problems in trials,
318, 322-323
relapse rates, 318, 320-321, 324-325
REM sleep and, 35
side effects, 274
treatment, 274, 297-298

stereochemical classification, 56-62, 265
teratogenicity, 277
toxic reactions, 274-279, 301
withdrawal effects, 277-279
in neonates, 279
L-Triiodothyronine (T_3), 24
effect on amitriptyline response, 24
effect on imipramine response, 24
Tryptophan, 34, 39-41, 50, 263
CSF levels in affective disorders, 40-41, 50
L-Tryptophan, 30, 44
as an antidepressant, 44
in mania, 44
Tryptophan hydroxylase, 33-34, 43
Tyramine, 286-287, 300
foods high in, 287
MAOI's, interaction with, 286-287
Twin studies, in genetic investigations, 81,
90-92, 101
L-Tyrosine, 30
Tyrosine hydroxylase, 34, 42
Unipolar affective illness, 20, 24, 36, 40, 52, 54,
86-89, 91-92, 94, 96-98, 100, 102-103, 131, 143,
145, 148, 184, 214, 228, 254, 310-326, 329-331
alcoholism in relatives, 148
antidepressant prophylaxis, 315, 318-325
relapse rates, 318, 321-325
antidepressants in, 254
early bereavement in, 184
early environmental stress, 184
lithium prophylaxis, 310-317, 323, 326,
329-331
relapse rates, 312-317
morbidity risk in relatives, 86, 88-89
premorbid personality patterns, 143, 145
prognosis in, 214
sex distribution, 24, 89
twin studies, 91-92
Ur-depression, 181
Urinary studies, 35-37, 46
biogenic amines, 35-37
cyclic AMP, 46
Validity, 158-161, 163, 175
criterion, 159, 161
of rating scales, 159
Visual Analogue Scale (VAS), 159, 160
Vivactyl (*See* Protriptyline)
Wakefield SADS, 159
Wechsler Scale, 161
WHO classification, 142, 156
Zung Depression Status Inventory, 161
Zung Self-rating Depression Scale, 159-161